100 Years of the Nineteenth Amendment

100 Years of the Nineteenth Amendment

AN APPRAISAL OF WOMEN'S
POLITICAL ACTIVISM

Edited by Holly J. McCammon
and
Lee Ann Banaszak

OXFORD
UNIVERSITY PRESS

OXFORD
UNIVERSITY PRESS

Oxford University Press is a department of the University of Oxford. It furthers
the University's objective of excellence in research, scholarship, and education
by publishing worldwide. Oxford is a registered trade mark of Oxford University
Press in the UK and certain other countries.

Published in the United States of America by Oxford University Press
198 Madison Avenue, New York, NY 10016, United States of America.

Portions of chapter 2 are from J. Kevin Corder and Christina Wolbrecht. 2016.
Counting Women's Ballots: Female Voters from Suffrage through the New Deal.
Cambridge University Press. Reprinted with the permission of Cambridge University Press.

Library of Congress Cataloging-in-Publication Data
Names: McCammon, Holly J., 1959– editor. | Banaszak, Lee Ann, 1960– editor.
Title: 100 years of the Nineteenth Amendment : an appraisal of women's
political activism / edited by Holly J. McCammon and Lee Ann Banaszak.
Other titles: One hundred years of the Nineteenth Amendment
Description: New York, NY : Oxford University Press, [2018] |
Includes bibliographical references and index.
Identifiers: LCCN 2017046486 (print) | LCCN 2017052238 (ebook) |
ISBN 9780190265168 (Updf) | ISBN 9780190876579 (Epub) |
ISBN 9780190265151 (pbk. : alk. paper) | ISBN 9780190265144 (hardcover : alk. paper)
Subjects: LCSH: Women—Political activity—United States—History. |
Women—Suffrage—United States—History. | Feminism—United States—History. |
Women's rights—United States—History.
Classification: LCC HQ1236.5.U6 (ebook) | LCC HQ1236.5.U6 A16 2018 (print) |
DDC 320.082/0973—dc23
LC record available at https://lccn.loc.gov/2017046486

1 3 5 7 9 8 6 4 2

Paperback printed by Webcom Inc., Canada
Hardback printed by Bridgeport National Bindery, Inc., United States of America

{ CONTENTS }

PART III Diversity in Women's Social Movement Activism: Illustrations from One Hundred Years of Engagement

100 Years of the Nineteenth Amendment

Introduction

FROM THE NINETEENTH AMENDMENT TO TODAY:
AN APPRAISAL OF 100 YEARS OF WOMEN'S
POLITICAL ENGAGEMENT

Holly J. McCammon and Lee Ann Banaszak

Rejoice that the struggle is over, the aim achieved, and the women of the nation about to enter into the enjoyment of their hard-earned political liberty.

——CARRIE CHAPMAN CATT, *SUFFRAGE LEADER, IN THE CALL FOR THE LAST CONVENTION OF THE NATIONAL AMERICAN WOMAN SUFFRAGE ASSOCIATION, 1920*

The Founding Fathers never envisioned black women being in this place, so every time another one of us comes, we jolt the system just a little bit more simply by being here.

——MAXINE WATERS, *DEMOCRATIC CONGRESSWOMAN FROM CALIFORNIA, EBONY, 1994*

Today, we have broken the marble ceiling.

——NANCY PELOSI, *DURING HER SWEARING-IN CEREMONY AS SPEAKER OF THE US HOUSE OF REPRESENTATIVES, 2007*

In order to see where we are going, we not only must remember where we've been, but we must understand where we have been.

——ELLA BAKER, *CIVIL RIGHTS LEADER, SPEECH BEFORE THE INSTITUTE OF THE BLACK WORLD, 1961*

One hundred years ago, suffragists in the United States won the right to vote with the adoption of the Nineteenth Amendment. Ratification of the amendment ended nearly seven decades of struggle for women's voting rights, with women across the United States pressing for the ballot until they won their goal in 1920. In honor of the one-hundred-year anniversary of enactment of the Nineteenth Amendment, we have assembled an edited volume that takes the long view and looks back over the past century to consider what women have achieved in the ensuing decades. The chapters are written by scholars from different disciplinary backgrounds—law, political science, sociology, and women's and gender studies—each with deep historical and contemporary knowledge of women's political participation in the United States.

The observations in these chapters tell a diverse and complex story. What was the immediate outcome of ratification of the Nineteenth Amendment? What is the legacy of the suffrage movement for women's political activism? And how has women's broad and varied political engagement unfolded over the last hundred years? Tracing these themes over a century illustrates similarities and differences between women's and men's political engagement, as well as important differences among women in their political agendas and varied identities, including race, ethnicity, and class. Sometimes the developments since the ratification of the Nineteenth Amendment are exhilarating for the progress that women have made; at other times, this long view of the past is discouraging, because barriers to equality and representation still need to be surmounted to reach gender parity and to ensure that all women have a voice in the US political arena.

In this chapter we introduce our volume by briefly revisiting the suffrage movement and ratification of the Nineteenth Amendment. We explore how this victory set the stage for two further political developments for women. First, gaining the vote opened US electoral politics to a large segment of the female population. This changed electoral landscape ushered in an era of growth in women's voting and in time an increasing presence of women in elected office and party politics. Second, the suffragists' success also revealed to women how effective their organized social movement activism could be. The victory of the suffrage movement helped fuel additional women's organized activism and participation in other movements, activism that continued well beyond winning the vote and that is easily evident today.

Our volume thus explores a one-hundred-year historical trajectory of women's engagement in both electoral politics and social movement activism. Since the creation of the United States, institutionalized politics (particularly electoral processes and party politics) and extra institutional politics (that is, associational and protest mobilizations) have constituted two core forms of citizens' political engagement, and women have been heavily involved in both forms. While our chapters cannot describe every development over the last hundred years, the contributions here reveal many of the rich and varied aspects of a century of women's political action in the electoral and protest arenas. As the volume shows, women's efforts in the political realm have grown substantially, and women today are important political leaders in diverse domains, from serving as members of Congress to leading important environmental organizations. Yet taking the long view and reviewing women's political history also shows that women have long experienced unequal treatment, and women still confront important cultural and structural barriers to their success, especially women of color and women without substantial economic resources. Our volume also shows that politics itself is gendered, and women can bring unique perspectives to politics—not as a single group but differentiated by the way that gender intersects, for instance, with race, ethnicity, sexual orientation, nativity, and class. We hope that the insights of this volume help readers understand the progress that women have achieved and the steps that still need to be taken.

The Woman Suffrage Movement and Ratification of the Nineteenth Amendment

Readers can find numerous detailed accounts of the US suffrage movement, from narratives written by suffragists themselves (e.g., Catt and Shuler 1923; Stanton et al. 1881 [1985]; Stevens 1920) to scholarly investigations (e.g., DuBois 1978; Flexner [1959] 1996; Terborg-Penn 1998) to popular film (*Iron Jawed Angels* 2004). Evident in the many portrayals is that ratification of the Nineteenth Amendment was an important victory in the long struggle for women's rights. From the earliest calls for woman suffrage at the 1848 women's rights convention in Seneca Falls, New York, until the final state vote for ratification in Tennessee on August 26, 1920, women agitated across the country for a formal political voice—forming suffrage organizations, lobbying lawmakers, and conducting public educational campaigns. Most women pressing for voting rights were white, middle-class women, but black women and working-class women also mobilized for the vote, confronting the intersections of sexist, racist, and classist opposition (Terborg-Penn 1998). Especially in the last decades of the movement, suffragists had an extensive network of state- and city-level organizations as well as strong national groups— the National American Woman Suffrage Association (NAWSA) led by Carrie Chapman Catt and the National Woman's Party led by Alice Paul. The Nineteenth Amendment passed largely because of women's concerted and collective efforts.

The suffragists used a variety of strategies in their battle for the vote. Catt's "Winning Plan" for NAWSA centralized leadership, deployed resources toward building a broader membership, and pressured lawmakers in both Washington and the states (Catt and Shuler 1923). At roughly the same time, Alice Paul's Congressional Union, which soon would become the National Woman's Party, launched a set of more militant tactics, including picketing the White House and holding hunger strikes (Adams and Keene 2008). While World War I diverted attention away from the movement, at the close of the war the contradiction of fighting in Europe for democracy when women at home were denied the vote gave rhetorical ammunition to the suffragists. Multiple explanations of the suffragists' victory have been offered, including the movement leaders' strategic actions in these later years, the broad-based mobilization itself, the changing nature of partisan politics, a gendered culture shifting more broadly in progressive directions, and the rhetorical leverage in the immediate postwar years (Banaszak 1996; Buechler 1990; Graham 1996; McCammon et al. 2001; McConnaughy 2013). In all likelihood, a confluence of these factors—that is, the combination of women's collective agency and a more hospitable cultural and political environment—worked to produce the suffrage victory.

After Congress passed the Nineteenth Amendment in 1919, it took another year until on a hot August day in Nashville, Tennessee, the final state ratified the

amendment. The suffragists viewed Tennessee as perhaps their last chance for gaining the required endorsement of three-quarters of the states (Flexner [1959] 1996).
In the Tennessee legislature, antisuffragist lawmakers appeared to have the upper
hand, but one eastern Tennessee legislator had recently received a letter from his
mother, and she encouraged him to vote for the suffragists (Spruill Wheeler 1995).
Because of his mother's sage advice, at the last minute the lawmaker changed his
vote, with a momentous result. The suffragists won. With the thirty-sixth state
approving the amendment, the United States now had a constitutional amendment giving women the right to vote. The Nineteenth Amendment, which took
some seventy years to achieve, offers a fairly simple but yet profound statement:
"The right of citizens of the United States to vote shall not be denied or abridged
by the United States or by any State on account of sex."

The Aftermath of Winning the Nineteenth Amendment

Even at the moment when woman suffrage was won, women activists disagreed
over how much had been achieved, whether it was necessary for women to continue organizing for additional political rights for women, and what women voters would bring to US electoral politics (Andersen 1996; Butler 2002; Cott 1987;
Terborg-Penn 1998). Some desired to keep the momentum of mobilization for
women's rights going. Following the Nineteenth Amendment's ratification, Alice
Paul continued to lead the National Woman's Party, stating that women must maintain their struggle until full equality was achieved. The National Woman's Party,
in time along with other women's organizations such as the National Federation
of Business and Professional Women's Clubs—and, by the late 1960s, the newly
founded National Organization for Women—ensured that an equal rights amendment (ERA) was introduced in Congress every year from 1923 until it passed
Congress in 1972 (Mansbridge 1986). Too few states, however, ratified the amendment and thus it did not ultimately succeed.

Carrie Chapman Catt, leader of NAWSA at the time suffrage was won, took
a different approach and led many of the suffragists into a new organization, the
League of Women Voters (LWV), a group stating that its mission was not women's
rights but rather broad voter education on a variety of issues. The LWV carried a
portion of the momentum of the suffrage movement in another direction, broadening organized women's focus to include welfare for women and children, governmental reforms, and international affairs (Goss 2013; Noun 1989). Some have
ventured that this step "short-circuited" the feminist vigor of the suffrage movement after the vote was won (Flexner [1959] 1996, 320). What is certain is that
divisions among women activists became quite visible, with the LWV declining to
support the ERA until the 1970s (Noun 1989).

In fact, in the decades following suffrage, some women's groups actively lob-
bied against the equal rights amendment, working instead to maintain hard-won
workplace protective laws (Harrison 1988). These ERA opponents argued that an
equal rights amendment would necessitate doing away with protective laws, laws

that shielded women from the harsh realities of the early-twentieth-century work-place. Women such as Ethel Smith in the Women's Trade Union League saw a need rather to strengthen women's roles in trade unions and viewed protective laws and trade union activism as a means of advancing women's economic as well as political status (Butler 2002; Kirkby 1987).

Moreover, while white women had been enfranchised by the Nineteenth Amendment, most African American women, particularly those living in the South, and many Latinas residing in the Southwest continued to be barred from voting through racist policies specifically designed to prevent people of color from participating in electoral politics (Keyssar 2009; Norman 1997; Terborg-Penn 1998). In fact, some white suffragists, at the time the Nineteenth Amendment was passed, favored steps to continue limiting black women's voting (Terborg-Penn 1998). Black women (and men) in the South were kept from voting until passage of the 1965 Voting Rights Act, and the ability of some Asian Americans, Latinos, and Native Americans to vote freely was restricted until revisions of the Voting Rights Act in the 1970s and 1980s (Desipio 2004; but see also Montoya in this volume). While the Nineteenth Amendment gave many women voting rights, it did not provide the same access to electoral politics for women of color that it did for white women. Women and men of color continued their activism to change voting restrictions well into the twentieth century (Norman 1997; Robnett 1997).

The late 1960s ushered in a period of heightened feminist activism, often referred to as the second wave of feminism. In 1970 the recently formed National Organization for Women (NOW) commemorated fifty years of women's voting by staging a Women's Strike for Equality, with women across the country not only looking back but forward as well, protesting continuing gender inequality and calling for reforms to give women greater economic and political equality. During the 1970s, many US women's groups, although not all, converged again around a specific issue, as they had done earlier in their support for woman suffrage. A core goal of second-wave feminism was passage of the ERA. Liberal and radical feminists, lesbians, and numerous feminist political leaders joined in the demand for greater rights and equality for women (Banaszak 2010; Echols 1989; Taylor and Whittier 1992). Women of color organized, sometimes side by side with white women but often in their own organizations (Roth 2004). But as support for the ERA grew, a countermobilization of conservative women and men came together. They vigorously and ultimately successfully fought ratification, and in 1982, the campaign for the ERA ended in defeat (Critchlow 2005).

Where Are We Today?

Reflecting on the past one hundred years of women's political engagement reveals a complex and diverse history, one that is not easily characterized. A cursory examination shows that women today have made significant strides in the political realm. Women's share of the voting electorate has increased over time, and by 1980, women's voter turnout rates surpassed those of men and have continued to outpace the male vote (Burns et al. 2001, this volume; Center for American Women and Politics 2017a). Women are now voting in elections in higher percentages than their male counterparts, and this is typically true across racial and ethnic groups. Women are also increasingly represented in elective and appointed office, although much of the increase in women's representation occurred in more recent decades (Center for American Women and Politics 2017b). For instance, until the early 1990s women held fewer than thirty-five seats in Congress. Today, this number has increased to over one hundred, and one-third of female congressional office holders are women of color (see Figure 1.1). In recent years, African American women's office-holding has climbed, while black men's has plateaued (Smooth 2014). Women also run exceedingly successful political campaigns. Research shows that female candidates overall are highly competitive in political races, including in their capacity to raise funds (Burrell 1994; Fox 2014). Women voters have also made their mark on political parties, altering party platforms and bringing issues important to women onto the center stage of politics (Freeman 2000; Wolbrecht 2000). In 2016, for the first time in the nation's history, a nominee for president from a major political party was a woman, and although Hillary Clinton did not win the election, she garnered a majority of the popular vote.

As women's efforts around the ERA attest, women continued to engage in social movement activism after suffrage. Women's protest and movement organizations have been pronounced over the past century and not only in feminist activism. Women have played pivotal roles in a variety of other social movements, including the civil rights (Robnett 1997), environmental (Unger 2012), lesbian/gay/bisexual/transgender (LGBT) (Rupp, Taylor, and Roth 2017), and labor movements (Bronfenbrenner 2005; Cobble 1993), to name just some examples. Today, as many have noted, feminist activism often takes place inside the primary institutions of

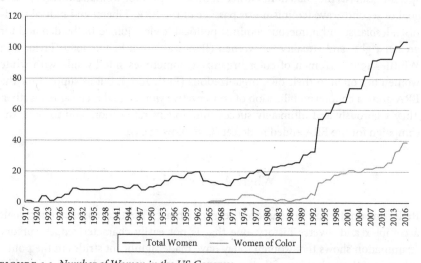

FIGURE 1.1 *Number of Women in the US Congress*
Manning, Brudnick, and Shogan 2015; US House of Representatives 2016.

US society (Banaszak 2010; Freeman 2000; Katzenstein 1998; Staggenborg and Taylor 2005). With substantial increases in women holding positions of formal institutional authority, including within the government, corporations, and religious institutions, feminists now often work as insiders enacting gender-equal policy from within political institutions. But grassroots women's collective action also remains commonplace, including in activism occurring across racial, ethnic, and class communities (Naples 1998) and in social movements in alignment with a variety of political ideologies (Benowitz 2015; Blee 1991). A young political generation of feminist activists enacts feminism today in new ways, including utilizing social media in their activism (Crossley 2015; Reger 2005, 2012; Snyder 2008).

On the other hand, while women have been highly engaged politically over the past hundred years, gender inequality continues today. Women are underrepresented in elected office and in political parties. Indeed, in recent years, women's representation in state legislatures has stagnated or actually declined (Center for American Women and Politics 2017b). Moreover, just as the Nineteenth Amendment did not enfranchise many African American women, women's achievements at the intersections of gender, race, ethnicity, and class in representation and within political institutions have moved at best slowly, albeit with important recent successes (Bejarano 2013; Scola 2006; Sierra 2010). Recent new restrictions on voters, including voter ID laws, have impacted poorer and less educated voters, including both women and men (Hershey 2009). Moreover, women living in poverty or who are members of the working class face continuing political disadvantage in a political system heavily controlled by the affluent (Nelson 1984). Women's experiences in social movements reveal ongoing gendered and patriarchal constraints on their roles, particularly in leadership positions (Evans 1979; McAdam 1992; Robnett 1997; Taylor 2015). Additionally, lesbian and transgender women have found that they are often marginalized, even within movements they have helped to mobilize (Gamson 1995; Taylor and Whittier 1992). As a result, in many respects, the progress in women's roles in politics overall has very real limits.

An Overview of the Book

This volume looks back at the decades since women won the right to vote, to analyze the progress, the limits, and the continuities in women's roles in the broad political sphere. Our volume not only speaks to important and far-reaching changes over the last hundred years, but the discussions here also analyze the achievements in representation and political equality—weighing the lingering and often pronounced shortcomings, with particular attention to women from a variety of racial, ethnic, educational, class, regional, and even ideological backgrounds. Our volume thus seeks to provide a broad appraisal of women's political engagement since enactment of the Nineteenth Amendment. Moreover, the book helps set the stage for understanding women's roles in the political system during the next hundred years. What can we expect from future developments in gender politics and women's political activism? What can be done to remedy continuing limits on women's voices in the political sphere? What can be done to strive for greater gender equality and for greater equality where gender combines with race, ethnicity, and class?

The chapters that follow are divided into three parts. Part I focuses on women's participation in electoral politics. The second and third parts both consider women's organizational and social movement activism, with Part II focused on women's activism, especially feminist activism, and Part III on women's roles in a variety of social movements.

The mobilization for and then adoption of the Nineteenth Amendment provided new access to institutionalized electoral politics for many women. Given this new access, chapters in Part I closely consider changes and continuities in women's participation in this realm across the last century, focusing on women's voter turnout, partisanship, and degree of political involvement, such as working for candidates running for office and communicating with public officials. Contributors to this section also consider women's office holding, examining trends in women's publicly elected positions over time.

The first chapter in this section (chapter 2) begins with a critical election just after women won the vote. J. Kevin Corder and Christina Wolbrecht consider the 1924 presidential election and how women's vote in this election set the electoral stage for the coming decades. Their analysis shows that the new women voters stabilized the electorate. Although women had been visible in the Progressive Party, compared to their male counterparts, they were less likely to vote for Progressive, third-party candidates. Female votes in 1924 tended to bolster the Republican Party and reduce Progressive Party inroads.

In chapter 3, Heather Ondercin studies shifts in women's partisanship over time. She compares women's support for the two major political parties to that of men's over the last century, charting the rise of the gender gap in partisan attachments. She also explores in detail how the gap differs among generations, racial and educational groups, and regions.

Chapter 4 investigates a variety of forms of women's political participation, ranging from placing a bumper sticker on a car to attending political rallies to working on a candidate's campaign. Nancy Burns, Kay Schlozman, Ashley Jardina, Shauna Shames, and Sidney Verba explain gender differences in various types of political participation, ultimately pointing to a "stubbornly persistent gender gap" (beyond voting) marked by greater participation overall among men compared to women in a number of important nonvoting forms of political action.

Celeste Montoya in chapter 5 also explores the theme of women's voting rights, offering a century-long overview, but she retells the historical narrative with an eye to racial disparities and voter suppression. Her chapter recounts the barriers to enfranchisement faced by women at the intersections of race and class and helps us understand the far-reaching impact of recent restrictions on voting, stemming from voter ID laws and court decisions involving the Voting Rights Act. Such developments suggest that the forward progress toward greater equality in politics is not at all a given, especially for women of color and poorer women.

In chapter 6, Jessica Lavariega Monforti offers a retrospective of Latina office holding, tracing how Latinas have moved into elective office since adoption of the Nineteenth Amendment. Her detailed biographies explore the intersections of ethnicity, class, citizenship status, and family influence as well as the role of self-identity as Latinas succeed in winning congressional office and navigate a variety of policy arenas in their work as lawmakers.

Chapter 7, the final chapter in Part I, takes a different approach to the study of institutionalized politics and examines women's election into state legislatures over time. Susan Welch's chapter shows how voting rights opened the door for women's election into state legislatures, slowly at first and then with increasing speed after 1970. But she finds striking differences among the states. Welch analyzes the possible explanations for these differences, looking at regions, women's economic and educational equity, and a number of other factors. At the same time she explores why the growth overall in women's representation since the 1990s has stagnated at the state level.

In the book's second and third parts, our contributors consider women's political engagement beyond the conventional politics of the electoral process. Parts II and III instead take a close look at women's extra institutional politics, politics characterized by organizational activism and often the protest politics of the streets. In Part II, our contributors focus specifically on women mobilizing as women, fighting to broaden women's rights and for issues women deem important for women. In Part III, our authors explore women's activist contributions in a diverse set of other social movements: civil rights, movements for nonviolence, white supremacy, environmentalism, and the Occupy movement. While some of these contributors find continuities in the gender bias women face even as they mobilize in contemporary social movements, often the message of these chapters concerns the critical nature of women's agency and contributions in this broad array of social movements.

In Part II, three chapters provide distinct investigations of women's activism as they mobilize as "feminists" or in "women's organizations"—in both cases, women engaging in political activism specifically as women and on behalf of what women deem women's issues. In chapter 8 Laura Nelson helps us conceptualize feminist activism, tracing continuities in feminist consciousness from the time of passage of the Nineteenth Amendment through second-wave feminism and up to the present. Nelson documents a century of feminist activists' collective focus on the ways in which "the personal is political." Her investigation reveals that consciousness-raising groups emerging in the 1960s and 1970s were preceded by "interpersonal feminism" among the earlier suffragists. Her chapter illuminates a continuity running through feminism over the last one-hundred-plus years. She finds that over this long period, across multiple generations, feminists have drawn on and shared their everyday experiences, and they have continued to conclude that "personal problems" are political and can be "open to collective change."

Kristin Goss's chapter (chapter 9) also helps orient our understanding of a century of women's social movement activism by offering a broad overview of a range of women's organizational efforts from 1880 until 2000. While many argue that women's groups died off just after women won suffrage in 1920, Goss's study shows quite the opposite: women's organizations, most of them national in scope, played critical and influential roles in lobbying Congress in the decades after winning the ballot. The influence continued through much of the twentieth century, only declining in the most recent decades for reasons Goss discusses.

In chapter 10 Tracey Jean Boisseau and Tracy Thomas describe nearly a century of struggle for an equal rights amendment, from its earliest history just after passage of women's voting rights in 1920 through second-wave feminism. These authors also bring the story up to the present, as a new coalition of feminist activists continues to press for a constitutional amendment guaranteeing women's legal equality. Boisseau and Thomas remind us of the divisions among women's groups in the ERA's history, both in the earlier part of the twentieth century when some groups claimed that the amendment would undermine women's workplace protective laws and in the 1970s and 1980s as conservative women argued that legal equality would encroach upon women's traditional roles as mothers and homemakers. Boisseau and Thomas conclude their chapter with a discussion of gender equality under contemporary law and an analysis of whether the ERA continues to be needed today.

Part III's chapters investigate women's influential roles in other key social movements, beyond specifically women's mobilizations, on both the left and the right. This section of our volume allows us to see the variety of women's social movement efforts. Brittany Hearne and Holly McCammon in chapter 11 examine multiple generations of black women cause lawyers using their legal expertise over the last century to fight within the legal system for civil rights for African Americans and gender equality for women. Today these legal activists have led the way in developing the intersectionality framework, allowing us to see how multiple interlocking systems of oppression constrain the lives of those with politicized identities.

In chapter 12 Selina Gallo-Cruz explores the intellectual and organizational effects women have had in movements of nonviolence in the twentieth century. She discusses the long-lived problem of how women's contributions to these efforts have been ignored or marginalized not only in activism but also in scholarship. Her chapter helps to right this wrong and allows us to see feminist nonviolence in a myriad of movement mobilizations and to appreciate the important contributions these women made to nonviolent activism.

Kathleen Blee in chapter 13 recounts changing women's roles in white supremacist movements over the last century. These racist movements were and continue to be an undertone in US political life; Blee explores women's links to men in these movement groups and reveals substantial ways in which gender influences women's (and men's) participation in white supremacy, often maintaining women's subordination within this movement.

Holly McCammon, Allison McGrath, David J. Hess, and Minyoung Moon, in chapter 14, explore women's leadership over the last hundred years in the environmental movement. The authors trace the varied and diverse roles of women environmentalists, including white women's preservation and conservation efforts in the early part of the twentieth century, African American women's critical leadership in the environmental justice movement, Native American women's spiritual connection to the land, and women's leadership in national environmental organizations in recent decades.

In chapter 15 Heather McKee Hurwitz and Verta Taylor reveal the gender conflicts that took place within the recent Occupy Wall Street movement. These authors illustrate how conflicts within a social movement that "disadvantage, threaten, or harm women, genderqueer persons and sexual minorities" can fuel a feminist collective identity. Their study demonstrates that today's feminist mobilizations often take place within other groups and settings, environments that are not initially explicitly feminist, but, because of continuing sexism and women's resistance of it, become enmeshed in gender politics and generate consciously feminist mobilizations.

We conclude the volume by summarizing its main themes and discussing ways in which these themes continue to be relevant for the US political scene. The 2016 presidential election contested by the first woman candidate from one of the two major parties and a contest itself that evidences the continued barriers to women in organized politics reflects many of these themes (Bordo 2017). Our conclusion also considers the ways these themes will continue into the second century of women's enfranchisement and political activism.

In 1906 in her last suffrage speech before her death, Susan B. Anthony left her listeners with the following words, "Failure is impossible" (Sherr 1995). These words became a motto for the suffragists as they continued to pursue and then succeeded in ratifying the Nineteenth Amendment. The words still hold much meaning for women today. Women have continued their struggle throughout the last one hundred years to achieve gender equality and a broader and more diverse political voice for women. In 1965, southern black women and men succeeded in gaining passage of the Voting Rights Act. Today, increasing numbers of women are running for political office, including many women of color. And women (and men) will continue to work to put a female president in the White House. Women's activism in the civil sphere, not only in the women's movement but in a large array of protests and social movement groups, helps shape the contour and content of US politics. Women over the last century have moved decisively and powerfully even further into the political arena. But as our appraisal of women's political engagement since the Nineteenth Amendment also shows, some clear goals still need to be reached. Women need equal representation in political office, and women from all backgrounds need to have a political voice and fair representation. Women are still striving to be equal participants in the US democratic system. We have more work to do, but Anthony's words from the past can provide optimism and courage as women continue to work for an equal presence for all women in the political arena.

References

Adams, Katherine H., and Michael L. Keene. 2008. *Alice Paul and the American Suffrage Campaign*. Urbana: University of Illinois Press.

Andersen, Kristi. 1996. *After Suffrage: Women in Partisan and Electoral Politics before the New Deal*. Chicago: University of Chicago Press.

Banaszak, Lee Ann. 1996. *Why Movements Succeed or Fail: Opportunity, Culture, and the Struggle for Woman Suffrage*. Princeton, NJ: Princeton University Press.

———. 2010. *The Women's Movement Inside and Outside the State*. New York: Cambridge University Press.

Bejarano, Christina E. 2013. *The Latino Advantage: Gender, Race, and Political Success*. Austin: University of Texas Press.

Benowitz, June Melby. 2015. *Challenge and Change: Right-Wing Women, Grassroots Activism, &the Baby Boom Generation*. Gainesville: University Press of Florida.

Blee, Kathleen M. 1991. *Women in the Klan: Racism and Gender in the 1920s*. Berkeley: University of California Press.

Bordo, Susan. 2017. *The Destruction of Hillary Clinton*. New York: Melville House Publishing.

Bronfenbrenner, Kate. 2005. "Organizing Women: The Nature and Process of Union Organizing Efforts among U.S. Women Workers since the Mid-1990s." *Work and Occupations* 32: 441–463.

Buechler, Steven M. 1990. *Women's Movement in the United States*. New Brunswick, NJ: Rutgers University Press.

Burns, Nancy, Kay Lehman Schlozman, and Sidney Verba. 2001. *The Private Roots of Public Action*. Cambridge: Cambridge University Press.

Burrell, Barbara. 1994. *A Women's Place Is in the House: Campaigning for Congress in the Feminist Era*. Ann Arbor: University of Michigan Press.

Butler, Amy E. 2002. *Two Paths to Equality: Alice Paul and Ethel M. Smith in the ERA Debate, 1921–1929*. Albany: State University of New York Press.

Catt, Carrie Chapman, and Nettie Rogers Shuler. 1923. *Woman Suffrage and Politics: The Inner Story of the Suffrage Movement*. New York: C. Scribner's Sons.

Center for American Women and Politics. 2017a. "Gender Differences in Voter Turnout." http://www.cawp.rutgers.edu/sites/default/files/resources/genderdiff.pdf.

———. 2017b. "Women in Elective Office 2017." http://www.cawp.rutgers.edu/women-elective-office-2017.

Cobble, Dorothy Sue, ed. 1993. *Women and Unions: Forging a Partnership*. Ithaca, NY: ILR Press.

Cott, Nancy F. 1987. *The Grounding of Modern Feminism*. New Haven, CT: Yale University Press.

Critchlow, Donald T. 2005. *Phyllis Schlafly and Grassroots Conservatism: A Woman's Crusade*. Princeton, NJ: Princeton University Press.

Crossley, Alison Dahl. 2015. "Facebook Feminism: Facebook, Blogs, and New Technologies of Contemporary U.S. Feminism." *Mobilization* 20: 253–269.

Desipio, Louis. 2004. "The Pressures of Perpetual Promise: Latinos and Politics, 1960–2003." Pp. 421–466 in *The Columbia History of Latinos in the United States since 1960*. New York: Columbia University Press.

DuBois, Ellen Carol. 1978. *Feminism and Suffrage: The Emergence of an Independent Women's Movement in America, 1848–1969*. Ithaca, NY: Cornell University Press.

Echols, Alice. 1989. *Daring to Be Bad: Radical Feminism in America, 1967–1975*. Minneapolis: University of Minnesota Press.

Evans, Sara. 1979. *Personal Politics: The Roots of Women's Liberation in the Civil Rights Movement and the New Left.* New York: Vintage Books.

Flexner, Eleanor. [1959] 1996. *Century of Struggle: The Woman's Rights Movement in the United States.* Cambridge, MA: Belknap Press of Harvard University Press.

Fox, Richard L. 2014. "Congressional Elections: Women's Candidacies and the Road to Gender Parity." Pp. 190–209 in *Gender and Elections: Shaping the Future of American Politics,* edited by Susan J. Carroll and Richard L. Fox. New York: Cambridge University Press.

Freeman, Jo. 2000. *A Room at a Time: How Women Entered Party Politics.* Lanham, MD: Rowman and Littlefield Publishers.

Gamson, Joshua. 1995. "Must Identity Movements Self-Destruct? A Queer Dilemma." *Social Problems* 42: 390–407.

Goss, Kristin. 2013. *The Paradox of Gender Equality: How American Women's Groups Gained and Lost Their Public Voice.* Ann Arbor: University of Michigan Press.

Graham, Sara Hunter. 1996. *Woman Suffrage and the New Democracy.* New Haven, CT: Yale University Press.

Harrison, Cynthia. 1988. *On Account of Sex: The Politics of Women's Issues, 1945–1968.* Berkeley: University of California Press.

Hershey, Marjorie Randon. 2009. "What We Know about Voter-ID Law, Registration, and Turnout." *PS: Political Science & Politics* 42: 87–91.

Iron Jawed Angels. 2004. Director, Katja von Garnier. HBO Films.

Katzenstein, Mary Fainsod. 1998. *Faithful and Fearless: Moving Feminist Protest inside the Church and Military.* Princeton, NJ: Princeton University Press.

Keyssar, Alexander. 2009. *The Right to Vote: The Contested History of Democracy in the United State.* New York: Basic Books.

Kirkby, Diane. 1987. "The Wage-Earning Woman and the State: The National Women's Trade Union League and Protective Labor Legislation, 1903–1923." *Labor History* 28: 54–74.

Manning, Jennifer E., Ida A. Brudnick, and Colleen J. Shogan. 2015. "Women in Congress: Historical Overview, Tables, and Discussion." *Congressional Research Service.* April 29. https://www.fas.org/sgp/crs/misc/R43244.pdf.

Mansbridge, Jane J. 1986. *Why We Lost the ERA.* Chicago: University of Chicago Press.

McAdam, Doug. 1992. "Gender as a Mediator of the Activist Experience: The Case of Freedom Summer." *American Journal of Sociology* 97: 1211–1240.

McCammon, Holly J., Karen E. Campbell, Ellen Granberg, and Christine Mowery. 2001. "How Movements Win: Gendered Opportunity Structures and U.S. Women's Suffrage Movements, 1866 to 1919." *American Sociological Review* 66:49–70.

McConnaughy, Corinne. 2013. *The Woman Suffrage Movement in America: A Reassessment.* Cambridge: Cambridge University Press.

Naples, Nancy A. 1998. *Community Activism and Feminist Politics: Organizing across Race, Class, and Gender.* New York: Routledge.

Nelson, Barbara J. 1984. "Women's Poverty and Women's Citizenship: Some Political Consequences of Economic Marginality." *Women and Poverty* 10: 209–231.

Norman, Martha Prescod. 1997. "Shining in the Dark: Black Women and the Struggle for the Vote, 1955–1965." Pp. 172–199 in *African American Women and the Vote, 1837–1965,* edited by Ann D. Gordon. Amherst: University of Massachusetts Press.

Noun, Louise M. 1989. *In the Public Interest: The League of Women Voters, 1920–1970*. New York: Greenwood Press.

Reger, Jo. 2005. *Different Wavelengths: Studies of the Contemporary Women's Movement*. New York: Routledge.

———. 2012. *Everywhere & Nowhere: Contemporary Feminism in the United States*. New York: Oxford University Press.

Robnett, Belinda. 1997. *How Long? How Long? African American Women in the Struggle for Civil Rights*. New York: Oxford University Press.

Roth, Benita. 2004. *Separate Roads to Feminism: Black, Chicana, and White Feminist Movements in America's Second Wave*. New York: Cambridge University Press.

Rupp, Leila J., Verta Taylor, and Benita Roth. 2017. "Women in the Lesbian, Gay, Bisexual, and Transgender Movement." Pp. 664–684 in *The Oxford Handbook of U.S. Women's Social Movement Activism*, edited by Holly J. McCammon, Verta Taylor, Jo Reger, and Rachel Einwohner. New York: Oxford University Press.

Scola, Becki. 2006. "Women of Color in State Legislatures: Gender, Race, Ethnicity, and Legislative Office Holding." *Journal of Women, Politics & Policy* 28: 43–70.

Sherr, Lynn. 1995. *Failure Is Impossible: Susan B. Anthony in Her Own Words*. New York: Times Books.

Sierra, Christine Marie. 2010. "Latinas and Electoral Politics: Movin' on Up." Pp. 144–164 in *Gender and Elections: Shaping the Future of American Politics*, second edition, edited by Susan L. Carroll and Richard Logan Fox. New York: Cambridge University Press.

Smooth, Wendy. 2014. "African American Women and Electoral Politics: Translating Voter Power into Officeholding." Pp. 167–189 in *Gender and Elections: Shaping the Future of American Politics*, third edition, edited by Susan L. Carroll and Richard Logan Fox. New York: Cambridge University Press.

Snyder, R. Claire. 2008. "What Is Third-Wave Feminism? A New Directions Essay." *Signs* 34: 175–196.

Spruill Wheeler, Marjorie. 1995. *Votes for Women! The Woman Suffrage Movement in Tennessee, the South, and the Nation*. Knoxville: University of Tennessee Press.

Staggenborg, Suzanne, and Verta Taylor. 2005. "Whatever Happened to the Women's Movement." *Mobilization* 10: 37–52.

Stanton, Elizabeth Cady, Susan B. Anthony, and Matilda Joslyn Gage. 1881 [1985]. *History of Woman Suffrage*. Volume 1. Salem, NH: Ayer Company Publishers.

Stevens, Doris. 1920. *Jailed for Freedom*. New York: Boni and Liveright.

Taylor, Dorceta E. 2015. "Gender and Racial Diversity in Environmental Organizations: Uneven Accomplishments and Cause for Concern." *Environmental Justice* 8(5): 165–180.

Taylor, Verta, and Nancy E. Whittier. 1992. "Collective Identity in Social Movement Communities: Lesbian Feminist Mobilization." Pp. 104–129 in *Frontiers in Social Movement Theory*, edited by Aldon D. Morris and Carol McClurg Mueller. New Haven, CT: Yale University Press.

Terborg-Penn, Rosalyn. 1998. *African American Women in the Struggle for the Vote, 1850–1920*. Bloomington: Indiana University Press.

Unger, Nancy D. 2012. *Beyond Nature's Housekeepers: American Women in Environmental History*. New York: Oxford University Press.

United States House of Representatives. 2016. "Women of Color in Congress." <http://history.house.gov/Exhibitions-and-Publications/WIC/Historical-Data/Women-of-Color-in-Congress/>.

Wolbrecht, Christina. 2000. *The Politics of Women's Rights: Parties, Positions, and Change.* Princeton, NJ: Princeton University Press.

{ PART I }

Women's Participation in Electoral Politics

ONE HUNDRED YEARS OF CHANGE
AND CONTINUITY

2

Disappointed Hopes?

FEMALE VOTERS AND THE 1924 PROGRESSIVE SURGE

J. Kevin Corder and Christina Wolbrecht

How do women employ their hard-earned right to vote? Since before the Nineteenth Amendment was ratified, observers and scholars have been interested in the possibility that women might use their ballots to support different parties, candidates, and causes than do men. As Heather Ondercin details in her chapter, we now have a significant body of research focused on understanding the modern gender gap, the popular term for differences in the partisan identification and vote choices of women and men. While the causes of the contemporary Democratic advantage among female voters remain contested, the fact of that difference in behavior has been well-established and tracked since at least the 1980 presidential election (Ladd 1997).

We know far less, however, about how the first women enfranchised by the Nineteenth Amendment cast their ballots. The conventional wisdom about the earliest female voters is often conflicting—that women voted just as their husbands did, that women favored the Republican Party, that women simply failed to use their new right. This conventional wisdom rests on very limited evidence. With rare exceptions, ballots are not distinguished by the sex of the person who drops them in the ballot box, so official records do not report the distinct vote choice of men and women. The modern solution to this problem, mass opinion polls, were either unavailable or unreliable during the first decades following enfranchisement. A few careful studies have provided insights into how women voted in a few elections in a small number of places (see, especially, Andersen 1994; Gamm 1986; Goldstein 1984). On the whole, however, we know very little about how the first female voters cast their ballots, despite confident assumptions—both at the time and over the past one hundred years—about how those women were likely to vote.

In this chapter, we examine one particularly widespread expectation—that the first women to enter polling places would vote in ways that reflected their sympathies toward Progressive movement goals and values. Women and women's organizations had been active and prominent participants in the Progressive movement, and many Progressive issues, such as child labor and especially Prohibition, were believed to be natural concerns of women. In much the same way that some analysts have attributed the modern gender gap in favor of the Democratic Party to women's (innate) inclination to care (see Huddy, Cassese, and Lizotte 2008), contemporaries of the first female voters assumed that essential gender differences in ethical perspective and moral values would translate into distinctive patterns of partisan support in favor of parties and candidates associated with the Progressive movement.

The presidential election of 1924 provides a unique opportunity to examine these expectations. The Republican Party had long been the party associated with Progressivism, and many expected that suffrage initially benefited Republican candidates (e.g., Brown 1991; Burner 1986). In the first presidential elections following the enactment of the Nineteenth Amendment, however, the two major parties differed little on Progressive issues; both largely ignored Progressive concerns in favor of pro-business policy positions. In response, activists mobilized behind the presidential candidacy of long-standing Progressive standard-bearer Senator Robert M. La Follette in 1924. For our purposes, La Follette's campaign provides a direct test of the expectation that women would be a natural constituency for a Progressive Party candidate. By 1924 women in every state of the nation had access to the voting booth and, in the intervening four years since the ratification of the Nineteenth Amendment, sufficient time to adjust to their new civic responsibility.

In this chapter we first review the electoral context and expectations for newly enfranchised female voters. We then introduce our unique estimates of women's turnout and vote choice in 1924. We overcome the challenges inherent in the lack of electoral records or survey data by employing recent innovations in ecological inference to estimate women's turnout and vote choice in ten states, part of a larger project analyzing women's electoral behavior in the period immediately following suffrage. We find that new female voters were not uniquely likely to defect from major party loyalties in order to support the Progressive candidate. If anything, male voters were more likely to cast third-party ballots; in a small number of Republican-dominated midwestern states, female voters were more Republican than men, and men were more Progressive than women, in their voting choices. In contrast to widely held expectations, we find that women tended to be mobilized by and were more loyal to the locally dominant political party than were men, even when offered a credible Progressive Party option. As a result, we ultimately conclude that the presence of large numbers of female voters actually stabilized the electorate, reinforcing the Republican advantage in most states and dampening the Progressive surge in the Midwest in particular. In the conclusion we put these findings in the broader perspective of the nearly one hundred years of female electoral participation that has followed.

The Election of 1924

Republican Calvin Coolidge assumed the office of the presidency following the death of Warren Harding in 1923 and was nominated on his own accord in 1924.

Coolidge was considered quite favorably inclined toward business interests (Hicks 1960); in addition to his famous quietude, Coolidge is perhaps best known for his claim that "the chief business of the American people is business" (Gould 2003: 242). On the Democratic side, the inability of various factions to agree on a nominee resulted in a convention that required more than one hundred votes before it could settle on John W. Davis, a fairly unknown compromise candidate (Burnham 1986; Hofstadter 1955).

Disappointed with the major-party candidates, various reform groups united behind the candidacy of Wisconsin senator Robert M. La Follette. La Follette was the leader of Progressive forces in Congress and a failed candidate for the Republican nomination (Burner 1971; Hicks 1960). La Follette's coalition sought to unite such disparate groups as organized labor, farm organizations, and Socialists (Burner 1971, 1986). Maintaining such a diverse coalition proved difficult for the campaign, but the radical and idealistic La Follette remained popular within the Progressive movement, and his candidacy provided the sole alternative to the more conservative platforms offered by the two major parties (Unger 2000).

In November, La Follette and the Progressive Party won almost 5 million votes—about 17% of the total—and carried his home state of Wisconsin (Burner 1986). In eleven other states, La Follette outpolled the Democratic nominee (MacKay 1947). Support tended to be largely focused in a handful of states in the Plains and Upper Midwest. Nationwide, Coolidge received 54% of the vote (down from the 60% Republicans polled in 1920), and Davis just 29% (Scammon 1965).

Expectations for Female Voters in 1924

While attention to female voters was not as great as it had been in the wake of ratification of the Nineteenth Amendment in 1920, the press and the public expressed considerable interest in the potential political behavior and influence of female voters in 1924. Many expected, or hoped, that with four years to acclimate to their new political role, women's turnout and impact would be improved over 1920.[1]

The state and national League of Women Voters, as well as other organizations, sought to mobilize female voters with both education and practical political training in 1924 (Breckinridge 1933).[2] Political parties also worked to appeal to and train female voters (Freeman 2000).[3] Party appeals tended to be gender-specific; the parties believed they would be most successful at mobilizing women *as women*, emphasizing how the party's candidates and positions were of particular appeal to the interests and concerns of women. Both Democrats and Republicans, for example, organized women's clubs in anticipation of the 1924 presidential election with the goal of increasing female turnout for each party over 1920 (Harvey 1998), and Democrats produced a 146-page Women's Democratic Campaign Manual that highlighted the party's positions on family and children's issues (Greenlee 2014).

The case of La Follette's Progressive Party presidential candidacy is a particularly fruitful opportunity to evaluate the different expectations for women's vote choice and partisanship. Certainly, most contemporary politicians and later scholars recognized that newly enfranchised female voters were diverse and expected women to cast ballots for a variety of parties and candidates (McConnaughy 2013). Yet many expected that women would be particularly likely to support candidates associated with Progressivism. Women and women's organizations were visible participants in the Progressive movement. Both had played an active role in Theodore Roosevelt's 1912 Progressive "Bull Moose" campaign (Freeman 2000). Progressive ideals, such as moral reform, were consistent with the qualities of purity, piety, and domesticity associated with women in the nineteenth and early twentieth centuries (Evans 1989; Baker 1984; Welter 1966). Progressives were early and ardent advocates for women's suffrage, and suffrage and Progressive organizations and parties had often been coalition allies (McConnaughy 2013). At the same time, opposition to women's suffrage had been motivated in no small part by the expectation that women would use the vote to achieve Progressive goals, particularly temperance (McDonagh and Price 1985; Flexner 1970), as Figure 2.1 suggests. Historians and early voting analysts expected that Progressive issues such as prostitution, child labor, workplace health and safety, good government, and especially prohibition weighed heavily in women's voting decisions (Allen 1930; Flexner 1970; McCormick 1928; O'Neill 1971; Ogburn and Goltra 1919; Rice and Willey 1924; Russell 1924; Tarbell 1924; Toombs 1929; Wells 1929; Willey and Rice 1924). Consistent with those expectations, Goldstein (1984) finds that women were more likely than men to cast votes for the Progressive candidates in University of Illinois Board of Trustee elections prior to 1920 (see also Andersen 1979).

The association of Progressivism and the campaign for women's suffrage also contributed to the expectation that women would be more committed to ideals than to any particular party, and thus more likely to defect from traditional party loyalties (Monoson 1990; Rogers 1930; Barnard 1928). While the strength of party allegiance was weakening from its late-nineteenth-century zenith, parties still constituted a strong bond between citizens and the political system in the 1920s. The Progressive movement denounced political parties as corrupt and inefficient, so to the extent women were associated with the Progressives, they were expected

FIGURE 2.1 *Antisuffrage Button*
From the suffrage collection of Dr. Kenneth Florey. Used with permission.

to be wary of the major parties (Andersen 1996, 1990; Lemons 1973; Russell 1924). More generally, the legacy of disenfranchisement meant that women had had fewer opportunities to reinforce their partisanship through voting, and might be expected to have weaker partisan attachments and greater likelihood of defection as a result (Converse 1969, 1976).

The election of 1924 thus provides a unique opportunity to observe gender differences in major party loyalty and support for Progressive ideals. La Follette himself had a long history of advocating for women's suffrage and women's rights, and his wife, Belle, had been a popular suffragist speaker (MacKay 1947; Thelen 1976). The Women's Division of the La Follette campaign sponsored speeches by prominent activists such as Hull House founder Jane Addams and Harriet Stanton Blatch, Elizabeth Cady Stanton's daughter and a well-known suffragist in her own right (Unger 2000). Yet few scholars have been able to even speculate as to the level of support for the Progressive Party among female voters in 1924. The analysis that follows thus offers unique answers to these questions.

Estimating Women's Vote Choice in 1924

Scholars and political observers have been lamenting the difficulty of observing the distinct electoral behavior of men and women since women first entered polling places. The challenge for scholars is described simply by Ogburn and Goltra (1919: 413): "women's ballots are not distinguished from those of men but are deposited in the same ballot box." As a result, in virtually all cases, official records report only the total number of votes cast and the number of votes cast for each candidate. With few, important exceptions, whether women cast ballots, for which candidates, and with what consequence cannot be directly determined from the actual vote record.

This chapter draws on our original estimates of women's turnout and vote choice in a sample of ten states, part of a broader project tracing the electoral behavior of women in the five presidential elections immediately following suffrage. We combine US Census and election return data, and employ a statistical technique known as *ecological inference* to estimate the turnout and vote choice of women and men. (The estimation strategy is described briefly in the appendix to this chapter and in detail in Corder and Wolbrecht 2016.) For those interested in evaluating the reliability of our estimates of the percentage of women and men turning out to vote and casting ballots for each party, we provide detailed evaluations of the estimator elsewhere (Corder and Wolbrecht 2016). We offer one kind of particularly compelling evidence here. As a rule, official election returns are not reported for distinct demographic groups. A brief, important exception is the state of Illinois, where from 1916 (1913 in the city of Chicago) through 1920, male and female ballots were recorded and reported separately. We can thus compare our estimates of male and female electoral behavior (based on aggregate Census and election return data) to the actual reported vote choice of men and women in Illinois during two presidential elections during this period.

Figure 2.2, which compares the estimated and observed Republican vote choice of women and men during the 1920 presidential election, demonstrates that our estimates do an impressive job of recovering the "true" electoral behavior of men and women in Illinois. Our estimates tend to fall quite close to the 45-degree line (perfect replication of the observed value by our estimated value), suggesting that despite the considerable challenges of ecological inference in general and for gender specifically, we can be confident in the ability of our methodological approach

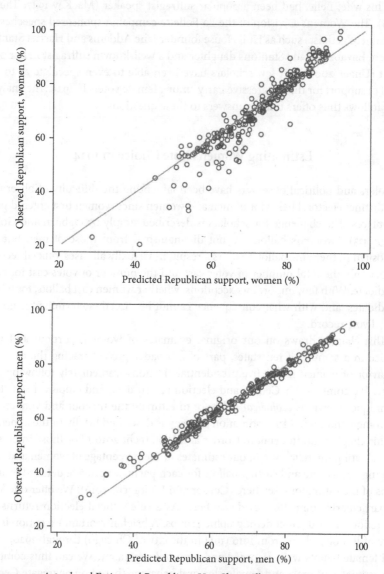

FIGURE 2.2 *Actual and Estimated Republican Vote Share, Illinois, 1920*

Note: Data points represent 96 counties, 103 minor civil divisions, and 35 wards. See the appendix for further information.

to provide reasonable estimates of the electoral behavior of men and women in the years following suffrage.

Given this and other reasons to be confident about our approach, we then apply this method to a total of ten states in 1924, listed and described in Table 2.1. Data availability challenges limit the geographic scope and representation of the states we are able to analyze, and thus our sample is not fully representative of the broader US electorate (see Corder and Wolbrecht 2016 for further information). Our sample is similar to the United States in Republican vote share in 1924 (54.2% in the US compared to 54.9% in our sample). Further, in terms of the percentage of the population that is white, foreign-born, and resides in urban areas, the ten state sample is representative of the nation as a whole. More importantly, these ten sample states permit us to evaluate the behavior of female voters for a broader and more varied set of states—in terms of such politically-relevant variables as region, partisanship, and competitiveness—than was possible in previous analyses, which were limited to a single state or city (e.g., Andersen 1994; Gamm 1986; Goldstein 1984).

The 1924 election took place during a period in which partisanship was very regional and most states were dominated by one or the other major party, with Democratic super-majorities in the South, and Republican dominance in the North and West (Burnham 1981). Our measure of party context is based on the percentage of seats held by each party in the state legislature, thus capturing local partisan power and influence, rather than a response to any particular presidential election (see Corder and Wolbrecht 2016). We organize our states by region and party context in the figures reported below: We start with our one-party Democratic southern state (Virginia) on the far left, then report on our two border states, with a one-party Democratic state (Oklahoma) followed by a competitive Democratic-leaning state (Kentucky). We then move on to our midwestern

TABLE 2.1 Description of sample states used in analysis

State	Date of Presidential Women's Suffrage[1]	Region	Electoral College Vote Share (1920)	Party Competition[2]
Connecticut	1920	Northeast	1.3	One-party Republican
Illinois	1913	Midwest	5.5	One-party Republican
Iowa	1919	Midwest	2.5	One-party Republican
Kansas	1912	Midwest	1.9	One-party Republican
Kentucky	1920	Border	2.5	Competitive Democratic
Massachusetts	1920	Northeast	3.4	One-party Republican
Minnesota	1919	Midwest	2.3	One-party Republican
Missouri	1919	Midwest	3.4	Competitive Republican
Oklahoma	1918	Border	1.9	One-party Democratic
Virginia	1920	Solid South	2.3	One-party Democratic

1. Credit: Keyssar (2000).

2. Credit: Burnham (1981) for 1914–1930. Burnham did not classify Minnesota since the legislature was nonpartisan. The Conservative Caucus (Republican in practice) was dominant in Minnesota.

states, starting with a competitive Republican-leaning state (Missouri) and then four one-party Republican states (Minnesota, Iowa, Kansas, and Illinois). Finally, to the far right we report the findings for our two one-party Republican states in the Northeast (Connecticut and Massachusetts).

Female Turnout in 1924

We begin with a general picture of women's electoral behavior in 1924. In our sample as a whole, women's turnout was 38%, a small increase over 1920, when we estimate women's turnout at 36%. Male turnout, on the other hand, is basically unchanged from 1920 to 1924: estimated male turnout in our sample is 68% in 1920 and 67% in 1924. In 1924, then, while women's turnout increased slightly, women continued to lag significantly behind men in exercising their right to vote.

Many factors likely contributed to women's overall lower levels of turnout, relative to men, in the elections immediately following suffrage. Disenfranchisement had denied women the opportunity to develop the habit of voting (Gerber, Green, and Shachar 2003; Plutzer 2002). Moreover, even with the achievement of suffrage, views about the inappropriateness of political activity for women remained persistent, and likely discouraged women from exercising their new right (Andersen 1990, 1996). Indeed, the experience of disenfranchisement would dampen women's turnout throughout their lives (Firebaugh and Chen 1995); nationwide, women's rate of turnout did not exceed that of men until 1980 (Center for American Women and Politics 2014).

Our state-level data tell a more complicated story, however. State-level turnout for each sample state is summarized in Figure 2.3. In every state save Iowa, fewer than half of women exercised their right to vote. Male turnout, on the other hand, exceeds 60% in every state except Virginia, and exceeds or approaches 70% in six of our ten states. In general, the turnout gender gap narrows as overall turnout in the state increases, suggesting that the factors encouraging (or discouraging) men's turnout did so to an even greater extent for women. Again excluding extremely low-turnout Virginia (which puts a ceiling on the size of the gender gap), the largest turnout gender gap is in Connecticut (37 points), where overall turnout was 44% (second lowest in our sample), while the smallest gender gap can be found in Missouri (22 points), where overall turnout was 61% (the third highest in our sample).

We emphasize that while women's turnout consistently lags behind that of men, and often to a considerable degree, the level of electoral mobilization among women, just four years after the ratification of the Nineteenth Amendment, is quite impressive in a number of places. Despite the legacy of disenfranchisement and social norms that continued to discourage political participation among women, more than half of age-eligible women in Iowa, and more than 40% in Kentucky, Missouri, Kansas, and Illinois, took advantage of their new right in 1924. On the other hand, fewer than 30% of women in Connecticut, Massachusetts, and Oklahoma—and fewer than 10% in Virginia—exercised their right to vote. The

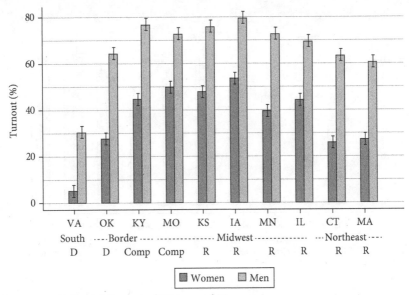

FIGURE 2.3 *Estimated Turnout of Women and Men, 1924*

states where more women turned out to vote tended to be more competitive and had fewer legal barriers to voting, such as poll taxes. The states where women were less likely to turn out tended to be less competitive and featured more barriers to electoral participation. The considerable variation in women's rate of turnout across states suggests that *where* women were first enfranchised, and the degree to which that context encouraged or discouraged their participation, was as important to their embrace of the vote as the fact that they were women.

The Partisan Mobilization of Women in 1924

How were women mobilized by parties—Democrats, Republicans, and uniquely, Progressives—in 1924? In our sample as a whole, the share of women's votes secured by the Republican Party declined from 63% in 1920 to 57% in 1924. Men's Republican vote share also declined, and by about the same amount, from 61% in 1920 to 53% in 1924. Thus, women in our sample were slightly more likely to vote Republican than were men, as they had been in 1920.

Our state-level estimates of Republican vote share, reported in Figure 2.4, once again tell a more complicated story. In one-party Democratic Virginia and Oklahoma, men's and women's vote choice is similar; our point estimates actually suggest that women in Virginia were mobilized by locally dominant Democrats to a greater extent than were men. The extremely low turnout of women in Virginia generates wide credible intervals that keep us from drawing strong conclusions, but even in this case, 79% of the simulations are consistent with the conclusion that women's Republican support was lower than men's.[4] Thus, where Democrats

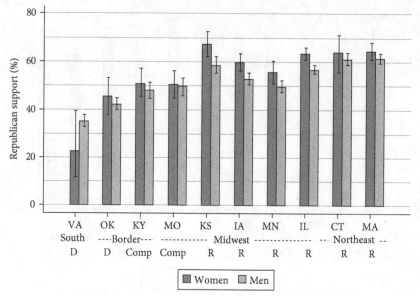

FIGURE 2.4 *Republican Vote Share of Women and Men, 1924*

were dominant, we have some evidence that women were even more Democratic in their voting behavior than were men. In competitive Kentucky and Missouri, on the other hand, men and women are equally likely to be mobilized by Republicans.

In all four of our one-party Republican states in the Midwest, however, women are more likely to be mobilized by Republicans than are men. The simulations suggest we can be very confident of this conclusion: In Minnesota, Iowa, Illinois, and Kansas, women's Republican support exceeds men's in 90% or more of the simulations in each state; in Illinois, that figure is more than 99%. In the traditionally Republican US East Coast (Massachusetts and Connecticut), on the other hand, the gender differences in Republican support are negligible. In Connecticut, for instance, women's Republican support exceeded men's support in only 66% of the simulations. Overall, then, the incorporation of new female voters appeared to reinforce the advantages for locally dominant parties in 1924.

Mobilization by Progressives

We now turn to the central question motivating this chapter: What about the long-held expectations that women would be weaker partisans and particularly likely to support candidates associated with the Progressive cause? Figure 2.5 reports the Progressive vote share for women and men in each of our sample states. Progressive Party support[5] in 1924 was extremely regional and concentrated in the upper Midwest—in our sample, Iowa and Minnesota, in particular. Progressives secured over 25% of the votes cast in Iowa and, astoundingly, over 40% in Minnesota.

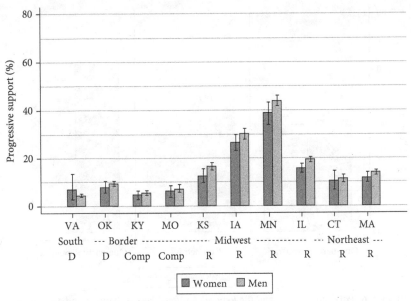

FIGURE 2.5 *Progressive Vote Share of Women and Men, 1924*

The key finding of Figure 2.5 is clear: Our estimates do not support the expectation that women were uniquely supportive of or mobilized by the Progressive Party. In only one state in our sample—Virginia—does the point estimate for female vote share for the Progressive Party exceed male vote share, but given the low turnout of women, we cannot be confident of this difference. In every other state in our sample, estimated male Progressive Party vote share exceeds estimated female vote share, contrary to expectations. In most states, we can only conclude with any confidence that male and female Progressive Party vote shares were not different from each other. However, in two states—Illinois and Kansas—we are confident that men were more supportive of La Follette than were women: male Progressive Party vote share exceeds female Progressive Party vote share in 99% of simulations in Illinois and in 91% of simulations in Kansas. These findings are consistent with the observed, recorded vote in 1916 and 1920 Illinois, where men's Progressive Party vote share exceeded women's in both elections (by a slim margin in 1916, but by a relatively large margin in 1920—7.7% Progressive vote share for men compared to 4.6% for women).

Overall, these estimates suggest that—at least in a few midwestern states—men and women responded differently to the presence of a popular Progressive Party candidate. While both men and women gave historically high levels of support to La Follette, men were as or more likely than women to abandon their loyalty to the major parties and support a Progressive candidate. Women—long associated with the causes and organizations of the Progressive movement and supposedly characterized by weaker party allegiance—were either slightly more reluctant or no more likely to defect from the major parties and register their support for La Follette. In at least two states, Progressives would have done better had women not

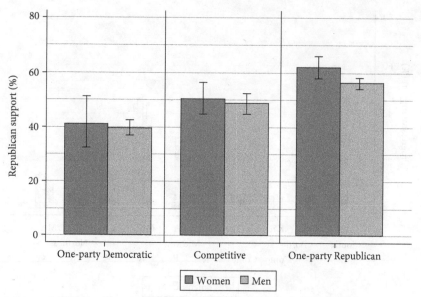

FIGURE 2.6 *Partisan Context and the Republican Vote Share of Women and Men, 1924*

been enfranchised, an ironic outcome for a movement at the forefront of suffrage advocacy for so long.

Organizing our states in terms of party context can provide further insight into these patterns. Figure 2.6 displays the average Republican vote share for women and men in our three different categories of states: one-party Democratic (two states), competitive (two states), and one-party Republican (six states). In the two competitive states—that is, states without a clearly dominant party—men's and women's Republican Party support differs very little. The same can be said of our two one-party Democratic states. In the six traditionally Republican-dominated states, however, women are more than 5 points more supportive of the GOP than are men. When we pool the six one-party Republican states, more than 99% of the simulations are consistent with higher female Republican support, so we can be confident about these conclusions even given the uncertainty associated with the estimates. Once again, we have evidence of mobilization of women into the locally dominant party in their state, despite the Progressive Party option.

Women's consistent loyalty to or mobilization by the locally dominant party had consequences for Progressive Party mobilization of women. Figure 2.7 reports average Progressive Party support for each of our partisan state groups. On average, men in the one-party Republican states were clearly more likely to support La Follette and the Progressive Party than were women. The point estimates suggest a difference of about 3 percentage points, and more than 99% of the simulations indicate men were more likely to support La Follette. Thus in 1924, men and women were either equally likely to support the Progressive candidate (in the Democratic-dominant and competitive states) or men were actually more likely to support La Follette than were women (in Republican-dominated states),

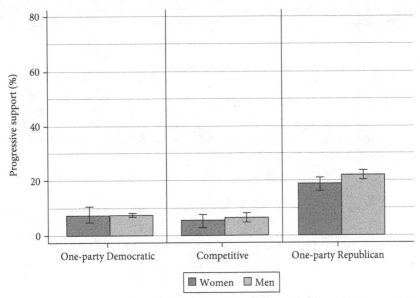

FIGURE 2.7 *Partisan Context and the Progressive Vote Share of Women and Men, 1924*

contradicting the hypothesis that women were less loyal or dependable voters or particularly attracted to the Progressive Party.

Generating Progressive Party Support

Where did Progressive voters come from? Were Progressive Party supporters largely established male and female Republican or Democratic voters? Or did the Progressive Party draw its support largely from newly mobilized voters? Did the same processes of third-party support characterize men and women, or was Progressive party support generated by a different process for recently enfranchised (and generally undermobilized) women than for long-enfranchised men?

Uncovering the divergent contributions of mobilization (entrance of new voters) and conversion (change among continuing voters) in accounting for electoral change, particularly major realignments, has been an ongoing challenge for social scientists and historians (for a thorough review, see Darmofal and Nardulli 2010). Like the enfranchisement of women, many of the dramatic and consequential cases of electoral realignment predate the widespread use of modern polling tools. Even when surveys exist, they rarely feature the panel design that permits researchers to track the entrance, exit, and changing party preference of voters. Researchers have employed a number of different approaches, some of which we follow here, to estimate the various contributions of conversion and mobilization to electoral change. While we cannot answer the question of conversion versus mobilization decisively with our data, the next set of figures, which report the actual *change* (from 1920) in the number of male and female ballots cast, overall

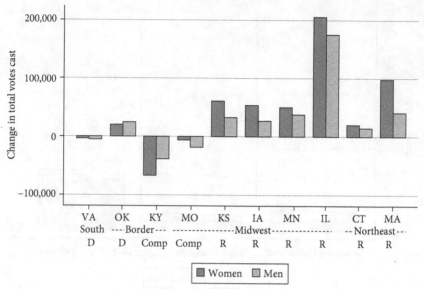

FIGURE 2.8 *Change in Number of Votes Cast by Women and Men, 1920 to 1924*

and for each party, can provide some insights into the processes that generated Progressive vote share in 1924.

Changes in the number of ballots cast overall are reported in Figure 2.8. Partly as a function of population growth, there were more ballots cast by both men and women in 1924 over 1920 in every state in our sample, save three. Those three include Virginia, where turnout remains low and is virtually unchanged among both men and women, and the traditionally competitive states of Kentucky and Missouri. Even with those declines, however, Kentucky and Missouri continue to boast some of the highest rates of turnout in our sample in 1924 (see Figure 2.3). In every state that experienced gains in the number of ballots cast, there were more new ballots cast by women than by men, as we might expect, given the larger numbers of previously nonvoting women available for mobilization.

We also can observe changes in the number of ballots cast for each party from 1920 to 1924. Figure 2.9 shows that the Republican Party lost votes among men in nearly every state. In some states the drop in Republican ballots was large (over 50,000 in Illinois and Iowa), but in all states the drop among men was larger than any corresponding drop among women, and sometimes much larger (e.g., Minnesota, Iowa). Of course, there were more male Republican voters in 1920 than there were female Republican voters in 1920, so more men were available to defect. Yet, in four states—traditionally Republican-dominated Illinois, Kansas, Connecticut, and Massachusetts—Republicans actually gained female voters while the number of male Republican ballots either declined or remained relatively flat.

Changes in the number of Democratic and Progressive Party votes cast are reported in Figures 2.10 and 2.11. Shifts are more consistent across the sexes. A party that gains ballots among men tends to gain among women; where support

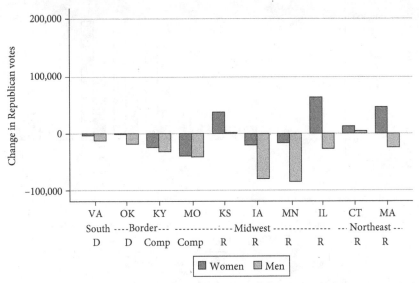

FIGURE 2.9 *Change in Number of Republican Votes Cast by Women and Men, 1920 to 1924*

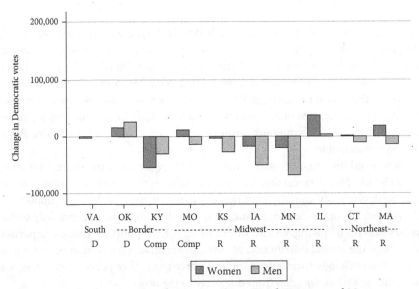

FIGURE 2.10 *Change in Number of Democratic Votes Cast by Women and Men, 1920 to 1924*

from men is unchanged, it tends to be unchanged among women. However, in Minnesota, Iowa, and Illinois—the states where the largest number of third-party ballots were cast—the number of new third-party ballots cast by men is nearly twice the number cast by women (Figure 2.11). Indeed, in most of the states in the sample, the number of new third-party votes among women is less than half that found among men. (Because so few third-party ballots were cast by either sex in

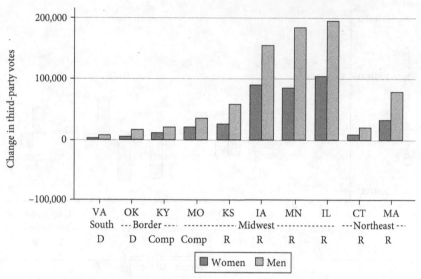

FIGURE 2.11 *Change in Number of Progressive Votes Cast by Women and Men, 1920 to 1924*

1920, the numbers of *new* Progressive ballots in Figure 2.11 represent nearly *all* Progressive votes cast in those states.) The twin patterns of generally similar or lower rates of Progressive support among women combined with overall lower female turnout meant Progressives owed far fewer votes to women than they did to men. If the electorate had been all male, Progressives would have done even better in 1924, and the two major parties would have done worse. The major parties continued to effectively mobilize women voters, even when a Progressive Party option was available.

Where did Progressive voters come from? There are two basic sources for electoral change. Mobilization is when new voters enter the active electorate in favor of a particular party and help shift the overall distribution of electoral support for the parties. The opposite of mobilization is demobilization, when previously active voters stop participating, and by withdrawing their support for particular parties also shape the overall distribution of votes. Alternatively, conversion occurs when active voters change their votes from one party to another between elections; we also refer to this as *defection* from one party to the other.

Our data cannot definitively identify the extent to which (de)mobilization or conversion are responsible for electoral change, but can offer some insight into likely processes. For example, consider a case where both Republicans and Democrats lose significant numbers of votes (from 1920) while Progressives gain significant numbers of votes, and the total number of ballots cast remains relatively stable from 1920 to 1924. In such a case, it seems likely that conversion (voters changing their party choice from one election to the next) is largely responsible; that is, we can assume that some or even many of those lost major-party votes became Progressive Party votes since there is little or no increase in total ballots cast (little evidence of new mobilization contributing to Progressive support) and the voters lost by one or both major parties are a logical source for the increased numbers of Progressive ballots. Yet, while such patterns may be *consistent* with conversion, we recognize that they are not definitive proof that such processes were at work. It is theoretically possible that a major-party vote decline and Progressive vote increase could be generated by significant demobilization by major-party voters that was offset by a large mobilization of new voters by the Progressive Party, rather than by conversion of major-party voters to the Progressive Party. Thus, we emphasize that our conclusions are tentative and do not extend beyond what the data can tell us.

In the six states where Progressive vote share exceeded 10%, our estimates suggest that both conversion (previous Democratic and Republican supporters switching to vote Progressive) and mobilization (previous nonvoters entering the electorate to cast ballots for the Progressive Party) were at work for both sexes. However, we have reason to believe that conversion from major-party support played a larger role among male voters than it did among female voters. In Minnesota, for example, Progressives gained more than 175,000 new male votes, an extraordinary level of third-party support. At the same time, Republicans lost about 85,000 male votes and Democrats lost about 65,000 male votes, for a total decline among men of about 150,000 two-party votes. It is possible that all of those lost major-party male voters just stayed home, and the Progressive Party support came entirely from new mobilization. It is more likely, we believe, that a good number of those major-party voters in 1920 cast Progressive Party ballots in 1924. Yet, even if all of them did so, they would still fall short of the 175,000 male Progressive ballots cast, suggesting a mobilization of at least 25,000 new male voters for the Progressive Party (Figure 2.8 shows an increase of about 35,000 male voters overall in Minnesota in 1924).

By contrast, mobilization seems to have played the larger role in generating Progressive votes among women in Minnesota, as we might expect of a generally undermobilized group. Republicans and Democrats lost about equal numbers of female votes in Minnesota in 1924 (totaling about 40,000), but Progressives gained about 80,000 female votes that same year. Again, keeping in mind that our assumptions could be incorrect (e.g., voters lost by Republicans and Democrats might have stayed home or voted for the other major party), it seems likely that as many or more than 40,000 new women voters were mobilized to cast their first ballots for the Progressive Party (Figure 2.8 shows about 50,000 new female ballots overall in Minnesota in 1924). Indeed, if we simply assume that all lost two-party votes went to the Progressives, we could attribute about half of women's Progressive Party votes to mobilization and half to conversion. For men, on the other hand, more than 85% of Progressive support (under the same assumptions) can be attributed to conversion, compared to just 15% attributed to new mobilization. While the details vary, Iowa and Massachusetts follow a similar pattern, suggesting a more significant role for conversion among men and a considerable role for mobilization among women.

Thus, we generally find more evidence of conversion among men than women in generating Progressive votes. Illinois, however, is distinctive as a state where both women's and men's Progressive support was clearly driven by mobilization.

In Illinois, both major parties gained female voters in 1924 (a total of about 100,000 across the two parties), while Progressives boasted about 90,000 new female voters. It is certainly possible—indeed, likely—that some previous female major-party voters defected to the Progressives and were compensated for by major-party mobilization exceeding the 100,000 reported in Figures 2.9 and 2.10. But given 200,000 new female voters overall in 1924, it appears likely that most of the female Progressive Party vote came from new voters, and not from women defecting from previous major-party support. The surprising feature of Illinois was that there are also an additional 175,000 male voters. Given the small net gains among Democrats (3,500 more male votes in 1924) and small net losses among Republicans (25,000 fewer male votes in 1924), the Progressive surge in Illinois was almost certainly due mainly to mobilization, rather than conversion, among men, contrary to the pattern in other states.

Implications for the One Hundred Years since Suffrage

Just four years after the ratification of the Nineteenth Amendment, newly enfranchised female voters were offered the opportunity to cast their ballots for an authentic Progressive Party candidate, Robert M. La Follette. Yet contrary to popular conceptions of women as natural Progressive allies, in no sample state (except possibly Virginia) were women more supportive of La Follette than men. Rather, we find that men were actually more likely to support Progressives than were women in two midwestern states. These results are broadly consistent with *observed* female and male vote choice in Illinois in 1916 and 1920—where combined female support for the Prohibition and Socialist Parties was roughly three-quarters the level of male support for the same parties.

Thus, the hopes of Progressive reformers that the enfranchisement of women would transform the electorate and usher in Progressive victories went unfulfilled in 1924. However great women's activism and preference for Progressive causes, as voters women acted more as party regulars than as ideologues, maintaining and expanding their support for the two major parties. Perhaps the specific form that the Progressive Party movement took in 1924 made Progressives less uniquely attractive to women than we might expect. The 1924 Progressive Party platform focused more on economic issues, political reform, and especially the plight of farmers than on the issues of moral reform and Prohibition associated with women's activism (Rosenstone, Behr, and Lazarus 1996; see Noel 2013 on ideological diversity within the Progressive movement). In any case, in 1924, rather than disrupting the system, the entrance of female voters tended to reinforce major party dominance at the state level.

The results of the election were shaped by the participation of women. For the most part, women's contribution was to shore up support for the major parties, especially the Republicans, and dampen the Progressive Party surge. For example, without female voters, Illinois would have witnessed massive third-party mobilization and consistent demobilization from both the Republican and (to a lesser extent) Democratic Parties. In Illinois, Republicans lost nearly 26,000 male voters, and third-party candidates picked up nearly 180,000 male voters. By contrast, Republicans gained 63,000 female voters, and third-party candidates picked up only about 92,000 female voters. Thus, in Illinois, as we observed in other states above, female voters stabilized the electorate and diminished the third-party showing.

That party loyalty also is reflected in the processes that generated Progressive support. Many expected women to be weaker partisans and less loyal to the major parties—because of their lesser knowledge and experience, because women were believed more committed to ideals than to (corrupt) parties, because of the Progressive critique of partisanship—yet we find evidence that women were more stable sources of major-party support than were men. While we cannot track conversion and mobilization definitively with our estimates, the changes between 1920 and 1924 suggest patterns in which male Progressive votes tended to come from major-party defection (conversion) while more of women's Progressive votes appeared to result from new voter mobilization. In one sense, we should not be surprised: Male mobilization was already significant in many states, so there were far fewer men available to be newly mobilized. Indeed, given the level of male mobilization, many weakly partisan men were likely already voting in 1920, and thus available for conversion, while perhaps weakly partisan women stayed home in 1920 and were available for mobilization by the Progressives in 1924. Nonetheless, to the extent we can conclude that women who cast major-party votes in 1920 were more likely to do so again in 1924 than were men, these findings undermine expectations that women would be less dependable partisans.

Women's relative disinterest in abandoning the major parties in favor of third-party options appears to have continued across the last one hundred years. Women were less likely than men to support third-party candidate George Wallace in 1968 (8% of women compared to 15% of men) and less likely to support the independent candidacy of Ross Perot in 1992 (14% compared to 23%). Women and men did not differ in their support for John Andersen in 1980 and Ross Perot's second run in 1996 (both less successful than the candidates in 1968 and 1992), however. The common expectation before suffrage was granted that women would be less reliable partisans was not borne out in 1924 or in 1968 and 1992 (American National Election Studies 2016). Instead, women appear to be more loyal to the major parties, or perhaps less willing to accept the risk of casting a ballot for a third-party candidate.

The expectations about women's support for the Progressive Party also presage the treatment of female voters throughout the one hundred years since the ratification of the Nineteenth Amendment. Assumptions about the inherent nature of women helped motivate expectations about Progressive Party support among women. Similar assumptions—particularly women's supposed natural inclination toward care, compassion, and moral values—have long been offered as a rationale for women's greater support for social welfare policies, which in turn is used to explain greater Democratic vote choice since the 1960s. Empirical support for this explanation has been weak or nonexistent, however (see Huddy, Cassese, and

Lizotte 2008). Similarly, in the same way that many expected women to reward the party that first supported women's suffrage, analysts often have expected women to favor candidates and parties who endorse specific women's issues, such as abortion rights or the Equal Rights Amendment, but research has consistently discredited these expectations as well (Chaney et al. 1998; Klein 1984; Mansbridge 1985; Cook and Wilcox 1991; but see Kaufmann 2002).

The election of 1924 also is not the only case in which electoral disruption, in this case a third-party surge, is more attributable to the defection of men than of women. While many expected women to be unreliable partisans and unpredictable voters (e.g., Converse 1969, 1976; Claggett 1980; Gosnell and Gill 1935; Russell 1924), our evidence, here and elsewhere, suggests women were often more loyal, particularly to the locally dominant party, than were men (see Harvey 1998 on the advantages of parties as mobilizers of early female voters). Similarly, when the modern gender gap in favor of the Democratic Party came to public and scholarly attention following the 1980 presidential election, explanations immediately and for some time focused almost exclusively on the behavior of women themselves: What caused women to shift their vote choice toward the Democratic Party? Yet scholars have since shown that much of the initial divergence in the partisan preferences of men and women in the second half of the twentieth century can be attributed to the defection of male voters from the Democratic Party, while female partisanship remained fairly stable (see Kaufmann and Petrocik 1999; Norrander 1999; Wirls 1986).[6]

Finally, the election of 1924 reminds us that, from the very start, women have been more similar to men in their electoral behavior than they have been different. While women's propensity to turn out to vote trailed men's substantially in 1924 (nationwide, women would remain less likely to turn out to vote than were men through the 1970s; Wolfinger and Rosenstone 1980), women's patterns of turnout were not dramatically different than those of men: Where men were more likely to turn out to vote, so were women, suggesting that both sexes responded to the same incentives and disincentives to vote and mostly (although not entirely) in the same way. Similarly, where men were Republican voters, so were women, and vice versa. We did uncover a greater likelihood for women to support the GOP, and men to support the Progressive Party, in a number of midwestern states, but the size of these differences were not huge. The same can be said of the political engagement of men and women today; differences exist—women are somewhat less likely to participate in some forms of political activism, but more likely to engage in others (Burns, Schlozman, and Verba 2001), women express different policy preferences (e.g., Shapiro and Mahajan 1986), and women are more likely to identify with and vote for Democrats (e.g., Kaufmann and Petrocik 1999), but differences are not stark relative to differences in political behavior observed between other social categories. These differences may still be substantively significant; as we saw in 1924, the participation of female voters helped stabilize the electorate. Yet on the whole, the evidence of the past one hundred years supports a characterization of women as citizens and political actors more similar than different from men, despite the legacy of disenfranchisement and the gender ideology that supported it.

Appendix

As we discuss in the text, we estimate female and male electoral behavior in 1924 by employing an approach to ecological inference described in Wakefield (2004). As with most approaches to ecological inference, Wakefield's methodology is based on a simple 2 x 2 table—comparing the choice to turn out or abstain for white and minority voters, for example (see King 1997). Building on a large body of related work in biostatistics and epidemiology (see Richardson and Monfort 2000), Wakefield develops a computationally manageable Bayesian strategy for 2 x 2 tables. We extend Wakefield's approach in two ways. First, we apply Wakefield's approach to the more complex 2 x 4 problem, estimating Democratic vote, Republican vote, other-party vote, and abstention (four possible outcomes) for men and women (two population groups). Second, we introduce the uncontroversial assumption that male turnout will exceed female turnout in each geographic unit. We emphasize that while we assume women turn out at a lesser rate than men, we make no assumptions about the size of that gap, and indeed, we find the size of the gap between female and male turnout to vary considerably across states.

Work on more complex tables (more than two rows [R] or two columns [C]) has appeared in the statistical and political science literature (Ferree 2004; Lau, Moore, and Kellerman 2007), but application of the RxC strategies is less common, and direct comparisons of alternative RxC estimation strategies are rare. We adopt an approach similar to the estimator proposed in Greiner and Quinn (2009), a Markov Chain Monte Carlo (MCMC) estimator that decomposes a large RxC problem into a series of 2 x 2 subtables. The 2 x 4 problem we confront (men and women distributed across Republican, Democratic, other party, and abstention) is decomposed into six 2 x 2 subtables. The advantage of this approach is that uncertainty about estimates in one subtable (the distribution of male and female votes across Republican and Democratic candidates, for instance), also reflects in uncertainty about estimates in other subtables (e.g., the distribution of votes across third-party candidates or abstentions). The approach developed by Greiner and Quinn ensures that each of the parameter estimates incorporates uncertainty related to all other parameters. While our approach differs in important ways (we rely, for instance, on cell proportions rather than counts), we follow the Greiner-Quinn strategy combined with Wakefield's (2004) approach to the estimation of 2 x 2 tables. The estimator is implemented in a modified version of a hierarchical ecological inference model in the R package MCMCpack (Martin, Quinn, and Park 2011). Replication details—the data and the modified C++ and R language, as well as the estimates (the full set of estimated probabilities) and parameters used to assess convergence diagnostics (state-level logits)—are available from the authors.

The MCMC simulation is repeated for each state-election year dataset, so ten simulations are required to generate the estimates for 1924. For 1924 Illinois, for example, a matrix of 282 rows (282 geographic units) and 6 columns (number of voting-age men; number of voting-age women; number of votes for Democratic, Republican, and third-party candidates; and implied number of voters abstaining) was passed through the simulation. These data are the column and row marginals for the 2 x 4 tables. We also specified a prior distribution, the value of the parameters that we would accept in the absence of any information in the data. The prior in each case was simply the observed combined or total turnout and vote choice—the same proportions Republican, Democratic, third-party, and abstaining for men and women. So, any information in the data would move our estimates away from these priors. Any difference we observe in the posterior distributions that describe the vote choices of men and women must be a consequence of the data introduced to the simulation, the likelihood function we choose, and the uncontroversial assumption that male turnout exceeded female turnout in each geographic unit, not the choice of prior distribution.

The estimator requires a lengthy simulation (10 million or more iterations); the point estimate for each geographic unit is the average of the last 1 million or so values of the simulation. We then average across those population-weighted units to generate state-level estimates of women's and men's turnout and vote choice for each of our ten sample states. These point estimates—for example, percentage female turnout in Connecticut—are reported in our figures. We also use the simulations to estimate measures of uncertainty. For each point estimate, we display the Bayesian Credible Interval (BCI), the range of values that includes the point estimates from 90% of the simulations. Critically, we also can directly compare simulated quantities for men and women to assess our degree of confidence in observed gender differences in the point estimates. In general, we are confident of findings observed in 90% or more of the simulations, moderately confident of those found in 80% or more, and cannot be confident of any substantive difference when it is found in less than 80% of the simulations.

MCMC approaches to Bayesian problems are becoming more common in the political science literature, but there are few conventions for assessing the performance of the estimator and reporting point estimates and confidence intervals. The key question to be assessed is whether the Markov Chain has converged in each case—that is, whether the estimator is sampling across the entire range of the posterior distribution in the observed simulations. To assess convergence, we rely on two commonly used diagnostics: Geweke's diagnostic and the Heidelberger-Welch diagnostic (for a brief introduction to each test, see Gill 2002). Geweke's diagnostic compares the mean of the estimated parameter in some early proportion of the chain to the mean in some latter proportion of the chain. We used two forms of this diagnostic: We tested the first 20% of each chain with the last 40%, and the first 10% with the last 50%. In each of the ten simulations we were able to extend the length of the chain to a point where convergence was unambiguous: each of the twelve state-level logits passed each of three tests for stationarity, and nearly all the parameters passed a second-stage diagnostic that assesses precision. Together with the validation checks using observed female and male electoral behavior in Illinois, described in the chapter text, we have considerable confidence that our estimates provide reliable measures of female and male turnout and vote choice in these ten states in 1924.

Notes

1. E.g., William H. Crawford, "A Big Woman Vote Seen by Mrs. Sabin." *New York Times*, October 27, 1924, p. 8.

2. See, for example, "Women Voters Will Have a Novel Booth at State Fair," *Duluth News Tribune*, September 2, 1924; "Thirty Million Women to Vote in November Elections: Leaders at Work: Move to Get Rural Vote Out," *Houston Press*, September 3, 1924; "W.C.T.U. Plans Campaign to Get Voters to Polls," *The Duluth News Tribune*, September 11, 1924.

3. "To Train Women Speakers," *New York Times*, September 8, 1924; "Maine Democrats Organize Women," *New York Times*, September 5, 1924; "Both Old Parties Woo Women Voters," *New York Times*, October 10, 1924: 5; "Appeals to Women to Vote for Davis," *New York Times*, November 2, 1924: 6; "Three Women Debate Campaign Issues," *New York Times*, November 2, 1924: 7; "G.O.P. Women of State Are Now Organized," *Duluth News Tribune*, October 6, 1924.

4. As we explain in the Appendix, we use the simulations that generate our estimates of female and male turnout and vote choice to create measures of uncertainty as well. For each point estimate, we display the Bayesian Credible Interval (BCI), the range of values that includes the point estimates from 90% of the simulations. We can directly compare simulated quantities for men and women to assess our degree of confidence in observed gender differences in the point estimates. In general, we are confident of findings observed in 90% or more of the simulations, moderately confident of those found in 80% or more, and cannot be confident of any substantive difference when it is found in less than 80% of the simulations.

5. The estimates are support for all third parties (including Prohibition, Socialist, and Miscellaneous Independent), but we refer to this as Progressive support since over 96% of the third-party ballots are for La Follette. Due to difficulties with ballot access, La Follette was listed as the candidate for four different parties, depending on the state (Rosenstone, Behr, and Lazarus 1996; Sundquist 1973).

6. The precise contributions of men and women to the trajectory of the partisan gender gap remain contested. American National Election Studies data suggests that prior to the 1990s—that is, for the first approximately twenty-five years of the modern gender gap—much of the gender gap can be attributed to men moving toward the Republican Party. Since the 1990s, however, women's partisanship has become more variable (Kaufmann 2006). Recent analysis of far more frequently administered Gallup polls, on the other hand, suggests that among the college-educated (where the gender gap emerged earlier than among the non-college-educated), women's greater shifts toward the Democrats account for much of the growth of the gender gap before 1980. After 1980, shifts toward the Republicans among both college- and non-college-educated men are responsible for more of the growing gender gap (Gillion, Ladd, and Meredith 2014).

References

Allen, Florence E. 1930. "The First Ten Years." *Woman's Journal*. August: 5–7, 30–32.

American National Election Studies (ANES). 2016. The ANES Guide to Public Opinion and Electoral Behavior. http://www.electionstudies.org/nesguide/nesguide.htm.

Andersen, Kristi. 1979. *The Creation of a Democratic Majority, 1928–1936*. Chicago: University of Chicago Press.

———. 1990. "Women and Citizenship in the 1920s." Pp. 177–198 in *Women, Politics, and Change*, edited by Louise Tilly and Patricia Gurin. New York: Russell Sage Foundation.

———. 1994. "Women and the Vote in the 1920s: What Happened in Oregon." *Women & Politics* 14(4): 43–56.

———. 1996. *After Suffrage: Women in Partisan and Electoral Politics before the New Deal*. Chicago: University of Chicago Press.

Baker, Paula. 1984. "The Domestication of Politics: Women and American Political Society, 1780–1920." *American Historical Review* 89 (June): 620–647.

Barnard, Eunice Fuller. 1928. "The Woman Voter Gains Power." *New York Times Magazine*, August 12: 1–2, 20, 28.

Breckinridge, Sophonisba P. 1933. *Women in the Twentieth Century: A Study of Their Political, Social, and Economic Activities*. New York: McGraw-Hill.

Brown, Courtney. 1991. *Ballots of Tumult: A Portrait of Volatility in American Voting*. Ann Arbor: University of Michigan Press.

Burner, David. 1971. "Election of 1924." Pp. 2458–2581 in *History of American Presidential Elections, 1789–1968*, edited by Arthur M. Schlesinger Jr. and Fred L. Israel. New York: Chelsea House Publishers in Association with McGraw-Hill.

———. 1986. *The Politics of Provincialism: The Democratic Party in Transition, 1918–1932*. Second edition. Cambridge: Harvard University Press.

Burnham, Walter Dean. 1981. "The System of 1896: An Analysis." Pp. 147–202 in *The Evolution of American Electoral Systems*, edited by Paul Kleppner, Walter Dean Burnham, Ronald P. Formisano, Samuel P. Hays, Richard Jensen, and William G. Shade. Westport, CT: Greenwood Press.

———. 1986. "Those High Nineteenth-Century American Voting Turnouts: Fact or Fiction?" *Journal of Interdisciplinary History* 16 (Spring): 613–644.

Burns, Nancy, Kay Lehman Schlozman, and Sidney Verba. 2001. *The Private Roots of Public Action: Gender, Equality, and Political Participation*. Cambridge, MA: Harvard University Press.

Center for American Women and Politics (CAWP). 2014. "Fact Sheet: Gender Differences in Voter Turnout." Center for American Women and Politics, Eagleton Institute of Politics, Rutgers University.

Chaney, Carole Kennedy, R. Michael Alvarez, and Jonathan Nagler. 1998. "Explaining the Gender Gap in U.S. Presidential Elections, 1980–1992." *Political Research Quarterly* 51(June): 311–339.

Claggett, William. 1980. "The Life Cycle and Generational Models of the Development of Partisanship: A Test Based on the Delayed Enfranchisement of Women." *Social Science Quarterly* 4(March): 643–650.

Converse, Philip E. 1969. "Of Time and Partisan Stability." *Comparative Political Studies* 2(July): 139–171.

———. 1976. *The Dynamics of Party Support: Cohort-Analyzing Party Identification*. Beverly Hills, CA: Sage Publications.

Cook, Elizabeth Adell, and Clyde Wilcox. 1991. "Feminism and the Gender Gap—A Second Look." *Journal of Politics* 53(November): 1111–1122.

Corder, J. Kevin, and Christina Wolbrecht. 2016. *Counting Women's Ballots: Female Turnout and Vote Choice from Suffrage through the New Deal*. New York: Cambridge University Press.

Darmofal, David, and Peter F. Nardulli. 2010. "The Dynamics of Critical Realignments: An Analysis of Time and Space." *Political Behavior* 32: 255–283.

Evans, Sara M. 1989. *Born for Liberty: A History of Women in America*. New York: Free Press.

Ferree, Karen. 2004. "Iterative Approaches to RxC Ecological Inference Problems: Where They Can Go Wrong and One Quick Fix." *Political Analysis* 12: 143–159.

Firebaugh, Glenn, and Kevin Chen. 1995. "Vote Turnout of Nineteenth-Century Women: The Enduring Effect of Disenfranchisement." *American Journal of Sociology* 100(January): 972–996.

Flexner, Eleanor. 1970. *Century of Struggle: The Women's Rights Movement in the United States*. Cambridge, MA: Harvard University Press.

Florey, Kenneth. 2013. *Women's Suffrage Memorabilia: An Illustrated Historical Study*. Jefferson, NC: McFarland.

Freeman, Jo. 2000. *A Room at a Time: How Women Entered Party Politics*. Lanham, MD: Rowman and Littlefield.

Gamm, Gerald. 1986. *The Making of the New Deal Democrats: Voting Behavior and Realignment in Boston, 1920–1940*. Chicago: University of Chicago Press.

Gerber, Alan S., Donald P. Green, and Ron Shachar. 2003. "Voting May Be Habit-Forming: Evidence from a Randomized Field Experiment." *American Journal of Political Science* 47(July): 540–550.

Gill, Jeff. 2002. *Bayesian Methods: A Social and Behavioral Sciences Approach*. Boca Raton, FL: Chapman and Hall.

Gillion, Daniel Q., Jonathan M. Ladd, and Marc Meredith. 2014. "Education, Party Polarization, and the Origins of the Partisan Gender Gap." Working paper. Washington, DC: Georgetown University.

Goldstein, Joel H. 1984. *The Effects of the Adoption of Woman Suffrage: Sex Differences in Voting Behavior—Illinois, 1914–21*. New York: Praeger.

Gosnell, Harold F., and Norman N. Gill. 1935. "An Analysis of the 1932 Presidential Vote in Chicago." *American Political Science Review* 29(December): 967–984.

Gould, Louis L. 2003. *Grand Old Party: A History of the Republicans*. New York: Random House.

Greenlee, Jill S. 2014. *The Political Consequences of Motherhood*. Ann Arbor: University of Michigan Press.

Greiner, D. James, and Kevin Quinn. 2009. "R x C Ecological Inference: Bounds, Correlations, Flexibility, and Transparency of Assumptions." *Journal of the Royal Statistical Society A*. Part I. 172: 67–81.

Harvey, Anna L. 1998. *Votes without Leverage: Women in Electoral Politics, 1920–1970*. Cambridge: Cambridge University Press.

Hicks, John D. 1960. *Republican Ascendancy, 1921–1933*. New York: Harper and Row.

Hofstadter, Richard. 1955. *The Age of Reform: From Bryan to F.D.R.* New York: Alfred A. Knopf.

Huddy, Leonie, Erin Cassese, and Mary-Kate Lizotte. 2008. "Gender, Public Opinion, and Political Reasoning." Pp. 31–49 in *Political Women and American Democracy*, edited by Christina Wolbrecht, Karen Beckwith, and Lisa Baldez. New York: Cambridge University Press.

Kaufmann, Karen M. 2002. "Culture Wars, Secular Realignment, and the Gender Gap in Party Identification." *Political Behavior* 24(September): 283–307.

———. 2006. "The Gender Gap." *PS: Political Science and Politics* 39(July): 447–453.

Kaufmann, Karen M., and John R. Petrocik. 1999. "The Changing Politics of American Men: Understanding the Sources of the Gender Gap." *American Journal of Political Science* 43(July): 864–887.

Keyssar, Alexander. 2000. *The Right to Vote: The Contested History of Democracy in the United States*. New York: Basic Books.

King, Gary. 1997. *A Solution to the Ecological Inference Problem: Deconstructing Individual Behavior from Aggregate Data*. Princeton, NJ: Princeton University Press.

Klein, Ethel. 1984. *Gender Politics: From Consciousness to Mass Politics*. Cambridge, MA: Harvard University Press.

Ladd, Everett Carll. 1997. "Media Framing and the Gender Gap." Pp. 113–128 in *Women, Media, and Politics*, edited by Pippa Norris. New York: Oxford University Press.

Lau, Olivia, Ryan T. Moore, and Michael Kellerman. 2007. "eiPack: RxC Ecological Inference and Higher Dimension Data Management." *R News* 7: 43–47.

Lemons, J. Stanley. 1973. *The Woman Citizen: Social Feminism in the 1920s*. Charlottesville: University Press of Virginia.

MacKay, Kenneth Campbell. 1947. *The Progressive Movement of 1924*. New York: Columbia University Press.

Mansbridge, Jane J. 1985. "Myth and Reality: The ERA and the Gender Gap in the 1980 Election." *Public Opinion Quarterly* 49(Summer): 164–178.

Martin, Andrew D., Kevin M. Quinn, and Jong Hee Park. 2011. "MCMCpack: Markov Chain Monte Carlo in R." *Journal of Statistical Software* 42(9): 1–21.

McConnaughy, Corrine M. 2013. *The Woman Suffrage Movement in America: A Reassessment*. New York: Cambridge University Press.

McCormick, Anne O'Hare. 1928. "Enter Woman, the New Boss of Politics." *New York Times Magazine* October 21: 3, 22.

McDonagh, Eileen L., and H. Douglas Price. 1985. "Woman Suffrage in the Progressive Era: Patterns of Opposition and Support in Referenda Voting, 1910–1918." *American Political Science Review* 79(2): 415–435.

Monoson, S. Sara. 1990. "The Lady and the Tiger: Women's Electoral Activism in New York City before Suffrage." *Journal of Women's History* 2(Fall): 100–135.

Noel, Hans. 2013. *Political Ideologies and Political Parties in America*. New York: Cambridge University Press.

Norrander, Barbara. 1999. "The Evolution of the Gender Gap." *Public Opinion Quarterly* 63: 566–576.

Ogburn, William F., and Inez Goltra. 1919. "How Women Vote: A Study of an Election in Portland, Oregon." *Political Science Quarterly* 34: 413–433.

O'Neill, William L. 1971. *Everyone Was Brave: A History of Feminism in America*. New York: Quadrangle.

Plutzer, Eric. 2002. "Becoming a Habitual Voter: Inertia, Resources, and Growth in Young Adulthood." *American Political Science Review* 96(March): 41–56.

Rice, Stuart A., and Malcolm M. Willey. 1924. "American Women's Ineffective Use of the Vote." *Current History* 20(July): 641–647.

Richardson, S., and C. Monfort. 2000. "Ecological Correlation Studies." Pp. 205–220 in *Spatial Epidemiology: Methods and Applications*, edited by P. Elliott, J. Wakefield, N. G. Best, and D. J. Briggs. Oxford: Oxford University Press.

Rogers, Edith Nourse. 1930. "Women's New Place in Politics." *Nation's Business* 18: 39–41, 124.

Rosenstone, Steven J., Roy L. Behr, and Edward H. Lazarus. 1996. *Third Parties in America: Citizen Response to Major Party Failure*. Second edition. Princeton, NJ: Princeton University Press.

Russell, Charles Edward. 1924. "Is Woman-Suffrage a Failure?" *Century Magazine* 35: 724–730.

Scammon, Richard M., ed. 1965. *America at the Polls: A Handbook of Presidential Election Statistics, 1920–1964*. Pittsburgh: University of Pittsburgh Press.

Shapiro, Robert Y., and Harpeet Mahajan. 1986. "Gender Differences in Policy Preferences: A Summary of Trends from the 1960s to the 1980s." *Public Opinion Quarterly* 50(Spring): 42–61.

Sundquist, James L. 1973. *Dynamics of the Party System: Alignment and Realignment in the United States*. Washington, DC: Brookings Institution.

Tarbell, Ida M. 1924. "Is Woman's Suffrage a Failure?" *Good Housekeeping*, October: 18.

Thelen, David P. 1976. *Robert M. La Follette and the Insurgent Spirit*. Boston: Little, Brown, and Company.

Toombs, Elizabeth O. 1929. "Politicians, Take Notice." *Good Housekeeping*, March: 14–15.

Unger, Nancy C. 2000. *Fighting Bob La Follette: The Righteous Reformer*. Chapel Hill: University of North Carolina Press.

Wakefield, J. 2004. "Ecological Inference for 2 × 2 Tables (with Discussion)." *Journal of the Royal Statistical Society* 167: 385–445.

Wells, Marguerite M. 1929. "Some Effects of Woman Suffrage." *Annals of the American Academy* 143: 207–216.

Welter, Barbara. 1966. "The Cult of True Womanhood: 1820–1860." *American Quarterly* 18(Summer): 151–174.

Willey, Malcolm M., and Stuart A. Rice. 1924. "A Sex Cleavage in the Presidential Election of 1920." *Journal of the American Statistical Association* 19: 519–520.

Wirls, Daniel. 1986. "Reinterpreting the Gender Gap." *Public Opinion Quarterly* 50: 316–330.

Wolfinger, Raymond E., and Steven J. Rosenstone. 1980. *Who Votes?* New Haven, CT: Yale University Press.

3

The Evolution of Women's (and Men's) Partisan Attachments

Heather L. Ondercin

The passage of the Nineteenth Amendment nearly doubled the size of the electorate in the United States. At the time, few understood the impact this expansion would have on the partisan makeup of the electorate. Many felt that women's votes would resemble their fathers', husbands', or brothers' votes (McConnaughy 2013). In contrast to this line of thinking, women's participation in the reform movements and entry into politics were structured by gender in important ways (Andersen 1996). Thus, gender could inform and structure women's partisan preferences independent of family connections. Understanding the influence of the Nineteenth Amendment on the US political system requires understanding the similarities and differences in men's and women's partisan attachments over the one hundred years since the amendment's passage.

The enactment of the Nineteenth Amendment not only codified voting rights for women, but also made gender a more salient political identity. In this volume, Corder and Wolbrecht examine women's turnout and voting in the 1924 election to understand the proximate electoral impact of the passage of the Nineteenth Amendment. I take a longer view of the consequences of the Nineteenth Amendment by analyzing men's and women's partisanship, or their psychological attachments to the political parties since the adoption of the Nineteenth Amendment. I contend that, over time, gender has become increasingly important in influencing both men's and women's partisan attachments. As a result, men's and women's preferences have diverged, forming a gender gap in partisanship.[1] We commonly associate the formation of the gender gap with the 1980 presidential election. The analysis in this chapter demonstrates that this conclusion is accurate for women as a whole, but differences in partisan attachments between men and women started to emerge earlier within subgroups in the population. Today, women find the policy positions of the Democratic Party more attractive than men, making women a central group within the Democratic Party's coalition of voters. This has resulted in the gender gap in partisanship having important electoral consequences for the political parties.

Along with understanding the similarities and differences between men and women in partisan attachments, this chapter examines the unity and disunity of women's partisan attachments. Women (and men) are members of heterogeneous groups within the electorate, holding multiple social and political identities that intersect to shape their partisan attachments. By examining the similarities and differences in men's and women's partisan attachments among subpopulations in the electorate we can better understand how gender works to shape partisanship.

This chapter proceeds as follows. First, I examine how women's organizational activism influenced women's partisan attachments and voting behavior before and in the immediate aftermath of the passage of the Nineteenth Amendment. Information on attitudes and behavior during this time period is limited due to a lack of systematic quantitative data; however, historians and political scientists provide us with fascinating and unique insights into men's and women's political behavior during this period. I then explore the partisan attachments of men and women between 1950 and 2012. To gain a more complete understanding of the gender gap, I examine how the gender gap varies in size and trajectory among demographic groups in the electorate in the fourth section. Specifically, I analyze generational gaps, gaps based on education, and gaps based on race and region. I conclude with some observations on how the gender gap shapes our modern political climate and how the gap will continue to influence politics in the future.

Partisanship from Suffrage to the New Deal

The first question newly enfranchised women faced was not only which party to join (as Wolbrecht and Corder discuss), but whether to adopt a partisan label. Prior to the adoption of the Nineteenth Amendment, politics was squarely located within the public sphere and, thus, mostly considered the domain of men. Moreover, politics was largely party politics, and aligning oneself with a political party was hitherto part of male political identity (Baker 1984; Gustafson 1997). Through activism women had slowly integrated themselves into politics, transforming their relationship with the political parties (Baker 1984; Zaeske 2003). The passage of the Nineteenth Amendment therefore fundamentally altered women's political roles and identities.

Their struggle to gain voting rights and participation in other social movements pulled women into public politics (Baker 1984; Zaeske 2003). Women's relationship to partisan politics through these movements was wide-ranging, as they oscillated between partisan politics and nonpartisan identities. Initially, many activists and organizations of the suffrage movement had allegiances with the Republican Party based on the issue of abolition. However, these ties were challenged with the passage of the Civil War Amendments (Fourteenth to Sixteenth), which extended suffrage to black men and ignored the claims for female suffrage (Evans 1989; Wolbrecht 2000). After this critical moment the ties to the political parties became more varied. At the organizational level, many suffrage organizations took largely nonpartisan, some might even say antipartisan stances (Andersen 1996; Graham

1996; Gustafson 1997). Several activists within the suffrage movement thought that partisan identification would hurt the movement. For example, suffragist Ida Husted Harper argued that women's partisan activities would distract from the suffrage movement and divide women's loyalties (Gustafson 1997). Other suffrage organizations, such as the American Women Suffrage Association, continued to work with the Republican Party to achieve their goals (Freeman 2000).

Among suffrage organizations, the National Women's Party (NWP) organized by Alice Paul embraced direct engagement with party politics (Cott 1984; Lunardini 1986).[2] The NWP worked to put pressure on antisuffrage lawmakers, regardless of their party membership. Even though they more directly engaged in partisan politics, Paul and the NWP often times considered their activism as nonpartisan because they were willing to target both parties (Lunardini 1986). While the NWP mobilized women in states where they had already achieved suffrage, there is not much evidence that women formed enduring attachments to the organization.

In addition to the suffrage movement, many women were also involved in other social movement activities during this time period. These organizations tended to be on the periphery of partisan politics. For example, temperance was one of the largest social reform movements of the era. Women actively participated in this movement via the Woman's Christian Temperance Union (WCTU), which was a major force within the Prohibition Party. After their defeat in the 1884 election, the Republican Party attempted to attract Prohibition and WCTU supporters. Frances Willard, the leader of the WCTU, aided this move. Willard came under criticism for her behavior, with many arguing that the organization should maintain a nonpartisan identity (Freeman 2000; Gustafson 1997). Women also were active in third parties that aligned with the moral and social reform agenda, such as the Populist Party (Freeman 2000) and the Progressive Party (Gustafson 1997).

While suffrage and other social movement organizations had a mixed relationship with the political parties, at the individual level many of the activists within the suffrage movement exhibited allegiances toward the parties. McConnaughy (2013) observes that "Regardless of whether they believed their partisan leanings ought to be invoked in their suffrage work, prominent suffrage advocates were identified with nearly every political party that entered national electoral politics during the seventy-plus years of the movement. . . ." (51). Both parties capitalized on women's talents and activities through auxiliary organizations. Women created banners, engaged in debates, wrote letters, and participated in other campaign activities (Freeman 2000; Gustafson 1997). Moreover, the parties felt that women could use their influence within the home to persuade their voting husbands (Freeman 2000). Despite their participation in party-sponsored events and activities, many women maintained a nonpartisan identity (Gustafson 1997).

When the Nineteenth Amendment was adopted, women had been more directly active in third parties that were tied to the social welfare and moral reform movements than traditional parties. Women served as delegates and on committees at the Prohibition Party convention in 1869 (Freeman 2000). Jane Adams, a leader in the social reform movement, seconded Theodore Roosevelt's nomination as the Progressive Party's presidential nominee in 1912 (Gustafson 1997). Women were more active in third or minor parties because these parties generally were more open to women's activities and their party platforms were aligned with social movements where women were highly engaged.

The passage of the Nineteenth Amendment resulted in women taking on the more traditional role of citizen as voter and, subsequently, changed female activists' perspectives on party politics. Partisan identities appeared easier for women to adopt in the postsuffrage era, particularly women who were just coming of age politically. As McCormick explains, "Women who went through the fight for equal suffrage were inclined to be skeptical and more non-partisan than men . . .. Women who inherited the vote without effort on their part are likely to be partisans; they were enfranchised into a party rather than into citizenship" (Andersen 1996: 75). As women became socialized into their new roles as voters, they also took on a greater role in party politics and developed more crystalized partisan identities.

After the enactment of the Nineteenth Amendment, both parties started to recruit and appeal to female voters in an attempt to gain an electoral advantage. The success of these activities was largely dependent on the local partisan context in which women were recruited. That is, the Democratic Party benefited from newly enfranchised women in areas where they already had a strong partisan base, while the Republican Party benefited where they already had a strong partisan base (Andersen 1996). For example, Corder and Wolbrecht report in their chapter in this volume that strong local parties were able to effectively mobilize female voters. They also find little difference between male and female voters' support for the Progressive Party in the 1924 election.

The New Deal realignment resulted in massive changes to party politics and partisan alignments. Modern party coalitions and partisan perceptions are based largely on the politics resulting from the New Deal realignment—the incorporation of, among other groups, the poor, the unionized, the urban population, Roman Catholics, and recent immigrants into the Democratic Party's winning coalition (Brewer and Stonecash 2009; Key 1955).[3] Much of the research on the New Deal coalition makes little reference to sex. However, Andersen's (1979) analysis of the realignment process in Chicago between 1928 and 1936 places women within the Democratic Party's coalition. In particular, she shows that women and other newly enfranchised groups were key to the growth of the Democratic Party coalition during this time period. Brewer and Stonecash (2009) also classify women as one of the social groups associated with the New Deal realignment. The lack of quality survey data makes it difficult to conclude with any confidence if men and women were attracted to the Democratic Party at different rates during this time period. While we cannot determine if a gender gap emerged during the New Deal realignment, we can gain a better understanding of the similarities and differences of men's and women's partisanship starting in the 1950s using survey data. I now turn to analysis of the modern gender gap between 1950 and 2012.

Partisan Attachments and the Modern Gender Gap

To trace the evolution of men's and women's partisanship, I have generated quarterly estimates of partisan attachments based on Gallup surveys from 1950 to 2012.[4] The quarterly estimates represent the percentage of men or women who identify with the Democratic Party out of all two-party identifiers.[5]

Figure 3.1 plots men's and women's identification with the Democratic Party between 1950 and 2012. Each diamond represents the quarterly estimate of women's Democratic partisanship and each circle represents the quarterly estimate of men's Democratic partisanship. Smoothed lines representing the weighted quarterly estimates are presented to help trace the movement of men's (dashed) and women's (solid) Democratic partisanship. Early in the series, men and women held very similar partisan attachments. During the 1950s men held a slight preference for the Democratic Party compared to women: on average, 59% of men identified as Democrats compared to 57% of women. These differences are even smaller during the 1960s and 1970s, when on average men and women differed in their partisan attachments by less than 1%.

We begin to see men's and women's partisan attachments separate at the end of the 1970s. Both men's and women's partisan identification with the Democratic Party starts to decline; however, men's attachments decline at a faster rate. The differences between men's and women's partisanship are moderate in the 1980s: on average 57% of men identified with the Democratic Party compared to 60% of women. The average across the entire decade masks the growing difference between men's and women's Democratic attachments: in 1980, 64% of men identified with the Democratic Party compared to 66% of women; by 1989, 51% of men and 57%

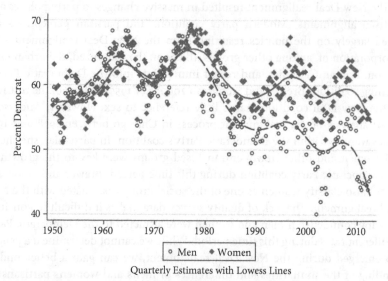

FIGURE 3.1 *Men and Women's Democratic Macropartisanship, 1950–2012*
Produced by author using Gallup surveys from 1950 to 2012.

of women identified with the Democratic Party. That is, the 2 percent difference in 1980 grew to a 6 percent difference by the end of the decade. Throughout the 1990s and 2000s, men's Democratic partisanship continued to decline, while women's Democratic partisanship remained level. In the 1990s, 60% of women identified with the Democratic Party compared to 54% of men. In the 2000s, 60% of women continued to identify with the Democratic Party, but Democratic Party identification dropped to 50% for men. These dynamics caused the difference between men's and women's partisan attachments to grow during the 1990s and 2000s.

The emergence and growth of these differences are easy to see when we look at the gender gap in partisanship in Figure 3.2. Starting in the 1980s it is clear that (1) women are more likely to identify with the Democratic Party than men and (2) the gender gap has grown over time. While these differences started to emerge in the late 1970s, by the 1980s there were modest differences between men and women's partisanship, averaging about 4%. The gap between men and women has grown in each decade since the 1980s. In the 1990s the gap averaged about 6.5%, and in the 2000s the gap averaged 8%. Between 2010 and 2012, the gap has grown even larger, averaging about 11%.

Men's and women's degrees of partisanship have exhibited a considerable amount of shared movement since the 1950s. However, starting in the late 1970s we see the formation of a gap that continues to grow. The gender gap carries important political consequences as well. Differences in partisanship translate into men and women casting their ballots differently at the federal and state level (Carroll

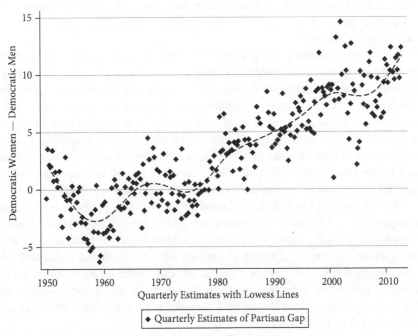

FIGURE 3.2 *Democratic Gender Gap in Partisanship, 1950–2012*
Produced by author using Gallup surveys from 1950 to 2012.

2006). Moreover, these differences are amplified by women's higher turnout rates in elections (Diekman and Schneider 2010; Huddy, Cassese, and Lizote 2008).

Explanations for the Gender Gap

Differences between men's and women's behavior and attitudes captured the attention of scholars, political parties, and the media in the aftermath of the 1980 presidential election. In postelection analyses, the media and National Organization for Women (NOW) used the term "gender gap" to describe how men and women cast their ballots (Mansbridge 1985). Men were more likely (54%) than women (46%) to support Ronald Reagan in the 1980 election, creating a gender gap of 8% (Center for American Women and Politics 2012). After the gap in vote choice was identified, other gaps in partisanship and public opinion were also discovered. But what caused these gender gaps?

Initially the gender gap was framed as a product of the second wave of the women's movement. Under this theory, the gender gap formed in the 1980 presidential election because women responded to the Republican Party dropping its support for the Equal Rights Amendment and adopting an antiabortion stance. Subsequent analysis of the 1980 election has shown that neither of these issues played a significant role in the gender gap (Frankovic 1982; Mansbridge 1985). Instead, men and women tend to hold very similar opinions on both abortion policy and the Equal Rights Amendment (Norrander 2008; Shapiro and Mahajan 1986). While these issues contribute little to the gender gap, differences in opinion on other issues do play a significant role in the formation of the gender gap partisanship and vote choice.

For decades, modest but important differences between men and women have existed on a wide variety of public policies. Some of the largest policy differences between women and men revolve around law-and-order issues domestically and the use of military force internationally. On the domestic side, women tend to be more supportive of gun control and less supportive of the death penalty (Howell and Day 2000; Norrander 2008; Shapiro and Mahajan 1986). In terms of the international use of force, women tend to be less supportive of sending troops to war and military spending. Women also are more likely to wish to see peaceful, non-military resolutions to international events (Fite, Genest, and Wilcox 1990).

Women also tend to hold more liberal domestic policy positions, supporting a larger role and scope of government (Kellstedt, Peterson, and Ramirez 2010; Shapiro and Mahajan 1986). Differences have been found for general social welfare policies, such as government-guaranteed jobs and expanded social services, and identified within the policy domains of health care, aid to the poor, Social Security, education, childcare, treatment for substance abuse, and programs for the homeless (Howell and Day 2000; Norrander 2008; Schlesinger and Heldman 2001; Shapiro and Mahajan 1986).

These opinion differences serve as the basis for gender differences in both vote choice and partisanship. Differences of opinion and salience on social welfare issues explain the gender gap in vote choice in the 1992 and 1996 elections (Kaufmann and Petrocik 1999). Additionally, men and women weigh their social welfare positions differently in their decisions about party identification (Kaufmann 2004). Generally, differences in men's and women's opinion on national and personal financial situations, foreign affairs, use of force, ideology, and social programs explain about three-quarters of the gender gap in vote choice between 1984 and 1992 (Chaney, Alvarez, and Nagler 1998).

Understanding why men and women hold different opinions on these issues is more complicated. Diekman and Schneider (2010) argue that the social roles an individual plays in society shape individual-level psychological processes that influence political attitudes. Women's and men's social roles have evolved considerably over the past several decades. A driving force behind these changes has been demographic changes that include women's increased participation in the paid labor force and women remaining single for longer in their lives. The extant research identifies two important implications of these changes. First, women have developed greater psychological and economic independence from men (Carroll 1988). This creates the potential for different political orientations to emerge from men and nonworking women (Iversen and Rosenbluth 2010). Second, women's workforce participation has not been on equal grounds with men. Women tend to be located in lower-paying jobs and therefore have greater dependence on government services (Erie and Rein 1988). Thus, these demographic changes imply that women are more likely to benefit from expansive social welfare programs both directly and indirectly than are men.

There is considerable evidence that these demographic changes and changes in women's social roles have resulted in changes in opinion, voting, and partisanship. In general these macro-level demographic changes have been linked to working women's greater support for social welfare programs cross-nationally (Iversen and Rosenbluth 2010). In the United States, women's workforce participation specifically has been linked to the gender gap in vote choice via changes in social welfare attitudes (Manza and Brooks 1998). Moreover, women in the workforce tend to hold different attitudes than women not in the workforce (Andersen and Cook 1985; Iversen and Rosenbluth 2010). At the aggregate level, Box-Steffensmeier, De Boef, and Lin (2004) show that the rise in percentage of single women increases differences between men's and women's partisan attachments. Additionally, men in occupations that rely more directly on government tend to be more supportive of social welfare programs, thus reducing the opinion differences between men and women (Howell and Day 2000). At the same time, women are more likely to be in redistributive occupations, leading to more feminist attitudes and less support for conservative ideological positions (Howell and Day 2000). This suggests that part of the gender gap is formed by men's and women's self-interest.

Along with creating differences in self-interest, differences in men's and women's social roles generate differences in personality and values (Eagly 1987). Small but consistent differences have been found between men and women on the "Big Five" personality traits, with women exhibiting more neuroticism, agreeableness, warmth, and openness to feelings and men demonstrating more assertiveness and openness to ideas (Costa, Terracciano, and McCrae 2001). These differences in personality translate into different values that are linked to political attitudes (Eagly, Diekman, Johannesen-Schmidt, and Koening 2004; Schwartz and Ruble 2005). Values play an important role in shaping differences in public opinion. Women are more likely to feel it is important to help others, which contributes to their more liberal positions on social welfare. More support for helping others actually appears to make men take a more conservative ideological position (Howell and Day 2000).

Differences in opinions are clearly linked to the political parties and lay the groundwork for ideological changes that also contribute to the gender gap. The issue differences discussed above more closely align women with the policies endorsed by the Democratic Party after the New Deal realignment, while men are more closely aligned with the policies endorsed by the Republican Party. Some of the differences we observe in men's and women's partisanship attachments reflect the process of individuals aligning and realigning with the political parties in the aftermath of both the New Deal realignment and Southern realignment (Ondercin 2017).

Generational Differences

Did women who came of age politically after the passage of the Nineteenth Amendment align with the political parties differently than women who came of age before the passage of the Nineteenth Amendment? Did women who came of age politically before and after suffrage hold different political preferences than men? What influence did the second wave of the women's movement have in shaping men's and women's partisan attachments? Examining how different political generations aligned with the political parties provides insight into the Nineteenth Amendment's influence on women's partisan identities.

The data set for this project provides unique leverage in understanding generational differences in partisanship before and after the passage of the Nineteenth Amendment. Most studies of the gender gap have focused on a post-1980 time period, meaning that very few individuals who came of age politically before the passage of the Nineteenth Amendment remain in the population. The first observations in the data set used here are recorded only thirty years after the passage of the Nineteenth Amendment, allowing us to better trace the partisan attachments of both the presuffrage generation and multiple postsuffrage generations.

The analysis examines men's and women's partisan attachments in four different political generations. Generation 1 is the presuffrage generation, defined as those who turned twenty-one years old before the passage of the Nineteenth Amendment in 1920.[6] Generation 2 is the immediate postsuffrage generation, defined as those who turned twenty-one between 1921 and 1960. Generation 3 captures those who came of age politically during the second wave of the women's movement in the United States. Individuals are coded as part of Generation 3 if they turned twenty-one between 1961 and 1970 or if they turned eighteen between 1971 and 1980. Generation 4 captures the last age group analyzed and comprises individuals who turned eighteen after 1980. To allow for enough respondents in each generation, the analysis of Generation 1 ends in 1980. Additionally, the analysis of Generation 3 starts in 1965 and Generation 4 starts in 1987.

Figure 3.3 examines women's Democratic partisan identification by generation. Focusing only on women allows us to consider whether different time periods had differential effects on women's allegiances to the political parties. For clarity's sake, Figure 3.3 presents the smoothed lines but omits the quarterly estimates of women's partisanship. Women who came of age politically before suffrage (Generation 1, solid line) exhibit different attachments with the political parties than the other political generations. In addition to gender, the larger political context should influence the partisan attachments of the different generations. As a result we would expect that the partisan attachments of the postsuffrage generation (Generation 2, dashed line) to be influenced by the New Deal realignment, making them more Democratic than the presuffrage generation (Miller and Shanks 1996). This expectation is confirmed. The presuffrage generation is less likely to identify with the Democratic Party than the immediate postsuffrage generation. Interestingly, the immediate postsuffrage generation (Generation 2) does not differ significantly from women who came of age politically during the second wave of the women's movement (Generation 3, dotted line). Generation 4 (dashed-dotted line) starts off less Democratic than Generations 2 and 3 but quickly increases its level of Democratic Party identification.[7]

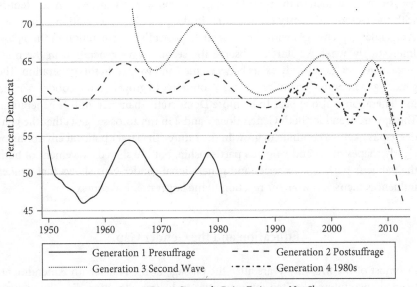

Lowess Lines, Quarterly Point Estimates Not Shown

FIGURE 3.3 *Women's Democratic Macropartisanship by Generations, 1950–2012*

Produced by author using Gallup surveys from 1950 to 2012.

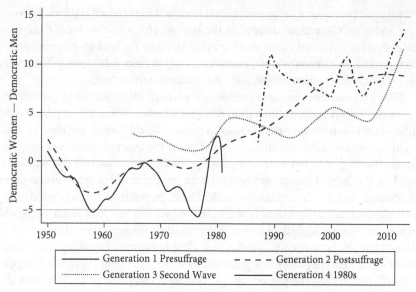

FIGURE 3.4 *Generational Gender Gaps in Democratic Macropartisanship, 1950–2012*
Produced by author using Gallup surveys from 1950 to 2012.

Did women in these different political generations significantly differ from men in the same generation? Figure 3.4 explores the Democratic gender gaps of the four political generations. The presuffrage generation exhibits a small, negative gender gap; on average, men in the presuffrage generation were 2% more likely to identify with the Democratic Party than women in the presuffrage generation. The modern gender gap emerges with the immediate postsuffrage generation in the 1980s. Interestingly, when we start to observe the second-wave generation in the mid-1970s, a gender gap already exists between men and women in this generation. The gender gap in both Generations 2 and 3 continues to grow into the 2000s. Women in Generation 4 also appear to be more Democratic than men in this generation. The upward trend for both Generations 3 and 4 in the 2010s suggests that the gender gap is likely to continue to grow in the future. The larger political environment clearly shapes men's and women's partisanship, but the shared movement of both the women's partisanship series and generational gender gaps shows that gender influences men's and women's reaction to the larger political context.

Education and the Gender Gap

For most of the first fifty years after the passage of the Nineteenth Amendment, women encountered limited opportunities in higher education. For the women who had the resources to attend college during this time period, the curriculum offered to women in higher education prepared them to take on traditional social

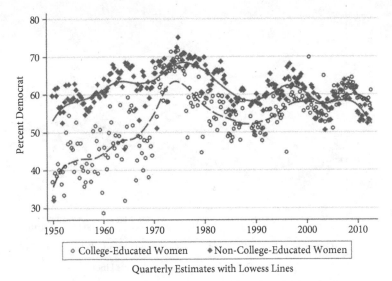

FIGURE 3.5 *Women's Democratic Macropartisanship by Education Level, 1950–2012*
Produced by author using Gallup surveys from 1950 to 2012.

roles. As the century progressed, more and more women sought higher education that was equal to men's. The passage of Title IX in 1972 greatly increased women's opportunities in higher education, mandating that colleges and universities that received public funds could not discriminate on the basis of sex. As a result, the number of women pursuing a college education has greatly increased. Women's increased educational attainment contributed to the transformation of women's social roles. Not only did it lead to women's increased workforce participation, but women entered different positions—more professional and white-collar occupations—in the workforce. Examining women's partisan attachments among those with a college and without a college education, therefore, can provide us further insight into how the changing social roles of women transformed their political behavior.

The Democratic partisan attachments of women by level of education are plotted in Figure 3.5. Smoothed lines are used to highlight the overall trends in the data, with the dashed line representing women with a college degree and the solid line representing women without a college degree. In the 1950s, women without a college education were considerably more Democratic than women with a college education. The difference between women with and without a college education decreases through the 1960s, but a gap remains until 2000. During this time period the Democratic partisanship of non-college-educated women declined slightly, while the Democratic identification of college-educated women increased. Since 2000, college-educated women are slightly more likely to identify with the Democratic Party than non-college-educated women.

Figure 3.6 shows the gender gap in Democratic partisanship among individuals with a college education and individuals without a college education.

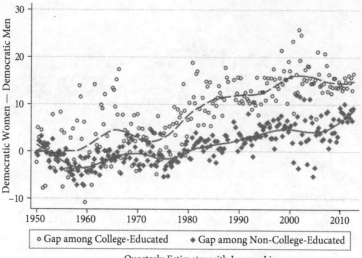

FIGURE 3.6 *Democratic Gender Gap by Education Level, 1950–2012*
Produced by author using Gallup surveys from 1950 to 2012.

The gender gap in partisanship emerges earlier among those with a college education than those without a college education. Starting in the 1960s the partisan preferences of men and women with a college education begin to diverge
to form the modern gender gap. During the 1960s and 1970s the gender gap
among the college educated averaged 3%. At the same time, a smaller gender
gap in the opposite direction existed among the non-college-educated. On
average, non-college-educated men were approximately 1.5% more Democratic
than non-college-educated women during the 1960s and 1970s. In 1980 a substantial gap of almost 11% existed between college-educated men and women,
but no gap existed between non-college-educated men and women. A small
gap among the non-college-educated emerged in the 1980s and then slowly
grew over the next several decades. Among the college educated the gap also
grows, but at a faster rate than the non-college-educated. Between 2010 and
2012 the gender gap among the college educated was almost twice the size of
the gender gap among the non-college-educated. The larger and earlier gender
gap among the college-educated highlights the importance of changes in men's
and women's social roles in shaping partisan attachments and the formation of
the gender gap.

Race and the Gender Gap

Some of the largest differences in both partisanship and voting are along racial
lines. Since Southern realignment, African Americans have overwhelmingly identified with the Democratic Party and supported Democratic candidates. Given the

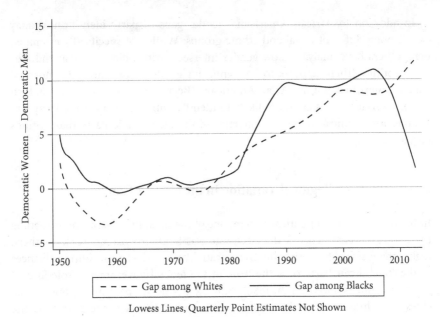

FIGURE 3.7 *Democratic Gender Gap by Race, 1950–2012*
Produced by author using surveys from 1950 to 2012.

cohesive political behavior of African Americans, there is likely little opportunity for gender differences in partisanship to emerge. However, some studies suggest that African American women are more likely to turn out to vote and support Democratic candidates than African American males (Huddy, Cassese, and Lizote 2008; Lien 1998).

Figure 3.7 examines that gender gap in Democratic partisanship among whites and African Americans between 1950 and 2012. Surprisingly, the gender gap among whites and African Americans show similar trends over time. The gender gap among African Americans emerges slightly before the gender gap among whites. Additionally, the gender gap among African Americans is larger than the gender gap among whites for most of the series. This is not to say that African Americans and whites hold Democratic partisan attachments at the same level; rather, these results indicate that the difference in Democratic Party identification between white men and women and African American men and women is similar. An analysis of men's and women's partisanship not shown here demonstrates that since Southern realignment, African Americans identify with the Democratic Party at much higher rates than whites. Throughout the 1950s and 1960s, identification with the Democratic Party increased considerably until it reached, on average, around 90% for African American men and women. However, African American women's identification with the Democratic Party is even greater than that of African American men. Between 1970 and 2012, on average 94% of African American women identified with the Democratic Party, compared to 87% of African American men.

In addition to African Americans, gender gaps in party identification may exist among different racial and ethnic groups. While not specifically examined here, others have analyzed how gender intersects with different racial and ethnic identities. There appears to be significant gender gaps among Latinos and Native Americans, but not Asian Americans (Bejarano 2014; Conway 2008; Lien 1998). Overall Latinos are more likely to identify with the Democratic Party, but Latinas are significantly more supportive of the Democratic Party than Latinos (Bejarano 2014).

Regional Variation in the Gender Gap

In the post–New Deal political system, one of the most important events shaping the partisan attachments of the electorate was Southern realignment. Southern realignment saw elites within the Democratic Party in the South shifting alliances to the Republican Party over the issue of the federal government's role in civil rights (Carmines and Stimson 1989). Moving at a slower pace in response to the elites, the white electorate in southern states shifted its allegiance away from the Democratic Party. The impact of Southern realignment can be seen in Figure 3.1, which indicates that both men's and women's Democratic partisanship declines in the 1970s and 1980s. As a result of this regional realignment process, the South went from being solidly dominated by the Democratic Party to strongly favoring the Republican Party (Black and Black 2002; Miller 1991).

Did men and women respond to the elite cue in the same manner, meaning there would be no gap in the South? Or do gender gaps in partisan identification exist across the different geographical regions? Norrander (1999a, 1999b) argues that the gender gap we observe in the population as a whole is largely about Southern realignment. Additionally, white women in the South have been more likely to retain their Democratic identification than white men (Miller 1991; Ondercin 2013).

Despite these possibilities, the gender gap in the South looks very similar to the gender gap in other regions of the country. Figure 3.8 examines the gender gap in partisanship in southern states and nonsouthern states.[8] The solid line is the estimate for the southern gender gap and the dashed line is the estimate for the nonsouthern gender gap (quarterly point estimates were omitted for presentational purposes). We can see the estimates of the gaps are virtually on top of each other, meaning that, essentially, there was no difference in the gap in southern and nonsouthern states. Analysis of men's and women's partisanship shows that both declined in the South as a result of Southern realignment. Moreover, that decline was larger among men compared to women, forming the gender gap in the South and offering aggregate confirmation to the individual-level findings. At the same time, gaps between men's and women's partisanship also were formed outside the South, with women maintaining their level of Democratic partisanship while men's Democratic partisanship declined.

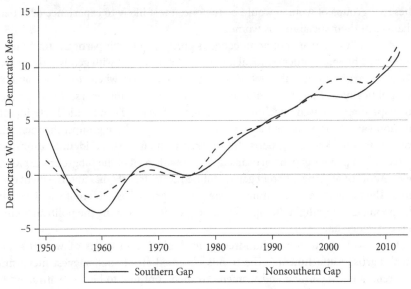

FIGURE 3.8 *Regional Gender Gaps in Democratic Macropartisanship, 1950–2012*
Produced by author using surveys from 1950 to 2012.

Conclusion

The electorate's partisan attachments have changed considerably since the passage of the Nineteenth Amendment. The New Deal realignment and Southern realignment in the later part of the twentieth century slowly caused both men and women to adjust their partisan attachments. In addition to these events, one important characteristic of the partisan changes over the past one hundred years has been the emergence and growth of the gender gap in partisanship. After the passage of the Nineteenth Amendment, women appear to have shared their partisan identities and voting preferences with their husbands, fathers, and brothers. But approximately sixty years after achieving the right to vote, women's and men's partisan preferences began to diverge. Today, the gender gap in partisanship represents an important electoral cleavage.

The 1980 presidential election set a significant milestone for the gender gap in partisanship because it was the first election where women's and men's preferences clearly differed. The analysis presented above also suggests that it was the first election where all groups of women, regardless of age, region, race, or education level, favored the Democratic Party compared to men. These analyses point out an often overlooked fact: the gender gap in partisanship existed before the 1980s among certain subgroups in the population. College-educated women and women coming of age politically during the second wave of the women's movement both favored the Democratic Party more so than men prior to 1980. Interestingly, these subgroups of women would be the ones most likely to experience or expect changes in their social role as women.

Men and women are not homogeneous groups, and their partisan attachments are shaped by many other political identities that intersect with gender. The analysis above explored how the political identities based on when someone came of age politically and their level of education, race, and region intersect with gender to shape their partisan attachments. While the level of Democratic Party identification varied for both men and women across all of these groups, the men and women within these subgroups still differed in their partisan identification. Put differently, a gender gap in partisanship exists within all of the subgroups explored here. Additionally, the different gaps exhibited considerable shared movement over time. The presence and dynamics of the gender gap across different subgroups in the population highlight the significance of gender in shaping the political identities of women and men.

What will the next one hundred years look like in terms of women's and men's partisan attachments? The trends observed since 2008 suggest increasing differences between men and women. Women continue to be more attracted to the Democratic Party while men appear to be shifting their attachments to the Republican Party. The generational analysis suggests that differences in men's and women's partisan attachments among the youngest generation are some of the largest and are growing. If these trends continue, as this generation becomes a larger portion of the electorate, we are likely to see even larger differences in men's and women's partisan attachments.

Another factor to consider regarding the future of the gender gap is the influence of the changing demographic makeup of the country. The analysis above focuses on the gender gap between whites and African Americans. However, the racial and ethnic makeup of the electorate is becoming increasingly diverse. More research is needed to understand the gender gap among different racial and ethnic groups. Christina Bejarano (2014) finds that in the 2012 election Latina women held distinct policy preferences from Latino men. This work indicates that the continued growth of the gender gap may be related to changing demographic patterns in the electorate.

The future of the gender gap will also depend on the political parties and the packages of policies they assemble to attract voters. The current issue advantages of the political parties are based on the New Deal realignment. Men and women have adjusted their partisan attachments as their social roles have evolved. When new issues enter the political agenda or old issues are reframed, it offers the opportunity for political parties to solidify existing voting blocs or try to attract new voters. While men and women exhibit significant differences in their partisan attachments, there are also a considerable number of similarities. Thus, parties and politicians are likely to focus on gender differences to influence their electoral chances. We therefore may see some of the largest changes in the gender gap in the future as men and women respond to changes in the policies championed by the political parties.

Notes

1. The *gender gap* is a term used to capture differences in the attitudes or behavior of men and women. The focus of this chapter is on men's and women's identification with the political parties, or the gender gap in partisanship. In the course of discussing the gender gap in partisanship, other gender gaps are addressed, such as the gender gap in vote choice and the gender gap observed in different policy issues.

2. Despite the inclusion of "party" in its name, the National Women's Party was more a single-issue pressure organization rather than a political party.

3. Interestingly, the coalition of voters that formed the New Deal was the same coalition of voters assembled by Massachusetts suffragists in their lobbying effects to secure the vote (Graham 1996).

4. The Gallup Organization has extensively surveyed the American public since the 1950s. The data for this project are based on a collection of Gallup surveys archived with the Roper Center. First, I started with all surveys that had as their sampling frame a national adult sample. This excluded surveys with an oversample of certain populations and surveys that were only conducted of registered voters. Second, given the importance of partisanship and sex for the analysis, the survey had to include both the partisan identification question and the respondent's sex.

Overall, 1,451 Gallup surveys were used to create the quarterly estimates. There is at least one survey every quarter, and on average there are six surveys per quarter. The third quarter of 2000, the fourth quarter of 2001, and the fourth quarter of 2004 only have one survey. The fourth quarter of 1992 has the largest number of surveys in a quarter at nineteen. On average there were 8,362 respondents per quarter. The smallest sample size was 1,002 respondents in the fourth quarter of 2004. The largest sample size was observed in the first quarter of 1964, which had a sample size of 22,262 individuals.

Some scholars have criticized the use of Gallup surveys because the partisanship question is different from the question used by other survey houses (Converse 1976; Abramson and Ostrom 1991). Gallup asks, "In politics today, do you consider yourself a Republican, Democrat, or Independent?" They argue that the phrase "In politics today" results in greater short-term variation than questions that use the phrase "Generally speaking." While there is evidence that the Gallup series do exhibit greater variation, this variation does not appear to greatly influence substantive results (Erikson, MacKuen, and Stimson 2002; MacKuen, Erikson, and Stimson 1992; Bishop, Tuchfarber, Smith, and Abramson 1994). Unfortunately, other surveys do not offer the rich time series that can be compiled from the Gallup surveys.

One potential obstacle with basing the time series on Gallup surveys is that Gallup changed its mode of interview from in-person to telephone. Many have observed that the telephone interviews produced samples that tended to be more Republican (Erikson, MacKuen, and Stimson 2002; Green, Palmquist, and Shickler 2002; Hugick 1991). If left uncorrected, there would be a drift toward the Republican Party starting in the 1980s not present in the in-person interviews or other survey houses. Past estimates of the bias reflected the population as a whole and did not examine whether differences existed in the bias for men and women. I estimated the Republican bias introduced by telephone interviews for men and women separately and then adjusted the telephone samples before incorporating them into the time series.

Gallup continued to use both modes of interviews in the 1980s and 1990s, with the majority of the transition occurring between 1984 and 1995. Following Erikson, MacKuen, and Stimson (2002), I use the in-person interviews as the baseline. I then estimate the difference between surveys with in-person interviews and those conducted over the telephone within the same quarter. The estimates of Democratic partisanship for telephone interviews are then corrected based on the estimated bias.

Democratic partisanship is calculated as the percentage of respondents who identify as Democrats out of two party identifiers. Women's Democratic partisanship is the percentage of women who identify with the Democratic Party out of all women who identify with the Democratic or Republican Party. Men's Democratic partisanship is the percentage of men who identify with the Democratic Party out of all men who identify with the Democratic Party or Republican Party. The gender gap is calculated by subtracting men's Democratic partisanship from women's Democratic partisanship. Positive gaps mean that women are more likely than men to identify with the Democratic Party. Negative gaps mean that men are more likely than women to identify with the Democratic Party. The same logic was used to calculate the Democratic attachments in subpopulations of the electorate. For example, to calculate the partisan attachments of women from the presuffrage generation, I calculated the percentage of women in Generation 1 out of all women in Generation 1 that identified with the Democratic or Republican Parties. Male Democratic partisanship for Generation 1 reflects the percentage of men in Generation 1 who identified with the Democratic Party out of all men in Generation 1 identifying with the Democratic or Republican Parties. The gender gap in Generation 1 reflects the percentage of women who identify in Generation 1 with the Democratic Party minus the percentage of men identifying with the Democratic Party.

Lowess smoothing lines are calculated using nonparametric locally weighted regressions of the quarterly estimates. The lowess lines allow us to see the general trends in the movement of men's and women's partisanship. The smoothness of the line or how much it responds to each quarterly estimate is determined by the bandwidth. A bandwidth of .2 was used for all the lowess estimates reported here. Essentially, the lowess line is a moving average of the quarterly estimates using 20% of the quarterly estimates to create each point in the lowess line. The data used in this analysis represent aggregate quarterly estimates of partisanship.

The quarterly estimate is calculated by taking the average weighted by sample size for all surveys in a quarter. Using both the lowess smoothing and quarterly averages has several advantages. They produce easy-to-read figures that are not overcluttered with the vast amount of data used to calculate them and help even out random movement. The central disadvantage to this process is that it is extremely difficult to accurately calculate confidence bans around the lowess smoothing lines that take into account the number of individual respondents in each of the quarterly estimates. However, as noted above, the sample sizes per quarter are rather large. This holds true when examining the subpopulations in the figure. For the most part, we have over 1,000 respondents falling into subpopulations. The analysis of race and political generations represents some of the smallest samples, but still averaged around 750 respondents. Thus we can naively estimate confidence intervals of about 3.5%.

5. Box-Steffensmeier et al. (2004) use the same definition of men's and women's Democratic partisanship. This definition parallels the broader definition of Democratic

partisanship by Erikson, MacKuen, and Stimson (2002). This measure omits independent identifiers, who have increased considerably over the past several decades in the electorate. Norrander (1997) points out that in the National Elections Studies, men are more likely to fall into the leaning-independent category.

6. Some of the women in this generation would have had full or partial suffrage before the passage of the Nineteenth Amendment. At the time the Nineteenth Amendment was ratified, three-quarters of states had some form of voting rights for women (McConnaughy 2013). As a result, many of the women in this generation were likely to have some form of voting rights.

7. We start observing both Generation 3 and Generation 4 during what scholars of political socialization refer to as the *impressionable years* (Alwin and Krosnick 1991; Beck and Jennings 1991). This is a time period during late adolescence and young adulthood where opinions and attitudes have yet to crystalize. When we observe Generation 3 move from being considerably more Democratic than Generation 2 early in the series to only slightly more Democratic than Generation 2 over time, we are observing the influence of life-cycle effects and attitude crystallization. The same is happening when we observe Generation 4 increasing its Democratic Party attachments early on in the series.

8. The South is defined based on Gallup's classification of regions. States classified as in the South are Virginia, North Carolina, South Carolina, Georgia, Florida, Kentucky, Tennessee, Alabama, Mississippi, Arkansas, Louisiana, Oklahoma, and Texas.

References

Abramson, Paul R., and Charles W. Ostrom Jr. 1991. "Macropartisanship: An Empirical Reassessment." *American Political Science Review* 85(1): 181–192.

Alwin, Duane F., and Jon A. Krosnick. 1991. "Aging, Cohorts, and the Stability of Sociopolitical Orientations over the Life Span." *American Journal of Sociology* 97(1): 169–195.

Andersen, Kristi. 1979. *The Creation of a Democratic Majority, 1928–1936.* Chicago: University of Chicago Press.

———. 1996. *After Suffrage: Women in Partisan and Electoral Politics before the New Deal.* Chicago: University of Chicago Press.

Andersen, Kristi, and Elizabeth A. Cook. 1985. "Women, Work, and Political Attitudes." *American Journal of Political Science* 29(3): 606–625.

Baker, Paula. 1984. "The Domestication of politics: Women and American Political Society, 1780–1920." *American Historical Review,* 89(3): 620–647.

Beck, Paul Allen, and M. Kent Jennings. 1991. "Family Traditions, Political Periods, and the Development of Partisan Orientations." *Journal of Politics* 53(3): 742–763.

Bejarano, Christina. 2014. *The Latino Gender Gap in US Politics,* New York: Routledge Press.

Bishop, George F., Alfred J. Tuchfarber, Andrew E. Smith, and Paul R Abramson. 1994. "Question Form and Context Effects in the Measurement of Partisanship: Experimental Tests of the Artifact Hypothesis." *American Political Science Review* 88(4): 945–954.

Black, Earl, and Merle Black. 2002. *The Rise of Southern Republicans.* Cambridge, MA: Harvard University Press.

Box-Steffensmeier, Janet, Suzanna De Boef, and Tse-min Lin. 2004. "The Dynamics of the Partisan Gender Gap." *American Political Science Review* 98(3): 515–528.

Brewer, Mark D., and Jeffrey M. Stonecash. 2009. *Dynamics of American Political Parties.* Cambridge: Cambridge University Press.

Carmines, Edward G., and James A. Stimson. 1989. *Issue Evolution: Race and the Transformation of American Politics.* Princeton, NJ: Princeton University Press.

Carroll, Susan J. 1988. "Women's Autonomy and the Gender Gap: 1980 and 1982." Pp. 236–257 in *The Politics of the Gender Gap: The Social Construction of Political Influence,* edited by C. M. Mueller. Newbury, CA: Sage Publications.

——. 2006. "Voting Choices: Meet You at the Gender Gap." Pp. 74–96 in *Gender and Elections Shaping the Future of American Politics,* edited by S. J. Carroll and R. L. Fox. Cambridge: Cambridge University Press.

Center for American Women and Politics. 2012. *The Gender Gap Voting Choices in Presidential Election.* Fact sheet prepared by Center for American Women and Politics (CAWP), Eagleton Institute of Politics, Rutgers University.

Chaney, Carole Kennedy, R. Michael Alvarez, and Jonathan Nagler. 1998. "Explaining the Gender Gap in U.S. Presidential Elections, 1980–1992." *Political Research Quarterly* 51(2): 311–339.

Converse, Philip E. 1976. *The Dynamics of Party Support: Cohort-Analyzing Party Identification.* Sage Publications: Beverly Hills.

Conway, M. Margret. 2008. "The Gender Gap: A Comparison across Racial and Ethnic Groups" Pp. 170–183 in *Voting The Gender Gap,* edited by L. D. Whitaker. Urbana: University of Illinois Press.

Costa, Paul, Jr., Antonio Terracciano, and Robert R. McCrae. 2001. "Gender Differences in Personality Traits across Cultures: Robust and Surprising Findings." *Journal of Personality and Social Psychology* 81(2): 322–331.

Cott, Nancy F. 1984. "Feminist Politics in the 1920s: The National Woman's Party." *The Journal of American History* 71(1): 43–68.

Diekman, Amanda B., and Monica C. Schneider. 2010. "A Social Role Theory Perspective on Gender Gaps in Political Attitudes." *Psychology of Women Quarterly* 34(4): 486–497.

Eagly, Alice. 1987. *Sex Differences in Social Behavior: A Social Role Interpretation.* Hillsdale, NJ: Erlbaum.

Eagly, Alice H., Amanda B. Diekman, Mary C. Johannesen-Schmidt, and Anne M Koening. 2004. "Gender Gap in Sociopolitical Attitudes: A Social Psychological Analysis." *Journal of Personality and Social Psychology.* 87(6): 796–816.

Erie, Steven P., and Martin Rein. 1988. "Women and the Welfare State." Pp. 173–191 in *The Politics of the Gender Gap: The Social Construction of Political Influence,* edited by C. M. Mueller. Newbury, CA: Sage Publications.

Erikson, Robert S., Michael B. MacKuen, and James A. Stimson. 2002. *The Macro Polity.* Cambridge: Cambridge University Press.

Evans, Sara M. 1989. *Born for Liberty: A History of Women in America.* New York: Free Press.

Fite, David, Marc Genest, and Clyde Wilcox. 1990. "Gender Differences in Foreign Policy Attitudes: A Longitudinal Analysis." *American Politics Research* 18(4): 492–513.

Frankovic, Kathleen A. 1982. "Sex and Politics—New Alignments, Old Issues." *PS: Political Science & Politics* 15(3): 439–448.

Freeman, Jo. 2000. *A Room at a Time: How Women Entered Party Politics.* Lanham, MD: Rowman and Littlefield.

Graham, Sara Hunter. 1996. *Women Suffrage and New Democracy*. New Haven, CT: Yale University Press.

Green, Donald, Bradley Palmquist, and Eric Schickler. 2002. *Partisan Hearts & Minds: Political Parties and the Social Identities of Voters*. New Haven, CT: Yale University Press.

Gustafson, Melanie. 1997. "Partisan Women in the Progressive Era: The Struggle for Inclusion in American Politics." *Journal of Women's History* 9(2): 8–30.

Howell, Susan E., and Christine L. Day. 2000. "Complexities of the Gender Gap." *Journal of Politics* 62(3): 858–874.

Huddy, Leonie, Erin Cassese, and Mary-Kate Lizote. 2008. "Sources of Political Unitary and Disunity among Women: Placing the Gender Gap in Perspective." Pp. 141–169 in *Voting the Gender Gap*, edited by L. D. Whitaker. Urbana: University of Illinois Press.

Hugick, Larry. 1991. "Party Identification: The Disparity between Gallup's In-Person and Telephone Interview Findings." *Public Perspective* 2(6): 23–24.

Iversen, Torben, and Frances Rosenbluth. 2010. *Women, Work, and Politics*. New Haven, CT: Yale University Press.

Kaufmann, Karen. 2004. "The Partisan Paradox Religious Commitment and the Gender Gap in Party Identification." *Public Opinion Quarterly* 68(4): 491–511.

Kaufmann, Karen, and John R. Petrocik. 1999. "The Changing Politics of American Men: Understanding the Sources of the Gender Gap." *American Journal of Political Science* 43(3): 864–887.

Kellstedt, Paul, David A. Peterson, and Mark D. Ramirez. 2010. "The Macro Politics of the Gender Gap." *Public Opinion Quarterly* 74(3): 477–498.

Key, V. O. 1955. "A Theory of Critical Elections." *Journal of Politics* 17(1): 3–18.

Lien, Pei-Te. 1998. "Does the Gender Gap in Political Attitudes and Behavior Vary across Racial Groups?" *Political Research Quarterly* 51(4): 869–894.

Lunardini, Christine A. 1986. *From Equal Suffrage to Equal Rights*. New York: New York University Press.

MacKuen, Michael B., Robert S. Erikson, and James A. Stimson. 1992. "Peasants or Bankers? The American Electorate and the US Economy." *American Political Science Review* 86(3): 597–611.

Mansbridge, Jane J. 1985. "Myth and Reality: The ERA and the Gender Gap in the 1980 Election." *Public Opinion Quarterly* 49(2): 164–178.

Manza, Jeff, and Clem Brooks. 1998. "The Gender Gap in U.S. Presidential Elections: When? Why? Implications?" *American Journal of Sociology* 103(5): 1235–1266.

McConnaughy, Corrine M. 2013. *The Woman Suffrage Movement in America: A Reassessment*. New York: Cambridge University Press.

Miller, Warren E. 1991. "Party Identification, Realignment, and Party Voting: Back to the Basics." *American Political Science Review*. 85(2): 557–568.

Miller, Warren E., and Shanks, J. Merrill. 1996. *The New American Voter*. Cambridge, MA: Harvard University Press.

Norrander, Barbara. 1997. "The Independence Gap and the Gender Gap." *Public Opinion Quarterly* 61(3): 464–476.

———. 1999a. "Is the Gender Gap Growing?" Pp. 146–161 in *Re-Election 1996: How Americans Vote*, edited by H. E. Weisberg and J. M. Box-Steffensmeier. New York: Chatham House Publisher.

———. 1999b. "The Evolution of the Gender Gap." *Public Opinion Quarterly.* 63(4): 566–576.

———. 2008. "The History of the Gender Gap." Pp. 9–32 in *Voting and the Gender Gap,* edited by L. D. Whitaker. Urbana: University of Illinois Press.

Ondercin, Heather L. 2013. "What Scarlett O'Hara Thinks: Political Attitudes of Southern Women." *Political Science Quarterly* 128(2): 233–259.

———. 2017. "Who Is Responsible for the Gender Gap? The Dynamics of Men's and Women's Democratic Macropartisanship, 1950–2012."

Schlesinger, Mark, and Caroline Heldman. 2001. "Gender Gap or Gender Gaps? New Perspectives on Support for Government Action and Policies." *Journal of Politics* 63(1): 59–92.

Schwartz, Shalom H., and Tammy Ruble. 2005. "Sex Differences in Value Priorities: Cross-Cultural and Multi-Method Studies." *Journal of Personality and Social Psychology* 89(6): 1010–1028.

Shapiro, Robert Y., and Harpereet Mahajan. 1986. "Gender Differences in Policy Preferences: A Summary of Trends from the 1960s to the 1980s." *Public Opinion Quarterly* 50(1): 42–61.

Wolbrecht, Christina. 2000. *The Politics of Women's Rights.* Princeton, NJ: Princeton University Press.

Zaeske, Susan. 2003. *Signatures of Citizenship Petitioning, Antislavery & Women's Political Identity.* Chapel Hill: University of North Carolina Press.

{ 4 }

What's Happened to the Gender Gap in Political Participation?

HOW MIGHT WE EXPLAIN IT?

Nancy Burns, Kay Lehman Schlozman, Ashley Jardina,
Shauna Shames, and Sidney Verba

Americans who wish to influence political outcomes have many ways to get involved, some of which depend on suffrage and others of which are surely enhanced by suffrage. They can vote or otherwise take part in the electoral process by displaying a bumper sticker, attending meetings or rallies, working for a candidate or party, or making a financial contribution to a candidate, party, or other electoral organization. They can express their opinions directly by getting in touch with a public official, attending a protest or demonstration, working with others to solve community problems, serving on a local board like the school board, or joining an organization that takes stands in politics. But not all citizens are equally active in politics. As the authors of the 1848 Declaration of Sentiments knew all too well, these channels for the exercise of political voice provide Americans with the opportunity to inform public officials about citizen preferences and needs for government action and to pressure those in office to comply with what they hear. As did the authors of the Declaration of Sentiments, students of democracy take inequalities in participation seriously and are concerned when some citizens have a megaphone to amplify their voices and others speak in a whisper or not at all. Inequalities of political participation become especially worrisome for a democracy when a group of quiescent citizens is large; when membership in that group is determined by birth, not choice; and when group members are likely to have distinctive needs and concerns that are relevant for politics.

When women in the United States were finally granted suffrage in 1920, their turnout in the first elections was disappointingly low. Over much of the twentieth century, women did not turn out at the polls at nearly the same rate as men. Indeed, for as long as we have had the tools to measure individual participation in politics—which means roughly since the end of World War II—there has been a stubbornly persistent gender gap in political activity broadly, with men participating at somewhat higher rates than women. Even in the face of significant changes in women's roles and their access to social and economic resources, women's deficit in political activity stayed about the same size from the 1950s to the early 2000s. Then, without warning, at some point in the middle of the first decade of the twenty-first century, this deficit more or less vanished. In this chapter, we ask why. We seek answers both in social changes that have nothing to do with politics and in politics itself.

Thinking about Gender Differences—and Changing Gender Differences—in Political Participation

Our goal is to understand the changing nature of gender gaps in participation. To make headway with this goal, we must know about the factors that facilitate political participation generally,[1] and we must understand how differences between women and men in either the *level* or the *effect* of these factors contribute to gender disparity in political activity. That is, women and men might differ, on average, in how much of the resources and political orientations associated with political participation they possess (*level*). Or women and men might differ in how efficiently they convert whatever resources they have into political activity (*effect*). For example, it is well known that an individual's income is a strong predictor of making sizable campaign donations. Since men have, on average, significantly higher incomes than women do, income differences would have consequences for the gender gap in making major contributions to campaigns (Bryner and Weber 2013; National Council for Research on Women et al. 2014). In other words, the *level* of a resource—in this case, income—contributes to a gender gap in participation. It is also well known that turnout is higher when an election is highly competitive and visible—for example, in an election for president or governor rather than an election for school board (Campbell et al. 1960; Miller and Shanks 1996; Lewis-Beck, Nadeau, and Elias 2008). Nevertheless, because men and women live in the same electoral districts, there would be no aggregate gender difference in the kinds of elections to which citizens are exposed. Any possible contribution to the gender gap in participation from variations in the visibility and competitiveness of elections, then, would have to derive from these factors having a differential *effect* on men and women.

For the gender gap in political activity to narrow or widen over time, there must be a change in the level or effect of some participatory factor, and that change in level or effect must be different for men and women. To continue the example above, if men's and women's incomes both increase but the ratio of the two remains stable, then we would expect no change in the disparity between men and women in political activity. If, in contrast, men's aggregate income were to rise while women's stayed the same, then we would expect to see a small widening of the gender gap in participation.

The Factors That Explain the Gap

More than a decade ago we used a very detailed survey of the American public, the Citizen Participation Study, to investigate the participatory disparity between women and men.[2] We found then that the gender gap in political activity could be explained almost entirely in terms of differential stockpiles of participatory factors (the resources leading to participation). We found very little evidence for gender differences in the impact of those factors on activity. In short, for the most part, the key to the gender gap in political participation was differences in level rather than effect.

No single factor was responsible for the gap. Instead, women's participatory deficit was a consequence of a series of small, cumulative inequalities rooted in resource disadvantages that originate in institutions outside of politics. Most fundamental was that, compared to men, women had, on average, lower levels of educational attainment. Not only is educational attainment related directly to political participation, but education is related to almost every other factor that enhances political activity.[3] For example, the well-educated are more likely to hold jobs that pay well, and income level is related to political participation. Furthermore, people with high levels of education are more likely to cultivate organizational and communications skills on the job or in other nonpolitical domains of adult life—for example, in church or other religious institutions, or volunteering/community service (Verba, Schlozman, and Brady 1995). Engaging in such seemingly routine activities as arranging meetings and making presentations in settings having nothing to do with politics turns out to develop skills that are readily transferable to politics. On average, men have an advantage when it comes to all these resources for politics: they are better educated; they have higher incomes; and because they are more likely to be in the workforce full-time—and, if so, to have the kinds of jobs that are skill-endowing—they acquire more civic skills in nonpolitical settings, especially at work.

In addition, those who are psychologically engaged with politics—who are politically interested and informed, and who think that they could make a difference in politics—are more likely to take part. With respect to all these measures of psychological orientations to politics, we found, on average, a masculine advantage. When we probed further, we found the disparity in psychological political engagement to be related to politics itself, by the extent to which politics was a "man's game" and, specifically, by the paucity of women in elected office. Women, but not men, who were exposed to women contesting or holding visible public office—governor, US senator, or member of the US House—were more likely to know and care about politics. This was the only example we found of a difference in the effect rather than the level of a participatory factor. The presence of visible political women in the environment had different effects on women than on men, and thus indirectly narrowed the gender gap in participation.

The Incredible Shrinking Gap in Political Activity

Data collected a quarter of a century ago show a small but statistically significant gender disparity with respect to several political activities. In the first two columns of Table 4.1, data from 1990 show that women were significantly less likely than men to make campaign contributions or to contact government officials. They were also somewhat less likely (although not statistically significantly so) to vote or to work on a campaign.

More recently, the contours of the gender gap in political activity have changed. In the four right-hand columns of Table 4.1, we show data from surveys conducted in July 2008 and August 2012 by the Pew Research Center's Internet and American Life Project. Those figures show a small deficit in women's political activity in 1990 that disappeared at some point in the two decades separating the studies (the Citizen Participation Study of 1990 and the more recent Pew Surveys). By 2008, men and women made campaign contributions and contacted government officials at similar rates. In fact, the only statistically significant gender difference in the 2008 and 2012 data is that women were *more* likely than men to be registered to vote.[4]

THE GAP IN POLITICAL PARTICIPATION: A CLOSER LOOK

Since the closing of the participatory gender gap shown in Table 4.1 was unexpected and unheralded, we ask whether a similar pattern emerges from other surveys as well. We turn to two sources of data that have been conducted over a long period using comparable samples, comparable questions, and comparable survey designs: the US Census Bureau's Current Population Surveys (CPS) and the American National Election Study (ANES) Times Series studies. Such comparability over time is critical for assessing whether and when the gender gap

TABLE 4.1 Rates of political participation over time

	Citizen Participation 1990		Pew 2008		Pew 2012	
	Men	Women	Men	Women	Men	Women
Voted	74%	71%				
Registered to vote			78%	83%*	73%	78%*
Worked in a campaign	9%	8%	9%	7%	6%	8%
Made a campaign contribution	27%	20%**	20%	17%	16%	16%
Contacted a government official	38%	30%**	31%	28%	29%	27%
Attended a protest	6%	6%	4%	3%	6%	5%

* Significant at <.05; ** Significant at <.01.

Number of cases provided in Appendix Table 4.A1. Citizen Participation Study asked respondents whether they voted; Pew asked respondents whether they were registered to vote.

Sources: Citizen Participation Study 1990; Pew Research Center's Internet and American Life Project July 2008 and August 2012.

in political activity narrowed. Unfortunately, while the Citizen Participation Study and the Pew Surveys include questions about a relatively broad array of activities—including not only participation associated with campaigns and elections but also direct communications to public officials through protests or contacts—the range of participatory acts on these two other surveys is more limited. The Census's CPS has information about voter turnout only, and the ANES largely focuses on the various activities associated with the electoral process.

We begin with the most basic and most common political act in a democracy, voting. In Figure 4.1, we present data from the Census's Current Population Surveys about turnout rates for women and men in presidential years between 1964 and 2012. In this and subsequent figures, we focus on presidential election years because turnout rates and levels of other citizen activity associated with elections are consistently higher in presidential years.[5] Turnout has varied over the period, but the overall trend has been down. Men's and women's turnouts have risen and fallen in tandem, but another pattern is especially germane to our concerns. At the beginning of the period, men were slightly more likely than women to go to the polls. The gap, which was roughly 5% in 1964, narrowed slowly until 1980, at which point there was virtually no difference between the two groups.[6] After that, the disparity grew slowly, with women slightly more likely to vote than men. By 2012, the gender gap in voting showed an approximately 4% deficit for men.

Figure 4.2 presents ANES data beginning in 1976 about the average levels of campaign participation—including working for a candidate or party, attending political meetings or rallies, and displaying campaign paraphernalia, like buttons or bumper stickers—for men and women. The trend lines demonstrate that over the 1980s and 1990s, men did indeed participate at higher rates than women, with about 8% of men taking part in campaigns, compared to about 6% of women (a statistically significant difference). When overall participation was at its highest in the mid-2000s, the gender difference narrowed quickly and dramatically. By 2008, women's level of participation surpassed that of men. In 2012, a very slight

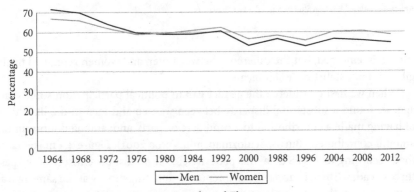

FIGURE 4.1 *Reported Voting Rates in Presidential Elections*
US Census Bureau, Current Population Surveys, 1968 to 2012 (Table A-9).

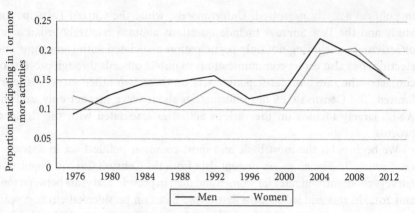

FIGURE 4.2 *Proportion Participating in Political Campaigns*

American National Election Studies, Cumulative File 1948 to 2012. Graph represents proportion of respondents who reported working for a party or candidate, attending rallies or political meetings during an election, or wearing a button or campaign sticker in support of a particular party or candidate.

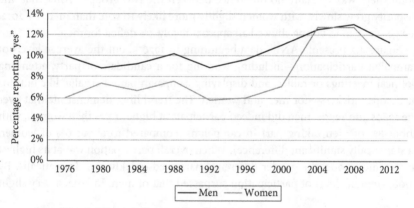

FIGURE 4.3 *Donate Money to Party or Candidate*

American National Election Studies, Cumulative File 1948 to 2012.

gap again emerged, but the difference between men and women remained negligible and not statistically significant.

When we first considered the gender gap in political participation some years ago, we found a substantial disparity between women and men in the likelihood of having made a contribution to a candidate or party and, among donors, in the amount contributed (Burns, Schlozman, and Verba 2001). Figure 4.3 makes clear that, according to ANES data, this pattern held for almost the entirety of the past three decades. Then, in 2004, women reported donating money at the same rate as men, a pattern that was replicated in 2008. In contrast to what we saw in the Pew data, a 2% gap reemerged in 2012, but this gap was fairly small and not statistically significant. We should note that in the rare instances that we have actually had data about the *size* of political contributions, men show an advantage, one deeply rooted in their higher levels of income and personal wealth.[7] Although the 2012 Pew Survey found no gender difference at all in the proportion who made a contribution to a political candidate or party, or any other political organization or cause, among donors, 24.3% of the men, but only 13.2% of the women, had made contributions totaling more than $250.

How Do We Account for These Changes?

What might explain this surprising shift in a long-standing pattern? Unfortunately, we do not have a study as admirably suited to answering this question as the 1990 Citizen Participation Study, which contained not only a broad set of political activities but also a rich array of participatory factors—for example, the civic skills developed at work, in organizations, or in church; affiliation with and activity in many kinds of organizations; family structure; leisure time available; level of political knowledge; experiences in high school activities; and requests to get involved in politics. Even without such measures, however, we can make some headway with the information at hand.

We seek our explanation in the changes that have taken place in American society and politics over the last four decades—changes with clear implications for men's and women's relative stockpiles of participatory resources. The first of these is the redefinition of gender roles over this period with its implications for the gender differences in employment and education that have figured so importantly in past accounts of the gender gap in participation. The second—as Welch (this volume) makes clear—is the increase of women in the ranks of those capturing visible elected offices.

CHANGING GENDER ROLES—CHANGING PARTICIPATORY RESOURCES

Among the most notable social changes of the past half century has been the narrowing of the gender gap in labor force participation, shown in Figure 4.4.[8] In 1960, 83% of adult men and 38% of adult women were in the labor force.[9] By 2010, the figures were 71% and 59%, respectively, and the disparity had shrunk from 45% to 12%. The principal and most widely noticed engine of this trend has been the dramatic increase in women's workforce participation—even among married women with young children.[10] However, another driver of the diminution of the gender disparity in workforce participation has been a long-term decline in the proportion of adult men who are in the labor force.[11]

While those who do paid work are, on average, more likely to take part in politics, the relationship between workforce participation and political participation is complex, and being in the labor force does not by itself facilitate political activity.[12] For one thing, selection into the workforce is not a random process. Members of the workforce have characteristics—in particular, higher average levels of educational attainment—that are

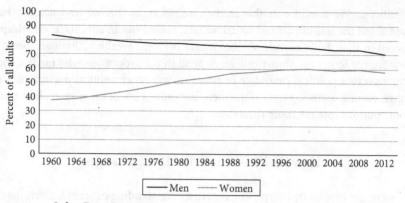

FIGURE 4.4 *Labor Force Participation*
US Bureau of Labor Statistics 2011.

associated with political activity. Thus, having nothing to do with what happens at work, we would expect those in the labor force to be more politically active. Besides, because paid work requires huge investments of time, we might expect that, all things being equal, being in the workforce would diminish participation in any form of political activity that takes time. Surprisingly, as hard as we looked, we could not find a relationship between the availability of leisure time and political participation.[13] In contrast, because the workplace fosters certain participatory resources, being in the workforce has a positive impact on participation: in particular, the income derived from paid work can be used, among other things, to make political contributions, and workers may develop civic skills from what they do on the job. Thus, even though among full-time workers, men have higher earnings and gain, on average, more civic skills than women do, it would seem that the narrowing of the gender gap in the labor force would be likely to diminish the gender gap in political activity.

That said, we must acknowledge that the sharp increase in women's labor force participation, which began as early as the 1940s and accelerated in subsequent decades, had leveled off by the 1990s and, thus, took place well before the convergence between women and men in political activity that we see around 2008. It is quite possible that, even though the narrowing of the gap in labor force participation did not coincide with the narrowing of the gap in political activity, women have continued to move into positions that brought their civic skills and incomes closer to parity with men.

Because we do not have information subsequent to the 1990 Citizen Participation Study about civic skills developed on the job, we are unable to investigate whether the gender difference in work-based civic skills continued to diminish during the first decade of the century, a time when women's workforce participation had ceased its upward climb. We can, however, assess whether women's wage deficit has decreased during this period as the result, presumably, of continued integration of women into high-paying jobs. Figure 4.5 presents data from the Current Population Survey about the ratio of women's to men's earnings for full-time year-round workers.[14] We can see that the relative disparity in earnings was cut roughly

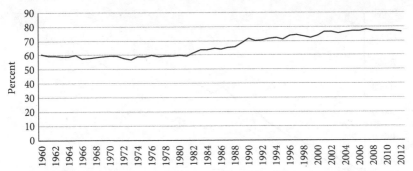

FIGURE 4.5 *Women's Earnings as a Percentage of Men's for Full-Time Year-Round Workers*
US Census Bureau, Current Population Survey, 1961 to 2013 Annual Social and Economic Supplements.

in half over the period. Once again, the changes took place unevenly over five decades, and the pattern is somewhat different from what we saw for the disparity in labor force participation. For twenty years, the earnings ratio—which was 59% both when Kennedy took office in 1961 and when Reagan took office in 1981—wobbled a bit but was essentially unchanged. Then it began to rise, slowly reaching 76% in 2001 when George W. Bush assumed the presidency. After that, the progress stalled. In 2012, the earnings ratio stood at 76.5% (meaning women, on average, earned 76.5 cents for every dollar earned by men). Thus, as with labor force participation, the narrowing of the gender gap in earnings from work did not coincide with the narrowing of the gender gap in political activity.

An individual's income is not derived simply from earnings, however. The financial resources that facilitate political participation, especially making political donations, include other sources, such as rents or interest as well as the earnings of other members of the household.[15] For several reasons, however, figuring out whether men's aggregate income advantage has changed over time is quite complicated. For one thing, it is not clear that the partners in married-couple households have equal command over the family's financial resources. Although there seems to be considerable consultation between the spouses in heterosexual couples when it comes to making substantial outlays of money, husbands seem to take considerably more responsibility than wives for "bigger financial decisions" (Burns, Schlozman, and Verba 2001: 188). In addition, the gender gap in income depends upon the distribution of, and relative incomes of, various types of households.[16] The data in Figure 4.6 demonstrate that married-couple families have long had higher household incomes than families consisting of a householder with no spouse present. That advantage, which has increased in recent decades, is especially pronounced if the householder without a spouse is female. At the same time, as shown in Figure 4.7, the number of households headed by a woman with no spouse has grown over the past several decades. This configuration of circumstances—growth in the share of households headed by women with relatively low incomes—suggests that the narrowing of the earnings gap between women and men might not have been accompanied by a narrowing of the income gap.

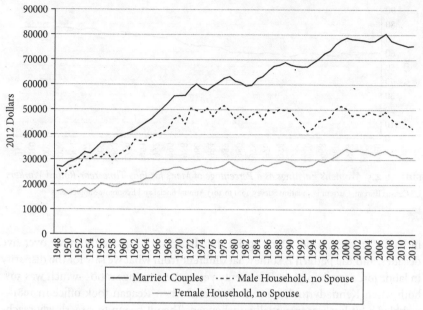

FIGURE 4.6 *Median Income (in 2012 US Dollars) by Household Type*

US Census Bureau, Current Population Survey, 1947 to 2012 Annual Social and Economic Supplements.

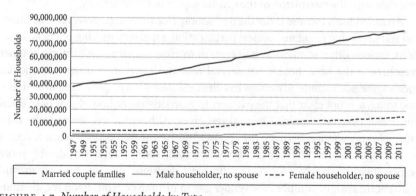

FIGURE 4.7 *Number of Households by Type*

US Census Bureau, Current Population Survey, 1947 to 2012 Annual Social and Economic Supplements.

CHANGING EDUCATIONAL ATTAINMENT

A less often noted development with potential consequences for participatory
inequalities is the striking progress made by women with respect to educational
attainment. As shown in Figure 4.8, men and women have both made advances in
education during the period since World War II. For men, the share of twenty-five-
to twenty-nine-year-olds who had graduated from college rose especially swiftly in

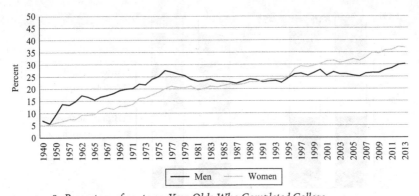

FIGURE 4.8 *Percentage of 25- to 29-Year-Olds Who Completed College*

1947 and 1952 to 2002 March Current Population Survey; 2003 to 2013 Annual Social and Economic Supplements to the Current Population Survey (noninstitutionalized population, excluding members of the Armed Forces living in barracks); 1950 Census of Population; 1940 Census of Population (resident population).

the late 1940s, when large numbers of recently discharged GIs marched into college classrooms courtesy of the GI Bill (Mettler 2005). The proportion of men in their late twenties who had graduated from college continued to increase until the mid-1970s, when it suddenly languished. In contrast, the share of women between ages twenty-five and twenty-nine with a bachelor's degree increased more slowly but continued to climb throughout the entire period. The result was that around 1990—coincidentally, at just the time that the "Title IX babies" born in 1972 were entering college—the lines crossed, and women began to surpass men in the share of those between ages twenty-five and twenty-nine who had earned a college degree. Women's advantage with respect to college graduation rates continued to widen in subsequent years.[17]

Of course, even though younger women were surpassing their male classmates in rates of college graduation, the male advantage in educational attainment built up over previous generations implied that, among all adults, women continued to be, in the aggregate, less well educated than men. As time went on, however, cohorts in which men held an educational advantage were replaced by cohorts for whom the opposite was true. The education gap between all adult men and women narrowed progressively to the point that, as shown in the right-hand bar graphs in Figure 4.9, women have now essentially achieved parity with men.[18]

To summarize, recent decades have witnessed trends with the potential to diminish men's relative advantage when it comes to the resources that facilitate political participation: the entry of women into the workforce and the erosion of men's workforce commitment, which have implications for two important participatory factors, civic skills developed on the job and earnings; and the closing of the aggregate gender gap in education. For several reasons, the fact that young women have quietly overtaken men in the proportion who finishes college is particularly important. First, of the trio of employment, income, and education, education has the consistently strongest relationship to political participation. Second, educational attainment is the only one of the three for which men do not retain

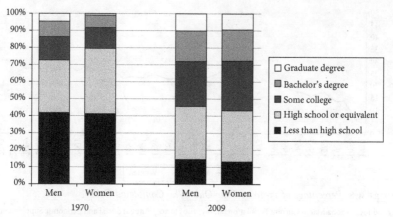

FIGURE 4.9 *Levels of Educational Attainment*
US Department of Commerce et al. 2011: 19.

an aggregate advantage. Moreover, the closing of the gender gap with regard to education occurred very recently and, thus, coincided with the narrowing of the gender difference in political activity.

WHAT ABOUT EFFECTS RATHER THAN LEVELS?

Earlier we made the point that understanding the gender gap in political participation requires that we investigate not only differences between women and men in the *levels* of the factors that influence participation but also the *effects* of those factors on activity. And understanding the *changing* gender gap requires that we investigate whether those effects have changed over time in ways that are different for men and for women. That is, we need to know whether these resources are converted to political participation at different rates now than in the past. If these resources have the same impact on political participation in 2012 as they did in the mid-1970s, and if that impact is the same for men and women, then one part of the story of the convergence in women's and men's political activity is that the changes in these resources translate into a smaller participatory gap. To accomplish this task, we use statistical models that assess the impact of a series of variables: gender, education, income, employment status, age, church attendance, and interest in campaigns and elections, on three forms of electoral participation—voting, campaign involvement, and monetary donations to candidates or parties. We estimate these models in repeated cross-sections of respondents from 1976 through 2012. We present full results of these analyses in the Appendix (Tables 4.A4, 4.A5, and 4.A6), where they can be scrutinized by the statistically curious. Here we just summarize in prose what we have found.

Our analyses produce several notable findings. First, there is a consistent pattern of difference among the three forms of electoral activity with regard to the strength of the association with education, income, and employment when other factors are taken into account: education, income, and employment are more strongly related to voting than to political giving and, especially, to campaign activity. Second, education, income, and employment are not equally strongly related to electoral activity. Across the entire period, compared to income, education is more strongly related to each of these forms of activity, and with other factors taken into account, employment has no significant association with electoral activity. Thus, education matters some for campaign participation, more for donating money, and perhaps most for electoral turnout. Income matters little for participating in campaigns, more for donating money, and even more for voter turnout.[19] On its own, employment status does not translate in any noticeable way into political action. Finally, there is striking continuity across the entire period in the way that these various factors are converted into the three kinds of electoral participation. In view of the extensiveness of the changes we have just reviewed, that these relationships have been consistent across the decades is almost startling. In other words, these analyses underscore that income and, especially, education have significant effects on political participation; that these effects are stable over time; and that these effects are not significantly different for women and men. Thus, the near disappearance of men's advantage with respect to educational attainment is very likely to have helped begin to close the gender gap in participation.

The Changing Political Landscape

At the same time, the world of politics has not been stagnant. Coinciding with these huge shifts in education, income, and workforce participation has been a steady change with the potential for substantial influence on the gender gap in participation. In 1975, politics was overwhelmingly a man's game. As shown in Figure 4.10, at that time, there were no women at all in the US Senate, and only 2% of governors, 4% of House representatives, and 8% of state legislators were women.

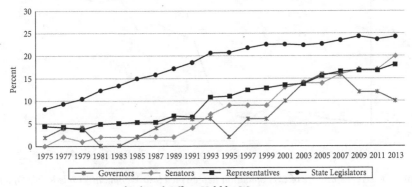

FIGURE 4.10 *Percentage of Political Offices Held by Women*
Women Candidates and Elected Officials Database (collected by the authors).

Since then, the number of women in office has increased slowly and—with the exception of governorships, for which the trajectory has included reversals—fairly steadily. By 2013, the share of women had risen to 10% among governors, 18% in the US House, 20% in the US Senate, and 24% among state legislators (see Welch, this volume).

The change in the gender composition of elected officials has garnered notice—with some applauding the steady increase and others ruing its slow pace. What has not captured notice is the dramatic growth in the proportion of the US population that has been represented by a woman holding visible public office—a governor, US senator, or US House representative. Consider the data in Figure 4.11.[20] In 1975, just under 6% of Americans were represented by a woman holding one of these offices. Within the next decade, that figure rose slowly. Then, an especially sharp increase occurred between 1991 and 1993. A major boost came in 1991 when women governors took office in Kansas (Joan Finney), Oregon (Barbara Roberts), and Texas (Ann Richards). In 1992, a special election in California brought Dianne Feinstein to the Senate, and the citizens of the nation's most populous state came into the group with a woman in visible elected office. Then, the elections that year, the "Year of the Woman," propelled nineteen new female representatives to the House and new female senators from Illinois (Carol Moseley Braun) and Washington (Patty Murray). By the new century, a majority of Americans were represented by a woman in at least one visible office. In 2013, 52% were.

POLITICAL REPRESENTATION BY WOMEN IN VISIBLE OFFICE AND POLITICAL PARTICIPATION

We are now in a position to assess for the nearly four-decade period from 1974 through 2012 whether the presence of women politicians in the environment functions as a factor—analogous to, say, education—that facilitates political

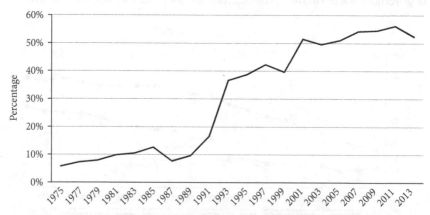

FIGURE 4.11 *Percentage of US Population Represented by a Woman in Visible Public Office*
Women Candidates and Elected Officials Database (collected by authors). Public office is defined here as governor, member of the US Senate, or member of the US House of Representatives.

participation. Because men and women live side by side in the same states and House districts, it is unlikely that there would be, in the aggregate, any significant gender disparity in *level* of exposure to visible political women. Thus, any impact on the gender gap in activity would have to derive from a difference between women and men in the *effect* on participation of the presence of visible political women in the individual's environment. In our analysis, we use data about individuals from the American National Election Studies and data about female office holders from our own Women Candidates and Elected Officials database.[21] Once again we summarize our findings in the text and place the analyses themselves in the Appendix.

Following the logic put forth earlier in the chapter for such variables as education, we investigated whether there is a direct influence on political participation of exposure to women contesting and holding visible public office—measured by the total number of female winners and female incumbents (governors, senators, or US House representatives) in the respondent's immediate political environment. The answer is unambiguously no. We did not find evidence that, over this period, the presence of women holding visible elected offices functions as a direct catalyst for participation (see Appendix Tables 4.A7, 4.A8, and 4.A9).[22]

However, we mentioned earlier that the link between the representation of women among elected officials and the disparity between men and women in political activity is likely to be indirect. Those who are psychologically engaged with politics—who are politically interested, informed, and efficacious (that is, who feel that they can make a difference)—are more likely to be active in politics. Indeed, we find consistently that electoral interest is a powerful predictor of political participation across genders. But we note that there is also a notable gender gap in this resource. That is, compared to women, men have traditionally displayed higher levels of such participation-enabling political orientations.

Figure 4.12, which presents data for women and men about the mean level of electoral interest for presidential years between 1976 and 2012, shows, not unexpectedly, that electoral interest varies over time, even in presidential election years when attention to politics tends to rise. More relevant to our concerns, it also shows a consistent disparity over the period, with men more interested than women in political campaigns.[23] Educational attainment is well-known to be a strong predictor of electoral interest—a result that shows up, with little variation across the years, in our analyses as well. Therefore, it is surprising that the gender gap in electoral interest persists in the 2000s, even though at that time, as we have discussed, men's educational edge in the adult population had eroded. In fact, for each of the years between 1976 and 2012, we find a small but statistically significant gender difference in electoral interest—even with other variables, including education and income, taken into account.[24]

We turn, therefore, to the question of whether the presence of women in the political environment has an effect on electoral interest and whether that effect differs for women and men. So far, every participatory factor we have considered has had a consistent relationship with political activity across a period of nearly forty years, an effect that is not only stable but the same for women and

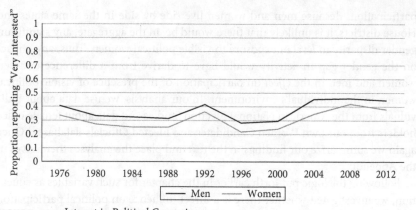

FIGURE 4.12 *Interest in Political Campaigns*
American National Election Studies, Cumulative File 1948 to 2012.

men. When it comes to exposure to women winning and holding visible public office, however, the patterns are different. We found that, quite unlike anything we have seen to this point, the impact of having visible women in the political environment on electoral interest is not stable across the periods, and it is not the same for men and women. Instead, the presence of visible women politicians is associated with higher levels of electoral interest only in the 1990s (Appendix Table 4.A10), the time when the percentage of women seeking and holding office increased dramatically, and it matters (in a statistically significant way) for women but not for men (Table 4.A11).[25] Thus, the gender gap in political participation would have been somewhat wider in the 1990s if the number of visible women in politics had remained at the low levels of the preceding decades.[26] However, after the turn of the century, this effect faded. Perhaps exposure to women gaining and holding visible public office lost its novelty as a majority of Americans experienced that exposure and as a small but growing number of women in politics—for example, Nancy Pelosi, Hillary Clinton, and Sarah Palin—achieved a national presence.

Conclusion

We began this chapter with an observation and a puzzle. The observation was that, quietly, while no one was noticing, the persistent gender gap in political participation that had been present since women became full political citizens in 1920 seems to have closed. The puzzle was why.

As is typical when it comes to understanding political participation, the account we give involves the interaction of several processes rather than a single cause. The last forty years have witnessed noteworthy changes both in women's and men's lives and in politics. However, these substantial changes have not always coincided with the shrinking of the gender gap in political participation, and they have not always proven to have the expected consequences for political activity. The single most important transformation for diminishing the gender difference in political participation has been the reversal in rates of educational attainment among younger cohorts of women and men. For more than two decades, women have been more likely than men to graduate from college. The result is, over time, the reduction to the vanishing point of the gender disparity in the most potent single predictor of political activity: education. Still, we are left with the conundrum as to why, at the same time that the education gap between men and women has disappeared, the gender disparity in electoral interest remained and only narrowed during the 1990s with the move of women into elite politics.[27]

Employment status is not, on its own, associated with political participation. However, the march of women into the labor force that took place in the era between World War II and the 1990s had the effect—when combined with the reality of men's stagnating wages and decreased workforce participation—of diminishing, but not eliminating, the gender gap with respect to another factor that is related to participation: earnings. Still, the narrowing of the disparity in earnings preceded the narrowing of the gap in participation and, thus, may not have contributed significantly to that outcome.

Similarly, the striking increase in the presence of women as high-profile and successful office seekers kept the gender gap in participation from being even wider during the 1990s through its impact on women's electoral interest at a critical period when the increase in those office seekers and incumbents was the greatest. As significant as that development has been for women's place in American politics and society, it has not contributed to the narrowing of the gender gap in participation during the twenty-first century. For unknown reasons, the continuing increase in the proportion of Americans who are represented by a woman in a visible public office did not have an impact on women's electoral interest after the 1990s. Further research might consider the possibility that younger cohorts of women are not responding to visible women office holders to the extent of earlier generations of women. We might also have reached a ceiling in the extent to which women are influenced by the presence of these candidates.

In 1892 Elizabeth Cady Stanton testified before the House Judiciary Committee and explained why a woman needs "all the opportunities for higher education, for the full development of her faculties, forces of mind and body . . . the most enlarged freedom of thought and action; a complete emancipation from all forms of bondage, of custom, dependence, superstition . . . a voice in the government under which she lives; in the religion she is asked to believe; equality in social life, where she is the chief factor; a place in the trades and professions, where she may earn her bread."[28] Stanton's vision has yet to come to pass. However, because these domains are not separate but are, instead, deeply intertwined, change in one realm has consequences for others. We are hopeful that the progressive integration of women into educational institutions, the labor force, and politics will contribute to a permanent closing of the gender gap in citizen political participation.

Appendix

TABLE 4.A1. Number of observations for Table 4.1

	Citizen Participation 1990		Pew 2008		Pew 2012	
	Men	Women	Men	Women	Men	Women
Voted / Registered to vote	297	305	3036	3169	3139	3318
Worked in a campaign	297	305	3055	3209	3175	3335
Made a campaign contribution	340	279	3050	3200	3169	3331
Contacted a government official	297	305	3052	3201	3171	3335
Attended a protest	297	305	3058	3204	3173	3334

TABLE 4.A2. Number of observations for Figures 4.1, 4.2, 4.3, and 4.12

	1976	1980	1984	1988	1992	1996	2000	2004	2008	2012
CAMPAIGN PARTICIPATION										
Male	1208	695	989	872	1153	782	793	588	1048	985
Female	1662	919	1268	1168	1335	931.9	1014	623.9	1274	1068
VOTING										
Male	991	615	874	765	1038	681	667	521	948	926
Female	1412	792	1115	1008	1219	823	875	540	1166	1003
DONATING										
Male	989	613	858	766	1036	679	667	521	947	932
Female	1405	792	1080	1007	1220	823	877	540	1166	1004
INTEREST IN POLITICAL CAMPAIGNS										
Male	1202	675	989	871	1150	782	793	588	554	985
Female	1654	890	1261	1165	1328	931	1014	623	653	1068

Source: American National Election Studies Cumulative File 1948 to 2012.

TABLE 4.A3. Number of observations for Figure 4.4

	1975	1977	1979	1981	1983	1985	1987	1990	1991	1993	1995	1997	1999	2001	2003	2005	2007	2009	2011	2013
Governors	1	2	2	0	0	1	2	3	3	3	1	3	3	5	7	8	8	6	6	5
Senators	0	2	1	2	2	2	2	2	4	7	9	9	9	13	14	14	16	17	17	20
Representatives	19	18	16	21	22	23	23	29	28	47	48	54	56	59	60	68	72	73	73	79
State legislators	604	688	770	908	991	1103	1170	1270	1368	1524	1532	1605	1664	1666	1654	1674	1732	1797	1750	1791

Source: Burns, Schlozman, and Verba (2001) data on female officeholders.

TABLE 4.A4. Predicting the level of campaign participation (OLS)

	1976	1980	1984	1988	1992	1996	2000	2004	2008	2012
Female	0.017*	-0.011	-0.004	-0.015	-0.028***	0.003	-0.007	-0.004	-0.000	-0.000
	(0.009)	(0.011)	(0.011)	(0.012)	(0.010)	(0.009)	(0.010)	(0.008)	(0.009)	(0.008)
Education	0.066***	0.061***	0.015	0.068***	0.049**	0.026	0.082***	0.041**	0.066***	0.045***
	(0.018)	(0.021)	(0.020)	(0.024)	(0.019)	(0.018)	(0.019)	(0.016)	(0.019)	(0.016)
Income	0.048***	0.011	0.017	-0.018	-0.033	0.015	0.028	0.015	0.002	0.030*
	(0.018)	(0.018)	(0.020)	(0.022)	(0.021)	(0.016)	(0.018)	(0.015)	(0.018)	(0.016)
Employed	0.003	0.007	0.003	0.028**	-0.004	0.022***	-0.016	-0.013	-0.002	-0.007
	(0.010)	(0.011)	(0.012)	(0.012)	(0.011)	(0.009)	(0.012)	(0.011)	(0.012)	(0.010)
Age	0.000	-0.038	0.024	-0.061	-0.084**	0.019	0.002	0.094***	0.016	0.065*
	(0.033)	(0.037)	(0.042)	(0.044)	(0.035)	(0.033)	(0.039)	(0.035)	(0.040)	(0.034)
Age over 65	0.013	0.002	-0.021	0.037*	0.006	-0.004	-0.000	-0.045***	-0.029	-0.027
	(0.016)	(0.019)	(0.019)	(0.021)	(0.017)	(0.016)	(0.018)	(0.017)	(0.018)	(0.019)
Freq. church attendance	0.016	0.024*	0.034**	0.034**	0.016	0.031***	0.022*	0.020**	0.011	0.033***
	(0.011)	(0.013)	(0.013)	(0.016)	(0.012)	(0.011)	(0.012)	(0.009)	(0.010)	(0.011)
Electoral interest	0.071***	0.154***	0.069***	0.139***	0.101***	0.115***	0.081***	0.086***	0.107***	0.074***
	(0.011)	(0.015)	(0.015)	(0.016)	(0.014)	(0.014)	(0.014)	(0.013)	(0.012)	(0.013)
Constant	-0.055***	-0.012	-0.018	-0.021	0.056**	-0.051***	-0.025	-0.048**	-0.028	-0.057***
	(0.021)	(0.022)	(0.025)	(0.027)	(0.023)	(0.019)	(0.024)	(0.019)	(0.021)	(0.019)
Observations	1,635	1,809	1,087	1,130	1,584	1,785	1,470	1,751	2,024	1,580
R-squared	0.055	0.094	0.039	0.098	0.054	0.082	0.066	0.067	0.062	0.065

Entries are Ordinary Least Squares coefficients. Standard errors in parentheses

*** $p<0.01$, ** $p<0.05$, * $p<0.1$

Source: American National Election Study Cumulative File 1948 to 2012.

TABLE 4.A5. Predicting donating money to campaign or political parties (OLS)

	1976	1980	1984	1988	1992	1996	2000	2004	2008	2012
Female	−0.039**	−0.018	0.009	−0.032*	0.000	0.005	−0.003	0.017	−0.016	−0.010
	(0.019)	(0.017)	(0.017)	(0.017)	(0.014)	(0.014)	(0.016)	(0.012)	(0.012)	(0.012)
Education	0.229***	0.170***	0.095***	0.159***	0.188***	0.112***	0.182***	0.138***	0.113***	0.084***
	(0.037)	(0.033)	(0.035)	(0.034)	(0.028)	(0.029)	(0.032)	(0.027)	(0.025)	(0.025)
Income	0.150***	0.173***	0.148***	0.159***	0.056**	0.165***	0.160***	0.075***	0.070***	0.121***
	(0.036)	(0.029)	(0.033)	(0.030)	(0.025)	(0.027)	(0.031)	(0.025)	(0.024)	(0.025)
Employed	0.000	0.012	0.027	−0.013	0.010	0.002	−0.025	−0.017	0.003	−0.008
	(0.021)	(0.018)	(0.018)	(0.019)	(0.015)	(0.016)	(0.017)	(0.017)	(0.013)	(0.014)
Age	0.240***	0.243***	0.148**	0.162***	0.213***	0.230***	0.213***	0.242***	0.229***	0.197***
	(0.071)	(0.060)	(0.060)	(0.062)	(0.052)	(0.056)	(0.056)	(0.049)	(0.051)	(0.049)
Age over 65	−0.088***	−0.027	0.023	0.015	−0.034	−0.018	0.029	−0.080***	−0.028	−0.011
	(0.034)	(0.033)	(0.031)	(0.032)	(0.027)	(0.029)	(0.032)	(0.027)	(0.027)	(0.029)
Freq. church attendance	−0.039	−0.012	0.036*	0.002	−0.061***	−0.013	0.028	−0.005	0.002	0.015
	(0.024)	(0.022)	(0.021)	(0.023)	(0.018)	(0.019)	(0.020)	(0.015)	(0.014)	(0.015)
Electoral interest	0.094***	0.119***	0.099***	0.153***	0.117***	0.134***	0.086***	0.115***	0.084***	0.074***
	(0.024)	(0.022)	(0.021)	(0.023)	(0.018)	(0.020)	(0.022)	(0.018)	(0.015)	(0.017)
Constant	−0.114***	−0.173***	−0.197***	−0.189***	−0.169***	−0.189***	−0.214***	−0.170***	−0.162***	−0.156***
	(0.042)	(0.035)	(0.038)	(0.036)	(0.029)	(0.033)	(0.032)	(0.028)	(0.025)	(0.024)
Observations	1,630	1,809	1,086	1,132	1,581	1,775	1,470	1,749	2,024	1,580
R-squared	0.091	0.096	0.088	0.133	0.099	0.105	0.122	0.097	0.068	0.084

Entries are Ordinary Least Squares coefficients. Standard errors in parentheses

*** p<0.01, ** p<0.05, * p<0.1

Source: American National Election Study Cumulative File 1948 to 2012.

TABLE 4.A6. Predicting voting (OLS)

	1976	1980	1984	1988	1992	1996	2000	2004	2008	2012
Female	-0.060***	0.016	0.002	-0.018	0.017	0.020	0.001	0.005	0.033*	0.003
	(0.023)	(0.023)	(0.025)	(0.026)	(0.020)	(0.021)	(0.022)	(0.021)	(0.017)	(0.024)
Education	0.307***	0.241***	0.330***	0.267***	0.265***	0.205***	0.300***	0.261***	0.324***	0.367***
	(0.042)	(0.043)	(0.051)	(0.049)	(0.043)	(0.041)	(0.041)	(0.041)	(0.033)	(0.050)
Income	0.185***	0.127***	0.116**	0.122**	0.258***	0.168***	0.279***	0.159***	0.221***	0.208***
	(0.046)	(0.040)	(0.051)	(0.049)	(0.041)	(0.042)	(0.045)	(0.041)	(0.037)	(0.050)
Employed	0.036	0.056**	0.095***	0.058**	0.028	0.050**	0.007	0.045*	0.044**	0.024
	(0.025)	(0.025)	(0.030)	(0.028)	(0.025)	(0.025)	(0.028)	(0.025)	(0.021)	(0.031)
Age	0.495***	0.832***	0.695***	0.822***	0.554***	0.893***	0.599***	0.835***	0.509***	0.650***
	(0.086)	(0.085)	(0.098)	(0.099)	(0.086)	(0.086)	(0.093)	(0.086)	(0.076)	(0.108)
Age over 65	-0.074*	-0.141***	-0.054	-0.124***	-0.048	-0.061	-0.042	-0.091**	-0.012	0.004
	(0.040)	(0.045)	(0.046)	(0.046)	(0.039)	(0.043)	(0.042)	(0.044)	(0.034)	(0.049)
Freq. church attendance	0.202***	0.112***	0.152***	0.099***	0.188***	0.147***	0.182***	0.126***	0.073***	0.117***
	(0.029)	(0.029)	(0.033)	(0.036)	(0.026)	(0.029)	(0.029)	(0.026)	(0.021)	(0.029)
Electoral interest	0.218***	0.395***	0.333***	0.448***	0.224***	0.458***	0.324***	0.455***	0.307***	0.401***
	(0.032)	(0.030)	(0.035)	(0.036)	(0.030)	(0.028)	(0.030)	(0.030)	(0.026)	(0.035)
Constant	0.068	-0.232***	-0.111*	-0.217***	0.010	-0.348***	-0.108**	-0.380***	-0.010	-0.289***
	(0.054)	(0.047)	(0.059)	(0.057)	(0.052)	(0.043)	(0.054)	(0.039)	(0.044)	(0.054)
Observations	1,637	1,806	1,086	1,130	1,614	1,786	1,468	1,753	2,023	1,580
R-squared	0.177	0.216	0.251	0.262	0.200	0.294	0.272	0.289	0.244	0.287

Entries are Ordinary Least Squares coefficients. Standard errors in parentheses

*** p<0.01, ** p<0.05, * p<0.1

Source: American National Election Study Cumulative File 1948 to 2012.

TABLE 4.A7. Campaign participation

	1976	1980	1984	1988	1992	1996	2000	2004	2008	2012
Female	0.017*	-0.004	-0.028***	-0.007	-0.000	-0.001	-0.006	-0.005	-0.007	-0.014
	(0.009)	(0.011)	(0.010)	(0.010)	(0.009)	(0.009)	(0.011)	(0.015)	(0.017)	(0.012)
Women candidates	0.037	0.026	-0.052	-0.093**	-0.021	-0.010	-0.044**	-0.108***	0.006	-0.024
	(0.055)	(0.054)	(0.033)	(0.042)	(0.022)	(0.029)	(0.019)	(0.024)	(0.034)	(0.019)
Education	0.066***	0.015	0.049**	0.081***	0.067***	0.057***	0.024	0.042	0.073*	0.062
	(0.018)	(0.020)	(0.019)	(0.019)	(0.019)	(0.017)	(0.024)	(0.028)	(0.040)	(0.040)
Income	0.048***	0.017	-0.033	0.029	0.003	0.005	0.011	0.002	-0.016	-0.013
	(0.018)	(0.020)	(0.021)	(0.018)	(0.018)	(0.021)	(0.024)	(0.028)	(0.040)	(0.019)
Employed	0.003	0.003	-0.004	-0.016	-0.002	0.026**	0.023**	-0.016	0.016	-0.030**
	(0.010)	(0.012)	(0.011)	(0.012)	(0.012)	(0.010)	(0.011)	(0.020)	(0.020)	(0.013)
Age	0.000	0.023	-0.082**	0.000	0.015	0.007	0.075	-0.081	0.078	-0.039
	(0.033)	(0.042)	(0.035)	(0.039)	(0.040)	(0.041)	(0.046)	(0.067)	(0.079)	(0.033)
Age over 65	0.013	-0.021	0.006	0.001	-0.028	0.007	-0.027	-0.016	-0.039	0.072***
	(0.016)	(0.019)	(0.017)	(0.018)	(0.018)	(0.018)	(0.022)	(0.032)	(0.032)	(0.026)
Freq. church attendance	0.015	0.034***	0.015	0.021*	0.010	0.025**	0.016	0.038*	0.019	0.041***
	(0.011)	(0.013)	(0.012)	(0.012)	(0.010)	(0.013)	(0.014)	(0.020)	(0.019)	(0.015)
Electoral interest	0.071***	0.069***	0.100***	0.082***	0.108***	0.095***	0.077***	0.147***	0.126***	0.098***
	(0.011)	(0.015)	(0.014)	(0.014)	(0.012)	(0.015)	(0.015)	(0.021)	(0.022)	(0.015)
Constant	-0.056***	-0.018	-0.057**	-0.023	-0.027	-0.051**	-0.035	0.047	-0.059	-0.002
	(0.021)	(0.024)	(0.023)	(0.024)	(0.021)	(0.023)	(0.026)	(0.034)	(0.042)	(0.027)
Observations	1,635	1,087	1,584	1,470	2,024	1,395	1,307	942	959	5,703
R-squared	0.055	0.039	0.055	0.068	0.062	0.070	0.049	0.089	0.066	0.092

Entries are Ordinary Least Squares coefficients. Standard errors in parentheses

*** p<0.01, ** p<0.05, * p<0.1

TABLE 4.A8. Donating money

	1976	1980	1984	1988	1992	1996	2000	2004	2008	2012
Female	-0.039**	0.010	0.000	-0.003	-0.016	-0.022*	-0.008	0.002	-0.022	-0.024
	(0.019)	(0.017)	(0.014)	(0.016)	(0.012)	(0.013)	(0.017)	(0.023)	(0.028)	(0.019)
Women candidates	-0.008	-0.011	-0.029	-0.107	-0.012	0.074	-0.057*	0.067	0.089	-0.016
	(0.101)	(0.085)	(0.057)	(0.065)	(0.032)	(0.052)	(0.031)	(0.043)	(0.065)	(0.036)
Education	0.229***	0.095***	0.188***	0.182***	0.114***	0.095***	0.059	0.174***	0.250***	0.335***
	(0.037)	(0.035)	(0.028)	(0.032)	(0.025)	(0.028)	(0.040)	(0.044)	(0.063)	(0.064)
Income	0.150***	0.148***	0.056**	0.162***	0.070***	0.111***	0.124***	0.099**	0.087	0.024
	(0.035)	(0.033)	(0.025)	(0.031)	(0.024)	(0.031)	(0.032)	(0.043)	(0.069)	(0.026)
Employed	0.000	0.026	0.010	-0.025	0.003	-0.017	-0.006	-0.009	-0.034	-0.046**
	(0.021)	(0.018)	(0.015)	(0.017)	(0.013)	(0.017)	(0.021)	(0.028)	(0.033)	(0.023)
Age	0.239***	0.148**	0.214***	0.211***	0.229***	0.265***	0.178**	0.309***	0.244**	0.140***
	(0.071)	(0.060)	(0.052)	(0.056)	(0.051)	(0.058)	(0.075)	(0.090)	(0.105)	(0.051)
Age over 65	-0.088***	0.023	-0.034	0.031	-0.028	-0.031	0.010	0.029	-0.019	0.053
	(0.034)	(0.031)	(0.027)	(0.032)	(0.027)	(0.032)	(0.039)	(0.052)	(0.057)	(0.043)
Freq. church attendance	-0.039	0.036*	-0.061***	0.028	0.002	-0.003	-0.012	0.019	-0.011	-0.018
	(0.024)	(0.021)	(0.018)	(0.020)	(0.014)	(0.019)	(0.021)	(0.030)	(0.033)	(0.023)
Electoral interest	0.094***	0.099***	0.116***	0.086***	0.084***	0.127***	0.155***	0.125***	0.129***	0.120***
	(0.024)	(0.021)	(0.018)	(0.022)	(0.015)	(0.023)	(0.028)	(0.029)	(0.035)	(0.023)
Constant	-0.113***	-0.197***	-0.168***	-0.211***	-0.162***	-0.188***	-0.143***	-0.259***	-0.231***	-0.215***
	(0.042)	(0.038)	(0.029)	(0.032)	(0.025)	(0.028)	(0.035)	(0.047)	(0.058)	(0.041)
Observations	1,630	1,086	1,581	1,470	2,024	1,395	1,307	942	959	5,702
R-squared	0.091	0.088	0.099	0.123	0.068	0.107	0.094	0.110	0.123	0.120

Entries are Ordinary Least Squares coefficients. Standard errors in parentheses.

*** $p < 0.01$, ** $p < 0.05$, * $p < 0.1$

TABLE 4.A9. Voting

	1976	1980	1984	1988	1992	1996	2000	2004	2008	2012
Female	-0.060***	0.001	0.017	0.001	0.033*	0.032	-0.001	0.056*	0.065**	0.016
	(0.023)	(0.025)	(0.020)	(0.022)	(0.017)	(0.025)	(0.026)	(0.029)	(0.031)	(0.025)
Women candidates	0.026	0.046	-0.377***	0.045	-0.006	-0.028	-0.026	-0.057	0.041	0.023
	(0.121)	(0.124)	(0.108)	(0.114)	(0.043)	(0.073)	(0.051)	(0.052)	(0.066)	(0.046)
Education	0.307***	0.329***	0.266***	0.300***	0.324***	0.333***	0.340***	0.226***	0.362***	0.401***
	(0.042)	(0.051)	(0.042)	(0.041)	(0.033)	(0.052)	(0.055)	(0.058)	(0.062)	(0.075)
Income	0.185***	0.115**	0.257***	0.278***	0.221***	0.271***	0.205***	0.215***	0.072	0.114***
	(0.046)	(0.051)	(0.041)	(0.045)	(0.037)	(0.050)	(0.053)	(0.053)	(0.060)	(0.039)
Employed	0.036	0.096***	0.031	0.007	0.044**	-0.013	0.006	0.054	-0.009	0.022
	(0.025)	(0.030)	(0.025)	(0.028)	(0.021)	(0.031)	(0.035)	(0.035)	(0.034)	(0.029)
Age	0.495***	0.692***	0.569***	0.600***	0.508***	0.534***	0.437***	0.181	0.288**	0.312***
	(0.086)	(0.098)	(0.086)	(0.093)	(0.076)	(0.119)	(0.122)	(0.117)	(0.125)	(0.078)
Age over 65	-0.074*	-0.054	-0.048	-0.043	-0.011	-0.005	-0.017	0.065	-0.024	-0.030
	(0.040)	(0.046)	(0.039)	(0.042)	(0.034)	(0.046)	(0.053)	(0.051)	(0.056)	(0.041)
Freq. church attendance	0.202***	0.152***	0.183***	0.182***	0.073***	0.140***	0.112***	0.040	0.033	0.095***
	(0.029)	(0.033)	(0.026)	(0.029)	(0.021)	(0.031)	(0.032)	(0.035)	(0.038)	(0.033)
Electoral interest	0.218***	0.333***	0.220***	0.324***	0.308***	0.316***	0.290***	0.327***	0.332***	0.322***
	(0.032)	(0.035)	(0.029)	(0.030)	(0.026)	(0.033)	(0.039)	(0.046)	(0.049)	(0.038)
Constant	0.067	-0.111*	0.019	-0.109**	-0.010	-0.049	0.043	0.175**	0.124*	0.047
	(0.054)	(0.059)	(0.052)	(0.054)	(0.044)	(0.070)	(0.070)	(0.076)	(0.075)	(0.061)
Observations	1,637	1,086	1,614	1,468	2,023	1,396	1,307	942	959	5,693
R-squared	0.177	0.251	0.208	0.272	0.244	0.265	0.226	0.203	0.203	0.205

Entries are Ordinary Least Squares coefficients. Standard errors in parentheses.

*** $p<0.01$, ** $p<0.05$, * $p<0.1$

TABLE 4.A10. Predicting the level of electoral interest

	1976	1980	1984	1988	1992	1996	2000	2004	2008	2012
Female	-0.043**	-0.050**	-0.068***	-0.057***	-0.036**	-0.041**	-0.044**	-0.070***	-0.043*	-0.047**
	(0.018)	(0.021)	(0.017)	(0.018)	(0.015)	(0.020)	(0.019)	(0.024)	(0.026)	(0.022)
Women candidates	-0.041	0.145	-0.106	0.089	0.103***	0.159***	0.057	-0.030	0.043	0.049
	(0.096)	(0.111)	(0.083)	(0.095)	(0.037)	(0.056)	(0.038)	(0.045)	(0.057)	(0.040)
Education	0.339***	0.372***	0.363***	0.316***	0.299***	0.245***	0.276***	0.238***	0.273***	0.435***
	(0.033)	(0.040)	(0.033)	(0.034)	(0.029)	(0.038)	(0.039)	(0.050)	(0.051)	(0.065)
Income	0.069*	0.075*	0.056*	0.085**	0.095***	0.028	0.053	0.077*	0.122**	0.060*
	(0.036)	(0.040)	(0.032)	(0.036)	(0.030)	(0.041)	(0.040)	(0.046)	(0.053)	(0.033)
Employed	-0.040**	-0.032	-0.035*	-0.015	-0.002	-0.041*	0.002	-0.056*	-0.048*	-0.060**
	(0.019)	(0.024)	(0.020)	(0.022)	(0.018)	(0.025)	(0.023)	(0.029)	(0.029)	(0.025)
Age	0.522***	0.500***	0.456***	0.327***	0.300***	0.309***	0.535***	0.443***	0.335***	0.403***
	(0.066)	(0.080)	(0.067)	(0.072)	(0.064)	(0.086)	(0.082)	(0.096)	(0.106)	(0.067)
Age over 65	-0.047	-0.052	-0.024	-0.027	0.008	-0.007	-0.057	-0.078*	-0.029	-0.048
	(0.035)	(0.042)	(0.036)	(0.037)	(0.032)	(0.041)	(0.041)	(0.046)	(0.048)	(0.038)
Freq. church attendance	0.058**	0.095***	0.097***	0.107***	0.029	0.119***	0.119***	0.022	0.069**	0.036
	(0.023)	(0.028)	(0.023)	(0.024)	(0.018)	(0.026)	(0.023)	(0.031)	(0.032)	(0.028)
Constant	0.199***	0.097**	0.140***	0.174***	0.273***	0.200***	0.065	0.333***	0.299***	0.174***
	(0.041)	(0.046)	(0.038)	(0.040)	(0.033)	(0.048)	(0.045)	(0.059)	(0.061)	(0.054)
Observations	1,907	1,239	1,803	1,665	2,212	1,555	1,505	1,066	1,064	1,833
R-squared	0.102	0.125	0.124	0.117	0.103	0.098	0.137	0.090	0.108	0.123

Entries are Ordinary Least Squares coefficients. Standard errors in parentheses

*** p<0.01, ** p<0.05, * p<0.1

Source: American National Election Study Cumulative File 1948 to 2012.

TABLE 4.A11. Predicting the level of electoral interest by gender

	Women			Men		
	Pre 1990	1990 to 2000	Post 2000	Pre 1990	1990 to 2000	Post 2000
Women office holders	-0.039	0.100***	0.006	-0.007	0.044	0.058
	(0.040)	(0.026)	(0.037)	(0.047)	(0.028)	(0.039)
Education	0.328***	0.273***	0.319***	0.311***	0.297***	0.273***
	(0.017)	(0.023)	(0.043)	(0.018)	(0.024)	(0.044)
Income	0.075***	0.086***	0.060*	0.047**	0.052*	0.067*
	(0.016)	(0.022)	(0.032)	(0.021)	(0.027)	(0.036)
Employed	-0.038***	-0.031*	-0.056**	-0.034**	-0.032*	-0.036
	(0.009)	(0.013)	(0.022)	(0.014)	(0.017)	(0.025)
Age	0.514***	0.391***	0.400***	0.470***	0.308***	0.467***
	(0.033)	(0.049)	(0.068)	(0.040)	(0.055)	(0.069)
Age over 65	-0.053***	0.006	-0.054	-0.069***	-0.002	-0.069*
	(0.017)	(0.024)	(0.034)	(0.022)	(0.027)	(0.037)
Freq. church attendance	0.078***	0.087***	0.044*	0.109***	0.089***	0.040
	(0.011)	(0.014)	(0.024)	(0.013)	(0.016)	(0.027)
Constant	0.058***	0.113***	0.224***	0.130***	0.214***	0.251***
	(0.017)	(0.025)	(0.044)	(0.023)	(0.029)	(0.043)
Observations	7,459	4,325	4,181	5,641	3,726	3,768
R-squared	0.108	0.106	0.098	0.101	0.100	0.110

Entries are Ordinary Least Squares coefficients. Standard errors in parentheses

*** p<0.01, ** p<0.05, * p<0.1

Source: American National Election Study Cumulative File 1948 to 2012.

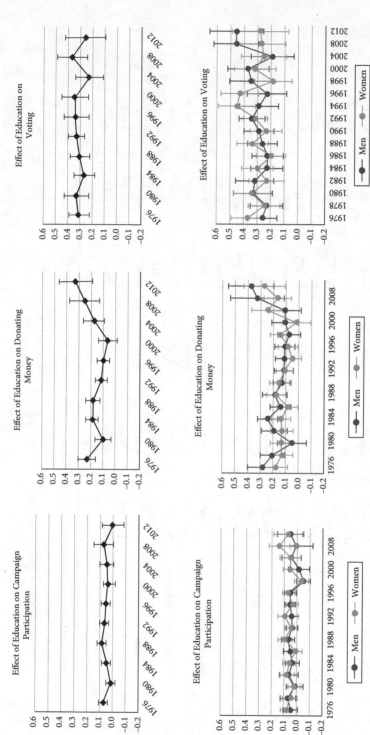

FIGURE 4.A1. *The Effect of Education on Levels of Political Participation over Time. Effects are Stable over Time and Not Significantly Different for Men or Women*

Source: American National Election Study Cumulative File 1948 to 2012. Data are weighted. All variables range from 0 to 1. Vertical bars represent 95% confidence intervals.

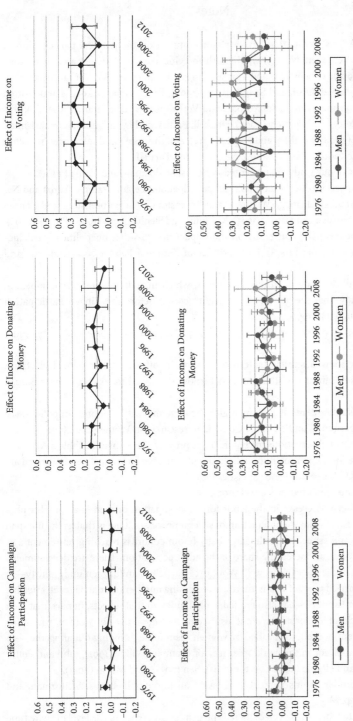

FIGURE 4.A2. *The Effect of Education on Levels of Political Participation over Time. Effects are Stable over Time and Not Significantly Different for Men or Women*

Source: American National Election Study Cumulative File 1948 to 2012. Data are weighted. All variables range from 0 to 1. Vertical bars represent 95% confidence intervals.

Notes

1. On the various factors that have a positive impact on the political participation of individuals, see Verba and Nie (1972); Milbrath and Goel (1977); Wolfinger and Rosenstone (1980); Junn (1991); Rosenstone and Hansen (1993); Leighley (1995); Verba, Schlozman, and Brady (1995); Nie, Junn, and Stehlik-Barry (1996); Brady (1999); Skocpol and Fiorina (1999); Conway (2000); Burns, Schlozman, and Verba (2001); Schlozman (2002); Zukin et al. (2006); Ostrander and Portney (2007); Driskell, Embry, and Lyon (2008); Ramakrishnan and Bloemraad (2008); Leighley and Nagler (2014); and the essays and references in Dalton and Klingemann (2007), Part VI; and Leighley (2010), Part III.

2. The results of our study are presented in Burns, Schlozman, and Verba (2001).

3. On the impact of education on political participation, see, for example, Verba and Nie (1972); Milbrath and Goel (1977); Wolfinger and Rosenstone (1980); Rosenstone and Hansen (1993); Verba, Schlozman, and Brady (1995); Nie, Junn, and Stehlik-Barry (1996); Bartels (2008). For a dissent from the consensus on the impact of education on political participation, see Kam and Palmer (2008). For a critique of Kam and Palmer, see Henderson and Chatfield (2011).

4. As we shall see, data from the US Census, which include much larger numbers of respondents, show that the gap in voter turnout closed before the Citizen Participation Study was conducted in 1990.

5. The number of observations for Figures 4.1, 4.2, 4.3, and 4.12 is provided in Appendix Table 4.A2.

6. CPS data show a similar pattern for voting in off-year congressional elections. However, it was not until 1986 that women's turnout surpassed men's (US Census Bureau 2013a).

7. As recent studies demonstrate, men give the large majority of money in politics; see Bryner and Weber (2013) and National Council of Research on Women et al. (2014).

8. The number of observations for Figure 4.4 is provided in Appendix Table 4.A3.

9. Figures are for the noninstitutionalized population sixteen years old and over and are taken from the US Bureau of Labor Statistics (2011).

10. See the data presented in Toossi (2002).

11. The long-term decrease in the labor force participation of men is a complex phenomenon that results from the interaction of several processes. One is that as the life span has lengthened, and especially as the large baby-boom cohort is reaching retirement age, the elderly constitute an increasing share of the adult population. There are developments at the other end of the life cycle as well. Workforce participation for men under thirty—in particular, unmarried men, of whom there are increasing numbers as marriage rates decline for those in their twenties—has also eroded, a phenomenon that reflects, in part, that men are staying in school longer. However, it also seems that men, but not women, who grow up in single-parent households headed by women seem to be dropping out altogether—to be neither in school nor in the workforce. See, for example, Wilkie (1991), Juhn and Potter (2006), Mosisa and Hipple (2006), Autor (2011), Sen (2012), and Morin (2013).

12. The remainder of this paragraph is based on findings in Burns, Schlozman, and Verba (2001, chap. 8).

13. Contrary to what we expected, there is no gender difference in the level of spare time available, and spare time has no effect on political activity. That is, in the aggregate, neither

men (who spend, on average, more time on paid work) nor women (who spend, on average, more time on home and child care) have an advantage when it comes to the amount of spare time available. Furthermore, the amount of spare time available does not predict an individual's participation. See Burns, Schlozman, and Verba (2001, pp. 184–187, 256–257).

14. The data are for the ratio of median annual earnings for full-time, year-round workers 15 years old and over. Before 1989, earnings are for civilian workers only. Analogous data for median weekly earnings (which exclude the self-employed and include full-time workers who work only part of the year) show slightly higher ratios. See Hegewisch et al. (2013, Figure 4.1).

15. Chang (2010) shows that even while the wage gap has narrowed, men as a group own considerably more wealth than women, in the form of property and investments like stocks.

16. The conclusions in the remainder of the paragraph are based on data about families (which exclude members of households of unrelated individuals) from the US Census Bureau (2013b).

17. Data from the ANES show that the average level of education for men in 1960 is .288 when the measure is rescaled to range from zero to one. By 2012, the average level was .640. The difference of .352 is statistically significant at p = .000. Among women, the average level of education in 1960 was .33. In 2012, it was .628. The difference of .298 is significant at p = .000. For helpful discussions of the rise of Title IX and its link to women's political action, see Sandler (2007) and Suggs (2005).

18. US Census data from 1960 and 2012 (Annual Social and Economic Supplements to the Current Population Survey) yield the following similar comparison:

		ELEMENTARY	SOME H.S.	H.S. GRADUATE	SOME COLL.	COLL. DEGREE
1960	Men	61%	21%		9%	10%
	Women	57%	28%		9%	6%
2012	Men	13%	31%		25%	31%
	Women	12%	30%		27%	31%

19. We illustrate these relationships in Appendix Figures 4.A1 and 4.A2.

20. We assembled the data in Figure 4.10 on an every-other-year, state-by-state basis using population figures for the states and nation from the US Census and information from the website of the Center for American Women and Politics at Rutgers, The State University of New Jersey (Center for American Women and Politics 2014). For each year in the time series, we compiled a total figure for the number of Americans having a woman in visible public office (governor, US senator, member of the US House). We created that sum by adding the entire state's population for any state with a governor or US senator. For most states having no female governor or senator, we then added 1/435th of the national population for every member of the US House from that state. For small states such as Wyoming or New Hampshire, we used a fraction of the actual state population for that year in calculating the increment from representation in the House. In the cases where a death or resignation from the House or Senate led to a replacement with a woman by appointment or special election, we coded the replacement if she ran and won in the next election. If not, we coded the person who held the seat for the majority of the term. We then divided that sum for the nation by the population for the nation in that year. We are grateful to Jenelle McNeill for her terrific work in assembling these data.

21. In order to undertake this analysis, we assembled an extensive database using the information contained in the successive volumes of the *Almanac of American Politics*, which have been produced since 1974 by Michael Barone and a series of coauthors and published by National Journal. For every female candidate for governor, US Senate, or US House, in each year she ran, we coded the year of the election; the state and, for candidates for the House, the district; the office being contested; the candidate's party; her incumbency status; and share of the vote in the general election. For candidates with ambiguous first names, we did additional research to ascertain gender. We are grateful to Anna Menzel and Jacqueline Park for their fabulous assistance in assembling these data.

22. Lawless (2004) finds a similar lack of a direct effect of "symbolic representation" on participation. Atkeson (2003) finds that women as citizens do increase their political engagement when they see other women run for office, but only if the female candidates are in competitive and visible races. Atkeson and Carrillo (2007) find evidence of non-dyadic representation effects, in that "higher levels of collective female descriptive representation [percentage of women in a state's legislature] promote higher values of external efficacy for female citizens" (p. 79). They, like Lawless (2004), find no direct effect of dyadic descriptive representation. In a comparative vein, Buhlmann and Schadel (2012) find strong effects across thirty-three European countries of descriptive representation on the political interest and motivation of women citizens, but not directly on their electoral participation. Reingold and Harrell (2010) suggest that whatever effects exist may also depend on party congruence. As in the previous literature, they do not find direct effects on participation narrowly, but instead find an interaction effect with gender, party, and candidate viability all mattering for the political engagement broadly of women as citizens. They write, "It is primarily female candidates of the same party who enhance women's interest in politics" (280). Relatedly, but looking specifically at young women, Campbell and Wolbrecht (2006) find that "where female candidates are visible due to visible campaigns for high-profile offices, girls report increased anticipated political involvement" (233). Their findings apply both to girls in the United States and cross-nationally. Ferreira and Gyourko (2011), however, find no evidence that more women run for office when exposed to women as mayors.

23. It would have been preferable if the ANES item had not specified political campaigns but had measured interest in politics more generally. Still, the availability of long time series using identical question wording outweighs the restriction to electoral interest.

24. Because relevant measures were not included in all surveys, we were unable to take into account several factors for which others have found an impact on electoral interest— and, perhaps, on the gender gap in such interest. Among these factors are the level of negativity, and especially incivility, in campaigns (Mutz and Reeves [2005]; Brooks and Geer [2007]; Mutz [2007]; Brooks [2010]) and the respondent's belief that politics matters in solving important problems (Shames [2014]).

25. The measure is the total number of female winners and incumbents for governor, US senator, and member of the US House in the respondent's environment. We considered a range of alternatives to this measure and learned that all of the effects depend on focusing on these high-profile winners and incumbents. Unsuccessful women candidates do not have this impact.

26. See Burns, Schlozman, and Verba (2001, chap. 13). Our findings have been elaborated in other studies finding indirect effects on participation of exposure to women as

candidates, working through variables such as external efficacy or political interest. For examples, see the studies cited in the previous note.

27. Scholars have looked for the roots of these differences in preadult political involvement and in adult institutions, state political culture, and the historical experience of state representation by women. Additionally, scholars have explored the nature of electoral mobilization. The gender gap in political interest is not explained by these factors (see Burns, Schlozman, and Verba 2001, chaps. 5 and 13).

28. The full text can be found in Stanton (1972 [1892]: 158).

References

Atkeson, Lonna Rae. 2003. "Not All Cues Are Created Equal: The Conditional Impact of Female Candidates on Political Engagement." *Journal of Politics* 65: 1040–1061.

Atkeson, Lonna Rae, and Nancy Carrillo. 2007. "More Is Better: The Influence of Collective Female Descriptive Representation on External Efficacy." *Politics and Gender* 3: 79–101.

Autor, David. 2011. "The Polarization of Job Opportunities in the US Labor Market: Implications for Employment and Earnings." *Community Investments Journal* (Federal Reserve Bank, San Francisco) 23: 11–41. http://www.frbsf.org/community-development/files/CI_IncomeInequality_Autor.pdf.

Bartels, Larry M. 2008. *Unequal Democracy: The Political Economy of the New Gilded Age.* New York: Russell Sage Foundation, and Princeton, NJ: Princeton University Press.

Brady, Henry E. 1999. "Political Participation." Pp. 737–801 in *Measures of Political Attitudes,* edited by John P. Robinson, Phillip R. Shaver, and Lawrence Wrightsman. San Diego, CA: Academic Press.

Brooks, Deborah Jordan. 2010. "A Negativity Gap? Voter Gender, Attack Politics, and Participation in American Elections." *Politics and Gender Journal* 6: 319–341.

Brooks, Deborah Jordan, and John G. Geer. 2007. "Beyond Negativity: The Effects of Incivility on the Electorate." *American Journal of Political Science* 51: 1–16.

Bryner, Sarah, and Doug Weber. 2013. "Sex, Money, and Politics." Center for Responsive Politics. http://www.opensecrets.org/news/reports/gender.php.

Buhlmann, Marc, and Lisa Schadel. 2012. "Representation Matters: The Impact of Descriptive Women's Representation on the Political Involvement of Women." *Representation* 48: 101–114.

Burns, Nancy, Kay Lehman Schlozman, and Sidney Verba. 2001. *The Private Roots of Public Action.* Cambridge, MA: Harvard University Press.

Campbell, Angus, et al. 1960. *The American Voter.* New York: Wiley.

Campbell, David E., and Christina Wolbrecht. 2006. "See Jane Run: Women Politicians as Role Models for Adolescents." *Journal of Politics* 68: 233–247.

Center for American Women and Politics (CAWP). 2014. "Facts on Women Officeholders, Candidates and Voters." http://www.cawp.rutgers.edu/facts.

Chang, Mariko Lin. 2010. *Shortchanged: Why Women Have Less Wealth and What Can Be Done about It.* Oxford: Oxford University Press.

Conway, M. Margaret. 2000. *Political Participation in the United States.* Third edition. Washington, DC: Congressional Quarterly Press.

Dalton, Russell J., and Hans-Dieter Klingemann, eds. 2007. *The Oxford Handbook of Political Behavior*. Oxford: Oxford University Press.

Driskell, Robyn, Elizabeth Embry, and Larry Lyon. 2008. "Faith and Politics: The Influence of Religious Beliefs on Political Participation." *Social Science Quarterly* 89: 294–314.

Ferreira, Fernando, and Joseph Gyourko. 2011. "Does Gender Matter for Political Leadership? The Case of US Mayors." NBER Working Paper No. 17671.

Hegewisch, Ariane, Claudia Williams, Heidi Hartmann, and Stephanie Keller Hudiburg. 2013. "The Gender Wage Gap: 2013." Institute for Women's Policy Research. http://www.iwpr.org/publications/pubs/the-gender-wage-gap-2013-differences-by-race-and-ethnicity-no-growth-in-real-wages-for-women.

Henderson, John, and Sara Chatfield. 2011. "Who Matches? Propensity Scores and Bias in the Causal Effects of Education on Participation." *Journal of Politics* 73: 646–658.

Juhn, Chinhui, and Simon Potter. 2006. "Changes in Labor Force Participation in the United States." *Journal of Economic Perspectives* 20: 27–46.

Junn, Jane. 1991. "Participation and Political Knowledge." Pp. 193–212 in *Political Participation and American Democracy*, edited by W. Crotty. New York: Greenwood Press.

Kam, Cindy D., and Carl L. Palmer. 2008. "Reconsidering the Effects of Education on Political Participation." *Journal of Politics* 70: 612–631.

Lawless, Jennifer L. 2004. "Politics of Presence? Congresswomen and Symbolic Representation." *Political Research Quarterly* 57: 81–99.

Leighley, Jan E. 1995. "Attitudes, Opportunities and Incentives: A Field Essay on Political Participation." *Political Research Quarterly* 48: 181–209.

Leighley, Jan, ed. 2010. *The Oxford Handbook of American Elections and Political Behavior*. Oxford: Oxford University Press.

Leighley, Jan E., and Jonathan Nagler. 2014. *Who Votes Now? Demographics, Issues, Inequality, and Turnout in the United States*. Princeton, NJ: Princeton University Press.

Lewis-Beck, Michael S., Richard Nadeau, and Angelo Elias. 2008. "Economics, Party, and the Vote: Causality Issues and Panel Data." *American Journal of Political Science* 52: 84–95.

Mettler, Suzanne. 2005. *Soldiers to Citizens: The G.I. Bill and the Making of the Greatest Generation*. Oxford: Oxford University Press.

Milbrath, Lester W., and M. Lal Goel. 1977. *Political Participation: How and Why Do People Get Involved in Politics?* Second edition. Chicago: Rand McNally.

Miller, Warren E., and J. Merrill Shanks. 1996. *The New American Voter*. Cambridge: Harvard University Press.

Morin, Rich. 2013. "The Disappearing Male Worker." Pew Research Center. http://www.pewresearch.org/fact-tank/2013/09/03/the-disappearing-male-worker/.

Mosisa, Abraham, and Steven Hipple. 2006. "Trends in Labor Force Participation in the United States." *Monthly Labor Review*. http://www.bls.gov/opub/mlr/2006/10/art3full.pdf.

Mutz, Diana C. 2007. "Effects of 'In-Your-Face' Television Discourse on Perceptions of a Legitimate Opposition." *American Political Science Review* 101: 621–635.

Mutz, Diana C., and Byron Reeves. 2005. "The New Videomalaise: Effects of Televised Incivility on Political Trust." *American Political Science Review* 99: 1–15.

National Council for Research on Women et al. 2014. "Money in Politics with a Gender Lens." New York: National Council for Research on Women.

Nie, Norman, Jane Junn, and Kenneth Stehlik-Barry. 1996. *Education and Democratic Citizenship in America.* Chicago: University of Chicago Press.

Ostrander, Susan A., and Kent E. Portney, eds. 2007. *Acting Civically: From Urban Neighborhoods to Higher Education.* Medford, MA: Tufts University Press.

Ramakrishnan, S. Karthick, and Irene Bloemraad. 2008. *Civic Hopes and Political Realities: Immigrants, Community Organizations, and Political Engagement.* New York: Russell Sage Foundation.

Reingold, Beth, and Jessica Harrell. 2010. "The Impact of Descriptive Representation on Women's Political Engagement: Does Party Matter?" *Political Research Quarterly* 63: 280–294.

Rosenstone, Steven J., and John Mark Hansen. 1993. *Mobilization, Participation, and Democracy in America.* New York: Macmillan.

Sandler, Bernice Resnick. 2007. "Title IX: How We Got It and What a Difference It Made." *Cleveland State Law Review* 55(4): 473–489.

Schlozman, Kay Lehman. 2002. "Citizen Participation in America: What Do We Know? Why Do We Care?" Pp. 433–461 in *Political Science: The State of the Discipline*, edited by Ira Katznelson and Helen V. Milner. New York: W. W. Norton.

Sen, Conor. 2012. "Why Is the Work Force Shrinking? Blame Young Men, Not the Economy." *The Atlantic.* http://www.theatlantic.com/business/archive/2012/10/why-is-the-labor-force-shrinking-blame-young-men-not-the-economy/263368/.

Shames, Shauna. 2014. "The Rational Non-Candidate: A Theory of (Uneven) Candidate Deterrence." PhD dissertation. Department of Political Science, Harvard University.

Skocpol, Theda, and Morris P. Fiorina, eds. 1999. *Civic Engagement in American Democracy.* Washington, DC: Brookings Institution Press; New York: Russell Sage Foundation.

Stanton, Elizabeth Cady. 1972 [1892]. "The Solitude of Self." Pp. 157–161 in *Feminism: The Essential Historical Writings*, edited by Miriam Schneir. New York: Random House, Vintage Books.

Suggs, Welch. 2005. *A Place on the Team: The Triumph and Tragedy of Title IX.* Princeton, NJ: Princeton University Press.

Toossi, Mitra. 2002. "A Century of Change: The U.S. Labor Force, 1950–2050." *Monthly Labor Review.* http://www.bls.gov/opub/mlr/2002/05/art2full.pdf.

U.S. Bureau of Labor Statistics. 2011. "Women at Work." http://www.bls.gov/spotlight/2011/women/.

U.S. Census Bureau. 2013a. "Historical Time Series Tables, Voting and Registration." http://www.census.gov/hhes/www/socdemo/voting/publications/historical/index.html.

U.S. Census Bureau. 2013b. "Current Population Survey, Annual Social and Economic Supplements." http://www.census.gov/hhes/www/income/data/historical/people/.

U.S. Department of Commerce Administration Economics and Statistics, and Executive Office of the President Office of Management and Budget. 2011. *Women in America: Indicators of Social and Economic Well-Being.*

Verba, Sidney, and Norman H. Nie. 1972. *Participation in America.* New York: Harper Row.

Verba, Sidney, Kay Lehman Schlozman, and Henry Brady. 1995. *Voice and Equality: Civic Voluntarism in American Politics.* Cambridge: Harvard University Press.

Verba, Sidney, Kay Lehman Schlozman, Henry E. Brady, and Norman Nie. 1990. *American Citizen Participation Study.* Ann Arbor, MI: Inter-university Consortium for Political and Social Research.

Wilkie, Jane Riblett. 1991. "The Decline in Men's Labor Force Participation and Income and the Changing Structure of Family Economic Support." *Journal of Marriage and Family* 53: 111–122.

Wolfinger, Raymond, and Steven Rosenstone. 1980. *Who Votes?* New Haven, CT: Yale University Press.

Zukin, Cliff, et al. 2006. *A New Engagement? Political Participation, Civic Life, and the Changing American Citizen*. New York: Oxford University Press.

{ 5 }

From Seneca to Shelby

INTERSECTIONALITY AND WOMEN'S VOTING RIGHTS

Celeste Montoya

Just seven years shy of the one hundredth anniversary of the Nineteenth Amendment, news broke about how a new and restrictive voting law passed in Texas might serve to restrict the ability of women to vote (Goodwyn 2013). Highlighted in these stories were two Texas women, District Judge Sandra Watts and state senator and gubernatorial candidate Wendy Davis. Both faced challenges at the polls for discrepancies between how their names were listed on voting registers and on their driver's licenses, a relatively common discrepancy related to marital name changes. Ultimately, both were able to avoid casting a provisional ballot, many of which are never properly certified and counted, by exercising an amendment that allowed them to sign an affidavit swearing to their identity. These stories were instrumental in highlighting one potential gender impact of current trends in voter restrictions. Changes in women's names may put them at higher risk of being excluded from voting.

At the same time, however, these examples drew the attention away from the pervasive racial and class dimensions of voter suppression. The implied message was that Texas's law is so strict that even these two politically prominent women who are *clearly* legitimate voters were impeded from exercising their constitutionally given right. That these two cases were highlighted over the numerous other examples of voting rights being impeded, in ways that are less easy to remedy, is reminiscent of earlier dilemmas in the history of women's suffrage, when the rights of middle-class white women were strategically emphasized and promoted over those of people (including women) who were marginalized by their racial, ethnic, or socioeconomic position, or all three. The potential exclusion of the two women mentioned here provide some of the few contemporary references to threats made to *women's* voting rights in the past century, despite the reality that millions of women, many of them women of color, have been impeded from voting since the ratification of the Nineteenth Amendment.

Diverging historical accounts of voting rights have emerged, one focusing predominantly on gender and the other centered primarily on race. Both leave an incomplete assessment of women's voting rights. The application of intersectional analysis to the woman's suffrage movement has been an important intervention to the hegemonic narratives that emphasize the experiences of white middle-class women (Hewitt 2010). Intersectional analysis moves beyond single-axis under-standings of gender oppression to recognize and examine multiple and intersect-ing dimensions of oppression, such as race and class (see Crenshaw 1989, 1994; Collins 1986; Hawkesworth 2003; McCall 2005; Hancock 2007). Intersectional interventions include probing the exclusionary elements of the mainstream move-ment and better incorporating the contributions and experiences of women from different social locations. Yet these intersectional accounts are far from univer-sal, and continued emphasis is placed on the struggle for formal voting rights over the actual practice of them. A more complete and ongoing assessment of women's voting rights has been limited by the Seneca Falls–to-suffrage narratives. Even narratives with stronger intersectional emphases stop with ratification of the Nineteenth Amendment. This temporal boundary reinforces a premature victory, particularly given that scholars have identified voter suppression as a pervasive and consistent feature of US political practice and institutions, accompanying and persisting beyond almost every expansionary voting effort, from historic constitu-tional amendments to contemporary efforts to increase accessibility (Bentele and O'Brien 2013; Keyssar 2000; Piven and Cloward 2000; Piven 2009; Wang 2012).

While analyses of women's suffrage have stopped short of examining voter sup-pression, examinations of voter suppression remain relatively silent on the issue of gender. Rather, historical and contemporary studies tend to emphasize race and, to a lesser extent, socioeconomic status. While the emphasis on racial oppression is a crucial part of understanding historical and contemporary patterns of voter suppression and exclusion, the lack of gendered analysis creates the same par-tial accounts that eclipse the experiences of women, particularly women of color. While gendering racially motivated voter suppression is more complicated, in that sometimes gender served to mediate oppressive measures, the importance of interrogating the experiences is crucial to developing a more complete under-standing of historical and contemporary voting rights.

In this chapter I seek to highlight the importance of more intersectional ana-lyses of both the impediments to and the mobilization for voting rights. This chapter is by no means meant to be a comprehensive intersectional analysis, but instead offers to highlight some of the ways that scholars have or might begin to address the complexities of intersecting oppressions in the evolution of US voting rights. In particular, I focus on the race-gendered dimensions of voting rights and suppression. The chapter is thus organized into three sections. In the first sec-tion, I discuss the intersectional interventions that have been or might be made in historical accounts of the woman's suffrage movement, highlighting the racial-ization and tactics of the movement, the varied participation and experiences of women, and efforts to further expand the boundaries of what is understood as the woman's suffrage movement. In the second section I focus on the historical practice of voter suppression subsequent to the ratification of the Fifteenth and Nineteenth Amendments, respectively, as well as the mobilization efforts aimed at ending suppression leading up to the adoption and amending of the Voting Rights Act of 1965. Here I highlight the experiences of differently situated women (in particular, women of color) in order to understand the ways in which racialized practices and experiences might have also been gendered. The third section shifts the focus to contemporary trends in voter participation and suppression, demonstrating how additional intersectional analyses might contribute to a more comprehensive evaluation of women's voting rights and practices.

Racing the Woman's Suffrage Narrative

Over the past several decades, critical scholars have worked to challenge and expand traditional and exclusionary narratives of women's suffrage. Yet, as argued by feminist historian Nancy Hewitt, the "Seneca Falls to suffrage" narrative remains prominent, heavily influenced by Elizabeth Cady Stanton and Susan B. Anthony's six-volume *History of Woman Suffrage* (Hewitt 2010: 17). This narrative focuses predominantly on the experiences of white, middle-class educated women in the Northeast; prioritizes the importance of de jure voting rights over de facto; and obscures the experiences of millions of women that remained excluded from the franchise even after the Nineteenth Amendment was ratified. This section of the chapter provides a brief overview of the ways in which scholars have amended and contested traditional narratives of woman's suffrage to decenter its focus on white, middle-to-upper-class, educated, northeastern women and instead highlights "the political claims that women [and men] from diverse racial, national, class, and regional backgrounds brought the US women's rights movement" (Hewitt 2010: 21). In this section I focus on three types of intersectional interventions scholars have made to this narrative: (1) the critique of racialized movement strategies and discourse (arising out of a lack of acting or thinking intersectionally), (2) the contributions made by women of color to the movement (located at the intersections of oppression), and (3) inquiries into women's voting rights that move beyond what is understood as the "woman's suffrage movement."

RACE AND RACISM IN THE WOMAN'S SUFFRAGE MOVEMENT

The genesis of the woman's suffrage movement was strongly linked to the abolition movement and efforts to establish the rights of blacks. Many of the well-known leaders—for instance, Susan B. Anthony, Elizabeth Cady Stanton, Lucy Stone, and Sarah and Angelina Grimké—were active in the antislavery movement (Wheeler 1995). They, along with black activists such as Sojourner Truth, Harriet and Margaret Forten, Caroline Remond Putnam, Josephine St. Pierre Ruffin, and Frederick Douglass, helped advocate for a "universal suffrage" (Terborg-Penn 1995, 1998). Angelina Grimké was especially vocal about the call to unity, stating, "I want to be identified with the Negro. Until he gets his rights, we shall never get ours" (Lerner 1967: 353). Attempts to forge solidarity went the other way as well.

Angela Davis (1983: 51) acknowledges Frederick Douglass "for officially introducing the issue of women's rights to the black liberation movement where it was enthusiastically welcomed."

Despite calls for solidarity, racial divisions were also rampant in the early struggles for women's rights. Although Frederick Douglass was present, not a single black woman was in attendance at the famous Seneca Falls convention (Davis 1983). It was not until two years later that Sojourner Truth would give her famous "Ain't I a Woman" speech at the 1851 women's convention in Akron, Ohio. The speech itself might be seen as an intersectional intervention to address not only the patriarchal stereotypes of female frailty but also to challenge the racism of white feminists who opposed her participation. The fragility of movement solidarity in some quarters, and the absence of it altogether in others, became more evident when the Fifteenth Amendment was passed in 1868, providing that the "right of U.S. citizens to vote shall not be denied or abridged by the United States or by any State on account of race, color, or previous condition of servitude." The omission of women from the Fifteenth Amendment caused a split within the movement for universal suffrage, igniting racial tensions that would last for decades (Terborg-Penn 1995, 1998; Newman 1999; Sneider 2008). Organizations advocating for universal suffrage, like the American Equal Rights Association, disbanded in the context of the amendment debate, and from this split emerged two rival woman suffrage organizations. The National Woman Suffrage Association (NWSA) headed by Stanton and Anthony represented those who opposed the amendment by virtue of its exclusion of women. The American Woman Suffrage Association (AWSA) headed by Stone included those who supported the amendment regardless, seeing it as a step in the right direction. Black suffragists were represented on both sides of the split, although Sojourner Truth notably continued to attend meetings for both (Terborg-Penn 1995, 1998).

Race played a divisive role in all levels of the movement, from the national to the local. In 1890 the AWSA and the NWSA merged into the National American Woman Suffrage Association (NAWSA), but the new organization was relentless in its pursuit of the franchise, using exclusionary strategies to court and maintain tenuous alliances with women's suffragist organizations in the South, many of which did not allow black members (Wheeler 1995). Criticisms of these tactics were written by Ida B. Wells and W. E. B. Du Bois. Wells, a black journalist best known for her antilynching work, was an active supporter of women's suffrage. She criticized Susan B. Anthony for refusing to support the efforts of black women and minimizing the visible participation of black allies such as Frederick Douglass, out of fear of alienating southern white women (Davis 1983). Du Bois, who had once expressed great optimism regarding women's suffrage and its potential to contribute to the voting rights both of black women and men, published reports on the movement's racism. In an editorial, he criticized Anna Shaw for stating "that all Negroes were opposed to woman suffrage" and notes that "In America . . . the war cry is rapidly becoming 'Votes for White Women Only'" (Yellin 2013: 400).

The segregation in the suffrage movement was fairly pervasive in the South, but also in the West. In both regions, women's clubs played a large role in regional and local movements, and these clubs were almost entirely segregated (McConnaughy 2013; Wheeler 1995). Even more problematic than the strategic exclusion of black women and other women of color from organizations and events as a mean of appeasing certain segments of the movement were the employment of racist frames or even outright opposition to racial rights by white suffragists. This includes discourse encouraging voter suppression, such as when Henry Blackwell asserted that the "negro problem" could be solved by attaching the literacy qualification to the right to vote. Blackwell along with other suffragists leveraged racism in support of the women's vote by arguing that southern white women would counterbalance the votes of black men and women, such that "the political supremacy of your white race will remain unchanged" (Wheeler 1995). But, even the "ostensibly 'neutral' stance assumed by the leadership of the NAWSA with respect to the 'color question' actually encouraged the proliferation of undisguised racist ideas within the suffrage campaign" (Davis 1983; Gilmore 1996).

Despite being overlooked within or more deliberately excluded from suffrage organizations, a growing number of African American women actively supported women's suffrage (Wheeler 1995). The National Association of Colored Women (NACW) was formed by black women in 1896, and included many prominent black female activists such as Harriet Tubman, Mary Church Terrell, Ida B. Wells, Adella Hunt Logan, and Frances E. W. Harper (Hooper 2012). The NACW worked for women's suffrage along with broader civil rights agendas. While these black women worked within their own organizations, some also staged small but meaningful interventions within the mainstream movement. A notable example came in the organization of a 1913 suffrage parade. Alice Paul, who would later form the more confrontational National Woman's Party, was responsible for organizing the march and had been quietly discouraging black women from participating, confiding to an editor, "As far as I can see, we must have a white procession, or a Negro procession, or no procession at all" (Walton 2010: 64). The Delta Sigma Theta sorority, an organization for black women, was the only group to participate in the march. Paul's compromise was to place these women at the end of the parade after the men's section. Ida B. Wells, also a member of Delta Sigma Theta, was vehement in her opposition to this segregation and defiantly marched with the Illinois delegation.

EXPANDING THE BORDER OF
THE "WOMAN SUFFRAGE MOVEMENT"?

Addressing the racism within the woman suffrage movement as well as the interventions made by black women and allies committed to universal suffrage helps challenge and expand popular narratives; however, it still provides a rather limited analysis of women's voting rights for the time period. A wider geographical and racial lens starts to better include the concerns of Native American women, Spanish American women, and various groups of immigrant women engaged in more encompassing struggles for citizenship that went beyond securing the vote. While these women were not necessarily excluded because of their gender, they nonetheless represent the need to broaden our understandings of the struggle for women's suffrage.

Examples of this are found by looking west. In an effort to court more women settlers, the territories and states of the West were among the first to offer women's suffrage. Starting with Wyoming in 1869, Colorado, Utah, Idaho, Washington, California, Oregon, Kansas, and Arizona all provided pre–Nineteenth Amendment voting rights to women. But these voting rights did not extend to all women. Asian Americans, Mexican Americans, and Native American women were all excluded (Hewitt 2010). Mexican American women lost many of the rights they had held under Spanish and later Mexican laws, when the borders of the Southwest were redrawn to establish what would become the modern United States (Hewitt 2010). Although technically granted citizenship, Mexican Americans were frequently prevented from exercising their rights, as discussed in the next section.

Other groups were outright excluded from citizenship. The 1882 Chinese Exclusion Act, which remained in place until 1943, not only halted Chinese immigration, but it also prohibited Chinese immigrants already living in the United States from becoming citizens. In the West, the Chinese faced similar discrimination to that of southern Blacks living under the Jim Crow laws (Scher 2010). Asians, in general, were often victims of violence and targets for discriminatory laws. South Asian Indians and Filipinos were not permitted to naturalize until 1946, and for Japanese, it was not until 1952.

Similar to Mexican American women, Native American women also experienced the loss of rights as the United States grew. Women who had held positions of religious and political authority in some of the tribes prior to colonization were displaced as more patriarchal forms of governance were imposed and tribes lost autonomy (Hewitt 2010). Throughout the United States and its territories, Native Americans were involuntarily treated as wards and excluded from voting. States and territories adopted exclusionary measures that kept tribal members from voting (Scher 2010). Some special local arrangements were made to grant citizenship to certain individuals or tribes, but these cases were tenuous exceptions and the process of naturalization was so demanding that few Native Americans could undertake it (McCool, Olson, and Robinson, 2007). Later, the Fourteenth Amendment and the Civil Rights Act of 1866 specifically excluded "Indians." The Indian Citizenship Act of 1924 was the first major federal step aimed at providing citizenship to enrolled members of tribes, those living on a federally recognized reservation, or those practicing Native culture. The 1924 law did not, however, ensure the right to vote.

The tenuous or nonexistent citizenship status of all of these groups excluded their women from exercising the voting rights granted to white women. To the extent that these women mobilized, it was often in seeking broader rights than just voting and with less emphasis on gender identity. That is not to say, however, that the experience was not gendered. The activist work within the black women's club movement in the South and its counterparts for Mexican American women in the Southwest demonstrate the relevance of women mobilizing as women of particular racial/ethnic orientations. One might also consider both the gendered and racial dimensions that the embodied experiences of women held when they struggled for the protections of citizenship. One might consider the example of Susette La Flesche, also called Inshata Theumba or Bright Eyes (Newman 1999). Part Ponca, a midwestern native tribe, Susette was a spokesperson for Native rights. She often traveled with male leaders of the Indian reform movement, serving as a translator. Alice Cunningham Fletcher, another member of the movement, describes her "clad in the garb of a white woman . . . The old stereotyped picture of the savage faded. . . . The skill with which the eloquence of the Chief was rendered into ringing English by the young Indian woman showed that the door of language could be unlocked and intelligent relations made possible between the two races" (Newman 1999: 121).

Gendering Voter Suppression and the Voting Rights Act

For many of the suffragists, the Nineteenth Amendment was celebrated as a momentous and long overdue victory for women's voting rights. But for some American women, the Nineteenth Amendment, not unlike the Fifteenth, was largely a symbolic victory. In practice, many would still be denied the right to vote. Southern black women were the largest contingent of female voters barred from the polls, although they were joined by millions of Asian and Mexican Americans in the West and Native Americans across the country (Hewitt 2010). For these women, the Voting Rights Act of 1965 (VRA) and its extensions in the 1970s represent more accurate markers for securing the right to vote (Hewitt 2010; Hine and Farnham 1994; Smooth 2006).

While African Americans were ostensibly granted the right to vote under the Fifteenth Amendment and women the right to vote under the Nineteenth Amendment, voter suppression countered expansion efforts as both parties attempted to manipulate voting populations (Wang 2012). Most of these strategies worked with and perpetuated racist and xenophobic narratives contextualized within different regions of the country. Because of this, the VRA and its subsequent additions, as well as voter suppression before and after its passage, are generally understood as affecting people of color. Yet while race was often the most salient dimension, the suppression, its resistance, and the impact of the VRA all had gendered dimensions. Wendy Smooth (2006) notes that the passage of the VRA significantly increased representation for women. She calls for an intersectional analysis of the VRA, recognizing the messiness of such considerations as it "requires race and politics scholars and activists to relinquish their proverbial hold on the Voting Rights Act as racial policy" and "women and politics scholars and activists [to make] an investment in the ongoing battles to protect and extend voting rights" (401).

GENDER AND VOTER SUPPRESSION

Gendering the civil rights narrative of voting rights requires messy intersectional work. In this section I start with a critical historical perspective of voter suppression following the ratification of the Fifteenth and then the Nineteenth

Amendments and provide an overview of struggles leading up to the passage of the Voting Rights Act and its extension. My discussion uses the experiences of women of color to demonstrate the ways in which the separate narratives of women's suffrage and racial voting rights converge and are necessary for providing a more inclusive analysis of women's voting rights.

The most noted form of systematic voter oppression occurred in the post-Reconstruction Jim Crow South. After the Fifteenth Amendment was ratified, an array of policies and tactics were developed to obstruct blacks (who were often Republicans at that time) from participating in elections. Jim Crow laws legalized the disenfranchisement of racial minorities through the imposition of literacy tests, poll taxes, property ownership requirements, grandfather clauses (that required voters to be eligible to vote prior to 1866 or to have a relative who was eligible), along with the more subjective "good character" tests. Although these laws might also exclude poor whites from voting, it was not unusual for actual poll practices to take place along racial lines. Poor and illiterate whites might be "allowed" to participate, while blacks who were literate or able to pay the poll taxes were turned away. Accompanying the formal institutions of restrictive voting laws were the informal institutions of violence and intimidation. In addition to arduous registration rules and practices, African Americans might also be punished for voting. In some cases, black voters were fired, evicted, or had loans recalled (Hillstrom 2009).

More extreme measures were used against black voters by members of white supremacist groups like the Ku Klux Klan (KKK), which used cross burnings, bombings, beatings, rapes, and even lynching as both punishment and warning (Hillstrom 2009). Du Bois, a supporter of women's suffrage, initially thought of it as a means of boosting black participation; "It is going to be more difficult to disenfranchise colored women than it was to disenfranchise colored men" (Yellin 2013: 406). After the Nineteenth Amendment, however, he provided important coverage of how black women's voting rights were now suppressed. For example, he published Walter White's exposé on the disenfranchisement of black women in Florida in which White recounted the ways in which a black woman might be tricked into and then arrested for perjury when attempting to vote. White stated, "I found many cases equally as flagrant where Negro women had been imprisoned for such 'offenses' as these" (Yellin 2013: 407–408). Black women were not exempt from the extreme physical violence enacted upon the African American community. Danielle McGuire (2004: 907) argues that "during the Jim Crow era, women's bodies served as signposts of the social order, and white men used rape and rumors of rape not only to justify violence against black men but to remind black women that their bodies were not their own."

While southern Democrats are often the focus of historical voter suppression discussions, the Republicans in the North were not much better, and voter suppression was widespread throughout the western US territories. In the North, similar tactics to those found in the South were employed against immigrants and factory workers who were more likely to vote for Democrats (Scher 2010). Irish, Italian, and other eastern and southern European immigrants were among those most commonly targeted for voter suppression. A common tactic employed was an earlier form of voter identification. Poll watchers might challenge the legitimacy of voters (often relying on racial and ethnic cues) and demand proof of citizenship. In addition to being subject to these formal exclusions, voters were also harassed, intimidated, and otherwise victimized.

Immigrants in other parts of the United States were subjected to other forms of exclusion In the Southwest, Mexican Americans were frequently denied the right to vote, even though many of them had been officially extended citizenship. Poll taxes and literacy tests were utilized, as well as more violent means of intimidation. The Texas Rangers used similar tactics against Latinos as were used against southern blacks, including lynchings, house burnings, and executions, in part to discourage them from voting (National Commission on Voting Rights 2014; Flores 2015). The challenges to voting for Mexican American women often lay at the intersection of gender, race, and class. Cotera (1997) speaks of the experiences of Chicanas in this part of the country: "If Chicanas could not afford the poll tax, they couldn't vote. If they could cross the tracks in the Anglo part of town only to work as domestics, they couldn't vote; if they were US citizens, but had no documents, they couldn't vote. If they were not physically able to resist the Sheriff's threats and blows, they couldn't vote. Finally, if the polling place was in a private home (a common practice in Texas) and if the homeowner did not allow Mexicans in, they couldn't vote" (214).

While there is little record of suppression efforts aimed solely at women after the passage of the Nineteenth Amendment, there are ways other than or in addition to race or ethnicity in which women might have fallen victim to suppression efforts. For example, given the low levels of women's education, particularly among poorer women, literacy tests provided a formidable obstacle even when women were given the right to vote. Similarly, given paternalistic inheritance and coverture laws, women might not be able to afford poll taxes without the financial support of male family members. Exercising an intersectional imaginary raises numerous questions that might be pursued in a more thorough analysis of women's voting rights in the decades following their formal inclusion to the franchise.

VOTING RIGHTS ACT OF 1965

The Voting Rights Act, signed into law on August 6, 1965, was seen as a significant victory for the black civil rights movement. First and foremost, the act established federal jurisdiction over what had previously been left up to the states, with the stated goal "To enforce the fifteenth amendment to the Constitution." The act had two main provisions. It prohibited states or public subdivisions from imposing any "voting qualification of prerequisite to voting, or standard, practice or procedure . . . to deny or abridge the right of any citizen of the United States to vote on account of race or color." This put an end to literacy tests and poll taxes. It also required that jurisdictions with a history of discrimination submit new election rules or plans to federal officials for "preclearance." The preclearance provision in the VRA required local officials to seek federal approval first for any changes in state law concerning voting. This shifted the burden to states to prove to federal officials that changes were not discriminatory on the basis of race, color, or language minority status.

Women, particularly black women, were a part of the activism leading up to the adoption of the VRA and surrounding its implementation. Their experiences within the movement reflect the complexity of gender at the intersection of race. Florenza Grant, a black woman from North Carolina who challenged local white authorities to obtain voting rights, states that "Women can have a more powerful impact on some things . . . than men can" (Valk and Brown 2010: 139). She argues that black women were less vulnerable to physical assault, making them able to join protests when men were unable, and were relatively immune from economic repercussions (Valk and Brown 2010). This is not to say that women did not suffer, because many did suffer retaliation, but rather that in some instances their gender identity provided them some modicum of protection.

The testimony of Fannie Lou Hamer, however, tells a different story. Hamer, one of the best known female civil rights leaders and a key organizer in the Mississippi Freedom Summer, was active in efforts to address voting rights. In her 1964 testimony before the Credentials Committee of the Democratic National Convention, she describes attempts to register and the subsequent violence. On the night of September 10, 1962, a house she was staying at was shot at sixteen times; that same night, two women were shot in Ruleville, Mississippi. In June 1963, after attending a voter registration workshop, she was violently arrested. In her testimony, she recounts the beating of her female cellmate, as well as her own. Danielle McGuire (2004: 910) provides this description of the story that Hamer told on national television "and continued to tell 'until the day she died.'"

> Hamer received a savage and sexually abusive beating by the Winona police. "You bitch," one officer yelled, "we're going to make you wish you were dead." He ordered two black inmates to beat Hamer with "a long wide blackjack," while other patrolmen battered "her head and other parts of her body." As they assaulted her, Hamer felt them repeatedly "pull my dress over my head and try to feel under my clothes."

Women like Hamer, as well as women's organizations and women in black churches, helped lead voter drives. But they were also a part of the violent confrontations. Women were among those beaten on Bloody Sunday in 1965, when police unleashed tear gas and billy clubs on the participants of a peaceful march for voting rights from Selma to Montgomery.

For some women, as well as some men, the threat of violence within this contentious public sphere was intimidating. Essie Alexander, a black woman living in a small city in the Mississippi Delta, recalls some of the hesitancies of black women: "So I felt like if the men needed to register, then the women did, too. But the first time, I had a time trying to get the other women to go. . . . I was kind of the spokesman for those few women, because they were kind of bashful" (Valk and Brown 2010: 152–153). For many of the women, participating in the civil rights movement would represent their entry into a new sphere of political participation and leadership that had heretofore been seen as a male domain, thus helping to facilitate both the consciousness and mobilizing skills necessary for the overlapping feminist movement of the 1970s.

Once the Voting Rights Act was adopted, circumstances began to change. The new law had an immediate impact on voter registration. During the first six months after it was signed, federal registrars processed over one hundred thousand applications for African American voters in the United States (Hillstrom 2009). African Americans registered to vote in Mississippi went from 6.7% to 59.8% in 1968, and most jurisdictions covered under the preclearance provision in the VRA saw a 25% increase in black registered voters by the 1968 presidential election (Hillstrom 2009)

The VRA would prove to be the mechanism for advancing voting rights for other groups as well. Although the VRA technically provided racial equality in voting rights, the act brought specific activism so that Native, Hispanic, and Asian Americans were covered by the law's provisions. In 1975 the VRA was renewed and expanded to protect these minority groups, due in no small part to the persistence of US House members Herman Badillo (New York), Ed Roybal (Los Angeles), and Barbara Jordan (Houston), who introduced the legislation, as well as representatives of the civil rights groups that testified in the congressional hearings about ongoing discriminatory practices (Berman 2015; Flores 2015). Included in the revised law was a prohibition on state laws requiring ballot and voting information exclusively in English and a provision for bilingual election requirements. The revised law also expanded preclearance to cover jurisdictions with large numbers of language minority groups that had low registration or turnout (Brown-Dean et al. 2015). In 1982 the VRA was renewed again with an added provision that gerrymandering could not be used to dilute minority voting strength. The 1982 change also allowed for assistance to blind, disabled, or illiterate citizens, and the act was also amended to clarify that discriminatory purpose was not required to bring a lawsuit to invalidate procedures that result in discrimination (Brown-Dean et al. 2015).

While technically the VRA did not address gender, it nonetheless expanded women's voting rights by virtue of expanding the rights granted to the groups to which women belonged. The added diversity to the "women's vote" has played a significant role in shifting some of the voting behaviors that are now considered to be gendered (such as trends in voter turnout and the gender gap). The next section starts with a look at contemporary voting patterns and the importance of adding intersectional dimensions to the analysis. The discussion also provides an overview of contemporary trends in voter suppression and considers the ways in which an intersectional analysis has been or might be incorporated to provide a more comprehensive analysis of women's voting rights in the twenty-first century.

Women's Voting Rights in the Twenty-First Century

Today, scholars note that women actively exercise their vote (Macmanus 2014; Dittmar 2015). Starting in the 1980s, women's voting participation began to exceed men's. This trend has continued into the twenty-first century. The consistency of gendered patterns in voter participation, even across race (discussed later), is perhaps why women's voting rights receive such scant attention. When contrasting gender patterns (as seen in Nancy Burns et al.'s chapter) and race patterns (see Figure 5.1), this emphasis might seem clear. In Figure 5.1, rates of voter turnout among whites are consistently higher than other racial groups, except in the 2008 and 2012 elections, with Barack Obama's candidacy. However, this type of analysis replicates problems of the past in which race and gender are treated as distinctive structural positionings, and overlooking the complex ways in which they, along with other relevant factors, intersect.

An intersectional analysis, however, illustrates patterns that are both gendered and raced (see Figure 5.2). As mentioned above, the gender gap in voting turnout is fairly consistent across races. In the past thirty years, women, regardless of race or ethnicity, in most cases have been more likely to vote than men of the same race. The single exception to this pattern is found for Asian American women. In 2000, Asian American men outvoted Asian American women; however, this is the last year in which this effect occurs. But these gendered patterns are also raced. Until 2008, white women had the highest level of voting turnout. In 2008, with the candidacy of Barack Obama, there is a decrease in white women's voting turnout at the same time that black women continue to increase their turnout, thus becoming the group with the highest level of voting turnout. In 2008 and 2012, a decrease in the racial gap between white men and black men occurred, although white men still participate at higher rates than black men. Although Latinas consistently outvote Latino men, both groups vote at significantly lower rates than whites or blacks of either gender. Asian Americans tend to have the lowest level of turnout, although sometimes their turnout exceeds that of Latino men, and in 2012 Asian women's voting rates rivaled that of Hispanic women.

This relatively simple intersectional analysis shows us that disaggregating women's voting patterns can expand our understanding of how women vote. It

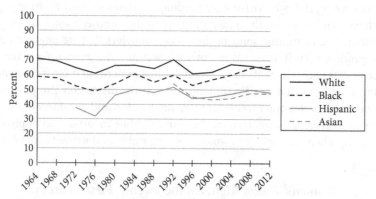

FIGURE 5.1 *Voter Turnout in Presidential Elections by Race, as Percentage of the Population*

US Census Bureau.

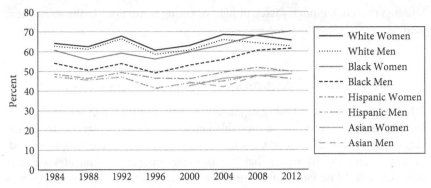

FIGURE 5.2 *Voter Turnout for Presidential Elections by Gender and Race, 1984–2012*
US Census Bureau data as reported by Center for American Women and Politics.

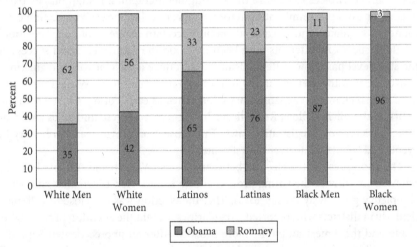

FIGURE 5.3 *Gender and Race Gap in Voter Support for Candidates, 2012 Presidential Election*

CNN Exit Poll (www.cnn.com/election/2012results/race/president).

also illustrates that women of color are an important part of the contemporary gender gap in voter turnout. In fact, they represent 74% of the growth in eligible women voters since 2000 (Harris 2014). They are arguably an even more important part of the modern partisan gender gap in presidential voting. In the last three presidential elections, the majority of white women and men have supported the Republican candidates; the political behavior of racial/ethnic minority women has maintained the contemporary partisan gender gap (Bejarano 2014). This was dramatically evident in the 2012 presidential election (see Figure 5.3). Intrarace gender gaps occurred for whites, Latinos, and blacks, but the overwhelming support for Democratic incumbent Barack Obama by Latinas and especially black women reinforced the partisan gender gap. Thus, when Republicans are characterized as having a "woman problem," it is really a problem in attracting women of color.

I discuss this contemporary issue in light of voting restrictions in the subsequent section.

REGULATING VOTING IN THE TWENTY-FIRST CENTURY

After the passage of the Voting Rights Act in 1965 and its expansion in the subsequent renewals, some of the more blatant forms of voter suppression become illegal. Suppression did not end, but its tactics simply became more sophisticated. Minnite (2010: 88–89) argues that "today, voter suppression strategies are pursued through subtle forms of intimidation and obstruction." While both parties historically have engaged in voter suppression, demographic shifts and trends in partisan voting in the new millennium have favored Democrats in ways that provide the party with incentives to expand voter turnout. Republicans have been left with two choices to capture the shifting demographics: realign on key party issues (for example, immigration reform as an appeal to the growing Latino electorate) or regulate voting so as to demobilize certain segments of the population. While unsuccessful attempts have been made on the former, electoral success at the state level has allowed Republicans to introduce a wave of voting regulations across the country (Bentele and O'Brien 2013 Hicks et al. 2015). While Democrats have helped champion expansionary efforts such as early voting, extended voting hours, and mail-in ballots, Republicans have countered these initiatives and promoted stricter voter registration laws. This subsection provides a brief history of events and trends in the twenty-first century.

The 2000 presidential election between George W. Bush and Al Gore brought renewed scrutiny to the voting process and to suppression efforts that had never completely gone away (Scher 2010). That the election was too close to call, particularly in districts with reported irregularities, caught the attention of civil rights group and the American public more broadly. After an unprecedented Supreme Court ruling halted recounts, the US Civil Rights Commission and the NAACP held a series of hearings scrutinizing possible obstructions made to curtail minority participation (Hillstrom 2009). They found that minority voters nationwide experienced problems, including but not limited to changes in poll locations without notice, the closing of polls while long lines remained, and the incorrect removal of names from voting registries. Florida, in particular, faced intensified scrutiny for its close count (Wang 2012). There it was reported that Republican Secretary of State Katherine Harris had ordered a purge of 57,700 names from the voter registry. Ninety percent of the voters purged were eligible voters, 54% of whom were black or Hispanic citizens. Studies also found that a high number of ballots were invalidated in counties where there were large numbers of African American voters (Wang 2012). Although Florida received the most media attention, similar trends were apparent throughout the country (Wang 2012).

The controversy surrounding the 2000 election instigated a number of new measures, not all of them conducive to increasing voter participation. The 2002 Help America Vote Act was a mixed piece of legislation that demonstrated divergent party efforts (Wang 2012). Democrats focused on addressing some of the problematic practices of the 2000 election, while Republicans emphasized voter fraud as their primary concern, an argument they have continued to use despite evidence that in-person voter fraud is extremely rare (Minnite 2010). The issue of voter identification was hotly debated, with Republicans arguing for the integrity of the process and reframing voting as a *privilege* instead of a *right*, and Democrats and civil rights advocates arguing that voter identification provisions would contribute to the disenfranchisement of Latinos, African Americans, the elderly, and the disabled (Wang 2012). The final bill included a compromise provision in which first-time voters must provide some sort of identification, the type of which each state could determine. Despite the legislation's initial intentions, voting rights advocates argued that the 2004 election was even worse in regard to the number of irregularities and policy manipulations (Wang 2012).

A more rigorous review of the voting process happened when the Voting Rights Act was up for reauthorization in 2006. Proponents of the renewal pointed to a number of controversial measures, including voter ID laws, redistricting, registration purges, and the invalidation of ballots (Hillstrom 2009). Bill Lann Lee, chair of the National Voting Rights Commission, testified on the findings of a study looking at voting rights from 1982 to 2005: "The evidence demonstrates unfortunately that the persistence, degree, geographic breadth, and methods of voting discrimination are substantial and ongoing" (Lee 2006). Opponents, meanwhile, focused on the provision of preclearance, arguing that preclearance placed an unfair burden on states based on reasons and violations that were now outdated. After a vigorous debate, the act was renewed with preclearance, passing in the House 390-33 and in the Senate 98-0.

A mere two years after the renewal, the battle continued in the 2008 presidential election. Voting rights advocates tried to counter mounting restrictive efforts (Wang 2012). Some states, many of which were considered battleground states, had very visible controversies. In Florida, a "no match, no vote" rule with few avenues of recourse was placed in effect, which impacted approximately twenty-two thousand voters, with Democrats being four times as likely as Republicans to have their registration rejected. Georgia instituted a "citizenship check" using out-of-date records on citizenship that incorrectly flagged a number of newer citizens as ineligible. Although a court injunction mandates that these voters be allowed to cast a "challenged" ballot, the Georgia law effectively disenfranchised a disproportionate amount of nonwhite voters. Purges using strict criteria and flawed data resulted in substantial purges in swing states Colorado and Ohio, a number of which were not entirely rectified. In Michigan (and elsewhere), foreclosure lists were used as the basis of mounting challenges at the polls. Across the country, voters faced prohibitively long lines and substandard polling resources, notably in poorer urban communities of color (Scher 2010; Barreto and Leal 2014).

Despite efforts to the contrary, the mobilization of nontraditional voters played a significant role in securing a victory for the country's first African American president, Barack Obama. The 2008 election was seen as a landmark for increased voter turnout among a range of demographic groups that have regularly been unrepresented. Overall, voter turnout increased by 5 million, from approximately 126 million to 131 million (U.S. Census Bureau 2010). The increase included approximately 2 million more African American voters, 2 million more Hispanic/Latino voters, and 600,000 more Asian American voters (U.S. Census Bureau 2010). Also notable was an increase in younger voters, particularly among those of college age. What followed this increase, however, was an electoral backlash (Wang 2012). The 2010 midterm election strengthened Republican representation at the state level, including a wave of Republican governors. This marked a major shift in the movement for restrictive voting that had begun stirring in 2000; from early 2011 until the 2012 election, state lawmakers introduced 180 restrictive voting bills in forty-one states, a trend that has continued in recent years (Weiser and Opsal 2014). In a study looking at restrictive voting proposals, scholars found that they occurred most frequently in competitive states under the control of Republicans, where African Americans are concentrated and both minority and low-income individuals have begun turning out at the polls more frequently (Bentele and O'Brien 2013; Hicks et al. 2015; Weiser and Opsal 2014).

The fight on voting rights was taken to a new level when the Supreme Court decided to hear *Shelby County v. Holder*. Shelby County, a preclearance jurisdiction in Alabama, sued the US attorney general in the US District Court for the District of Columbia, making the claim that sections 4(b) and 5 of the Voting Rights Act are facially unconstitutional and seeking to place a permanent injunction against their enforcement. In 2011 Judge John D. Bates found against the plaintiffs and upheld the provisions, arguing that evidence used to justify reauthorization by Congress in 2006 was sufficient. The US Court of Appeals for the DC Circuit affirmed the decision of the District Court in 2012, also finding the evidence in the *Congressional Record* to be sufficient to justify reauthorization. But on June 25, 2013, in a 5-4 decision, the Supreme Court struck down Section 4(b), the provision on preclearance. In the majority opinion (joined by fellow conservatives Antonin Scalia, Anthony Kennedy, Clarence Thomas, and Samuel Alito) Chief Justice John Roberts argued that the basis for covered jurisdictions was outdated, "Nearly 50 years later, things have changed dramatically. . . . Blatantly discriminatory evasions of federal decrees are rare . . . The tests and devices that blocked access to the ballot have been forbidden nationwide for over 40 years" (*Shelby v. Holder* 2013).

In a scathing dissent Ruth Bader Ginsburg argued that the Court had overstepped its bounds, overturning a precedent in which it has "repeatedly reaffirmed Congress' prerogative to use any rational means in exercise of its power in this area [to protect the rights to vote, and in particular to combat racial discrimination in voting]." Furthermore, she argued that preclearance works, citing the fact that "between 1982 and 2006, DOJ objections blocked over 700 voting changes based on a determination that the changes were discriminatory." In fact, more than three thousand voting changes were prevented under preclearance between 1965 and 2013, and this figure does not include likely thousands of additional proposed changes deterred from emerging by preclearance (National Commission on Voting Rights 2014).

The ruling effectively returned power to the states and shifted the burden of proof back to plaintiffs. "Without the preclearance requirements, plaintiffs will always be playing catch-up against recalcitrant jurisdictions" (Short 2014: 106). It did not take long to see the ramifications of the ruling, particularly in states that had heretofore been covered under preclearance (Brandeisky, Chen, and Tigas 2014). On the day of the Supreme Court ruling, Texas attorney general Abbott stated that Texas should immediately enact measures regarding a stringent voter ID law and redistricting that had both been rejected previously by a federal court. Additionally, two months after the Supreme Court decision, North Carolina passed a number of measures, including a law with strict new photo ID requirements. The state also eliminated same-day voter registration and instituted a shortened early voting period (Brandeisky et al. 2014). Virginia passed a number of new voting laws, including measures to restrict accepted voter identification and to purge voter rolls using the federal Systematic Alien Verification Entitlements database, which critics argue uses faulty data. Similar trends continued in other preclearance states. But it was not just the preclearance states changing their policies. Several non-preclearance states also strengthened voting restrictions. Republican legislators in Arkansas overrode the governor's veto of a strict new voter ID law, and Nebraska shortened early voting by ten days. The dramatic increase in more stringent voting laws that occurred after *Shelby* demonstrated that the "issue is not how to combat discrimination in areas previously covered for preclearance, but how to combat it across the country" (Short 2014: 107).

THE DISPARATE IMPACT OF VOTER RESTRICTIONS— INTERSECTIONAL CONSIDERATIONS

The National Commission on Voting Rights (2014: 135) issued a report in 2014 focusing on the "new generation of tactics for limiting minority voters' access to the ballot." The commission identified what it argues are some of the most concerning trends, including "new state laws that limit acceptable types of voter identification to those types that racial minorities are least likely to possess, substantial cutbacks to the days and hours of early voting periods popular with minority voters, and polling place relocations and closures in heavily-minority communities" (2014: 135). It also discussed redistricting plans that dilute minority voters, restrictions on voter drives (which bring in almost twice the rate of Latino and African American than white voters), proof of citizenship requirements, voter purges, and felony disenfranchisement. Although race is frequently, if not always, one of the primary dimensions of discrimination in these policies, there are others. Gendered impacts can also be a product of new polling practices. Here I suggest how an expanded intersectional analysis might be developed to more fully assess the growing restrictive policies.

This chapter began with a discussion of voter identification laws—Texas's law in particular, and its discriminatory impact. These ostensibly neutral state laws are a popular tactic, framed by supporters as maintaining the integrity of the vote. Prior to 2000, states generally had ID requirements that were fairly easy to satisfy, with most allowing voters to simply attest to their identity (National Commission on Voting Rights 2014). Between 2001 and 2012, 910 voter ID bills were introduced across a variety of states (Hicks et al. 2015). By the 2014 elections, thirty-one states had voter identification laws in force, although only about a third of them today are considered strict (Underhill 2014).

Voter identification laws have been criticized by opponents for their discriminatory impact, described by some as a modern-day poll tax. Because these laws vary in the type and degree of restriction, their impact also varies. A 2006 survey by the Brennan Center, however, suggests the disparate impact they might have. According to the survey, as many as 11% of US citizens (just over 21 million individuals) do not have government-issued photo identification. This is disproportionately higher among African Americans (25%), Latinos (16%), those over age sixty-five (18%), those ages eighteen to twenty-four (18%), and those earning less than thirty-five thousand dollars a year (15%). In particular, the Brennan Center reported that only 66% of voting-age women with ready access to any proof of citizenship (already a restricted number) have a document with their current legal name. This translates into roughly 32 million women who might be excluded due to inadequate voter identification. While these trends represent different dimensions of discrimination that are problematic when viewed in isolation, they are complicated by virtue of their intersections. Women, and women of color in particular, are overrepresented among lower socioeconomic groups, and women make up a disproportionate percentage of the elderly (Eichner and Robbins 2015; Ortman, Velkoff, and Hogan 2014). Also relevant are missed dimensions, such as how voter ID laws might impact voters with disabilities or voters who are transgender.

In the wake of the new laws, stories have emerged highlighting the intersectional gendered dimensions of discrimination. For example, Virginia Lasater, a ninety-one-year-old white woman who had voted and worked on campaigns for seventy years, was physically unable to obtain a photo ID when she faced a one-hundred-person wait at the Tennessee Department of Motor Vehicles, with no place to sit and no assistance from state workers (Macnamara 2011). Dorothy Cooper, a ninety-six-year-old African American woman also from Tennessee, showed up with her rent receipt, a copy of her lease, her former voter registration card, and her birth certificate, but was denied a photo ID because her birth certificate had her maiden name on it. She later stated on MSNBC that she did not have as many problems when trying to vote under the Jim Crow laws (Macnamara 2011). Sammie Louise Bates, who remembers counting the money needed to pay poll taxes with her mother, could not afford to pay the forty-two dollars for the birth certificate needed to register under Texas's new voter ID law (Weiser 2015).

In addition to voter identification restrictions, a number of measures have been proposed or adopted that impact the accessibility of voting. Eight states passed laws cutting back on early voting days and hours, many eliminating weekend and evening hours when minority voters are more likely to vote (National Commission on Voting Rights 2014; Wesier and Opsal 2014). These types of restrictions have

TABLE 5.1 Reasons cited for not voting in 2012 presidential election, by gender and race

	White		Persons of Color	
	Men	Women	Men	Women
Not interested, felt my vote wouldn't count	17.8%	14.9%	16.7%	11.5%
Too busy, conflicting work or school schedule	19.7%	16.0%	21.7%	22.2%
Illness or disability (own or family's)	9.6%	18.6%	9.5%	16.7%
Transportation problems	2.0%	3.4%	3.8%	5.7%

Data from US Census Bureau as reported by Harris 2014.

complex intersectional impacts. A survey inquiring about reasons people did not vote in the 2012 presidential election (before many of the most restrictive policies were put into practice) shows interesting patterns across race and gender (see Table 5.1). For example, 22.2% of the women of color surveyed cited they were too busy, followed by men of color (21.7%), white men (19.7%), and then white women (16%). White women were most likely to cite illness or disability (their own or a family member's), followed by women of color, both at almost twice the rate of men regardless of race. White women and women of color were more likely than men to have transportation problems, and people of color were more likely than those who are white to have such problems. Interestingly enough, low levels of interest or efficacy were less likely reported by women and particularly women of color.

Felony disenfranchisement provides another challenge to women's ability to vote, although its race-gendered impact has been woefully underexplored. While studies focus on the racial impact of voter disenfranchisement, any attention given to gender generally focuses on the plight of black men (for exceptions see Alexander 2010 and Smooth 2006). The Sentencing Project (2013) has provided some of the rare studies on black women. They report that in 2000 black women were incarcerated in state and federal prisons at six times the rate of white women. By 2009, this ratio decreased to about three times the rate. Given these persisting racial disparities, additional studies that focus on the intersections of gender and race in regard to voter disenfranchisement are much needed.

While this survey provides some suggestive support for considering the race-gendered impact of polling practices, numerous other considerations might be made. For example, while most laws allow voters to bring their children to the polling station, some states place restrictions on the number of children who may accompany a parent, making it difficult for women with more than two children (in the case of Indiana) to vote unless they have childcare. How are these voters, along with those who are disabled, to deal with long, cumbersome lines at inadequate polling sites? What intersectional impact is there in the increased purging of voter registration lists? Do face-to-face challenges at the polls by groups such as True the Vote have an intersectional impact? These are just a few intersectional considerations relating to the types of restrictions being put in effect across the country. Many of these questions remain unanswered and therefore point to the need for more systematic studies looking across multiple, intersecting social locations to more fully assess the wide-ranging and often gendered impact of restricting voting policy and practices.

Conclusion

Celebrating the centennial anniversary of the Nineteenth Amendment is important. It is right that we recognize this historical moment in the evolution of women's political rights. At the same time, it is imperative that we also recognize just what we are celebrating. This anniversary does not represent one hundred years of women voting; there have been too many exclusions of women voters over the past one hundred years to celebrate such an achievement. An intersectional analysis of this history demonstrates that the fight continued well beyond ratification and goes on even today. One might instead consider this moment in time as a juncture requiring a rallying cry. One hundred years later, not only are many women still effectively excluded from the franchise, but new threats continue to emerge. While 1920 was a momentous occasion in the path to women's suffrage, we must recognize other events that were just as important, if not more so, such as the 1965 Voting Rights Act. Better yet, we must recognize that the battle is far from over. Rights gained must be put into practice, exercised, and continuously protected lest they be lost.

References

Alexander, Michelle. 2010. *The New Jim Crow: Mass Incarceration in the Age of Colorblindness.* New York: New Press.

Barreto, Matt, and David Leal. (2014). *Race, Class, and Precinct Quality in American Cities.* New York: Springer.

Bejarano, Christina. 2014. *The Latino Gender Gap in U.S. Politics.* New York: Routledge.

Bentele, Keith G., and Erin E. O'Brien. 2013. "Jim Crow 2.0? Why States Consider and Adopt Restrictive Voter Access Policies." *Perspectives on Politics* 11(4): 1088–1116.

Berman, Ari. 2015. "The Lost Promise of the Voting Rights Act." *The Atlantic.* August 5. http://www.theatlantic.com/politics/archive/2015/08/give-us-the-ballot-expanding-the-voting-rights-act/399128/.

Brandeisky, Kara, Hanqing Chen, and Mike Tigas. 2014. "Everything That's Happened Since Supreme Court Ruled on Voting Rights Act." ProPublica. http://www.propublica.org/article/voting-rights-by-state-map.

Brown-Dean, Khalilah, Zoltan Hajnal, Christina Rivers, and Ismail White. 2015. "50 Years of the Voting Rights Act: The State of Race in Politics." Washington, DC: Joint Center for Political and Economic Studies.

Collins, Patricia Hill. 1986. "Learning from the Outsider Within: The Sociological Significance of Black Feminist Thought." *Social Problems* 33(6): S14–S32.

Cotera, Marta. 1997. "Among the Feminists: Racist and Classist Issues: 1976." Pp. 213–220 in *Chicana Feminist Thought*, edited by A. M. García. New York: Routledge.

Crenshaw, Kimberle. 1989. "Demarginalizing the Intersection of Race and Sex: A Black Feminist Critique of Antidiscrimination Doctrine, Feminist Theory, and Antiracist Politics." *University of Chicago Legal Forum* 1989(1): 139–167.

———. 1994. "Mapping the Margins: Intersectionality, Identity Politics, and Violence against Women of Color." Pp. 93–118 in *The Public Nature of Private Violence*, edited by Martha Alberson Fineman and Rixanne Mykitiuk. New York: Routledge.

Davis, Angela. 1983. *Women, Race, and Class*. New York: Vintage Books.

Dittmar, Kelly. 2015. "Women Voters." Pp. 99–126 in *Minority Voting in the United States*, edited by Kyle L. Kreider and Thomas J. Baldino. Santa Barbara, CA: Praeger.

Eichner, Alana, and Katherine Gallagher Robbins. 2015. "National Snapshot: Poverty among Women and Families." *National Women's Law Center*. https://nwlc.org/wp-content/uploads/2015/08/povertysnapshot2013.pdf.

Flores, Henry. 2015. *Latinos and the Voting Rights Act: The Search for Racial Purpose*. Lanham, MD: Lexington Books

Gilmore, Glenda Elizabeth. 1996. *Gender and Jim Crow: Women and the Politics of White Supremacy in North Carolina, 1896–1920*. Chapel Hill: University of North Carolina Press.

Goodwyn, Wade. 2013. "Texas Voter ID Law Creates a Problem for Some Women." *National Public Radio*. October 20. http://www.npr.org/2013/10/30/241891800/texas-voter-id-law-creates-a-problem-for-some-women.

Hancock, Ange-Mari. 2007. "When Multiplication Doesn't Equal Quick Addition: Examining Intersectionality as a Research Paradigm." *Perspectives* 5(1): 63–79.

Harris, Maya L. 2014. *Women of Color: A Growing Force in the American Electorate*. Center for American Progress. https://cdn.americanprogress.org/wp-content/uploads/2014/10/WOCvoters3.pdf.

Hawkesworth, Mary. 2003. "Congressional Enactments of Race-Gender: Toward a Theory of Race-Gendered Institutions." *American Political Science Review* 97(4): 529–550.

Hewitt, Nancy A. 2010. "From Seneca Falls to Suffrage? Reimagining a 'Master' Narrative in U.S. Women's History." Pp. 15–38 in *No Permanent Waves: Recasting Histories of U.S. Feminism*, edited by Nancy A. Hewitt. New Brunswick, NJ: Rutgers University Press.

Hicks, William D., Seth C. McKee, Mitchell D. Sellers, and Daniel A. Smith. 2015. "A Principle or a Strategy? Voter Identification Laws and Partisan Competition in the American States." *Political Research Quarterly* 68(1): 18–33.

Hillstrom, Laurie Collier. 2009. *The Voting Rights Act of 1965*. Detroit: Omnigraphics.

Hine, Darlene Clark, and Christine Anne Farnham. 1994. "Black Women's Culture of Resistance and the Right to Vote." Pp. 204–219 in *Women of the South: A Multicultural Reader*, edited by C. A. Farnham. New York: New York University Press.

Hooper, Cindy. 2012. *Conflict: African American Women and the New Dilemma of Race and Gender Politics*. Santa Barbara, CA: Praeger.

Keyssar, Alexander. 2000. *The Right to Vote: The Contested History of Democracy in the United States*. New York: Basic Books.

Lee, Bill Lann. 2006. "Voting Rights Act: Evidence of Continued Need." Testimony before the House of Representatives Committee on the Judiciary, Subcommittee on the Constitution, March 8.

Lerner, Gerda. 1967. *The Grimké Sisters from South Caroline: Pioneers for Women's Rights and Abolition*. Boston: Houghton Mifflin.

Macmanus, Susan. 2014. "Voter Participation and Turnout." Pp. 80–118 in *Gender and Elections: Shaping the Future of American Politics*, edited by Susan J. Carroll and Richard. L. Fox. New York: Cambridge University Press.

Macnamara, Elisabeth. 2011. Testimony at "Excluded from Democracy: The Impact of Recent State Voting Change." *League of Women Voters of the United States*. Washington, DC. November 14, 2011. (http://lwv.org/files/voteHouseID_TestimonyNov142011.pdf).

McCall, Leslie. 2005. "The Complexity of Intersectionality." *Signs* 30(3): 1771–1800.

McConnaughy, Corrine M. 2013. *The Woman Suffrage Movement in America: A Reassessment*. New York: Cambridge University Press.

McCool, Daniel, Susan M. Olson, and Jennifer L. Robinson. 2007. *Native Vote: American Indians, the Voting Rights Act, and the Right to Vote*. New York: Cambridge University Press.

McGuire, Danielle. 2004. "'It Was Like All of Us Had Been Raped': Sexual Violence, Community Mobilization, and the African American Freedom Struggle." *Journal of American History* 91(3): 906–931.

Minnite, Lorraine. 2010. *The Myth of Voter Fraud*. Ithaca, NY: Cornell University Press.

National Commission on Voting Rights. 2014. *Protecting Minority Voters: Our Work Is Not Done*. Washington, DC.

Newman, Louise Michele. 1999. *White Women's Rights: The Racial Origins of Feminism in the United States*. New York: Oxford University Press.

Ortman, Jennifer M., Victoria A. Velkoff, and Howard Hogan. 2014. "An Aging Nation: The Older Population in the United States. Population Estimates and Projections." Washington, DC: U.S. Census Bureau.

Piven, Frances Fox. 2009. *Keeping Down the Black Vote: Race and the Demobilization of American Voters*. New York: New York University Press.

Piven, Frances Fox, and Richard Cloward. 2000. *Why Americans Still Don't Vote: And Why Politicians Want It That Way*. Boston: Beacon Press.

Scher, Richard K. 2010. *The Politics of Disenfranchisement: Why Is It So Hard to Vote in America?* New York: M. E. Sharpe.

The Sentencing Project. 2013. "The Changing Racial Dynamics of Women's Incarceration." http://www.sentencingproject.org/publications/the-changing-racial-dynamics-of-womens-incarceration/.

Shelby County v. Holder, 570 U.S. 2 (2013).

Short, John Rennie. 2014. "The Supreme Court, the Voting Rights Act, and Competing National Imaginaries in the USA." *Territory, Politics, Governance* 2(1): 94–108.

Smooth, Wendy. 2006. "Intersectionality in Electoral Politics: A Mess Worth Making." *Politics and Gender* 2(3): 400–414.

Sneider, Allison L. 2008. *Suffragists in an Imperial Age: U.S. Expansion and the Woman Question 1879–1929*. New York: Oxford University Press.

Terborg-Penn, Rosalyn. 1995. "African American Women and the Woman Suffrage Movement." Pp. 135–156 in *One Woman, One Vote: Rediscovering the Woman Suffrage Movement*, edited by M. S. Wheeler. Troutdale, OR: New Sage Press.

———. 1998. *African American Women in the Struggle for the Right to Vote, 1850–1920*. Bloomington: Indiana University Press.

ity and Women's Voting Rights* 127

Underhill, Wendy. 2014. "Voter Identification Requirements: Voter ID Laws." National Conference of State Lawyers. http://www.ncsl.org/research/elections-and-campaigns/voter-id.aspx.

U.S. Census Bureau. 2010. "Voting and Registration in the Election of November 2008." https://www.census.gov/prod/2010pubs/p20-562.pdf.

Valk, Anne, and Leslie Brown. 2010. *Living with Jim Crow: African American Women and Memories of the Segregated South*. New York: Palgrave Macmillan.

Walton, Mary. 2010. *A Woman's Crusade: Alice Paul and the Battle for the Ballot*. New York: Palgrave Macmillan.

Wang, Tova Andera. 2012. *The Politics of Voter Suppression*. Ithaca, NY: Cornell University Press.

Weiser, Wendy R. 2015. "New Voting Laws Show That the Struggle Continues." New York: Brennan Center for Justice. https://www.brennancenter.org/blog/new-voting-laws-show-struggle-continues.

Weiser, Wendy R., and Erik Opsal. 2014. *The State of Voting in 2014*. New York: Brennan Center for Justice. http://www.brennancenter.org/sites/default/files/analysis/State_of_Voting_2014.pdf.

Wheeler, Marjorie Spruill. 1995. *One Woman, One Vote: Rediscovering the Woman Suffrage Movement*. Troutdale, OR: NewSage Press.

Yellin, Jean Fagan. 2013. "Du Bois's *Crisis* and Woman's Suffrage." *Massachusetts Review* 53(3): 399–409.

6

One Hundred Years since Women's Suffrage

MANAGING MULTIPLE IDENTITIES AMONG LATINA CONGRESSIONAL LEADERS

Jessica Lavariega Monforti

This chapter assesses the emergence of Latinas in the US Congress that began in the late 1980s. This assessment places the lives and careers of these Latina elected officials over the last decades in a historical, political, and cultural context reflecting the increasing political participation of Latinx[1] across the United States. The theoretical foundation of this chapter is based on an understanding of the lives, careers, and actions of Latina congressional members in light of a sociopolitical landscape that includes multiple marginalities and the intersection of ethnicity, gender, immigration, and socioeconomic status. I also evaluate the pathways these *congresistas*[2] have taken to their respective electoral victories.

The historical backdrop for the successes of women of color in politics includes the development of women's suffrage as well as various civil rights movements in the United States. A century has passed since women won the right to vote in federal elections, yet the representation of women in elected office falls far below proportionality. The disparity is even greater for women of color. While significant and growing proportions of the US population are Asian American, Black, and Latina[3] women, few women of color hold elective office. The first woman was elected to Congress in 1917, but the first woman of color was not elected to the institution until Hawaii's Patsy Mink was elected to the US House of Representatives in 1964. Carol Moseley Braun was the first, and to date only, African American woman elected to the US Senate. She was elected in 1992, was the first woman to defeat an incumbent senator in an election, and was the first and to date only female senator from Illinois. The first African American woman representative, Shirley Chisholm, was not elected to serve in the US House until 1968, and in 2012 Hawaii elected Mazie Hirono, the first Asian American woman, to the US Senate. As of 2016 no Native American woman has been elected to Congress. Ileana Ros-Lehtinen, who is of Cuban descent, in 1989 was the first Latina elected to the US House—and no Latina has served in the Senate to date.[4] Of the ninety-seven women who were elected in 2012 and served in the 113th Congress, only nine were Latina.[5]

So why examine Latinas in Congress? Women face multiple challenges when seeking elective office. Women are less likely to initiate office seeking themselves, and they often only run for office after being invited to do so (Carroll 1994). Women face greater fundraising challenges and are considered less serious candidates by both male and female voters.[6] Beyond these gender-based challenges are the additional challenges faced by women of color. They are marginalized by their ethnorace—a concept that combines the experiences of race and ethnicity—as well as their gender. Latinas, in particular, often have to contend with stereotypes held by many in the electorate as well as *machismo*[7] in their communities, and choosing to seek elective office can therefore generate hostility and backlash among both non-Latino and Latino voters (Hardy-Fanta 1993; Petersen, Hardy-Fanta, and Armenoff 2005; Lavariega Monforti and Gershon 2016). In short, Latinas face an intersection of gender and ethnorace challenges.

In this chapter I examine Latina political candidates who successfully ran for federal-level office and the multiple marginalities they faced and conquered in order to win those elections. These Latinas are political pioneers, yet very little has been written about them. Their names are unknown to most, and their accomplishments have gone unacknowledged despite their electoral and policy victories. What their stories reveal is that there is no one single way to become a Latina congresswoman—there is no formula to follow. However, there are commonalities at the core of their familial histories—close personal relationships with people who have been politically active and life experiences that helped them supersede intersecting barriers of racism and ethnocentrism, sexism and sometimes classism, and connect with voters in their respective districts.

Setting the Context

Many American women won the vote August 26, 1920, with ratification of the Nineteenth Amendment. By this time in US history, Hispanic communities had been living in the United States, primarily in the South and West, for over four hundred years—a legacy of the Spanish conquistadors—and the population grew significantly between 1906 and the 1930s. Nevertheless, and in spite of a treaty granting the Mexican-origin community US citizenship, most Hispanics were treated as second-class citizens. While there was some scant political representation of Hispanics in elected office—such as Joseph Hernández, who served as a representative from the Territory of Florida from 1822 to 1823—many Hispanics were subject to significant discrimination, segregation, and violence, such as beatings and lynchings, during this period (Delgado 2009).

The repressive treatment of Latinos in the United States has included the use of racist rhetoric such as "wetbacks" and "spics," segregation in public spaces and schools, theft of property, and mob violence directed against them (Carrigan and Webb 2013). The most extreme actions ended in death. For example, Mexicans and Mexican Americans were lynched for acting "too Mexican." If Mexicans were speaking Spanish too loudly or showcasing aspects of their culture too defiantly, they were in some cases lynched by racist whites. Mexican women could also be lynched if they resisted the sexual advances of Anglo (white) men. Many of these lynchings occurred with active participation of law enforcement such as the Texas Rangers. Considering that Mexicans had little to no political power or social standing, they had no recourse. Popular white opinion was that Mexicans should be eradicated in the Southwest (Martínez 2005). The incidence of lynching of Mexicans in the southwestern United States is second only to that of the African American community during that period (Delgado 2009).

In 1922, just two years after passage of the Nineteenth Amendment and despite these significant barriers for Latinos, the country witnessed its first Latina victory in a statewide election; Soledad Chávez de Chacón of Albuquerque, New Mexico, became secretary of state (Chávez 1996). However, it took another sixty-seven years for a Latina candidate to win a seat in the US Congress. Why did it take so long? Demographics, slowly increasing access to the ballot for Latinx voters, and racial and sex discrimination are major factors contributing to this lag. For example, the 1940 US Census reported that 1.8 million people of Hispanic origin lived in the country, which was about 1.4% of the US population. At this time, and some would argue still today, many non-Hispanic voters were unwilling to support Latinx candidates, regardless of gender. It took time for the Latino population in the United States to grow and gain access to the ballot. By 1970 the Hispanic population in the United States constituted about 4.7% of the population and reached almost 10 million people. By 1974, the first major Latino voter registration organization, the Southwest Voter Registration Education Project, began registering Latino voters. But in the mid-1970s, Latino representation in elective office continued to trail. According to Vilma Martinez's[8] testimony before the US Commission on Civil Rights in 1975,

> Throughout the Southwest, Mexican Americans have not been able adequately to make their weight felt at any level of government. In Texas, where Mexican Americans comprise 18% of the population, only 6.2% of the 4,770 elective offices—298 of them—are held by Chicanos. California is worse. There, Mexican Americans comprise 18.8% of the total population. Yet, in 1970, of the 15,650 major elected and appointed positions at all levels of government—federal, state, and local—only 310 or 1.98% were held by Mexican Americans. This result is no mere coincidence. It is the result of manifold discriminatory practices which have the design or effect of excluding Mexican Americans from participation in their own government and maintaining the status quo.[9]

Five years later, in 1980, the Hispanic population grew to over 14 million, or 6.4%.[10] We still did not see any Latinas elected to serve in either chamber of the US Congress. By 1990, more than 8 million Hispanics were added to the US population—about 9% of the population (Tienda and Mitchell 2006). As the new millennium began, there were 35.3 million Hispanics living in the United States, comprising 12.5% of the country's population (excluding the Commonwealth of Puerto Rico and the US Island Areas).[11] The demographic change in itself is important because numbers are political power in a democracy based on majority rule, but the geographic concentration of the growth in certain states like Florida, along with changing attitudes about women of color in politics, was even more important for the electoral success of Ileana Ros-Lehtinen—the first Latina elected to Congress in 1989.

Like many groups of women of color in the United States, Latinas have a long tradition of involvement in building community organizations, movements, and political agendas; volunteerism in civic and religious life; and a tradition of resistance and informal struggle against marginalization and exclusion.[12] In essence, Latinas have always been actors in the sociopolitical landscape of the United States. This chapter focuses on Latinas' pursuit of "traditional" political roles, particularly that of elected officials at the national level that were made possible by and can be considered an extension of this history (Cruz Takash 1997; Garcia Bedolla, Tate, and Wong 2005; Sierra 2009; Sepulveda 1998).

Beyond the increasing population size and geographical concentration, Latinx gaining access to vote at the ballot box was another central piece of the puzzle for Latina electoral gains in Congress. Similar to work on African American elected officials (Darling 1998), there is a clear relationship between the removal of race- and language-based barriers to Hispanic voter registration and participation (e.g., poll taxes, literacy tests, property requirements, English-only ballots, and physical intimidation and violence) and the number of Hispanics elected to public office across the United States. In 1964, the year that the Civil Rights Act was passed, there were only three Hispanics—one senator and two representatives, all male— serving in the US Congress. The significance of the Voting Rights Act (VRA), and its extension in 1975, as well as the redistricting of congressional districts for the election of Hispanic candidates, both male and female, to public office cannot be overstated. In 1975, when the VRA extension was passed, there were six male Hispanic members of the House and no senators. Since that time, the number of Latinxs in Congress has almost tripled.

However, such changes in access to the vote are not the only factor driving the increase in Latinas in office. Today, only one of the Latinas in Congress was elected in a majority-Hispanic district: Linda Sánchez from California's Thirty-Eighth Congressional District.[13] The vast majority of Latinas in Congress were elected in districts with multiple identity-based constituencies where Hispanics comprise 34% to 48% of eligible voters. The election of Jaime Herrera Beutler in Washington State, where the Latino share of the voter-eligible population is less than 5%, shows that Latinas can achieve electoral victories outside districts with a high proportion of Latina/o-eligible voters. Bejarano (2013) argues that Latinas may be aided by the intersection of their racial and gender identities. She suggests that Latina candidates can secure public support by appealing to a wide array of communities and voter coalitions, particularly women and minority communities. Additionally, she points out that Latina candidates are often better prepared for office holding and are perceived as less threatening than their male counterparts by white voters.

Despite historical barriers and their legacies, Latinas have made important inroads into the political arena, making study of *las políticas* important.

García (2001: 112) argues that "Chicanas and Latinas approach mainstream political participation differently than do their white female counterparts because of their unique experiences and political history as minority women." Hardy-Fanta's work (1993, 2002) demonstrates that Latinas emphasize the connections between their private and public lives. Latinas involve themselves in public elective office because such service is a further extension of their private life experiences and their efforts to promote community uplift. This can manifest itself in a different type of political behavior—one that includes electoral politics as well as community activism and leadership. Thus, another reason for the increase in Latina office holding is the preparation, determination, and community orientation of the candidates themselves.

As the research in this chapter shows, Latinas who have been elected to the US Congress hold multiple and intersecting identities. Identifying as Latina evokes both gender and ethnicity, and the office holders often exhibit concerns stemming from their class and their families' immigration backgrounds as well. These intersecting identities can lead to attempts to marginalize them, attempts that they often resist. Their political and policy efforts, then, can be said to be an outcome of this blend of identities and their ongoing efforts to achieve greater equality and justice in the face of intersecting barriers. Thus, as is pointed out by Darling's (1998: 151–152) work on African American women in state elective office in the South, analysis of women of color in elective office is "compelling because it requires us to ask what the real-world consequences are of the impact of race, gender, class, and sexuality and the ways oppositional and linear beliefs, paradigms, and actions create and sustain marginality and operate to establish multiple discriminations."

Latinas in Elective Office

Hispanics generally have experienced lower representation in nearly all elected bodies than have other demographic groups in the United States when compared to their presence in their communities (Garcia and Sanchez 2008). Nevertheless, Latinas have enjoyed greater increases in electoral success than their Latino male counterparts (Sierra 2009). Between 1996 and 2009, the number of Latina elected officials grew more quickly than the number for Latino males; the total number of Latina officials doubled (a 100% increase) compared to a 36% increase for Latinos (Sierra 2009). Local offices are an important entry point into politics for Latinas; for example, about 42% of Latina office holders in Texas can be found here (S. García et al. 2008). Bejarano (2013) even finds that Latinas have an advantage in winning races compared to their male coethnics and Anglo women at the local level. If these patterns hold, Latinas are the future of Latinx politics in the United States.

Overall, however, we find few Latinas in national-level offices. The underrepresentation of Latinas in national elected offices is an important reflection on the health of US democracy, with real-world implications for descriptive and substantive representation. *Descriptive representation* refers to whether elected officials mirror their constituents in terms of ethnorace, class, or sex, while *substantive representation* refers to the ability of the representative to act for the interests of the represented (Pitkin 1967).

First, in terms of descriptive representation, proportional representation of Latinas (and other major subgroups) serves as a measure of the strength and health of a representative democracy, indicating the capacity of all citizens to participate in governance in meaningful ways. If the political voice of any group that exists within a society is muted or silenced, then representation, and ultimately democracy, fades. Moreover, Mansbridge (1999) argues that minority and women representatives engender feelings of trust and legitimacy on the part of people of color in cases where a history of discrimination exists. They also represent the views of that group at the policymaking table and can bring new issues into consideration. Minority and women representatives can advocate, speak with moral authority as group members, and serve as role models for others. Additionally, Burrell (1996: 6) notes that, "When citizens can identify with their representatives they become less alienated and more involved in the political system."

Turning to substantive representation, Fraga et al. (2005) and Jaramillo (2010) posit that elected Latinas have a distinctive approach to politics as a result of their intersectional identities as women and Hispanics. That is to say, their intersecting identities of ethnorace and gender—along with other sociopolitical identities, such as language, immigration status, and history—shape their political worldviews. The disparity between constituencies and the demographics of the members of elected governmental institutions such as the US Congress raise doubts about the representativeness of the policies these leaders adopt. This representation gap is likely to increase given the dramatically changing demographics and Latino population growth in the United States, particularly in the Southwest. In other words, representation and democracy themselves are threatened when governance is not inclusive (Thomas and Welch 1991; Tate 2003; Swers and Larson 2005). Latinas in office, then, can play an essential role in broadening the scope of voices making policy for the country, just as has been the case for other cross-sections of the population. For instance, research shows that the ethnorace and gender of elected officials can effect substantive policy outcomes (Pinney and Serra 1999).

I now turn to a discussion of the Latinas who have been victorious in their pursuit of elective office in Congress. Nine Latinas have held congressional office, and they are shown in Figure 6.1. Table 6.1 lists all Latinos who have held office in Congress, including the nine female members (names bolded). These nine Latina congresswomen are a diverse group. The group includes women born in Latin America and the United States; the children of immigrants; women whose families have been in the United States for over ten generations; women of Cuban, Puerto Rican, and Mexican origin; bilingual and monolingual English speakers; and Democrats and Republicans, to name just a few characteristics that differentiate them. So what do these women share in common beyond gender and ethnicity?

FIGURE 6.1 *Las Políticas*
http://www.scpr.org/blogs/politics/2014/02/18/15874/rep-negrete-mcleod-to-leave-congress-after-one-ter/.

What are the commonalities in their biographies? In addition to holding intersecting identities and confronting intersecting ethnoracial and gender barriers, all of
them were socialized in families that were politically involved, either in the United
States or abroad. Additionally, the majority of these congresswomen came to elective office from service-oriented careers like teaching, government and nonprofit
work, and organizing, often with prior political experience at the state or local
level or both. In short, the training ground for Latinas in Congress has been family and community. These women have all blended various aspects of their private
lives into their public, elective leadership roles, all while confronting and overcoming intersecting ethnoracial and gendered barriers to their success.

BLENDING OF PUBLIC AND PRIVATE

As highlighted in the work of Hardy-Fanta (1993) and Michelson (2013), decisions of Latinas to become *políticas*, to throw their hats into the ring, are often the
result of a combination of private lives and prior public service. This rings true
for Ileana Ros-Lehtinen, the first Latina congresswomen. She said she decided to
enter public life "largely because of the influence of her father, Emilio Ros, a certified public accountant who also dabbled in local politics."[14] Additionally, Ros-
Lehtinen, a Cuban American Republican representing South Florida since 1989,
was a teacher before entering politics and has publicly stated that it was through
getting to know the parents of her students, and the problems they had with
immigration, Social Security, and Medicare that inspired her to run for office.
Her goal was to make these complicated policies work for the people in her community.[15] Further, the Ros family lived in a highly politicized community where

TABLE 6.1 Latino members of the 113th Congress

Senate		House	
FL	Marco Rubio (R)	AZ-3	Raul Grijalva (D)
NJ	Robert Menendez (D)	AZ-7	Ed Pastor(D)
TX	Ted Cruz (TX)	CA-29	Tony Cardenas (D)
		CA-32	**Grace Flores Napolitano (D)**
		CA-34	Xavier Becerra (D)
		CA-35	**Gloria Negrete McLeod (D)**
		CA-36	Raul Ruiz (D)
		CA-38	**Linda Sanchez (D)**
		CA-40	**Lucille Roybal-Allard (D)**
		CA-46	**Loretta Sanchez (D)**
		CA-51	Juan Vargas (D)
		FL-25	Mario Diaz-Balart (R)
		FL-26	Joe Garcia (D)
		FL-27	**Ileana Ros-Lehtinen (R)**
		ID-1	Raul Labrador (R)
		IL-4	Luis Gutierrez (D)
		NJ-8	Albio Sires (D)
		NM-1	**Michelle Lujan Grisham (D)**
		NM-3	Ben Lujan (D)
		NY-7	**Nydia Velazquez (D)**
		NY-15	Jose Serrano (D)
		TX-15	Ruben Hinojosa (D)
		TX-17	Bill Flores (R)
		TX-20	Joaquin Castro (D)
		TX-23	Pete Gallego (D)
		TX-28	Henry Cuellar (D)
		TX-34	Filemon Vela (D)
		WA-3	**Jaime Herrera Beutler (R)**

Source: http://www.naleo.org/downloads/US_Congress_Table_2012.pdf

the key issues were Cuba and communism—issues that were deeply personal to most Cubans and that pushed many in the community into the Republican Party (Torres 2001).

There is a similar storyline for Nydia Velázquez, a Puerto Rican Democrat serving New York's Seventh Congressional District since 1992. Like Ros-Lehtinen, she entered politics from the education field and was influenced by the political engagement of one of her parents. She came from a modest background with a father who was a sugar cane worker in Puerto Rico, and she was inspired to engage in electoral politics by her dad's political activism. How did the daughter of a sugar cane worker, born in Yabucoa, Puerto Rico, become a member of Congress? Politics was part of Velázquez's childhood socialization. Growing up, dinner conversations about politics were commonplace. Her father cut sugar cane but was also a local political activist and started a political party. Although he never finished elementary school, he was a political leader in her hometown of Yabucoa, and hearing him speak at political rallies inspired her to engage in politics (Geer, Schiller, and Segal 2013). Her dad focused on the rights of sugar cane workers and denounced the abuses of wealthy farmers.[16] One can see her father's focus on human rights evident in Velázquez's political career.

Another example is that of Jaime Herrera Beutler, who was elected to Congress in 2010 to represent southwestern Washington State. Herrera Beutler, a moderate Republican born in California and raised in southwestern Washington, is one of the youngest women currently serving in the US Congress, and she is the first Hispanic in history to represent Washington State in the US House of Representatives.[17] As a young girl, she worked alongside her parents going door to door for former Republican congresswoman Linda Smith. Homeschooled through ninth grade, Herrera Beutler's parents encouraged an interest in politics, including a trip to the state capital, Olympia, in the fifth grade. Herrera Beutler has said that that trip was what first sparked her interest in a career in public office. Visiting the capital inspired the idea, along with the encouragement of her parents' political activism in Republican congresswoman Linda Smith's campaign.

Lucille Roybal-Allard is the first Democrat, woman, and Hispanic to represent her greater Los Angeles district since its creation in 1973. Roybal-Allard's story also illustrates the general theme of familial political socialization, but her biography also reveals another common theme among Latinas in Congress, that of having a family member in elective office. Roybal-Allard is the eldest daughter of the late congressman Edward R. Roybal. Like the Latinas who preceded her, Roybal-Allard was exposed to politics at an early age. Her father in 1949 was the first Hispanic elected to the Los Angeles City Council, and her mother was active in his campaigns. Roybal-Allard has acknowledged her parents as Latino pioneers in California politics, and her father is called the "dean of California Latino legislators." She is quoted as saying, "My mom has been a tremendous role model, she's really the one who has helped to support and spearhead my father's career."[18]

Michelle Lujan Grisham's story provides another example. She was elected as a Democrat to the 113th Congress in New Mexico's First District in 2012. Her grandfather Eugene Lujan was the first Hispanic chief justice of the New Mexico Supreme Court. Additionally, former representative Manuel Luján (R-NM) and current representative Ben Ray Luján (D-NM) are her relatives.[19] A final example is that of Loretta and Linda Sánchez, both Democrats elected in 1996 and 2002, respectively, to represent California congressional districts. They are the first sisters and the first women of any relation ever to serve in Congress.[20] Having a politically active family, therefore, is a theme among these Latinas and shows us how their private lives influence their pursuit of public political office.

CAREERS OF SERVICE AND THE IMPORTANCE
OF LOCAL EXPERIENCE

Another commonality shared by Latinas in Congress is their differing pathways to federal office holding when compared to other office holders. While most members of Congress move from careers in law and business, Latinas have entered from work in communities and public service in local politics. The aforementioned examples of Ileana Ros-Lehtinen and Nydia Velázquez came to public office after working as educators. However, both women had political experience prior to running for Congress. Similar to Ros-Lehtinen, who served in the Florida House of Representatives from 1982 until 1986, Velázquez entered local politics prior to becoming a member of Congress. She taught political science and Puerto Rican studies through the early 1980s. By 1983 she was appointed as a special assistant to Congressman Edolphous Towns (D-Brooklyn) in the Tenth District of New York. Then in 1984 she became the first Latina to serve on the New York City Council, eventually becoming the national director of the Migration Division Office in the Department of Labor and Human Resourses of Puerto Rico.

Similarly, Jaime Herrera Beutler went from being a university student to holding temporary positions in both the Washington State Senate and in Washington, DC, at the White House Office of Political Affairs, which further ignited her interest in government and public service. Before running for Congress, she gained political experience as a senior legislative aide for Congresswoman Cathy McMorris Rodgers (R-Spokane), where Beutler served as the congresswoman's lead adviser on health care policy, education, and veterans' and women's issues.[21]

Latinas also often first gain valuable political experience through community, social, or church activism (S. García et al. 2008: 131). This community activism, often underappreciated as political engagement, teaches valuable skills, such as how to bring people together, build connections, and plan and execute successful meetings and events (Hardy-Fanta 1993). As a result of her community work, Grace Napolitano, a liberal Democrat and daughter of Mexican immigrants, was elected to serve California's Thirty-Fourth Congressional District in the greater Los Angeles area in 1998. She built her political resume in the same way as most Latinas in Congress—entry into local electoral politics. Her road to Congress began in 1974 when Napolitano was appointed a commissioner on the International Friendship Commission and was charged with cultivating a sister-city relationship between her city of residence and Hermosillo, Mexico. The program's focus on cultural exchanges and the experience of being politically engaged pulled Napolitano into public service.[22] Though she "hated politics," she says she got involved to show her children and "other youngsters on this side how lucky they were."[23] Here again, we see the interconnectedness of local engagement in public service and the decision to run for elective office.

Similarly, Roybal-Allard worked for the nonprofit sector before becoming a stay-at-home mother. She was approached to enter politics by political activists in California after she had raised her two children. In an interview about her entrance into electoral politics, she said she "shocked everyone including myself" when she decided to run.[24] Since then, Roybal-Allard has never lost an election.

Another example of how community work can lead to electoral pursuits is that of Loretta Sánchez. She was a financial planner who became the first Mexican American to represent Orange County in Congress in 1996. When she was asked what inspired her to run for Congress, however, Sánchez replied,

> When I was working as a financial planner, I spent some of my free time volunteering in summer school classes and mentoring programs in math and science. The experience inspired me to go to the Anaheim School Board members and try to get these programs in all the schools. But they did not act. I then tried to make an appointment with my congressman, Bob Dornan, but he refused to meet with me. I remember thinking that if I wanted to talk about a defense issue he would have been all over it, but it seemed he had no interest in education. If he was treating me this way I know he was probably treating others that way and he had to go. At that point I went home and said, "I'm going to run for Congress." I wanted to see change and I felt that I could do it. (Lavariega Monforti 2015)

It was her volunteer activity, not her career in business, that kindled her interest in politics.

In 2002 Linda Sánchez joined her sister Loretta in Congress, representing California's Thirty-Ninth Congressional District, which includes southeastern Los Angeles County. These sisters are the first sisters and the first women of any relation ever to serve in Congress. After working her way through school as a bilingual aide and an English as a Second Language (ESL) instructor, Linda Sánchez earned her law degree from the University of California, Los Angeles in 1995. She then worked in a private law practice, specializing in labor law, before going to work for the International Brotherhood of Electrical Workers Local 441 and the National Electrical Contractors Association in 1998. Prior to her congressional election, Sánchez served as the executive secretary-treasurer for the Orange County Central Labor Council, AFL-CIO. She started her political career after a new Thirty-Ninth Congressional District was created following the 2000 Census. Although the Sánchez sisters, as a financial planner and attorney, to a degree embody the more traditional professional pathway of the majority of members of Congress, both were also active in community service, suggesting once again the importance of this community activism in preparing Latinas for the political arena.

INTERSECTING IDENTITIES, INTERSECTING BARRIERS, AND POLICY FOCUSES

Another commonality across the Latinas in Congress is that their respective policy focuses stem from the multiple marginalities they face, as Puerto Rican, Cuban, and Mexican American women—that is, as Latinas and women of color. Here, it is important to pause from the use of pan-ethnic identifiers like Latina, and focus our attention on the fact that this group includes one Cuban American, one Puerto Rican, and seven Mexican American members of Congress, and all are women who have significant interests in the well-being of families and communities. The specific country-of-origin backgrounds held by these women, however, intersect with their stories as Latinas and congresswomen and the issues they choose to pursue as elected officials.

Ileana Ros-Lehtinen, the first Latina and to date the only Cuban American woman to hold a seat in the US Congress, represents a district including the cities of Miami and Miami Beach. In 1980, 50% of the district's population was of "Spanish origin," and parts were heavily Cuban (Barone 1987). Ros-Lehtinen ran in a special election after the death of incumbent Democratic congressman Claude Pepper, who had held the seat for twenty-eight years. With her experience as a state senator, Ros-Lehtinen defeated Democrat Gerald Richman, 53% to 47%. During her years in the Florida legislature, Ros-Lehtinen became identified with local and foreign policy issues, including the cause of a "free Cuba," a concern of hers stemming from her Cuban heritage. Moreno and Rae (1992) argue that her election is one of the clearest examples of a campaign in which ethnic factors predominated over all others. The election of Ros-Lehtinen continued a process of Cuban American empowerment in Dade County that began in 1982 and was a response in part to the targeting of Cubans and the Spanish language itself as being anti-American.[25]

The 1980s witnessed Cuban Americans winning seven seats in the Florida State House of Representatives, three seats in the state senate, plus the mayorships of Miami, West Miami, North Miami, Sweetwater, and Hialeah Gardens. The empowerment by Cuban Americans in South Florida has come almost exclusively under the Republican banner, and the 1989 special election strengthened and reinforced the trend of increasing Cuban American support for the GOP (Moreno and Rae 1992). Much was made of electing the first Cuban American to Congress in 1989. However, Ros-Lehtinen was also the first Republican woman elected to the House from Florida. Yet little was made of the fact that she is a woman (Moreno and Rae 1992). Ros-Lehtinen has been in Congress for more than twenty-five years and now serves Florida's Twenty-Seventh Congressional District. Today Ros-Lehtinen is the most senior Republican woman in the US House, and in 2011 she gave the first Republican response to the State of the Union address in Spanish.[26]

As a result of their intersectional identity, Latinas may pursue policies and ideas that others do not. For instance, Nydia Velázquez made two significant contributions that perhaps would not have been achieved in her absence. The first contribution was the nomination and confirmation of Sonia Sotomayor to the US Supreme Court, and the second is the pronounced support for women and minority-owned businesses. Her support for both issues is connected to her identity as a Puerto Rican woman. The former is tied to her commitment to advancing Latinas, and the latter, organizing for workers' rights, is the legacy of her father's activism in Puerto Rico. During the press conference held to announce the Congressional Hispanic Caucus's endorsement of Sonia Sotomayor, Velázquez said,

> As a woman, as a Latina, as a New Yorker, as a Puerto Rican and as the chairwoman of the Congressional Hispanic Caucus, it gives me great pride to see that President Barack Obama has nominated such a highly qualified and distinguished individual. Her experience and qualifications speak for themselves. . . . For Latinas and Latinos across the country this is a historic nomination. We feel a sense of pride when we see someone from our community rise past so many obstacles and challenges and earn her place—and I repeat, earned her place—on the highest court of our land.[27]

Her statement reveals Velázquez's gendered and ethnic identity as well as her knowledge of the barriers confronted by Puerto Ricans in the political establishment. The gendered, ethnic, and immigrant identities she focuses on in this quotation are turned into sources of power and legitimacy, turning the intersection of her Latina marginality on its head (Hancock 2007; Simien 2007). Sotomayor's identity as a Puerto Rican woman is transformed from an identity that would stereotypically be seen as negative or limiting to one that accentuates her success—despite the typical double stereotype of being a woman and a Latina.

The other policy contribution is Velázquez's strong support for women and minority-owned businesses as the ranking member on the House Committee on Small Business, for which she was named the inaugural Woman of the Year by *Hispanic Business* magazine. For example, she sponsored HR 3867, the Small Business Contracting Program Improvements Act, in 2007, which passed the House and was designed to expand opportunities for women and disabled veteran entrepreneurs. Her support for the bill reveals her intersecting identities, harkening back to her and her father's engagement with the business community in Puerto Rico while also advocating for women in business.

Lucille Roybal-Allard was the first of a series of Mexican American woman in the Southwest elected to Congress in 1992, and she represents the most Latino district (based on total population) in the nation, at 86.5% Latino. The congresswoman accomplished many firsts, as she was the first woman to chair the Congressional Hispanic Caucus and the first Latina appointed to the House Appropriations Committee.[28] Congresswoman Roybal-Allard has spent her time in the House focused on issues of central importance to women and Mexican Americans, such as health care, with a particular focus on women and children's health care needs, domestic violence, and immigration. Roybal-Allard has consistently held ratings of 100% from groups such as the National Organization for Women and the League of United Latin American Citizens.

As a Mexican American woman, she labored on the DREAM Act as one of its original coauthors. The act carries particular importance in Mexican American communities in that it is designed to ensure undocumented students a path to citizenship and college attendance in the United States with in-state tuition. Royal-Allard also led the Congressional Women's Working Group on Immigration and said she feels "we are losing the focus of the catastrophe and the humanitarian crisis of the children and these women" who arrive at the Texas-Mexico border in the hundreds daily from Central America and particularly Mexico.[29]

While Roybal-Allard has publicly stated that her work is aimed to benefit her primarily Hispanic district, it may have a residual effect on Hispanics everywhere. She uses a sweeping definition of what the issues of importance are to Hispanics. "Latinos in the past have been placed in a very narrow slot, [one that assumes] that we only care about immigration and bilingual education when the reality is that all the issues of American society are also our issues," she says. She goes on to say that in her view, the Latino movement has graduated from the politics of protest to the politics of inclusion. "It's no longer about howling at the door and shouting in the streets," she states. "Hispanics have garnered strength from their numbers and are finally getting the attention that their emerging political power demands."[30]

Loretta Sánchez has a strong record on human rights (with an 85% approval rating from the Human Rights Campaign) and is a member of the bipartisan Congressional Human Rights Caucus.[31] Her parents were immigrants from Mexico, and she has advocated for increased educational benefits for children, such as Head Start programs. In an interview, one can see how her personal experiences and intersecting ethnic, immigrant, and class identities blend to shape her policy goals. She states, "Head Start had an incredible impact on me.... I spoke my first words in Head Start. I believe that a preschool education program is important for all children, but particularly low-income and immigrant kids. In Orange County, 7,500 children qualify for Head Start, but we only have funding for 3,500. And while the Republicans might have tried to make it a requirement, the fact is in 1995 they tried to cut the entire program and have since continued to cut funding."[32] Linda Sánchez, Loretta Sánchez's sister and thus also the daughter of immigrants, focuses legislatively on issues of labor, trade, and families. And like her Latina contemporaries, Linda Sánchez has been an outspoken opponent of Arizona-style anti-immigrant legislation. As is true for the sisters profiled here, the Sánchezes' backgrounds as children of Mexican immigrants have greatly influenced their policy goals.

We learn from this discussion that intersecting identities, including the country of origin of Latina congresswomen and their families, play a significant role in the policy agendas of these political leaders. But how do these women experience and think about their intersectional identities as women and Latinx, now that they are in Congress? Does their intersectionality matter now that they are members of Congress and face complex decision making in policy choices and everyday interactions? I turn to this question in the next section.

NAVIGATING THE COMPLEXITIES OF MULTIPLE MARGINALITIES AND MAKING DIFFICULT DECISIONS

The intersectionality of Latinas in Congress and the multiple marginalities they face can make their political roles highly complex and require difficult decisions by the lawmakers. An instructive case is that of Loretta Sánchez, whose political career includes highlights such as her involvement in the Congressional Hispanic

Caucus (CHC) and her powerful committee appointments. In 2006 Sánchez withdrew from the CHC's Political Action Committee because the caucus chairman, Joe Baca, authorized political contributions to members of his family who were running for election (Hearn 2007). There were also claims that he was improperly elected chairman of the caucus because the vote failed to use secret ballots, as bylaws required. Sánchez claimed that the chairman repeatedly treated the CHC's female members, including her, with disrespect (Hearn 2007). She rejoined once the CHC chairman was replaced. Her response shows how managing multiple marginalities can require her to make difficult choices in her allegiances—in this case, calling into question the behavior of a male colleague with whom she shared an ethnic identity in part because of his actions against women. Sánchez's decision to make public her objections about a coethnic colleague caused many to question her sense of ethnic solidarity (Hearn 2007).

When asked how she has managed such complexities, Sánchez responded,

> As hard as it is to be a Latina some days, it's even harder to be a woman in politics. Okay? So my congressional friends that are black and women say, it's the double whammy. First, we get it because we are women, and then we get it because we are a minority—and I have seen that play out over and over, even within the Congress, as we try to get our work done.[33]

This tension for Sánchez reveals circumstances that may compel political leaders to have to choose between their identities—as in this case, when Sánchez decided to stand with women when a coethnic male colleague treated females unfairly.

Latina congressional leaders have to make other choices in difficult situations, deciding, for instance, how to portray their identity. Sánchez reveals another case in point:

> When Nancy Pelosi became the first woman Speaker of the House . . . we saw one of those barriers being broken down. . . . I was rushing to vote, and I jumped into an elevator as the doors were closing, and there were two southern gentlemen there who were trying to be polite and make conversation with me. And one turned to me and he said, "So, whose office do you work in?" And I'm wearing a suit, I'm wearing my member pin—and I was angry and just about to blast this guy. Then I remember my mom always telling me, "You catch more flies with honey than vinegar," right, so I turned to him, and I said very sweetly, "I don't work for somebody in this building, I have my own office in the building." And he turned and looked at his friend and they looked at each other like deer in the headlights, and the elevator doors opened and they scurried out because even though we had a female Speaker of the House, the assumption was that if I'm in the elevator in the Capitol, I must be the secretary or the staffer or the intern. I think there are huge perception problems that women have to overcome. I think we're judged by far harsher standards. . . . We still have many, many double standards or harder standards and hurdles that we have to overcome in order to be taken seriously.

Sánchez decided how to respond in this situation, simply emphasizing her identity as a member of Congress, and not highlighting her feminism overtly. She added, "I definitely see it as part of my charge as a member of Congress to challenge people when they have assumptions about whom or what I am or who or what I can accomplish . . . but it's very tough."[34]

We can see other instances in which intersecting identities call upon Latina congresswomen to make difficult choices. Ros-Lehtinen's public policy stances and her private life intersected in such ways. In 2010 the *Miami Herald* first reported that Ros-Lehtinen's daughter Amanda was living openly as Rodrigo, a transgender man and lesbian/gay/bisexual/transgender (LGBT) rights activist. Shortly thereafter, Ros-Lehtinen in a complex choice became the first Republican member of the US Congress to cosponsor the Respect for Marriage Act, which would repeal the Defense of Marriage Act.[35] In July 2012 Ros-Lehtinen also became the first Republican in the House to support same-sex marriage.[36] Here her family ties trumped her political party identity.

Finally, Gloria Negrete McLeod also made a difficult decision. She has written about the need for women, and Latinas, in particular, to run for elected office, as well as the barriers they may face. Like Ros-Lehtinen and Velázquez before her, Negrete McLeod entered politics from the field of education. She is Los Angeles–born but has a relatively close connection to her family's immigrant roots. Like many of the Latinas I examine, she is a mother and began her journey to Congress through local-level political positions. Her multiple identities influenced her political work in Congress. For instance, her role as a mother drew her to volunteer to serve on the Committee on Agriculture because she was concerned with issues of children's nutrition. But these issues were also what pushed her to make the decision to return to local politics.[37] She said, "My desire to represent this community locally, where I have lived for more than 40 years, and where I have long served as an elected official, won out."[38] She described her decision to run for Congress as an extension of the public service career she had been building over the previous two decades. In February 2014 she announced her intention not to run for reelection for her congressional seat and instead to run for the San Bernardino County Board of Supervisors. "My heart is here in the district," Negrete McLeod said in a written statement.[39] Her campaign for the San Bernardino County Board of Supervisors was unsuccessful, as she lost the November 2014 election to Republican state assemblyman Curt Hagman.

One can easily see that the intersecting identities of Latinas in Congress can result in situations where difficult decisions must be made, often where one identity will take precedent in guiding the decision making. Earlier work on women of color who were elected officials serving at the state and local levels shows that "their political ambition to achieve higher office may be influenced by factors such as their current level of office, prior socialization, initial political motivation, perceptions of biases or fairness in the political structure, and sociodemographic and political characteristics" (Lien et al. 2008: 10). According to Hardy-Fanta, "Women focus on participation rather than on power, on connecting people to other people to achieve change" (Hardy-Fanta 1993: 13). The intersectional lens through which office seeking is viewed by women of color is reaffirmed by the example of Negrete McLeod, where her commitment to serving Latino communities' interests rather than climbing the ladder of political power drove her decision not to run for congressional reelection.

Conclusion and Discussion

We are often presented with dichotomous views of elected officials as either female or male, minority or majority, Anglo or ethnic (Hancock 2007). For example, this is the kind of reporting we are exposed to from official sources:

> One hundred three women (a record number) serve in the 113th Congress: 83 in the House, including 3 Delegates, and 20 in the Senate. There are 43 African American Members of the House and 2 in the Senate. This House number includes 2 Delegates. There are 37 Hispanic or Latino Members (a record number) serving: 33 in the House, including 1 Delegate and the Resident Commissioner, and 4 in the Senate. Thirteen Members (10 Representatives, 2 Delegates, and 1 Senator) are Asian American or Pacific Islanders. Two American Indians (Native Americans) serve in the House.[40]

But such representations are highly problematic because they limit our view of the multiple and intersecting identities held by elected leaders. I have demonstrated in this research that these intersecting identities are important in that they impact decisions made about whether to seek office, policy preferences, and simply navigating the complex roles of political leadership. Latina elected officials can and have been overlooked when categories such as ethnicity and gender representation in Congress remain separate and fail to use an intersectional approach. My examination of Latina office holders in Congress reveals that these intersecting identities have important ramifications for these political leaders.

Previous literature demonstrates that the political leadership of Latinas is motivated by their desire to improve public policies that affect families and Latino communities (Hardy-Fanta 1993). Naples (1998) shows that Latinas enter politics because they are disappointed that the issues that concern them are ignored. My investigation in this chapter reveals as well that Latinas have intersecting and marginalized ethnic and gender identities that influence their politics. These blended identities stem from their personal life experiences, in their families and in their early experiences in local and community activities and politics. For most Latinas, politics is more than merely an election or voting. For the Latinas profiled here, politics is what they experience in their daily lives, and these experiences spark their interest in political office holding. The political experiences of family members and their careers in public service combine with their intersecting identities and guide them as they decide to run for office, pursue policy agendas, and navigate complex decision making.

As demographics continue to shift and we see increased voting by women as well as across Latino communities, we are likely to see an increase in the number of Latinas being elected. There is a need for greater representation of Latinas in elected office. Bejarano (2013) argues that women of color going forward may be aided rather than hurt by how the intersection of their racial and gender identities influences American voters. She argues that women of color, as candidates, can secure more public support by appealing to a wider array of communities and voter coalitions, including both women and minority communities. She points out that these women are often better prepared for office holding, and they are perceived as less threatening than their male counterparts by white voters. If these predictions are borne out, we may witness a wave of Latinas being elected over the next generation—which may importantly change the nature of political debate at the local as well as national level.

Democracy rests on the foundation of open access and equal voice. Latinas, as elected officials and as voters, strengthen that foundation. Latino communities are growing at a rapid pace, and in a number of states such as California and Texas, Latino children constitute the majority of students in public schools. The demographic shift is already under way, and the elementary students of today are the voters of tomorrow.

Notes

1. The word *Latinx* (pronounced *La-teen-ex*) is the gender-neutral alternative to *Latino*, *Latina*, and *Latin@*, and is used interchangeably with the word *Hispanic*.

2. *Congresistas* means *congresswomen*.

3. The terms *Latina/o* and *Hispanic* are used interchangeably throughout this chapter.

4. Barbara Farrell Vucanovich was elected to serve in Congress in 1983. She was a Republican from Nevada who served until 1997. Until recently her Hispanic ancestry was unknown, and she did not run as a Hispanic candidate. Her father was of Irish ancestry, and her mother was of English and Hispanic ancestry from Southern California.

5. http://www.cawp.rutgers.edu/fast_facts/women_of_color/FastFacts_LatinasinOffice. php.

6. See Carroll 1994; Burrell 1996, 1998; Fiber and Fox 2005; Fox and Lawless 2011; Lawless and Fox 2008; Dolan 2008; Ford 2010; Norris and Inglehart 2008; Sanbonmatsu 2013.

7. The Spanish term *machismo* is a common reference to Latino masculinity, particularly the gender construction of extreme traditional masculinity in Latin American and Caribbean societies. Here I use the term to refer to any form of sexism or attitudes that place males in a dominant position over females and other males. For more on this, see http:// link.springer.com/referenceworkentry/10.1007%2F978-1-4419-5659-0_475.

8. Martinez, a San Antonio native, was general counsel and president of the Mexican American Legal Defense and Education Fund during this time.

9. Vilma Martinez, Testimony before the US Commission on Civil Rights (1975) (from Mexican American Voices, Political Power, at Digital History: http://www.digitalhistory. uh.edu/disp_textbook.cfm?smtID=3&psid=622.

10. http://www.census.gov/population/www/documentation/twps0056/tab01.pdf.

11. http://www.census.gov/prod/2001pubs/c2kbr01-3.pdf.

12. Latinas have a long history of activism in the ranks of civic, social, and political organizations such as Cruz Azul Mexicana (1920s), Spanish-Speaking Parent-Teacher Associations and the Ladies League of United Latin American Citizens (1930s), the American G.I. Forum (1940s), the Political Association of Spanish-Speaking Organizations (1960s), the Raza Unida party (1970s), and Texans for the Educational Advancement of Mexican Americans (1970s), as well as the Industrial Area Foundation and organizations such as Communities Organized for Public Service (1980s). In the 1970s the Mexican American Legal Defense and Educational Fund established the Chicana Rights Project. Latinas also have a long history of labor activism.

13. See http://www.pewhispanic.org/interactives/mapping-the-latino-electorate-by-congressional-district/for more information.

14. http://ros-lehtinen.house.gov/.

15. http://www.makers.com/ileana-ros-lehtinen.

16. http://www.loc.gov/rr/hispanic/congress/velazquez.html.

17. http://www.oregonlive.com/hovde/index.ssf/2010/12/washington_states_new_congress.html and http://seattletimes.com/html/localnews/2014663775_congresswoman02m.html.

18. http://www.somosprimos.com/sp2010/spdec10/spdec10.htm.

19. Grisham's family experience also motivated her in an additional way. Her sister was diagnosed with a brain tumor at age two and she passed away at the age of twenty-one. Grisham's parents' substantial medical bills have led Grisham to emphasize health care policy and insurance reform.

20. Concurrent filial service has a bit of a history. From 1995 to 2009, such service was exemplified by Senator Ted Kennedy (D-MA), who died in August 2009, and his youngest child, Representative Patrick Kennedy (D-RI), who retired this year. Also Rand Paul (R-KY), son of eleven-term representative Ron Paul (R-TX) served simultaneously. The Levin brothers have served in Congress together as well. For more, see http://www.npr.org/2014/01/28/267309975/brothers-levin-near-the-end-of-a-32-year-congressional-partnership. See also http://www.politicsdaily.com/2010/11/09/congress-as-a-family-business-brothers-and-sisters-and-sons-i/ for more detailed information on family ties in Congress.

21. http://seattletimes.com/html/localnews/2014663775_congresswoman02m.html.

22. http://books.google.com/books?id=Dw2ZjkgjchkC&pg=PA678&lpg=PA678&dq=grace+napolitano+norwalk+hermosillo+sister+city&source=bl&ots=hBIF8mvGFK&sig=V2VV5uEvheA7kwXuVpBeAhUqCiI&hl=en&sa=X&ei=vesgVKykFdSfyATDuoGgDg&ved=0CDMQ6AEwAw#v=onepage&q=grace%20napolitano%20norwalk%20hermosillo%20sister%20city&f=false.

23. http://napolitano.house.gov/about-me/full-biography.

24. http://www.latinamericanstudies.org/latinos/roybal-allard.htm.

25. In 1988, Proposition Eleven, for "English as the official language," was placed on the Florida ballot. Hispanics were the only group that consistently opposed the amendment, voting over 80% against the measure.

26. http://issuu.com/humanrightscampaign/docs/winter_2013-equality-magazine/23?e=0/1818540.

27. http://votesmart.org/public-statement/436826/press-conference-with-rep-nydia-velazquez-d-ny-chair-congressional-hispanic-caucus-the-supreme-court-nomination-of-judge-sonia-sotomayor-transcript#.VCB7fvldUmk.

28. After serving three terms in the California State Assembly, Roybal-Allard ran for her father's congressional seat after his retirement in 1992.

29. http://www.nbcnews.com/storyline/immigration-border-crisis/roybal-allard-focuses-attention-girls-arriving-border-n157726.

30. http://www.latinamericanstudies.org/latinos/roybal-allard.htm.

31. See http://members-of-congress.insidegov.com/l/302/Loretta-Sanchez.

32. http://www.washingtonpost.com/wp-srv/liveonline/politics/freemedia111599.htm

33. http://www.c-span.org/video/?321775-2/roundtable-hispanic-caucus-institute-conference.

34. Ibid.

35. Ryan J. Reilly (2011). "Ros-Lehtinen First GOPer to Sponsor Bill Repealing DOMA." *Talking Points Memo*. September 23.

36. Grindley, Lucas 2012. "A First: GOP Congresswoman Supports Marriage Equality." *The Advocate*. July 13. https://www.advocate.com/politics/marriage-equality/2012/07/13/gop-congresswoman-first-house-her-party-support-marriage.

37. http://www.agri-pulse.com/Meet-the-Freshman-Negrete-McLeod-California.asp.

38. http://www.latimes.com/local/political/la-me-pc-gloria-megrete-mcleod-house-quit-20140218-story.html.

39. Ibid.

40. http://www.senate.gov/CRSReports/crs-publish.cfm?pid=%26oBL%2BR%5CC%3F%oA.

References

Barone, Michael. 1987. *The Almanac of American Politics*. Washington, DC: National Journal.

Bejarano, Christina E. 2013. *The Latina Advantage: Gender, Race, and Political Success*. Austin: University of Texas Press.

Burrell, Barbara. 1996. *A Woman's Place Is in the House*. Ann Arbor: University of Michigan Press.

———. 1998. "Campaign Finance: Women's Experience in the Modern Era." Pp. 26–37 in *Women and Elective Office: Past, Present and Future*, edited by S. Thomas and C. Wilcox. Oxford: Oxford University Press.

Carrigan, William D., and Clive Webb. 2013. *Forgotten Dead: Mob Violence against Mexicans in the United States, 1848–1928*. New York: Oxford University Press.

Carroll, Susan J. 1994. *Women as Candidates in American Politics*. Bloomington: University of Indiana Press.

Chávez, Dan D. 1996. *Soledad Chávez Chacon: A New Mexico Political Pioneer, 1890–1936*. Albuquerque: University of New Mexico Printing Services.

Cruz Takash, Paula. 1997. "Breaking Barriers to Representation: Chicana/Latina Elected Officials in California." Pp. 412–434 in *Women Transforming Politics: An Alternative Reader*, edited by C. J. Cohen, K. Jones, and J. Tronto. New York: New York University Press.

Darling, Marsha J. 1998. "African American Women in State Elective Office in the South." Pp. 150–162 in *Women and Elective Office: Past, Present, and Future*, edited by Sue Thomas and Clyde Wilcox. Oxford University Press.

Delgado, Richard. 2009. "The Law of the Noose: A History of Latino Lynching." *Harvard Civil Rights–Civil Liberties Law Review* 44: 297–312.

Dolan, Kathleen. 2008. "Women as Candidates in American Politics: The Continuing Impact of Sex and Gender" Pp. 110–127 in *Political Women and American Democracy*, edited by C. Wolbrecht, K. Beckwith, and L. Baldez. New York: Cambridge University Press.

Fiber, Pamela, and Richard Fox. 2005. "A Tougher Road for Women? Assessing the Role of Gender in Congressional Elections" Pp. 64–80 in *Gender and American Politics: Women, Men, and the Political Process*, edited by S. Tolleson-Rinehart and J. Josephson. 2nd ed. Armonk, NY: M. E. Sharpe.

Ford, Lynne. 2010. *Women and Politics: The Pursuit of Equality*. Boston: Cengage Learning.

Fox, Richard, and Jennifer Lawless. 2011. "Gendered Perceptions and Political Candidacies: A Central Barrier to Women's Equality in Electoral Politics." *American Journal of Political Science* 55(1): 59–73.

Fraga, Luis Ricardo, Valerie Martinez-Ebers, Linda Lopez, and Ricardo Ramírez. 2005. "Strategic Intersectionality: Gender, Ethnicity, and Political Incorporation." Presented at the annual meeting of the American Political Science Association, August 31–September 4. Washington, DC.

Garcia, Chris, and Gabriel Sanchez. 2008. *Moving (into) the Mainstream? Latinos in the U.S. Political System?* Upper Saddle River, NJ: Pearson/Prentice Hall.

García, Sonia R. 2001. "Motivational and Attitudinal Factors amongst Latinas in U.S. Electoral Politics." *National Women's Studies Association Journal* 13: 112–122.

García, Sonia R., Valerie Martinez-Ebers, Irasema Coronado, Sharon A. Navarro, and Patricia A. Jaramillo. 2008. *Políticas: Latina Public Officials in Texas*. Austin: University of Texas Press.

García Bedolla, Lisa, Katherine Tate, and Janelle Wong. 2005. "Indelible Effects: The Impact of Women of Color in the U.S. Congress" Pp. 235–252 in *Women and Elective Office: Past, Present, and Future*, edited by S. Thomas and C. Wilcox. New York: Oxford University Press.

Geer, John, Wendy Schiller, and Jeffery Segal. 2013. *Gateways to Democracy: An Introduction to American Government*. Boston: Cengage Learning.

Hancock, Ange-Marie. 2007. "When Multiplication Doesn't Equal Quick Addition: Examining Intersectionality as a Research Paradigm." *Perspectives on Politics* 5(1): 63–79.

Hardy-Fanta, Carol. 1993. *Latina Politics, Latino Politics: Gender, Culture, and Political Participation in Boston*. Philadelphia: Temple University Press.

———. 2002. "Latina Women and Political Leadership: Implications for Latino Community Empowerment." Pp. 192–212 in *Latino Politics in Massachusetts: Struggles, Strategies, and Prospects*, edited by C. Hardy-Fanta and J. N. Gerson. New York: Routledge.

Hearn, Josephine. 2007. "Sanchez Accuses Democrat of Calling Her a 'Whore,' Resigns from Hispanic Group." *Politico*, January 31. http://www.politico.com/news/stories/0107/2572.html.

Jaramillo, Patricia A. 2010. "Building a Theory, Measuring a Concept: Exploring Intersectionality and Latina Activism at the Individual Level." *Journal of Women, Politics and Policy* 31(3): 193–216.

Lavariega Monforti, Jessica. 2015. Personal interview with congresswoman.

Lavariega Monforti, J., and Sarah Allen Gershon. 2016. "Una Ventaja? A Survey Experiment of the Viability of Latina Candidate." Pp. 23–29 in *Latinas in American Politics: Changing and Embracing Political Tradition.* Edited by Sharon A. Navarro, Samantha L. Hernandez, and Leslie A. Navarro. Lanham, MD: Rowman and Littlefield.

Lawless, Jennifer L., and Richard L. Fox. 2008. *Why Are Women Still Not Running for Public Office?* Brookings Institute: Issues in Governance Studies. Washington, DC. http://www.brookings.edu/~/media/research/files/papers/2008/5/women%20lawless%20fox/05_women_lawless_fox.pdf.

Lien, Pei-te, Carol Hardy-Fanta, Dianne M. Pinderhughes, and Christine M. Sierra. 2008. "Expanding Categorization at the Intersection of Race and Gender: 'Women of Color' as a Political Category for African American, Latina, Asian American, and American Indian Women." Presented at the annual meeting of the American Political Science Association, August 27–31. Boston, MA.

Mansbridge, Jane. 1999. "Should Blacks Represent Blacks and Women Represent Women? A Contingent 'Yes.'" *Journal of Politics* 61(3): 628–657.

Martínez, Elizabeth. 2005. "Beyond Black/White: The Racisms of Our Time." *Social Justice* 20(1/2): 51–52.

Martinez, Vilma. 1975. "Testimony before the US Commission on Civil Rights" Mexican American Voices, Political Power, at Digital History. http://www.digitalhistory.uh.edu/disp_textbook.cfm?smtID=3&psid=622.

Michelson, Melissa R. 2013. "The Fight for School Equity in Chicago's Latino Neighborhoods" Pp. 73–80 in *The Roots of Latino Urban Agency,* edited by S. Navarro and R. Rosales. Denton: University of North Texas Press.

Moreno, Dario, and Nicol Rae. 1992. "Ethnicity and Partnership: The Eighteenth Congressional District in Miami." Pp. 186–204 in *Miami Now,* edited by G. Grenier and A. Stepick. Gainesville: University Press of Florida.

Naples, N. 1998. *Grassroots Warriors: Activist Mothering, Community Work, and the War on Poverty.* Routlege: New York.

Norris, Pippa, and Ronald Inglehart. 2008. "Cracking the Marble Ceiling: Cultural Barriers Facing Women Leaders." Harvard University: Kennedy School of Government. Cambridge, MA. http://www.hks.harvard.edu/fs/pnorris/Acrobat/Marble%20ceiling%20professional%20of ormat.pdf.

Petersen, Kristen A., Carol Hardy-Fanta, and Karla Armenoff. 2005. "'As Tough as It Gets': Women in Boston Politics, 1921–2004." *Center for Women in Politics and Public Policy Publications.* Paper 13. http://scholarworks.umb.edu/cwppp_pubs/13.

Pinney, Neil, and George Serra. 1999. "The Congressional Black Caucus and Vote Cohesion: Placing the Caucus within House Voting Patterns." *Political Research Quarterly* 52(3): 583–608.

Pitkin, Hanna. 1967. *The Concept of Representation.* Los Angeles: University of California Press.

Sanbonmatsu, Kira. 2013. "The Candidacies of U.S. Women of Color for Statewide Executive Office." Presented at the Annual Conference of the American Political Science Association, August 29–September 1. Chicago.

Sepulveda, Emma. 1998. *From Border Crossing to the Campaign Trail: Chronicle of a Latina in Politics.* Falls Church, VA: Azul Editions.

Sierra, Christine. 2009. "Latinas and Electoral Politics: Movin' on Up." Pp. 144–164 in
    Gender and Elections, second edition, edited by S. J. Carroll and R. L. Fox. Cambridge:
    Cambridge University Press.

Simien, Evelyn. 2007. "Doing Intersectionality Research: From Conceptual Issues to
    Practical Examples." *Politics & Gender* 3(2): 36–43.

Swers, Michelle L., and Carin Larson. 2005. "Women in Congress: Do They Act as
    Advocates for Women's Issues?" Pp. 100–128 in *Women and Elective Office: Past, Present,
    and Future*, edited by S. Thomas and C. Wilcox. New York: Oxford University Press.

Tate, Katherine. 2003. *Black Faces in the Mirror: African Americans and Their Representatives
    in the U.S. Congress*. Princeton, NJ: Princeton University Press.

Thomas, Sue, and Susan Welch. 1991. "The Impact of Gender on Activities and Priorities of
    State Legislators." *Western Political Quarterly* 44: 445–456

Tienda, Marta, and Faith Mitchell, eds. 2006. "Multiple Origins, Uncertain Destinies:
    Hispanics and the American Future." National Research Council (US) Panel on Hispanics
    in the United States; Washington (DC): National Academies Press (US); 2, Multiple
    Origins, Hispanic Portrait. http://www.ncbi.nlm.nih.gov/books/NBK19804/.

Torres, María de los Angeles. 2001. *In the Land of Mirrors: Cuban Exile Politics in the United
    States*. Ann Arbor: University of Michigan Press.

7

Women in State Legislatures from the Gilded Age to the Global Age

Susan Welch

Only a few historians remember that the first woman governor in America was Hannah Callowhill Penn, who governed Pennsylvania and parts of Delaware and New Jersey from 1712 to 1726, after her husband, William Penn, became incapacitated and then died. A tough politician, she successfully fought attempts by the Crown and her own stepsons to remove her. But her example of women's leadership in an American state was not to be repeated for nearly two hundred years. And Hannah Penn was the sole woman in Pennsylvania's provincial government. There were no women in Pennsylvania's legislature nor in the legislatures of any other American colonies at the time.

It was not until 1894, 148 years after Hannah Penn's death, that the first women were elected to state legislatures. In that year, Colorado voters elected three Republican women to the Colorado lower house, only a year after women were given full suffrage rights in the state.[1] All three had migrated to Colorado from the East Coast, and all three had been active in public life: one as a member of the school board, another in securing veterans' rights, and a third as a newspaper writer. Just two years later, Utah elected the first woman upper house member, a doctor and a Democrat (Cox 1996).

The passage of the Nineteenth Amendment dramatically accelerated the pace at which these pioneers were joined by other women elected to state legislatures and other offices. At the time of the amendment's ratification debates, only twelve states had ever elected women to their state legislatures; and three years after the amendment's passage, that number nearly tripled to thirty-three.[2] The number of women serving in the legislatures increased from merely 25 who were able to vote on ratification in 1920 to 150 a decade later (Cox 1996: 23).[3]

But the pace of change slowed, and in 1940, there were still only 150 women state legislators. Today, there are more than 1,800, about 25% of all state legislators and about half what we would expect based on population proportion alone. Women in two states have more than 40% legislative membership, within shouting distance of equality, whereas, at the other extreme, in six states, including Wyoming, less than 15% of their legislatures are women, a token minority.[4]

As we draw near the one hundredth anniversary of the Nineteenth amendment, we examine the significant changes it has brought about in the composition of state legislatures. We first consider how women's legislative membership has grown during this near-century, and the societal factors that seem to have influenced the overall rate of growth. Then we explore what factors explain some of the differences among the states that are more and less advanced in their women's membership.

Historical Trends in Women's State Legislative Representation

No women held state or federal office for 105 years after the US Constitution was ratified. Nor, during 83 years of that time, could any women vote for state and national offices in any state. Women did have partial suffrage rights in a few states around the time of the Revolution. The last state, New Jersey, withdrew women's suffrage in 1807. From 1807 to 1890, some states offered very limited suffrage. For example, Kentucky allowed certain women to vote in school elections after 1838, and some women were elected to school boards.

Beginning in 1890, when Wyoming was added to the union and was already granting women the right to vote, states began adopting broader suffrage laws. In most states that adopted these laws, election of women to the state legislatures followed within a few years. Before the turn of the century, Idaho voters joined Colorado and Utah in electing women to their legislatures, and a total of sixteen women had served in those three states (Cox 1996: 13). Women were also elected to the legislatures in nine additional states between 1900 and 1920, when the Nineteenth Amendment was ratified.

Despite the significant increase in women legislators after ratification in 1920, in some states women were not able to run for legislative office in 1920—or in a few states, even after (Cox 1996: 23–24). In some states, ratification came after the filing deadline for the 1920 elections, so women were not on the ballot. In southern states, poll taxes were required to vote and run for office, and in some states, the deadline for payment was early in 1920. Other states had explicit gender qualifications for state legislative offices, so their constitutions had to be amended. Indeed, it was not until 1928 when the last state, Iowa, amended its constitution to allow women to run for state legislative office.

Following the initial burst of energy when the Nineteenth Amendment was passed, progress in increasing women's legislative representation was slow. Early analyses of women in state legislatures focused on this sluggish rate of growth (Martin and van de Vries 1937; van de Vries, 1948; Young 1950). Thirty years after the passage of the Nineteenth Amendment, women were still only 4% of state legislators. Eleanor Roosevelt (Roosevelt 1954) pointed to that as a bright spot compared to women's election to other offices. But it took nearly twenty more years (1973) for 4% to inch up to 5%. After that, progress accelerated, and by 1979 women were 10% of state legislators, a number that continued to climb for more than a decade. But then in the early 1990s, the rate of progress slowed, and today, nearly a century after the amendment, women still comprise only 25% of all state legislators.

Figure 7.1 illustrates patterns of growth in numbers of women state legislators: a fairly flat line before 1920, then, after the amendment, a modest uptick until about 1927, then another period of stagnation. Werner (1968) had also pointed to this pattern in her analysis of women's memberships through the middle 1960s. She attributed the slow progress during the 1930s to the social disruptions of the Depression.

Werner also noted a gain during World War II and a slowing afterward. The wartime election years of 1942 and 1944 added about 80 women to the ranks of state legislators. This was a tiny percentage of all state legislators, but it was a more than 50% increase over the 154 women serving in 1941. With millions of men overseas, new opportunities were opened for women in business, industry, public service, and other areas of the economy. Women volunteered in many organizations helping the war effort, such as the Red Cross and USO. It is not surprising, then, that more women were found in elected office, too.

In 1947, after most of the troops came home, women's representation decreased by about 20 women, followed by slow growth until 1955, when the number first passed the 300 mark. We know that women's roles shrank in much of the post–World War II economy when men returning from the war displaced women who had entered the workforce during the war. But we see only a pale reflection of this in women's state legislative membership, largely because the growth of women legislators during the war had been small in numbers even if larger in percentage terms.

Sluggish growth in the number of women members continued until the early 1970s, when in 1973, the number of women reached 400. Then, as Figure 7.1 demonstrates, growth accelerated and continued at this faster rate until the mid-1990s. Women

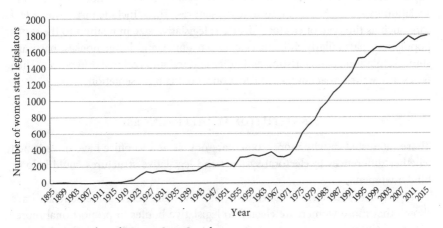

FIGURE 7.1 *Number of Women State Legislators, 1895–2015*
Cox 1996; Center for American Women and Politics 2016.

were 4.5% of legislators in 1971, barely more than when Roosevelt wrote twenty years earlier, but two decades later, women comprised more than 20% of legislative membership. During that period, in each session there were more women than in the past one.[5]

That growth spurt corresponded with congressional passage of the Equal Rights Amendment (ERA) followed by the political battles in the states for ratification. Those campaigning for ratification of the ERA in the states also worked to elect more women legislators as part of their strategy. In that sense, the passage of the ERA by Congress was a causal explanation for the election of more women. On the other hand, it is also the case that some conditions both accelerated the push to elect more women and the campaign to ratify the ERA. The feeling that the time had come for women to have an equal place in society affected both movements.

Growth slowed after 1993, but until 2003 more women were elected at each election. The numbers fell back by 12 in 2003, a loss more than made up in 2005. Modest upward growth resumed in 2005 until 2011, when, after an election dominated by Republican victories, once again the number of women legislators declined, this time by nearly 50. Nonetheless, in 2017, the number of female state legislators reached an all-time high of 1,844.

Factors Predicting Differences in Women's Representation

Several factors have shaped the growth in women's state legislative representation. Some factors, like the passage of the Nineteenth Amendment, World War II, and the women's rights movement, affected patterns in all states. Other factors are more specific to each state or region or to each legislative body. Nearly fifty years after Emmy Werner (Werner 1968)[6] observed that women's legislative membership reflected partisanship, membership size (women were a greater proportion of members of legislatures in smaller states with large legislatures), and region, scholars continue to propose new explanations for these interstate differences. We now explore several of the factors that, over the years, have been thought to explain variation in women's election to state legislatures. These include institutional factors, such as the type of electoral districts; legislative size in relation to the state's population, particularly differences between upper and lower houses; partisanship; population characteristics; and other cultural and regional differences. Then we examine the impact of those factors on women's representation.

INSTITUTIONAL DIFFERENCES

Those interested in why more women are not elected to office have investigated whether differences in electoral systems and legislative structures could help or hinder women.

Type of electoral district. Over time, and over the years, some scholars have shown that more women are elected to legislative bodies in proportional representation (PR) systems, where parties put up slates of candidates and voters elect multiple legislators in proportion to votes cast for each party (Darcy, Welch, and

Clark 1994; Kunovich and Paxton 2005; Rule 1987, 1994). American state legislators have rarely been elected in PR systems,[7] though multimember, non-PR districts (MMD) have been common. As late as 1950, thirty-nine states used multimember districts to elect at least some of their representatives (Kurtz 2011). In this form of election, often used in city councils, voters cast more than one vote, electing two or more candidates who run individually, sometimes on nonpartisan tickets.

Scholars have not agreed about the influence of non-PR multimember districts. The preponderance of the evidence suggests that women may do slightly better in multimember than single-member districts (Arceneaux 2001; King 2002; Moncrief and Thompson 1992; Welch and Studlar 1990, 1996).[8] Women might find it easier to run in districts where they are not the sole focus, or voters may like the idea that they could vote for both men and women in one district. To the extent party leaders have a say, they might believe it strategic to run both men and women. Nonetheless, MMD state legislative systems have declined significantly during the past fifty years, with only ten legislatures currently using them (Kurtz 2011).[9] In eight of these states, MMD are used only for the lower house. In those eight states in 2016, women are better represented in the lower house than the upper house in three states, less represented in three states, and tied in the other two.

It is difficult, if not impossible, to track the influence of multimember districts over time. Even if we could identify the years when multimember districts were used in each state, they are often not used for all seats.

Population per district. Over the years, women have been somewhat more likely to be elected in states with large legislatures relative to the size of their populations. An exemplar was New Hampshire, a small-population state with a lower house of more than four hundred members (Diamond 1977; Werner 1968). Legislatures with smaller memberships had proportionally fewer women members (see Nechemias 1987; Ondercin and Welch 2009; Sanbonmatsu 2002; Squire 1992). Observers speculated that seats in larger legislatures were less desirable than seats in smaller legislatures where there is more competition and individual members have more clout.[10]

Lower and upper houses. The first women state legislators were elected to the lower house, and since then, the proportion of women in the lower houses has always exceeded the proportion in the upper (Figure 7.2).[11] Upper houses are smaller in size than lower houses in every state that has two houses, so they are more elite and members are elected from larger population districts. Currently the median population per seat in upper houses is 119,000; in lower houses, 40,000. Only eight lower houses have a median population per seat of more than 100,000.

Immediately after the Nineteenth Amendment, the majority of states elected women to their lower houses. In the 1923 session, for example, only fifteen of the forty-eight states had no women lower house members. But it wasn't until 1973 that the majority of upper houses had at least one women member, and not until 2003 did all. In recent years, the gap between the upper and lower houses in women's membership has narrowed slightly.

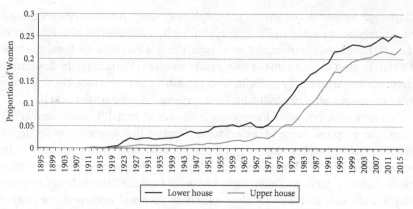

FIGURE 7.2 *Proportion of Women Legislators by Upper and Lower Houses*
Cox 1996; Center for American Women and Politics 2016.

PARTY AFFILIATIONS OF WOMEN LEGISLATORS

In 1895, the first session after women were elected to state legislatures, Democrats outnumbered Republicans three to one, there being four women elected. During the next twenty years, when women were elected at all, there were usually a few more Democrats than Republicans.

The tide then turned, and for nearly five decades between 1917 and 1965, as Figure 7.3 illustrates, there were always more Republican than Democratic women legislators, except for the sessions after the elections of 1930, 1932, and 1934—the first elections after the beginning of the Great Depression. In 1932, the voters swept in Franklin Delano Roosevelt and turned twelve state legislatures (plus Congress) from Republican to Democratic majorities. In 1934, voters removed a few more Republicans and instituted Democratic majorities in three more states. These Democratic victories brought in Democratic women as well as men, and cleared out some Republican women.

After 1935, though, it was not until 1965 that female Democrats again outnumbered Republicans (see Rule 1981, 1990). In fact, scholars writing in the 1960s and 1970s sought to explain why Republicans dominated the partisan affiliation of women legislators (see Werner 1968). Looking at the partisan gender gap now, this may seem incongruous. But in the first two-thirds of the twentieth century, many Democratic Party organizations were machine driven and hardly welcoming to women. Other Democratic strongholds were in the South, bastions of traditional and exclusionary structures, also inhospitable to women. Many politically active women focused their activity on the League of Women Voters and similar organizations that had a distinctly middle-class Republican composition.

From 1965 through 1970, the lead in women legislators switched between Democrats and Republicans. But beginning in 1971, and continuing until the present, Democratic women legislators outnumber Republican ones, a gap

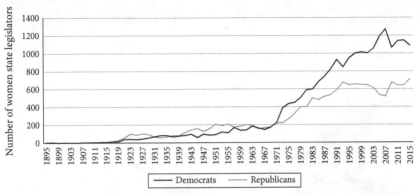

FIGURE 7.3 *Women State Legislators by Party*

that grew from a handful in 1971 to 379 in 2015 (for analyses of partisan divides in the 1970s through 1990s, see Matland and Brown 1992; Nechemias 1987; Sanbonmatsu 2002).

In the last few years, Republicans have captured the majority in more and more state legislatures. Though the number of women Republican legislators is increasing, it is only slowly advancing, another factor reducing the overall growth in women legislators. In 2016, Democratic women were 34% of all Democratic legislators. Republican women held only 17% of their party's seats, a striking difference (Center for American Women in Politics 2016; National Council of State Legislatures 2016).

The change in the locus of women's representation in the parties is additional evidence of the parties' increasingly gendered nature (Freeman 1999; Wolbrecht 2000). As the Republican Party grew more conservative with the shift of the South to a Republican stronghold, and as women's issues became defined as part of the culture wars, the Democratic Party became the party of women's issues. Women state legislators were less likely to enter politics through channels such as the League of Women Voters and more likely to be part of the women's movement or the expanding professional class of women. Not surprisingly, then, in recent decades, Democratic congressional districts have become more "women friendly" (Ondercin and Welch 2009; Palmer and Simon 2008a), and many Republican women have been discouraged about running (Thomsen 2015).

Figure 7.4 illustrates the differential strength of Republican and Democratic women in state legislatures in 2016. Western states such as Idaho and Colorado, pioneers in electing women to legislatures in the late nineteenth and early twentieth centuries, still are among the leaders in women's representation within each party today (maps a and b). But because they are Republican-dominated states, and Republican women have much lower legislative representation than Democratic ones, these states are not among the highest proportion of women overall (map c). Montana's and Utah's Democratic women are well represented within the Democratic caucus in those states, but Republican women are not. In fact, Republican women in Utah are in the lowest bracket of representation.

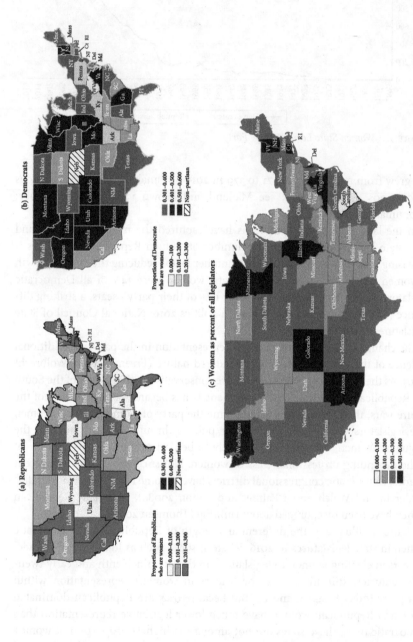

(a) Republicans

Proportion of Republicans
who are women

- 0.000–0.100
- 0.101–0.200
- 0.201–0.300
- 0.301–0.400
- 0.40–0.500
- Non-partisan

(b) Democrats

Proportion of Democrats
who are women

- 0.000–100
- 0.101–0.200
- 0.201–0.300
- 0.301–0.400
- 0.401–0.500
- 0.501–0.600
- Non-partisan

(c) Women as percent of all legislators

- 0.000–0.100
- 0.101–0.200
- 0.201–0.300
- 0.301–0.400

FIGURE 7.4 *Proportion of Women among State Legislators, Total and by Party*

Data from Center for the American Women and Politics, Rutgers University.

POPULATION CHARACTERISTICS

During the decades since the Nineteenth Amendment, scholars have sometimes found that women were somewhat better represented in states with more urban and educated populations and more population near the state capital (for a review, see Arceneaux 2001; Darcy et al. 1994; Dolan and Ford 1997; King 2002).

The logic behind having greater representation in states with more urban and educated populations is that there would be a greater pool of women from the business and professional occupations from which legislators typically and increasingly are drawn (Cammisa and Reingold 2004; Dolan and Ford 1995; Kirkpatrick 1974; Thomas 1994; Welch 1978). Studies of individual women legislators confirm this, and district-level analysis of congressional districts inform us that women are more likely to be elected in urban districts with a more educated population (Ondercin and Welch 2009; Palmer and Simon 2008b). However, there is little evidence from state legislative districts. Garnering data from thousands of individual legislative districts is nearly prohibitive. Correlations of urban and educated populations on the state level with the proportion of women state legislators have not been strong or consistent over the years.

Population density around the state capital plays a role in women's representation. Especially in the earlier part of the twentieth century, women were more location-bound than men. In an era when sex roles were more tightly circumscribed than now, married women, especially those with young children, would be unlikely to leave their families to spend days and weeks at the state capitol. After all, until the 1980s, women legislators with young children were quite rare, and women typically stifled their political ambitions until their children were grown (Sapiro 1982; Stoper 1977). Nechemias (1987, 1985) sought to test a logical outcome of this argument by examining whether women were found more often in legislatures where members had short average driving distances to the state capitol. Maybe, she speculated, women are more likely to run in states where the average distance to the capitol is thirty miles (Maryland) rather than three hundred (South Dakota). Family life would be less disrupted in the former than the latter, where daily commutes would be impossible for most members. In fact, she found that in most, but not all, of the sixteen states she examined, women legislators tended to live closer to the capitol than did men.

In the nearly thirty years since that study, geographic information system methodologies allow measures more directly related to the hypothesis. Thus, we examined a measure of the proportion of the population within fifty miles of the state capitol.[12] This measure sorts the states on accessibility within driving distance of the capitol. Of course, the measure does not take into account traffic patterns that could make a sixty-mile trip in Nebraska shorter than a twenty-mile trip in New Jersey, nor does it include public transportation options that might make longer distances more feasible for commuting.

We expected that the relationship between the proportion of women state legislators and geographic distance from the capitol would be stronger in earlier rather than recent years because of better transportation in more recent years. But that was not the case. Bivariate correlations with the proportion of the population within fifty miles of the capitol were significant in every session from 1953 to 2013 for the upper houses (with 1943 having a significance level of .054) and every session from 1933 to 2013 for the lower houses.[13]

REGION AND CULTURE

Region is another factor shaping women's proportions in state legislatures. Region reflects political culture, though is not a perfect correlate (Erickson, McIver, and Wright 1987; Johnson 1976). In the United States, the geographical base of political cultures is strong, especially for the traditional cultures of the South (Elazar 1984; Erickson et al. 1987; Sharkansky 1969) and what has been called the moralistic cultures of the upper Midwest, New England, and West (Elazar 1984; Sharkansky 1969). Dominant populations of *traditionalistic* states seek to preserve established ways of political and social life, especially relationships among races, between men and women, and in terms of authority structures. States with *moralistic* political cultures and values operate on an ethos that government functions to improve society (Elazar 1984). A third culture, found in the industrial East and Midwest, is labeled the *individualistic* and is characterized by political activity designed to further the interests of one's group or oneself. Of course, these are archetypes, and many states display characteristics of more than one of them.

These regional differences are directly relevant to the progress of women in elected office. In mid-twentieth-century America, the largest proportion of women legislators were elected in the moralistic states of New England and the West (Arceneaux 2001; Diamond 1977; Kirkpatrick 1974). In fact, in the 1960s, three of the New England states (Connecticut, New Hampshire, and Vermont) contained nearly half of all women legislators (Nechemias 1987). States with traditional political cultures, mostly found in the South (Elazar 1984), lagged behind other regions in women's representation even when the one-party Democratic South turned Republican (Hill 1981). In more recent years, evidence for a regional impact has been mixed (Nechemias 1987; Ondercin and Welch 2009; Sanbonmatsu 2002).

Region is also a stand-in for many factors that shape a state's politics, ranging from the racial composition of the electorate to the partisan preferences and intensities of the voters. Regional differences also shape policies, including women's rights. For example, in the fierce debate of the 1970s over the ERA, most southern states did not ratify it; all states in the Northeast did. States in the Northeast and West led the fight for the rights of lesbian/gay/bisexual/transgender (LGBT) citizens; the South lagged.

Occasionally, observers have suggested that women are less likely to be found in more professional legislatures (longer sessions, smaller memberships, higher salaries), and these characteristics also reflect regional differences. Part-time legislatures with few staff tend to be concentrated in the mountain and New England states, while full-time legislators with large staffs are largely found in the industrial Midwest and East.

Figure 7.5 shows regional differences in women's legislative membership over time using the Census's nine-category regional breakdown: Northeast,

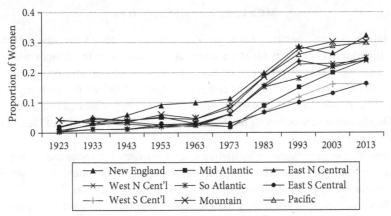

FIGURE 7.5 *Regional Differences in Proportion of Women in Lower House*

Mid-Atlantic, East North Central, West North Central, South Atlantic, East South Central, West South Central, Mountain, and Pacific. All regions have shown growth patterns, but regions differed as to when and how fast the increase in women legislators has been.

In the early postsuffrage years, New England was distinct in its larger women's representation. From about 1940 to the beginning of the accelerated increase in 1973, more women were elected in New England than anywhere else. In 1973, the southern and southwestern states fell behind the rest of the country in sending women to state legislatures.

Today, three distinct regional differences have emerged. New England, the Mountain, and the Pacific coast states have the largest women's representation; the South, the worst; and the East, Mid-Atlantic, and Southwest are in the middle. These differences are aptly illustrated in the ranking of state legislatures by women's representation. In 2016, for example, seven of the top ten were New England or western states, with only Illinois, Maryland, and Minnesota intruding, and seven of the bottom ten are southern or southwestern states, with only Utah, West Virginia, and Wyoming from other regions (see Figure 7.4).[14]

Explaining Interstate Differences in Women's Representation

We now turn to state-by-state differences in the proportion of women in each house in light of the factors we have examined: district size relative to population, partisanship, proportion of population within fifty miles of the state capitol building, region, and time.[15] The unit of analysis is the state at a particular time period, each year ending in 3 from 1923 to 2013, inclusive. With ten time periods in the analysis, the fifty states yield 492 cases.[16] Examples of cases would be Illinois in 1943 or California in 1983.

MEASURING THE FACTORS

To tap the overall partisan leanings of the state, we coded the case 1 if their presidential majority was for the Democratic candidate in the concurrent election (that is, if there were a presidential election in the year ending in 2) or the immediately preceding one (year ending in 0) and coded 0 if the majority voted Republican. We also assessed whether (1) or not (0) upper houses had a majority of Democrats and whether or not the lower houses had a majority of Democrats (Dubin 2007).

The ratio of population to legislative seats is measured in thousands of population per seat.[17] We measure population density around the capital as the proportion of the state's population within fifty miles of the state capital.[18]

Regional variables combined the East South Central and West South Central into one denoting the southern states, New England is the second measure, and the third is a combination of the Mountain and Pacific states. The rest of the country served as the omitted category in this set of variables.[19]

Of course, as we have shown in several ways, the proportion of women legislators is strongly related to time. There has been a nearly inexorable growth over time, albeit at different rates in different states. Controlling for time in the analysis is crucial in order to adequately interpret the effect of other variables that change over time, such as the proportion of the population within fifty miles of the capital or the ratio of seats to population.

EXPLAINING THE RESULTS

Table 7.1 presents the analyses' results for the lower and upper houses separately and for the mean of the two. Overall, our five predictors explain more than 80% of the variation in women's legislative membership over time and across states. All of these factors, except district size, play an important role in predicting the proportion of women in a legislature.

Starting first with the changes over time, we know that the proportion of women increases as the years roll by. The shape of that increase is slightly different for the lower and upper houses. In the lower houses, in 1953, the proportion of women becomes significantly more than in 1923 (all time differences are compared to 1923). But in the upper houses, the proportion of women is not significantly different from 1923 until 1973, at the time of the accelerated growth in women's representation. Thus, growth in the proportion of women took place in the lower houses first. Figure 7.2 illustrates this. The 1933 and 1943 coefficients are negative but not significant for the upper and lower houses, indicating the stagnation in the proportion of women during that time.

We have already shown (see Figure 7.3) that there were slightly more Republican than Democratic women in the 1940s through the early 1960s, but during the accelerated growth period after 1973, Democratic women became much more numerous. Table 7.1 indicates that if the Democratic presidential candidate carries a state in the election just before or coincident with the last legislative election, there are likely to be more women elected to the

TABLE 7.1 Impact of time and political and social factors on the proportion of women in the state legislatures

	All legislatures		Upper houses		Lower houses	
	b	(s.e.)	b	(s.e.)	b	(s.e.)
DEMOCRATIC CONTROL						
Upper house	.008	(.006)	.001	(.005)	—	
Lower house	−.010	(.006)	—		−.005	(.005)
% Demo state presidential vote	.001*	(.000)	.001*	(.000)	.001*	(.000)
REGION						
New England	.040*	(.008)	.040*	(.009)	.035*	(.008)
West	.035*	(.005)	.026*	(.006)	.040*	(.005)
South	−.033*	(.006)	−.029*	(.007)	−.037*	(.006)
% population within 50 miles	.031*	(.009)	.034*	(.011)	.030*	(.013)
POPULATION PER LEGISLATIVE SEAT						
All	.000	(.000)	—		—	
Upper house	—		.000	(.000)		
Lower house	—		—		.000	(.000)
TIME						
1933	−.015	(.010)	−.015	(.012)	−.011	(.010)
1943	−.009	(.010)	−.010	(.012)	−.004	(.010)
1953	.010	(.009)	.005	(.010)	.017*	(.009)
1963	.011	(.009)	.006	(.011)	.018*	(.009)
1973	.039*	(.009)	.032*	(.010)	.047*	(.009)
1983	.107*	(.009)	.084*	(.010)	.131*	(.009)
1993	.182*	(.009)	.171*	(.011)	.197*	(.009)
2003	.199*	(.009)	.189*	(.011)	.210*	(.009)
2013	.213*	(.009)	.199*	(.011)	.230*	(.009)
constant	−.036*	(.010)	−.045*	(.012)	−.023	(.011)
R^2	.83		.83		.83	
N	492		492		484	

Results of a Generalized Least Squares regression with random effects. The dependent variable is the proportion of the upper and lower houses who are women. The mean of those two numbers is the dependent variable in the "all legislatures" model. The omitted category is 1923. * indicates significant at .05 or better.

state's legislature. On both sides of the aisle, many women are challengers to incumbents or contestants for open seats, but there are more women candidates on the Democratic side. Thus, a swing to the Democrats will elect more Democratic challengers and open-seat candidates, and among Democrats more of those challengers are women (for data on congressional female challenges, see Ondercin and Welch 2009). On the other hand, Democratic control of the chambers had no significant impact on the proportion of Democratic or Republican women in the legislature.

The regional differences that we saw in Figure 7.5 are clear in this analysis. Compared to the eastern, Mid-Atlantic, Midwest, and Prairie states, women are more likely to be elected in the New England and western states, and less likely to be elected in the South. These effects are significant in both the upper and lower houses, and amount to between a 3% and 4% difference in proportion of women in state legislatures. For example, in the upper houses, the southern states, on average, have about 2.9% fewer women than the Mid-Atlantic, Midwest, eastern, and Prairie states, and the New England states have about 4% more.

If we examine the other two factors included in our equation, unlike some previous findings, we see little impact of district size in either the lower or upper houses.[20] Past findings that did show an impact were largely based on earlier eras when the states with the most women legislators were the New England states with very large lower houses and relatively few inhabitants. We see a confirmation of earlier work showing that population density around the capitol facilitates the election of women. The effect is obvious in the lower and upper houses. Overall, then, Table 7.1 has helped us understand more fully the dynamics of the increases in women state legislators.

In Table 7.2, we examine factors predicting women's representation in the earlier (1923 to 1963) and later (1973 to 2013) periods. Not only does this temporal division separate the membership into two equal chronological parts, it also divides the membership into the slow-growth era before 1972 and the much faster growth era after.

The factors examined here explain much more of the state-to-state variation in the later period than the earlier period, as evidenced by the R^2 values of .38 and .72, respectively. That is, variation among states in the latter period can be more easily explained by our five variables than in the former period.

The dynamics of growth are much the same in our 1973 to 2013 analysis as in Table 7.1, which describes the entire nearly one-hundred-year period. The presidential election matters, with Democratic presidents sweeping in more women. Regional differences are well developed, with the South significantly behind and the West and New England states significantly ahead of the rest of the country. Density around the capitol positively affects the proportion of women in the legislature, and the size of the legislature has no impact. Each variable measuring year has a significant effect, and the coefficients are larger through time, indicating that the pace of growth has accelerated, even since 1973.

The factors predicting women's representation in the earlier period were somewhat different. The first two time indicators, 1933 and 1943, were tiny and insignificant, indicating stagnant growth in these first twenty years. The measures for 1953 and 1963 are positive and significant, indicating the beginning of a small increase in the proportion of women. Measures of party success were mixed. The victory or defeat of a Democratic presidential candidate had no impact during this first half century. The direction of party control in the legislature did matter, though in inconsistent ways. Democratic upper houses had a few more women than those controlled by the Republicans, though the reverse was true in the lower houses. The latter finding is consistent with the greater number of Republican women legislators during this 1940s–1960s period. The upper house finding is difficult to explain, although throughout much of this period, several upper houses had no women at all. Population density around the capital was significantly related to

TABLE 7.2 Impact of time and political and social factors on the proportion of women in the state legislatures, by era

	1923–1963		1973–2013	
	b	(s.e.)	b	(s.e.)
DEMOCRATIC CONTROL				
Upper house	.009*	(.004)	−.001	(.011)
Lower house	−.009*	(.004)	−.012	(.011)
% Demo state presidential vote	−.000	(.000)	.001*	(.001)
% population within 50 miles	.023*	(.007)	.038*	(.015)
POPULATION PER LEGISLATIVE SEAT	−.000	(.000)	.000	(.000)
REGION				
New England	.021*	(.006)	.052*	(.013)
West	.015*	(.003)	.052*	(.009)
South	.000	(.004)	−.051*	(.010)
TIME				
1933	.005	(.005)	—	
1943	.008	(.005)	—	
1953	.015*	(.004)	—	
1963	.020*	(.004)	—	
1983	—		.066*	(.011)
1993	—		.141*	(.011)
2003	—		.155*	(.011)
2013	—		.164*	(.011)
constant	.001	(.006)	−.017	(.019)
R^2	.38		.73	
N	242		250	

Results of a Generalized Least Squares regression with random effects. The dependent variable is the mean proportion of the upper and lower houses who are women. The omitted category is 1923 in the 1923–1963 analysis and 1973 in the 1973 to 2013 analysis. * indicates significant at .05 or better.

women's legislative membership, though less than in later years. Regional differences are clear, but also not as strong as in the later period. The South is not so distinctive in this early period, perhaps because many other states also had few elected women legislators.

And as we have already seen, the pace of growth in women's representation accelerated over time. Other things being equal, the 1963 coefficient indicated that there were 2% more women than in 1923. The 2013 coefficient indicated there were 17% more women legislators than in 1973.

Conclusion

The Nineteenth Amendment gave impetus to a previously rare phenomenon in US politics: elected office holders who were women. The amendment required full suffrage rights for women in all states. Once empowered to vote, many women decided to take the next step to run for office. Though women had been elected to a few state legislatures before national suffrage, and indeed some women legislators were able to vote for ratification of the Nineteenth Amendment, the amendment opened the door to more frequent election of women. By 1933, two-thirds of all lower houses had women members; the onetime rarity became merely unusual, though still far from common. The amendment set the stage for a gradual, very incremental growth in women's representation that continued for about fifty years.

Moreover, suffrage and the small growth in women elected officials soon made a difference in some public policies in ways we might imagine. Suffrage was followed by nonincremental increases in local public health spending, decreases in child mortality (Miller 2008), and an increase in local school expenditures (Carruthers and Wanamaker 2015). The impact of women legislators persists in many ways (Thomas 1991; Swers 2001).

It wasn't until fifty years had passed that the proportions of women in legislatures began to grow steadily. After 1973, the resurgent women's movement worked to obtain ratification of the ERA and to add women to local, state, and national political offices. After that, for the next twenty years, the growth in women's representation occurred at a much steeper rate. In the past twenty years, the growth slowed.

This analysis is the first to look systematically at factors predicting women's state legislative representation through the entire history of women in American state legislatures. We see that state-to-state differences in women's representation are as vast as over-time differences have been. Several factors have shaped the growth in women's legislative representation.

Time is the best predictor of how many women are legislators. We know that the percentage of women members has grown steadily; only occasionally have there been fewer women elected than the prior year. As time has progressed, the gap between the states leading in women's representation and those lagging has increased substantially. In the years right after suffrage, the interstate range in women's representation was 0% to 2%. Today, the gap is from 13% to 42%, a substantial variation. Clearly, different states have taken different paths with regard to women's representation. Neighbors Wyoming and Colorado were among the first states to adopt full women's suffrage, and yet today Colorado is at the top and Wyoming near the bottom of women's legislative representation, reflecting, in part, the partisan differences between the states.

Women's representation was much slower to develop in upper houses than in lower houses. For example, some upper houses as late as 1983 had no women members, whereas every state lower house had women members by 1963. Even today, women's representation in the upper houses is, on the whole, smaller than in the lower houses. There would appear to be significant opportunities for women to obtain seats in the upper houses, given their numbers in lower houses.

Regional differences remain striking. In the New England and western states, women's representation is about 7% more than in the southern states, with the rest of the country in between. These differences are closely tied to partisan differences. Notably, the states lagging in women's representation are among the most conservative states.

All but one of the top ten states in women's representation are blue states, Arizona excepted. All of the states at the bottom of the list are red states. This situation suggests that the gendering of political parties may be most distinct in those states because the Republican Party is extremely conservative and has only half, proportionally, the number of women representatives that Democrats do. Republican women tend to be somewhat more moderate than their male counterparts, which presents a disincentive to run for office (Thomsen 2015). This may be less of an inhibiting factor in states that are less conservative. Then, too, in the most conservative states, Democrats are unable to mount enough votes to elect either men or women. The issue of partisan control of state legislatures as it affects women's representation deserves further attention.

National elections can have an impact, too. Democratic presidential years tend to be accompanied by a larger growth in women state legislators, as more Democratic legislators are elected and more women run on that ticket. The 2016 election, though it brought defeat to Hillary Clinton at the top of the Democratic ticket, did promote another increase in women state legislators in both parties. Thirty-four more Democratic and fifty more Republican women were elected, moving the number of women state legislators to another all time high of 1844, just shy of 25 percent of all members.

Geography is also relevant in that women are more likely to be elected in states with a greater population cluster around the state capitol. We can speculate that with more women living near the capital city, more will be interested in running for office because holding the job would be less disruptive to their family lives. But it may also be that women are more attracted to state politics in those areas because the statehouse gets more media coverage there.

The slowing of the rate of progress in the past twenty years has been discouraging to those who seek better women's representation. Had the rate of increase of women in state legislatures evidenced from about 1971 to 1993 continued, women would now hold 720 more seats than they do, about 34% of the seats in state legislatures instead of 24%. On the other hand, if growth continues at the post-1993 rate, women will not hold 34% of the seats until 2052, a daunting prospect.

Despite the impetus of the Nineteenth Amendment, nearly one hundred years later, women still have a long way to go in achieving proportional representation or anything close to it in the state legislatures, as in most other elected bodies.

Notes

1. Carrie Clyde Holly, Francis S. Klock, and Clara Cressingham.

2. Women were serving in eleven states during the ratification votes: Arizona, California, Colorado, Idaho, Kansas, Montana, New York, Oregon, Utah, and Washington. Wyoming had previously elected a woman but did not have one serving in 1919–1920.

3. Joining the three pioneer states were Wyoming (1911), Washington (1913), Arizona (1915), Oregon (1915), Montana (1917), and California, Kansas, Nevada, and New York in 1919. By 1919 all western states except New Mexico granted women the vote.

4. Contemporary data in this paragraph and others come from the Center for American Women and Politics, Rutgers University. http://www.cawp.rutgers.edu/women-state-legislature-2016.

5. These data are drawn from Cox (1996) for 1895 through 1993 and from the state legislative fact sheets of Rutgers University, Center for the American Woman and Politics, for subsequent data. The data are comparable as best as can be determined, but the gender of some early state legislators cannot be determined for certain. Moreover, the numbers of legislators change even within a session as prolonged vote recounts, deaths, and resignations produce changes throughout the session.

6. For a reflection on the importance of Emmy Werner's (1968) article, see Carroll (2008).

7. Illinois used a system of cumulative voting between 1870 and 1982 where voters chose three representatives from each lower house district, two from one party and one from another.

8. Other works comprising the rich literature on the influence of multimember districts include Darcy, Welch, and Clark 1994; Matland and Brown 1992; Sanbonmatsu 2002; Dolan and Ford 1997; Kenworth and Malami 1999; Palmer and Simon 2001. However, we do not have complete data on the existence of multimember districts historically.

9. Multimember districts tend to diminish the representation of racially segregated minorities, particularly African Americans (Arceneaux 2001; King 2002). See also Ballotpedia at https://ballotpedia.org/State_legislative_chambers_that_use_multi-member_districts for information about multimember districts in state legislative elections.

10. Within each set of houses (upper, lower), the correlation is about .2 between proportion of women and population per district.

11. Except for 1905 and 1907, when there were no women legislators at all.

12. The computations of population within fifty miles of the capital were done by Patrick Hagge, Department of Geography, Arkansas Tech.

13. The twenty-five-mile radius measure is less consistently related to women's representation. Counter to our expectations, it is more related in recent years than earlier.

14. Data from the Center for American Women in Politics, http://www.cawp.rutgers.edu/women-elective-office-2016.

15. The fifty miles is measured from the state capitol building.

16. Actually 492 because Alaska and Hawaii are not included before statehood in 1958 and 1959, respectively.

17. Since the 1962 Supreme Court's decision in *Baker v. Carr*, state legislative seats must be approximately equal in size. Before that time, there were significant variations from the mean.

18. The computations of population within fifty miles of the capital were done by Patrick Hagge, Department of Geography, Arkansas Tech.

19. The comparison of each regional variable is to that omitted category of eastern and midwestern states.

20. Comparing the ten states with the largest percentage of women per the Center for American Women in Politics with the ten states with the lowest percentage shows that the average density ranking of the first group is 28.2 and the latter group is 29.1, essentially indistinguishable.

References

Arceneaux, Kevin. 2001. "The 'Gender Gap' in State Legislative Representation: New Data to Tackle an Old Question." *Political Research Quarterly* 54(1): 143–160.

Cammisa, Anne Marie, and Beth Reingold. 2004. "Women in State Legislatures and State Legislative Research." *State Politics & Policy Quarterly* 4: 181–210.

Carroll, Susan J. 2008. "Commentary on Emmy E. Werner's 1968 Article, 'Women in the State Legislatures.'" *Political Research Quarterly* 61(1): 25–28.

Carruthers, Celeste, and Marianne Wanamaker. 2015. "Municipal Housekeeping: The Impact of Women's Suffrage on Public Education." *Journal of Human Resources* 50(4): 837–872.

Center for American Women in Politics. 2016. "Women in State Legislatures, 2016." http://www.cawp.rutgers.edu/women-state-legislature-2016.

Cox, Elizabeth M. 1996. *Women State & Territorial Legislators, 1895–1995*. Darby, PA: Diane Pub Co.

Darcy, R, Susan Welch, and Janet Clark. 1994. *Women, Elections, & Representation*. Lincoln: University of Nebraska Press.

Diamond, Irene. 1977. *Sex Roles in the State House*. New Haven, CT: Yale University Press.

Dolan, Kathleen, and Lynne Ford. 1995. "Women in the State Legislatures." *American Politics Quarterly* 23(1): 96–108.

———. 1997. "Change and Continuity among Women Legislators: Evidence from Three Decades." *Political Research Quarterly* 50: 137–151.

Dubin, Michael J. 2007. *Party Affiliations in the State Legislatures: A Year-by-Year Summary, 1796–2006*. Jefferson, NC: McFarland.

Elazar, Daniel Judah. 1984. *American Federalism: A View from the States*. New York: Harper and Row.

Erickson, Robert, John McIver, and Gerald Wright. 1987. "State Political Culture and Public Opinion." *American Political Science Review* 81(3): 797–813.

Freeman, Jo. 1999. *A Room at a Time: How Women Entered Party Politics*. Lanham, MD: Rowman and Littlefield.

Hill, David B. 1981. "Political Culture and Female Political Representation." *Journal of Politics* 43(1): 159–168.

Johnson, Charles A. 1976. "Political Culture in American States: Elazar's Formulation Examined." *American Journal of Political Science* 20(3): 491–509.

Kenworth, Lane, and Melissa Malami. 1999. "Gender Inequity in Political Representation." *Social Forces* 78(1): 235–268.

King, James D. 2002. "Single-Member Districts and the Representation of Women in American State Legislatures: The Effects of Electoral System Change." *State Politics & Policy Quarterly* 2(2): 161–175.

Kirkpatrick, Jeane J. 1974. *Political Woman*. New York: Basic Books.

Kunovich, Shen, and Pamela Paxton. 2005. "Pathways to Power: The Role of Political Parties in Women's National Political Representation." *American Journal of Sociology* 111(2): 505–552.

Kurtz, Karl. 2011. "Declining Use of Multi Member Districts." *The Thicket at State Legislatures*. National Council of State Legislatures. July. http://ncsl.typepad.com/the_thicket/2011/07/the-decline-in-multi-member-districts.html.

Martin, M. E., and B. T. van de Vries. 1937. "Women in State Capitols." *State Government* 10: 213–215.

Matland, Richard E., and Deborah Dwight Brown. 1992. "District Magnitude's Effect on Female Representation in U.S. State Legislatures." *Legislative Studies Quarterly* 17(4): 469–492.

Miller, Grant. 2008. "Women's Suffrage, Political Responsiveness, and Child Survival in American History." *Quarterly Journal of Economics* 123(3): 1287–1327.

Moncrief, Gary, and Joel Thompson. 1992. "Electoral Structure and State Legislative Representation." *Journal of Politics* 54(1): 246–256.

National Council of State Legislatures. 2016. "State Partisan Composition." http://www.ncsl. org/research/about-state-legislatures/partisan-composition.aspx#2016.

Nechemias, Carol. 1985. "Geographic Mobility and Women's Access to State Legislatures." *Western Political Quarterly* 38(1): 119–131.

———. 1987. "Changes in the Election of Women to U.S. State Legislative Seats." *Legislative Studies Quarterly* 12(1): 125–142.

Ondercin, Heather, and Susan Welch. 2009. "Comparing Predictors of Women's Electoral Success: Candidates, Primaries, and the General Election." *American Politics Research* 37: 593–613.

Palmer, Barbara, and Dennis Michael Simon. 2001. "The Political Glass Ceiling: Gender, Strategy, and Incumbency in U.S. House Elections." *Women & Politics* 23(1/2): 59–78.

———. 2008a. *Breaking the Political Glass Ceiling: Women and Congressional Elections.* New York: Routledge.

———. 2008b. *Breaking the Political Glass Ceiling: Women and Congressional Elections.* Second edition. Women in American Politics Series. New York: Routledge.

Roosevelt, Eleanor. 1954. *Ladies of Courage.* New York: Putnam.

Rule, Wilma. 1981. "Why Women Don't Run: The Critical Contextual Factors in Women's Legislative Recruitment." *Western Political Quarterly* 34(1): 60–77.

———. 1987. "Electoral Systems, Contextual Factors, and Women's Opportunity for Election to Parliament in Twenty-Three Democracies." *Western Political Quarterly* 40(3): 477–498.

———. 1990. "Why More Women Are State Legislators: A Research Note." *Western Political Quarterly* 43(2): 437–448.

———. 1994. "Women's Underrepresentation and Electoral Systems." *PS: Political Science and Politics* 27(4): 689–692.

Sanbonmatsu, Kira. 2002. "Political Parties and the Recruitment of Women to State Legislatures." *Journal of Politics* 64(3): 791–809.

Sapiro, Virginia. 1982. "Private Costs of Public Commitments or Public Costs of Private Commitments? Family Roles versus Political Ambition." *American Journal of Political Science* 26(2): 265–279.

Sharkansky, Ira. 1969. "The Utility of Elazar's Political Culture." *Polity* 2(1): 66–83.

Squire, Peverill. 1992. "Legislative Professionalization and Membership Diversity in State Legislatures." *Legislative Studies Quarterly* 17(1): 69–79.

Stoper, E. 1977. "Wife and Politician: Role Strain among Women in Public Office." In *A Portrait of Marginality: The Political Behavior of American Women.* New York: David McKay.

Swers, Michele. 2001. "Understanding the Policy Impact of Electing Women." *PS: Political Science and Politics* 34: 217–220.

Thomas, Sue. 1991. "The Impact of Women on State Legislative Policies." *Journal of Politics* 53: 958–976.

———. 1994. *How Women Legislate*. New York: Oxford University Press.

Thomsen, Danielle. 2015. "Why So Few (Republican) Women? Explaining the Partisan Imbalance of Women in the U.S. Congress." *Legislative Studies Quarterly* 40(2): 295–323.

van de Vries, B. T. 1948. "Housekeeping in the State Legislature." *State Government* 21: 127–128.

Welch, Susan. 1978. "Recruitment of Women to Public Office: A Discriminant Analysis." *Western Political Quarterly* 31(3): 372–380.

Welch, Susan, and Donley T. Studlar. 1990. "Multi-Member Districts and the Representation of Women." *Journal of Politics* 52(2): 391–412.

———. 1996. "The Opportunity Structure for Women's Candidacies and Electability in Britain and the United States." *Political Research Quarterly* 49(4): 861–874.

Werner, Emmy E. 1968. "Women in the State Legislatures." *Western Political Quarterly* 21(1): 40–50.

Wolbrecht, Christina. 2000. *The Politics of Women's Rights: Parties, Positions, and Change*. Princeton, NJ: Princeton University Press.

Young, Louise. 1950. *Understanding Politics: A Practical Guide for Women*. New York: Pellegrinia and Cudahay.

{ PART II }

Feminism and Women's Movement Activism

A CENTURY OF STRUGGLE

8

"Feminism Means More Than a Changed World. . . . It Means the Creation of a New Consciousness in Women"

FEMINISM, CONSCIOUSNESS-RAISING, AND CONTINUITY BETWEEN THE WAVES

Laura K. Nelson

Spiritual freedom evolves out of consciousness of powers possessed, a sense of self and opportunity, and it is only out of spiritual freedom that the whole individual evolves.

—— ROSE YOUNG, 1914

Agitation for specific freedoms is worthless without the preliminary raising of consciousness necessary to utilize these freedoms fully.

—— SHULAMITH FIRESTONE, 1968

The simple act of talking openly about behavioral patterns makes the subconscious conscious. . . . Talking can transform minds, which can transform behaviors, which can transform institutions.

—— SHERYL SANDBERG, 2014

On a cold evening in February, hundreds of men and women crowded into the nearly packed Great Hall at Cooper Union in New York City. The subject: "What Is Feminism?" The event cycled through twelve speakers, six men and six women, each discussing what feminism meant to them. "Feminism means trouble; trouble means agitation; agitation means movement; movement means life," said one. "Feminism means revolution, and I am a revolutionist," said another. Feminism means access to more rights, the group agreed: we deserve the "right to a profession," the "right to keep our own name," the "right to ignore fashion," and the "right to organize." "We want woman to have the same right as man to experiment with her life," concluded one speaker. Others spoke about how feminism would lead to more fulfilled lives for women: "We're sick of being specialized to sex!" one of the women speakers cried. "We intend simply to be ourselves, not just our little female selves, but our whole, big, human selves" ("Talk on Feminism Stirs Great Crowd," 1914: 2).

With language reminiscent of the freedom-loving activists of the 1960s, this event in fact occurred in 1914, fifty years before the second-wave feminist movement would permanently change American culture. This first event was followed three nights later by an equally well-attended meeting called "A Feminist Symposium." These two "mass meetings" were arguably the first of their size to center on feminism as a distinct political identity in the United States, and they marked the beginning of a vibrant, but all too brief, feminist uprising.

This feminist movement existed alongside the more widely known, and better documented, suffrage movement. The suffrage movement comfortably fits the popular image of a "real" social movement: it sought a particular political change—the extension of the right to vote to women—and employed tactics common to many social movements: mass demonstrations, pickets, and political lobbying. In general, scholars who research nineteenth- and twentieth-century social movements, including those who study women's movements, tend to focus their attention on these types of confrontational tactics.

If, however, we shift our attention from the suffrage movement as the center of the first-wave women's movement, and instead focus on the early feminists who organized the mass meetings detailed above, we get a much different picture of the way women organize. These early-twentieth-century feminists did not march in the streets or lobby politicians; instead, they employed a strategy I call *narrative-based consciousness-raising*. This form of feminism asserts that, in order to change institutions and achieve complete equality, movements must first change the hearts and minds of individuals themselves. Narrative-based consciousness-raising uses personal life stories, or life narratives, to reveal the collective roots of personal problems in order to effect this personal change. More precisely, narrative-based consciousness-raising includes four main tenets: (1) knowledge should be grounded in the everyday experience of women, (2) sharing everyday experiences will expose the roots of personal problems in collective patterns of interpersonal social relationships, (3) this will in turn change women's and men's consciousness about their social position, and (4) only then will institutions such as marriage, the nuclear family, and the state change. Unlike suffrage, this strategy focuses on personal issues rather than political issues, and it identifies psychology and interpersonal relations as the driver of inequality, rather than states and political institutions.

In this chapter I trace the history of this form of feminism, from its origins in the 1910s during the first-wave women's movement, up to its most contemporary appearance. This history, I argue, demonstrates that, despite its extra-institutional focus, narrative-based consciousness-raising should be placed alongside demonstrations, picketing, and political lobbying as a staple social movement strategy. The history of narrative-based consciousness-raising challenges our understanding of social movements in three ways. First, it shifts this personal strategy to the center, rather than the periphery, of the women's movement as a whole. Second, it helps us better understand contemporary cases of the women's movement, as well as cases between heightened waves of activism. Scholars have attempted to contort the traditional view of social movements, which focuses on politics and confrontational tactics, in an attempt to convince others that phenomena such as self-help groups, "Lean In Circles," and Twitter hashtags are indeed social movements. The story I tell in this chapter instead suggests that this type of organizing is simply a continuation of a form of feminism that has always been a core strategy of the women's movement. Third, this history reinforces the notion that the women's movement has been a continuous movement over time, and provides an alternative way of understanding social movement continuity. Scholars have sought to explain connections within women's movements over time, proposing concepts such as overlapping generations (Reger 2012) and abeyance structures (Taylor 1989) to explain movement continuity. To these concepts I add another concept: the institutionalization of knowledge. In addition to direct connections between generations of women, women also draw on institutionalized knowledge to form their own organizations and movements, producing a "rolling inertia" that leads to movement continuity over time (see, e.g., Greve and Rao 2012; Molotch, Freudenburg, and Paulsen 2000).

The chapter is structured as follows. I first provide the historical and theoretical background necessary to understand why discussing the continuity of narrative-based consciousness-raising is important. I then describe a group of feminist activists in the first wave who developed this particular form of feminism, followed by a discussion of similar activism in the second wave and third wave. I end by suggesting how institutionalized knowledge, not overlapping generations, may have led to the continuity of this strategy over time.

Women's Movements over Time

Despite multiple challenges (Cobble 2005; Roth 2004; Staggenborg 1996; Taylor 1989), the wave metaphor remains the dominant way of describing the history of the US women's movement. There have been at least three peaks, or waves, of heightened political activity by women, and each wave has focused on different issues and introduced new social movement tactics. The first wave, existing from roughly 1837 to 1920, is commonly known for its focus on woman suffrage and the variety of tactics—including large parades, lobbying, and direct action—used to win suffrage. The first wave went far beyond suffrage, however, addressing the right to an equal education, equal property rights in marriage, equal access to jobs, and legalizing access to birth control (Stansell 2010). The second wave, which began in 1964, is known both for mass-membership organizations like the National Organization for Women (NOW) and smaller, local organizations that focused on "raising consciousness" and making "the personal, political" (Evans 1980; Ferree and Hess 2000; Rosen 2000). This wave addressed issues around equal pay, sexual harassment in the workplace, and images of women in the media. The third wave, beginning around the 1990s, shifted to a more micropolitics approach, favoring acts of personal expression and the recognition of intersecting identities over political lobbying and mass demonstrations (Reger 2005, 2012).

A BRIEF HISTORY

The woman suffrage movement, culminating in the passage of the Nineteenth Amendment in 1920, is viewed as the center piece of the *first wave* of the women's movement. The first wave began around the mid-1800s, with the first conference discussing women's rights held in 1837 in New York City (Gordon 1996; Giddings 2007) and the first convention devoted to women's rights in Seneca Falls, New York, in 1848. The Seneca Falls convention focused on a number of rights that at that time were denied to women, including the right to own property, keep their own wages when married, receive an education, and divorce on the same grounds as men, among others (Stanton, Gordon, and Anthony 1997). While the vote eventually became the movement's focal point, the first-wave women's movement as a whole focused on many issues, including reproductive rights, equal pay, and social issues such as marriage, sex, and prostitution. These women worked through established mainstream groups like women's clubs and settlement houses, leftist organizations such as the Socialist Party and the Liberal Club, as well as their own feminist organizations such as Heterodoxy and the Feminist Alliance.

After women won the right to vote, women's movement activity waned, and while women remained active in politics, they were not as publicly visible as the pre-1920s' years (Rupp and Taylor 1987). This changed in the early 1960s when the second-wave women's movement rocketed into the public sphere. This *second wave* was started largely by what scholars call *liberal feminists*—feminists who work for women's equality through political, legal, and customary reforms (Tong 2013). This wing of the second-wave movement, called the *women's rights wing*, consisted of large, mass membership organizations like NOW and the Women's Political Equity League (Evans 1980; Ferree and Hess 2000; Stansell 2010).

An additional wing of the second-wave movement expanded the scope of women's rights activism to include social, cultural, and in particular, interpersonal issues; this wing is commonly called *women's liberation* (Evans 1980; Echols 1989). Women's liberationists were typically younger than those in the women's rights wing, and many had been active in the civil rights and new left movements of the 1960s. Those involved in the women's liberation wing wanted more than reforms; they wanted a complete social revolution, believing in the need for system-wide changes that would penetrate every social institution, including marriage, sexual relationships, and the nuclear family (Echols 1989; Rosen 2000).

The second-wave movement, composed of both the women's rights and the women's liberation wing, peaked in the late 1970s. Following a failed attempt to ratify the Equal Rights Amendment (ERA), by the mid-1980s the movement was in retreat and a full-fledged backlash was under way (Faludi 2006). Starting around the mid-1990s the purported *third wave* of the US women's movement began, and it continues today. Drawing on work produced near the end of the second wave (e.g., Hull, Scott, and Smith 1982; Lorde 1984; Moraga and Anzaldua 1984; hooks 2000), the third-wave women's movement emphasized *intersectionality*: the notion that different social identities—for example, race, class, and gender—intersect in complex ways so that not all women experience gender oppression the same way.

The third wave as a whole also shifted from a focus on political lobbying and direct action to more of a micropolitics approach, where women saw the expression of personal identity and cultural change as a way to "be" feminist and "do" feminist politics (Reger 2005, 2012). The third wave has also introduced multiple new tactics into the feminist toolkit, including the use of online tools to promote and practice feminist politics (Crossley 2015), evidenced in part by popular hashtags such as #YesAllWomen, #EverydaySexism, and #SayHerName, as well as offline tactics such as the rapid worldwide diffusion of the SlutWalk demonstration. We have yet to see the full range of issues addressed and tactics developed by the contemporary feminist movement, as it continues to grow and change today.

CONTINUITIES BETWEEN THE WAVES

The wave metaphor, while useful in describing the general shape of feminist activism over the years, can also be misleading. Almost as soon as the wave metaphor was used to describe feminist activism, researchers have challenged it, looking in particular at the different temporal shape of nonwhite feminisms (Roth 2004), identifying important activity that happened between major waves (Cobble 2005), and recognizing crucial continuities between these waves (Rupp and Taylor 1987; Staggenborg 1989; Taylor 1989; Whittier 1995; Reger 2012; McCammon 2012). This work has collectively demonstrated that each moment in the history of feminism has consisted of *overlapping generations* (Reger 2012), where individuals and organizations from an earlier wave coexist with individuals and organizations from the new wave. These overlapping generations exist in and through *abeyance structures* (Rupp and Taylor 1987), defined as organizations and institutions that persist through periods of backlash against social movements and provide support and structure for movements as they reemerge in times of general political upheaval.

Research on feminist activity in the 1980s and 1990s revealed that these abeyance structures are often not formal social movement organizations but institutions such as feminist subcultures, feminist-owned businesses, and cultural festivals that enable feminism to persist through these decades of popular backlash (Staggenborg 1989; Whittier 1995; Reger 2012).

THE MULTI-INSTITUTIONAL APPROACH

These *extra-institutional* abeyance structures, structures that exist outside of the formal political sphere, emphasize something that social movement scholars have long asserted: social movements use a variety of strategies and tactics, and have diverse goals, that often go beyond coordinated public action targeted at explicitly political institutions. Armstrong and Bernstein (2008) articulate this in their call for a "multi-institutional" approach to social movements, highlighting social movement goals that go beyond changing public policies or laws, such as building identities, challenging cultural categories, or seeking symbolic change in the larger culture. In line with the multi-institutional approach, Staggenborg and Taylor (2005) argue that the feminist movement has been so successful, and has lasted for so long, precisely because it has developed a wide range of tactics that include less visible, but no less important, tactics and goals, and they urge researchers to include these less visible tactics in their analysis of the women's movement. Because this extra-institutional activity often happens outside of the public view, however, it is not easy to find or measure.

In the next two sections of this chapter I use writings and documents produced and published by feminists in the 1910s and the 1970s to trace the history of a type of feminist activity that centers on a less visible source of extra-institutional change: collective self-expression. I argue that, far from being peripheral to the women's movement, or a product of any one moment in history, collective self-expression was in fact central to every moment in the history of US women's movement. This form of feminism, narrative-base consciousness-raising, represents both a staple tactic of this movement and a key aspect of continuity within this movement over time.

Self-Expression in the 1910s: "Creating a New Consciousness in Women"

The 1910s were a crucial decade for the woman suffrage movement. During this decade, the suffrage movement introduced a variety of new and influential tactics, including massive suffrage parades and direct-action "Silent Sentinels" in front of the White House. These innovative tactics, combined with the aftermath of World War I, resulted in the passage of the Nineteenth Amendment in 1920, ending a battle that had been waged for over sixty years.

This decade, however, was not just important for the suffrage movement or for these public, confrontational tactics; the 1910s also saw the introduction of the word *feminism* into the United States for the first time, the subsequent rise of feminism as an identity distinct from the movement for suffrage, and the introduction of a less visible tactic into the social movement repertoire: "background talks." Before describing this new tactic, I first describe the general importance of feminism to the historical moment.

According to historian Nancy Cott, the introduction of the word *feminism* was a turning point for the women's movement, providing a label that named a group of women who believed that women's shared socially constructed position provided the opportunity to develop a common consciousness among women that would, in itself, "impel change" (Cott 1987: 5). The impact of these early feminists is recognized now by a few notable historians, but according to their contemporaries, feminists made a deep impact on the Progressive Era left, beyond what historians recognize. While rare in 1910, by 1913 the word *feminism* appeared frequently in the United States (Cott 1987), and by 1914 the left and the general press agreed that feminism, distinct from suffrage, had become a significant social movement. Figure 8.1 illustrates this rapid rise (and then decline) of the word *feminism* in the mainstream press.[1] In 1910, 15 articles in the *New York Times* mentioned the word *feminism*, usually referencing feminism in France. In 1912 the number of

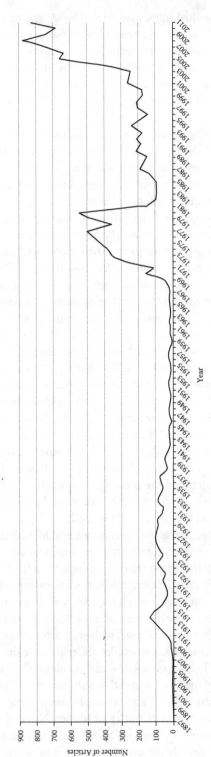

FIGURE 8.1 *Mentions of Feminism in the* New York Times

articles mentioning *feminism* had more than tripled to 68, and in 1914 that number again more than doubled, with 142 articles mentioning the word *feminism*. This level of frequency was not reached again until the 1970s, six years into the second-wave movement.[2] Beyond the *New York Times*, by 1913, articles about feminism occurred in periodicals as diverse as *Harper's Weekly, Good Housekeeping, McClure's Magazine* (credited with having started the tradition of muckraking), and the *Century Magazine*.

There was a general feeling at this time, particularly on the left, that feminism was becoming one of the most important social movements of the time. In August 1911, for example, when feminism was still associated with suffragists, socialist Josephine Conger Kaneko wrote in the popular left magazine *The Masses* that there "are two significant movements in the world to-day—that of the working class for economic freedom, and that of the woman for political freedom" (Kaneko 1911: 16). In December of that year, *The Masses* devoted an entire issue to women. In February 1913, when feminism as a theory distinct from suffrage was gaining momentum, the popular magazine *McClure's* started a Department for Women, headed by feminist and famous suffragist Inez Milholland.[3] The goal of this department was to treat the new feminist movement in "a sensible, straightforward manner," claiming, "No movement of this century is more significant or more deep-rooted than the movement to readjust the social position of women" ("A New Department for Women" 1913: 185). By May 1914 feminism had fully infiltrated US culture. In an editorial titled "The Revolt of the Woman" printed in *The Century* magazine and republished in the *New York Times*, editors declared that feminism would win, and that when it did, the world would be a better place: "The time has come to define feminism.... The germ is in the blood of our women.... The doctrine and its corollaries are on every tongue.... Like every demand for human freedom, feminism will succeed; and, when it does come to pass, the human race will attain for the first time its full efficiency" ("The Revolt of the Woman" 1914: 964–965). By 1914 the left and the press were generally united in the belief that feminism (distinct from suffrage) was a significant and profound new movement, and was one that would change society for good.

All of these feminists were suffragists,[4] and many, like Milholland, were quite central to the suffrage movement. But feminism was much broader than the suffrage movement. One of the main features that distinguished feminists from suffragists was their insistence that political reforms, such as suffrage, would not be enough to reach gender equality; a much broader and deeper revolution was needed. In an article in *Harper's Weekly* titled "The Younger Suffragists," Winnifred Harper Cooley argued that women's suffrage, while important, was only one part of a larger revolution. Feminists, she claimed, "consider the vote the merest tool, a means to an end—that end being a complete social revolution" (Cooley 1913: 16). Suffrage was only the beginning of a social revolution that Cooley believed was "sweeping every civilized country, and is the prophecy of the dawn of a tomorrow far brighter and better than yesterday or to-day" (Cooley 1913: 19). This social revolution did not mean a few changes allowing more equality for women; it rather meant an entirely new definition of what it meant to be a man and a woman: "Feminism is not a female with fewer petticoats; it does not seek to crinoline men," claimed one prominent feminist. "It asks a new fashion in the social garments of each" ("Talk on Feminism Stirs Great Crowd" 1914: 2).

While feminists active in the 1910s agreed on the need for a revolution, like the feminist movement in the second wave and again today, these activists disagreed on how to achieve that revolution. In the remainder of this section I focus on a specific strategy and tactic used by 1910s feminists, a form I call *narrative-based consciousness-raising*.

"BACKGROUND TALKS" AND CREATING
A NEW CONSCIOUSNESS IN WOMEN

The feminist movement consisted of more than a few individuals writing for the press; there were also feminist organizations in New York City with membership lists in the hundreds (Cott 1987). The earliest, largest, and longest-lasting feminist organization of this period was an organization called Heterodoxy. Heterodoxy was founded in Greenwich Village, New York City, in 1912 by twenty-five women "who did things and did them openly" (Luhan 1985: 144). The membership list quickly expanded to over one hundred and included the most prominent leftist women of the time, including Crystal Eastman, Elizabeth Gurly Flynn, Charlotte Perkins Gilman, Emma Goldman, and Eleanor Roosevelt (Beasley, Shulman, and Beasley 2000). All of the members of Heterodoxy were self-sufficient in some way, and most were writers, educators, doctors, lawyers, and small business owners. Most of these women were fighting for larger reforms affecting women, such as working for suffrage or to abolish the Comstock Laws.[5]

Heterodoxy's main goal was to act as a support group for women who were breaking social, political, and professional norms, as well as to change and expand women's awareness about their social position as women. To do so, Heterodoxy had weekly meetings that commonly consisted of what they called "background talks," where a member would narrate their personal histories and experiences, focusing on intimate issues in a way they could not do in public. Heterodoxy member Inez Milholland articulated the theory behind these background talks. In order to achieve any sort of lasting social change, she claimed, women had to first inquire "into every phase of life," in order "to act with some authority regarding it" (1913: 185). This form of inquiry, she claimed, would penetrate "into the remotest, obscurest corners of life, searching boldly under the premises of everything profane and sacred," and once they understood their own lives, women could then broadcast "their discoveries" to the world (Milholland 1913: 185). First and foremost, she claimed, women needed to learn how to be frank with one another and talk about problems facing women, like sex and prostitution, abusive husbands, and beauty norms.

Heterodoxy member Inez Irwin described how these background talks would start with a member telling "whatever she chose to reveal about her childhood, girlhood and young womanhood" (quoted in Schwarz 1982: 20). As women shared these experiences, the group would note the common themes that ran throughout the stories and would discuss possible collective causes of these themes. One theme that continually arose was childrearing, which was encouraged by Heterodoxy member and noted psychologist Leta Hollingworth. The members would talk about how they were raised with certain expectations because they were women, and how their brothers were raised with different expectations. They would then discuss why this was the case. Out of these discussions many of the members, more or less successfully, consciously attempted to raise their children in gender-neutral environments in order to break the cycle of gendered expectations (Schwartz 1982: 21). Women in Heterodoxy also used this woman-only protected space to examine how women internalized men's and society's view that women were inferior, with the goal of overcoming their "inferiority complex." Their goal was to increase their own beliefs about what they, as women, could do, and then impart this knowledge to their children and other women (Wittenstein 1991). Their ultimate goal was the creation of an entirely new consciousness in women.

This focus on changing women's consciousness was widespread among 1910s feminists. Feminist Ellen Glasgow, in 1913, claimed "the feminist movement is a revolt from a pretense of being—it is at its best and worst a struggle for the liberation of personality" (Glasgow 1913: 21).[6] "Spiritual freedom evolves out of *consciousness of powers possessed*," claimed Heterodoxy member Rose Young, "a sense of self and opportunity, and it is only out of spiritual freedom that the whole individual evolves" (1914: 25, emphasis in original). If women did not know their own capabilities, if women believed in the inferiority prescribed to them by men, women could never utilize political rights or achieve true equality. At its heart, claimed Heterodoxy founder Marie Jenny Howe, "feminism means more than a changed world. It means a changed psychology, the creation of a new consciousness in women" (Howe 1914: 29).

THE PERSONAL IS POLITICAL

One outcome of this tactic—using personal narratives to understand the collective roots of common problems—was to open personal problems to collective change, or in other words, to make the personal political. Milholland went on to argue that as women explored their own oppression they would find that "her 'home' has, in the complex of social life of our time, become entangled in a thousand ways with the outside life of the community and the nation" (1913: 188). As women explored their own lives and the causes of common problems, they would inevitably target interpersonal issues such as marriage, the home, and sexual relationships with men. Milholland emphasized this process in 1913: as women, as a political class, together dig into their own lives, they will, she claimed, naturally focus on the institutions most important to them: "home and marriage itself," and change, she claimed, must be brought to these institutions (1913: 188). Society cannot liberate women, Milholland stated, "without ultimately finding ourselves facing radical changes in [women's] relations with man" (1913: 188). Many women in Heterodoxy actively attempted to effect radical changes in their own lives by exploring alternative types of relationships with each other and with men. Some of them lived with men who were not their husbands, some lived apart from their husbands in order to maintain their freedom in marriage, some lived with other women, and some had multiple sexual partners in their lives, including married women living in open relationships.

In sum, while women in the suffrage movement were participating in parades, direct actions, and political lobbying, an influential subset of these women were additionally focused on extra-institutional change: changing patterns of relationships between men and women. They did so by using personal narratives to expose the collective roots of personal problems and to change men's and women's understanding of the social world and eventually interpersonal relations themselves. This form of feminism was reproduced in almost an exact form in the 1960s and 1970s.

1960s Radical Feminism: "Studying the Whole Gamut of Women's Lives"

Women's formation of discussion groups with the express aim of personal and social change was most memorably named during the second-wave movement, where it was coined *consciousness-raising* (Sarachild 1979; Evans 1980; Brownmiller 2000). Consciousness-raising was developed, theorized, and named by women in early second-wave radical feminist organizations in New York City. The first of these organizations was New York Radical Women (NYRW), formed in 1967 by feminists Pam Allen and Shulamith Firestone.[7] In 1969 NYRW split, and one side changed its name to Redstockings. A separate radical feminist group called the Feminists was formed in 1968 by women who split from the New York City chapter of NOW, led by former New York City NOW president Ti Grace Atkinson. In late 1969 Firestone broke away from Redstockings and founded yet another radical feminist organization, New York Radical Feminists (NYRF), with the purpose of integrating the masses of women interested in radical feminist politics. Some of the women who formed these groups were committed activists and veterans of the civil rights movement and New Left; many were professional writers and artists, trying to make it in male-dominated fields.[8]

Women's liberation was thrust onto the public scene during one of the first and most successful public actions led by NYRW and the Feminists: a protest outside of the 1969 Miss America Pageant in Atlantic City, New Jersey. Feminists targeted this event because they believed beauty pageants perpetuated the idea that beauty, grace, and aesthetically pleasing men should be women's main life goal and the only measure of their worth. Outside of the auditorium hosting the pageant, feminists put "instruments of female torture," like bras, girdles, false eyelashes, and high heels, into a "freedom trash can" and crowned a sheep "Miss America" to illustrate their claim that women in the pageant were mindless followers (Hanisch 1968; Freeman 1969). Inside the pageant, women unfurled a banner reading "Women's Liberation," which was picked up by the TV cameras and broadcast to the nation, drawing national attention to the burgeoning movement. This action exposed what every young, well-off woman felt: women existed for men, not themselves, and men wanted them for their looks, not their minds.

While this public protest put women's liberation on the social and cultural map, sparking the lasting stereotype of feminists as angry, men-hating, bra-burners (Campbell 2010), the more common tactic used by radical feminists was in fact consciousness-raising. Kathy Sarachild, a member of NYRW, recounted the initial expression of the idea of consciousness-raising as a political tactic in the second wave. After the Miss America protest, women in NYRW were wondering what to do next. Borrowing from her experience in the civil rights movement, NYRW member Ann Forer spoke up and said, "I think we have a lot more to do just in the area of raising our consciousness" (Sarachild 1979: 144). Consciousness-raising, claimed Sarachild, involved "studying the whole gamut of women's lives, starting with the full reality of one's own," and was a way to prevent the women's movement from getting sidetracked by reforms and single-issue organizing (Sarachild 1979: 145). When women had a better understanding of how their lives related to the general condition of women, it would make them better fighters "on behalf of women as a whole," she claimed (Sarachild 1979: 145).

To put this idea into action, these radical feminist organizations began to organize consciousness-raising sessions. During these consciousness-raising or "rap" sessions, small groups of women would get together to talk about their personal experiences with various issues, like beauty standards, sex with men, sex with women, working as mothers, and so on. Their goals were to find common issues facing all women and to explore the common roots of these issues. It was out of these consciousness-raising activities that radical feminists coined the term *The personal is political*, which became a general rallying cry for feminists (Hanisch 1970). The goal of these sessions was to change the consciousness of women by revealing to them how their lives and their ambitions were shaped by patterns of social relationships that benefit men, a system that 1960s feminists labeled *patriarchy*. This change in consciousness was a necessary precursor to wider political and social change, claimed radical feminists, as women would not know what issues to target, nor would they be able to utilize newly won rights, unless they first expanded their idea of what it meant to be a woman.

As women explored and questioned their lives in these sessions, they found, just as the 1910s feminists concluded, that even the most intimate relationships between men and women were shaped by patriarchy. Sex, relationships with men, and the nuclear family were at the center of many of the discussions held in these groups (e.g., O'Brien 1978; Leon 1978). Some feminists, as well as the group the Feminists, played around with officially limiting the number of hours women could spend with men, some called for abstaining from sex altogether, and others advocated lesbianism as the only way women could be truly liberated (Echols 1989). Everything about the interpersonal relationships between men and women was up for discussion—and change—for the consciousness-raising feminists in the second wave.

Consciousness-raising as a political tactic partially arose out of, and partially shaped, the specific theory of women's oppression articulated by these early radical feminist organizations, a theory that set them apart from other women's liberation organizations such as the Chicago Women's Liberation Union. Radical feminist organizations claimed that women's oppression was caused by a system of interpersonal patriarchal gender relationships in which all men, politically, legally, socially, and morally, subordinated all women. This patriarchal system was fundamentally rooted in men's psychological need to dominate women, and women's psyches had long developed under the psychological domination of men (e.g., Redstockings 1969; Millett 2000 [1970]). Changing laws to better incorporate women, as organizations like NOW were doing, or even a full-fledged socialist revolution as other leftist organizations were working toward, would leave this patriarchal system, and thus women's oppression, intact. What was needed, believed radical feminists, was a revolution in the interpersonal relationships between men and women and a fundamental change in the psychology of both.

This history highlights four important continuities between 1910s feminism and 1970s feminism: collectively exploring the realities of individual lives as a way to understand women's position in society, their insistence that personal problems are in fact political, a focus on changing interpersonal relationships between men and women as part and parcel of overall social change, and, importantly, the insistence on the importance of changing consciousness as a prerequisite to larger social change (see Table 8.1 for a summary of these similarities).

Contemporary Feminism: Self-Help, Lean In Circles, and Online Communities

As feminist scholars explore contemporary feminist groups and organizing, they continue to uncover examples of narrative-based consciousness-raising. In the 1980s and 1990s, for example, there was a rise in women's self-help groups, which again employed a type of narrative-based consciousness-raising to heighten awareness of, but also change individual consciousness about, issues such as breast cancer and postpartum depression (Taylor 1996). Taylor, who explored postpartum depression support groups, claimed "self-help communities start out as sites where participants can find personal support through sharing their problems," but "the experience of being intensely immersed in a shared women's community," Taylor asserts, "offers participants the opportunity to reframe their individual biographies in socially and politically meaningful terms" (1996: 104). This was precisely the goal of narrative-based consciousness-raising in the 1910s and 1960s. Nonetheless, these self-help groups have never been incorporated into the common narrative of the history of the women's movement. Situating these groups in the framework of narrative-based consciousness-raising places them firmly in the continuum of the women's movement and highlights the importance of this tactic.

Today, as we are experiencing yet another period of heightened political action, we are again seeing a resurgence of a more public type of consciousness-raising as a women's movement tactic.[9] As in the first and second waves, this tactic is

TABLE 8.1 Continuities between the first and second waves

	Exploring your own life	The personal is political	Personal institutions	Raising consciousness
First Wave Organizations: *Heterodoxy*	"[Women will insist] on her right to inquire into every phase of life, and to act with some authority regarding it."[1]	"[Women have] discovered that her 'home' has, in the complex of social life of our time, become entangled in a thousand ways with the outside life of the community and the nation."[3]	". . . the institutions most certain to be touched and changed are the institutions in which the sex, as a sex, is most peculiarly and vitally interested. And these institutions, it is hardly necessary to point out, are the home and marriage itself."[3]	"Spiritual freedom evolves out of *consciousness of powers possessed*, a sense of self and opportunity, and it is only out of spiritual freedom that the whole individual evolves."[2]
Second Wave Organizations: *NYRW Redstockings The Feminists NYRF*	Consciousness-raising means "studying the whole gamut of women's lives, starting with the full reality of one's own."[4]	"One of the first things we discover in these groups is that personal problems are political problems. There are no personal solutions at this time. There is only collective action for a collective solution."[6]	"When male supremacy is completely eliminated, marriage, like the state will disappear."[7]	"Agitation for specific freedoms is worthless without the preliminary raising of consciousness necessary to utilize these freedoms fully."[5]

Source: [1]Milholland 1913: 185; [2]Young 1914: 25; [3]Milholland 1913: 188; [4]Sarachild 1979; [5]Firestone 1968; [6]Hanisch 1970; [7]Kathy Sarachild quoted in Echols 1989: 146.

being used by professional women who are in male-dominated careers or who are attempting to fight for women's rights in other areas.

One example of this is Sheryl Sandberg's book *Lean In* (2014) and the phenomenon based on this book: Lean In Circles. The home page of the website leanincircles.org describes their mission:

> Lean In Circles are small groups who meet regularly to learn and grow together. . . . Women are asking for more and stepping outside their comfort zones, and men and women are talking openly about gender issues for the first time. (LeanIn.org 2016).

Women in these groups help each other ask for raises, ask for promotions, or develop organizations aimed at winning more rights for women, but the general aim of these circles is to understand common ways in which women are prevented from advancing in their careers and to help each other overcome those obstacles. The website claims that there are twenty-one thousand circles in ninety-seven countries, and more are forming every day (LeanIn.org 2016).

Sandberg explains the importance of women talking about their issues with one another in her book *Lean In*: "The simple act of talking openly about behavioral patterns makes the subconscious conscious. . . . Talking can transform minds, which can transform behaviors, which can transform institutions" (Sandberg 2014: 157–158). Here Sandberg is rearticulating an approach to feminism that, as we have seen, was first expressed in the 1910s.[10]

Another example of contemporary narrative-based consciousness-raising, with a modern technological twist, is the Everyday Sexism Project. The Everyday Sexism Project, started by Laura Bates in 2012, established an online platform where women can share their personal experiences of sexism with one another. Women from all over the world post stories of examples of sexism they have faced, from catcalls on the street to domestic violence to harassment in their workplaces. Their goal: to "show the world that sexism does exist, it is faced by women everyday and it is a valid problem to discuss" (The Everyday Sexism Project 2016). With project branches in twenty-five countries, the creators have grouped these stories into themes such as media, politics, and college campuses, and are publishing them in book format (Bates 2016).

In addition to this project, trending hashtags meant to highlight the experience of different groups of women on Twitter serve the same purpose: collective self-expression as a political act. #YesAllWomen, which details stories of sexual harassment, and #SayHerName, which publicizes police brutality against black women, are just two examples of how women are using Twitter to express common problems. These women are using the Internet to transcend geographical boundaries and provide a global space for women to collectively explore sexism through personal narratives.

Knowing the history of the feminism recounted above puts self-help groups, Sandberg's Lean In Circles, the Everyday Sexism Project, and hashtags in perspective. This approach to feminism has been at the core of the women's movement from its earliest moments; it continued to be central to the movement in the 1960s and 1970s, reemerged in self-help groups in the 1990s, and is still central today. While the history of mass demonstrations and political lobbying is a critical component of women's movements throughout history, I argue that so is narrative-based consciousness-raising.

Disruption, Recurrence, and Continuity

We have seen that narrative-based consciousness-raising has been a central strategy of the women's movement from the first wave through the contemporary moment. What explains the continuity, or recurrence, of this strategy over time? An examination of how and why the first-wave feminist movement ended suggests that overlapping generations or abeyance structures, the popular ways of explaining continuity to date, likely did not contribute to the continuity of this form of feminism over time. To illustrate, I briefly discuss the political conditions in the United States following the First World War, and how this affected the feminist movement.

In the 1910s feminism as a political identity made an impressive, but brief, showing. The end of the decade was as bad for left-leaning political movements as the beginning of the decade was good. In 1917 all of American society, including large and vibrant Progressive movements, was interrupted by the entrance of the United States into World War I. This entrance shifted public attention away from government corruption and Progressive reform, the focus during the first years of the 1910s, and united public opinion firmly behind nationalism and the war effort. After the 1917 Russian Revolution raised the possibility of a socialist revolution in the United States, this hypernationalism quickly turned to suspicion of anyone not born in the United States and anyone involved in leftist movements. The public at large rallied behind this general fear, and the years between 1918 and 1920 are now called the *First Red Scare*.

The Sedition Act of 1918 made any speech-act criticizing the government or the war efforts an arrestable and deportable crime. Beginning in 1919 the Department of Justice, led by Attorney General A. Mitchell Palmer and under the legal cover of the Sedition Act, raided the headquarters of leftist organizations, stealing literature, meeting notes, and other organizational property as "evidence" of seditious activity. Over ten thousand people were arrested during what were eventually called the Palmer Raids, and hundreds were deported for "offenses" as small as writing an article that criticized the government (Finan 2007). These expansive raids and the general nationalist hysteria following the war very effectively silenced the left, including the feminist movement. As early as 1919 political activists were using the term *postfeminist* (Cott 1987: 282), and much like the 1980s, there was a general backlash against feminism in the 1920s.

In the 1920s the government continued to target social movements, feminism and women's movement organizations in particular. The Military Intelligence Division had begun collecting information on feminism and its connection to socialism during World War I. This information was compiled and published in

May 1923 by a librarian at the Chemical Warfare Service of the War Department in a document that is now called the "Spider Web Chart" (Catt 1924). The chart focused on the Women's Joint Congressional Committee (WJCC), an umbrella organization connecting the work of a number of mainstream women's organizations, including the League of Women Voters and the Woman's Christian Temperance Union. In the chart, individual members of the WJCC were named and connected to socialist and communist groups, and their "radical" opinions were quoted. The lines linking individuals and organizations made the chart look like a web, giving it its arachnoid nickname. At the bottom of the chart the librarian wrote a poem she called "Miss Bolshevik," which began,

> Miss Bolsheviki has come to town,
> With a Russian cap and a German gown,
> In women's clubs she's sure to be found,
> For she's come to disarm America. (Quoted in Catt 1924: 32)

This chart was published along with a detailed story about feminism and socialism in two installments (Catt 1924). This chart was eventually used as evidence by legislators who opposed the social legislation introduced by the WJCC, and it was read into the *Congressional Record* in 1926, accompanied by charges of "bolshevism" and "socialized medicine," during a hearing about renewing the Sheppard-Towner Act—pioneering legislation first passed in 1921 that gave mothers guaranteed health care for themselves and their children (Freeman 1995). During and following the tense atmosphere created by the First Red Scare and the Palmer Raids, a chart such as this, targeting mainstream feminist organizations, would have had a chilling effect. As a result, the women's movement struggled during this period and the history of feminism recounted above was effectively buried and almost forgotten.

Second-wave women's liberationists worked to publicize the history of women's activism, and they believed they were continuing the work of presuffrage radical women, including the work by the National Woman's Party (NWP). Interestingly, however, despite their commonalities with early feminists like Milholland, Young, and Howe of Heterodoxy, second-wave feminists did not reference these writers; as a result, second-wave feminists believed their focus on consciousness-raising and psychological change made what they were doing decidedly different from first-wave feminists. In 1968, Firestone, for example, the founder of three different radical feminist organizations, wrote an article taking inspiration from the early women's movement but also describing how she thought her movement was distinct. The main difference, she claimed, was that the early movement was too focused on "hot" issues, such as Prohibition and suffrage, and failed to "raise the general consciousness" of women's overall position in society (Firestone 1968). Kate Millett, another feminist involved with NYRW, had a similar analysis of what she called the "first phase" of the "sexual revolution." The first phase was unable to last beyond winning the right to vote because, according to Millett, it failed to "challenge patriarchal ideology at a sufficiently deep and radical level to break the conditioning process of status, temperament and role" (2000 [1970]: 85).

What was needed, and the first phase did not attempt, she claimed, was a change in "social attitudes *and* social structure, in personality *and* institutions" (Millett 2000 [1970]: 85, emphasis added). Given the dearth of information on women's history available in the 1960s and early 1970s, second-wave feminists knew an impressive amount about the first-wave movement, and certainly learned from it. Nonetheless, it is unlikely that they got their focus on consciousness and "personality" directly from their knowledge of first-wave activists.

What, then, can explain the near identical use of consciousness-raising as a tactic and the focus on personal and interpersonal change in both the first and second waves? While decidedly answering this is not possible within the scope of this chapter, I suggest that this particular form of continuity was a result of the institutionalization of political knowledge.

The general institutionalization of knowledge leads to what Robert Merton calls "multiple independent discoveries" of the same ideas or the same solutions to a problem. Multiple independent discoveries happen when the knowledge and tools necessary for a discovery "accumulate in man's [*sic*] cultural store" and when attention is focused on a particular problem by "emerging social needs" (Merton 1973: 371). This may be at work for the feminists in the second wave, who were facing similar historical and social circumstances as women in the 1910s and were able to draw on this institutionalized knowledge as they were building their political organizations. Once the narrative-based consciousness-raising approach was institutionalized by feminists in the 1910s, and as women were faced with similar problems in the 1960s, they (re)discovered the same solution, independent of their direct knowledge of these early feminists but as a result of drawing on latent (or hidden) institutionalized knowledge. This happened again in the 1990s, and once again in the 2010s. The women's movement, thus, has exhibited a sort of "rolling inertia" as women draw on the same base of knowledge to form their movements in different periods (Greve and Rao 2012).

Conclusion

Taking seriously Staggenborg and Taylor's (2005) call to analyze continuities between feminist waves, I examined the continuity in one feminist approach—narrative-based consciousness-raising—through three waves of feminism. By emphasizing this history, collective self-expression as politics becomes a core, rather than peripheral, aspect of the women's movement over time.

Contemporary feminist theories reinforce that this form of feminist activism gets to the root of persistent gender oppression. Ridgeway's contemporary feminist theory, for example, focuses on the role of interpersonal behavior in continuing gender inequality: "Key processes at the interpersonal level," she claims, and "institutionalized cultural beliefs about gender that shape expectations for behavior at the interpersonal level . . . are especially important for the persistence of gender inequality in the modern world" (Ridgeway 2011: 16–17). Precisely these institutionalized cultural beliefs and interpersonal behavior are the targets of narrative-based consciousness-raising. The root of gendered oppression in these interpersonal institutions justifies the continued use of narrative-based consciousness-raising as a feminist strategy.

This approach to feminism and feminist activism, however, is one of many forms of feminism that has existed in the United States and abroad. Feminism is made up of a plurality of theories, and feminist activism includes a wide range of tactics; this particular tactic is not without its limitations. This approach assumes a sort of gender universalism—that all women will be able to relate to one another and find common ground between their experiences. Many feminists and women's rights activists have pointed out that not all women experience women's oppression in the same way, and gender universalism typically privileges a certain type of woman: most often white and typically middle to upper class (Lorde 1984; Moraga and Anzaldua 1984; Roth 2004; hooks 2000; Cobble 2005). Indeed, it does take a certain type of privilege to have to talk about one's oppression in order to recognize it, and to have the time and resources to do so.

As women continue to raise awareness today by telling personal narratives, drawing connections between personal problems, and supporting one another through platforms such as Twitter, Facebook, and other global organizations, this form of feminism includes underrepresented women, such as black and transwomen, and narratives of difference are being articulated alongside narratives of commonalities. As the movement continues to grow, we can be heartened and inspired by the traditions they are carrying on, even as we critique them. Hopefully we will reach the day when consciousness-raising is no longer needed.

Notes

1. This was done with a keyword search for "feminism OR feminist" using the *New York Times* online archives, recording the numbers of articles per year mentioning either of the words.

2. In 1970, 158 articles mentioned feminism, and this number continued to increase through 1980.

3. Milholland was the famous woman in white, wearing a long white cape astride a white horse, leading the suffrage parade in Washington, DC, in 1913.

4. Emma Goldman is one exception. She was a feminist but not a suffragist.

5. The Comstock Laws made it illegal to disseminate information about contraception, under the guise that this information was "obscene." Even doctors were forbidden from disseminating this information. These laws were not fully repealed until 1972, when the Supreme Court decision on *Eisenstadt v. Baird* finally allowed physicians to disseminate information about contraception to married and unmarried persons (Gordon 1976).

6. The word *personality* was a generally leftist term at the time, meaning the "full development of subjectivity, free from institutional constraints and all preexistent psychological forms and social expectations" (Keetley and Pettegrew 2005: 4).

7. Historical details come from Echols 1989; Rosen 2000; and Stansell 2010.

8. Ellen Willis, for example, was a popular music critic when the field was dominated by men and was the first popular music critic for the *New Yorker*, Firestone was a trained painter and author, and Robin Morgan was an author and involved in the publishing industry.

9. Figure 8.1 suggests that we are indeed in the middle of a third wave of feminism, as evidenced by the number of mentions of feminism in the *New York Times*.

10. There are plenty of valid criticisms of Sandberg and her movement, and many would not accept her as a bearer of the feminist tradition. The same criticisms of Sandberg, however, can be made of the radical feminists of the 1960s and of Heterodoxy: they mainly target middle-class, professional women; they ignore institutional constraints; and they ignore the diversity of experiences among women. Making the connections between these three moments in this way, I believe, can help us understand the place of this particular tactic in the larger feminist movement.

References

Armstrong, Elizabeth A., and Mary Bernstein. 2008. "Culture, Power, and Institutions: A Multi-Institutional Politics Approach to Social Movements." *Sociological Theory* 26(1): 74–99.

Bates, Laura. 2016. *Everyday Sexism*. New York: A Thomas Dunne Book for St. Martin's Griffin.

Beasley, Maurine Hoffman, Holly Cowan Shulman, and Henry R. Beasley. 2000. *The Eleanor Roosevelt Encyclopedia*. Westport, CT: Greenwood.

Brownmiller, Susan. 2000. *In Our Time: Memoir of a Revolution*. New York: Dell.

Campbell, W. Joseph. 2010. *Getting It Wrong: Ten of the Greatest Misreported Stories in American Journalism*. Berkeley: University of California Press.

Catt, Carrie Chapman. 1924. "Poison Propaganda." *Woman Citizen* 14(May): 32–33.

Cobble, Dorothy Sue. 2005. *The Other Women's Movement: Workplace Justice and Social Rights in Modern America*. Princeton, NJ: Princeton University Press.

Cooley, Winnifred Harper. 1913. "The Younger Suffragists." Pp. 16–19 in *Public Women, Public Words: A Documentary History of American Feminism: Volume 2: 1900–1960*, edited by D. Keetley and J. Pettegrew. Lanham, MD: Rowman and Littlefield.

Cott, Nancy Falik. 1987. *The Grounding of Modern Feminism*. New Haven, CT: Yale University Press.

Crossley, Alison Dahl. 2015. "Facebook Feminism: Social Media, Blogs, and New Technologies of Contemporary U.S. Feminism." *Mobilization: An International Quarterly* 20(2): 253–269.

Echols, Alice. 1989. *Daring to Be Bad: Radical Feminism in America, 1967–1975*. Minneapolis: University of Minnesota Press.

Evans, Sara. 1980. *Personal Politics: The Roots of Women's Liberation in the Civil Rights Movement and the New Left*. New York: Vintage Books.

The Everyday Sexism Project. 2016. http://everydaysexism.com/about.

Faludi, Susan. 2006. *Backlash: The Undeclared War against American Women*. New York: Three Rivers Press.

Ferree, Myra Marx, and Beth B. Hess. 2000. *Controversy and Coalition the New Feminist Movement across Three Decades of Change.* New York: Routledge.

Finan, Christopher M. 2007. *From the Palmer Raids to the Patriot Act: A History of the Fight for Free Speech in America.* Boston: Beacon Press.

Firestone, Shulamith. 1968. "The Women's Rights Movement in the U.S.A.: A New View." Pp. 1–7 in *Notes from the First Year,* edited by New York Radical Women. New York: New York Radical Women.

Freeman, Jo. 1969. "No More Miss America! (1968–1969)." http://www.jofreeman.com/photos/MissAm1969.html.

———. 1995. "The Spider Web Chart." http://www.jofreeman.com/polhistory/spiderweb.htm.

Giddings, Paula J. 2007. *When and Where I Enter: The Impact of Black Women on Race and Sex in America.* Second edition. New York: William Morrow Paperbacks.

Glasgow, Ellen. 1913. "Feminism." Pp. 19–22 in *Public Women, Public Words: A Documentary History of American Feminism: Volume 2: 1900–1960,* edited by D. Keetley and J. Pettegrew. Lanham, MD: Rowman and Littlefield.

Gordon, Ann. 1996. "Introduction." Pp. 1–9 in *African American Women and the Vote, 1837–1965.* Edited by A. Gordon, B. Collier-Thomas, J. H. Bracey, A. V. Avakian, and J. A. Berkman. Amherst: University of Massachusetts Press.

Gordon, Linda. 1976. *Woman's Body, Woman's Right: A Social History of Birth Control in America.* New York: Grossman.

Greve, Henrich R., and Hayagreeva Rao. 2012. "Echoes of the Past: Organizational Foundings as Sources of an Institutional Legacy of Mutualism." *American Journal of Sociology* 118(3): 635–675.

Hanisch, Carol. 1968. "What Can Be Learned: A Critique of the Miss America Protest." http://carolhanisch.org/CHwritings/MissACritique.html.

———. 1970. "The Personal Is Political." In *Notes from the Second Year,* edited by S. Firestone and A. Koedt. New York: Radical Feminism.

hooks, bell. 2000. *Feminist Theory: From Margin to Center.* Second edition. Cambridge, MA: South End Press.

Howe, Marie Jenney. 1914. "A Feminist Symposium: Feminism." Pp. 29–34 In *Public Women, Public Words: A Documentary History of American Feminism: Volume 2: 1900–1960,* edited by D. Keetley and J. Pettegrew. Lanham, MD: Rowman and Littlefield.

Hull, Gloria T., Patricia Bell Scott, and Barbara Smith. 1982. *But Some of Us Are Brave: All the Women Are White, All the Blacks Are Men—Black Women's Studies.* New York: Feminist Press at CUNY.

Kaneko, Josephine Congo. 1911. "Woman Suffrage and Socialism." *The Masses* 1(2): 10.

Keetley, Dawn and John Pettegrew. 2002. *Public Women, Public Words: A Documentary History of American Feminism: 1900–1960.* Vol. 2. Lanham, MD: Rowman and Littlefield.

LeanIn.Org. 2016. "Lean In Circles." http://leanincircles.org/.

Leon, Barbara. 1978. "The Male Supremacist Attack on Monogamy." Pp. 128–129 in *Feminist Revolution/Redstockings of the Women's Liberation Movement,* edited by K. Sarachild. New York: Random House.

Lorde, Audre. 1984. *Sister Outsider: Essays and Speeches.* Trumansberg, NY: Crossing Press.

Luhan, Mabel Dodge. 1985. *Movers and Shakers.* Albuquerque: University of New Mexico Press.

McCammon, Holly J. 2012. "Explaining Frame Variation: More Moderate and Radical Demands for Women's Citizenship in the U.S. Women's Jury Movements." *Social Problems* 59(1): 43–69.

Merton, Robert K. 1973. *The Sociology of Science: Theoretical and Empirical Investigations*. Chicago: University of Chicago Press.

Milholland, Inez. 1913. "The Liberation of a Sex." *McClure's Magazine*, 181–185.

Millett, Kate. 2000 [1970]. *Sexual Politics*. Urbana: University of Illinois Press.

Molotch, Harvey, William Freudenburg, and Krista Paulsen. 2000. "History Repeats Itself, But How? City Character, Urban Tradition, and the Accomplishment of Place." *American Sociological Review* 65(6): 791–823.

Moraga, Cherrie, and Gloria Anzaldua, eds. 1984. *This Bridge Called My Back: Writings by Radical Women of Color*. New York: Kitchen Table / Women of Color Press.

"A New Department for Women." 1913. *McClure's Magazine*, 181.

O'Brien, Joyce. 1978. "In Favor of True Love Over Settling." Pp. 123–125 in *Feminist Revolution/Redstockings of the Women's Liberation Movement*, edited by K. Sarachild. New York: Random House.

Redstockings. 1969. "Redstockings Manifesto." http://redstockings.org/index.php/42-uncategorised/76-rs-manifesto.

Reger, Jo. 2012. *Everywhere and Nowhere: Contemporary Feminism in the United States*. New York: Oxford University Press.

Reger, Jo, ed. 2005. *Different Wavelengths: Studies of the Contemporary Women's Movement*. New edition. New York: Routledge.

"The Revolt of the Woman." 1914. *The Century: A Popular Quarterly* 87: 964–965.

Ridgeway, Cecilia L. 2011. *Framed by Gender: How Gender Inequality Persists in the Modern World*. New York: Oxford University Press.

Rosen, Ruth. 2000. *The World Split Open: How the Modern Women's Movement Changed America*. New York: Penguin Books.

Roth, Benita. 2004. *Separate Roads to Feminism: Black, Chicana, and White Feminist Movements in America's Second Wave*. Cambridge, MA: Cambridge University Press.

Rupp, Leila J., and Verta Taylor. 1987. *Survival in the Doldrums: The American Women's Rights Movement, 1945 to the 1960s*. New York: Oxford University Press.

Sandberg, Sheryl. 2014. *Lean In: Women, Work, and the Will to Lead*. New York: Alfred A. Knopf.

Sarachild, Kathie. 1979. "Consciousness-Raising: A Radical Weapon." Pp. 144–150 in *Feminist Revolutions/Redstockings of the Women's Liberation Movement*, edited by K. Sarachild. New York: Random House.

Schwarz, Judith. 1982. *Radical Feminists of Heterodoxy: Greenwich Village, 1912–1940*. Lebanon, NH: New Victoria Publishers.

Staggenborg, Suzanne. 1989. "Stability and Innovation in the Women's Movement: A Comparison of Two Movement Organizations." *Social Problems* 36(1): 75–92.

———. 1996. "The Survival of the Women's Movement: Turnover and Continuity in Bloomington, Indiana." *Mobilization: An International Quarterly* 1(2): 143–158.

Staggenborg, Suzanne, and Vera Taylor. 2005. "Whatever Happened to the Women's Movement?" *Mobilization: An International Quarterly* 10(1): 37–52.

Stansell, Christine. 2010. *The Feminist Promise: 1792 to the Present*. New York: Modern Library.

Stanton, Elizabeth Cady, Ann D. Gordon, and Susan B. Anthony. 1997. *The Selected Papers of Elizabeth Cady Stanton and Susan B. Anthony*. New Brunswick, NJ: Rutgers University Press.

"Talk on Feminism Stirs Great Crowd: Freedom for Women, Speakers Agree, Is Goal of the Movement. IT DEVELOPS THE INDIVIDUAL Rose Young at Cooper Union Discussion Says the Battle Is to Overcome Convention." 1914. *The New York Times*, February 18: 2.

Taylor, Vera. 1989. "Social Movement Continuity: The Women's Movement in Abeyance." *American Sociological Review* 54: 761–775.

———. 1996. *Rock-a-by Baby: Feminism, Self-Help, and Postpartum Depression*. New York: Routledge.

Tong, Rosemarie. 2013. *Feminist Thought: A More Comprehensive Introduction*. Boulder, CO: Westview Press.

Whittier, Nancy. 1995. *Feminist Generations: The Persistence of the Radical Women's Movement*. Philadelphia: Temple University Press.

Wittenstein, Kate E. 1991. *The Heterodoxy Club and American Feminism, 1912–1930*. Ann Arbor, MI: University Microfilms International.

Young, Rose. 1914. "What Is Feminism?" Pp. 22–26 in *Public Women, Public Words: A Documentary History of American Feminism*, edited by D. Keetley and J. Pettegrew. Lanham, MD: Rowman and Littlefield.

9

US Women's Groups in National Policy Debates, 1880–2000

Kristin A. Goss

When the United States enacted a constitutional amendment guaranteeing female suffrage in 1920, many observers believed women would declare victory and retire from the political struggle. Suffrage leaders insisted that, on the contrary, the "woman movement" was just getting started, with new modes of collective action and an ambitious policy agenda. There was nothing particularly "wonderful in being able to put some marks on a piece of paper and drop it into a box three or four times a year," said one leading women's advocate. "We thought of the ballot as a tool with which great things were to be done."[1]

On the one hundredth anniversary of the Nineteenth Amendment's ratification, this chapter examines whether women working together after suffrage indeed did try to get great things done. Early assessments of suffrage insisted that it had been a dud: Women hadn't fully embraced their new right to take part in the nation's governance. However, the findings here suggest that such gloomy assessments were mistaken. The amendment had a significant, long-term impact on American democracy by emboldening women's organizations to advance ambitious, wide-ranging policy agendas. What is more, the most interesting developments after suffrage may not have been at the polls but rather in the halls of the US Congress, where women's groups helped lawmakers to imagine and build the modern American state.

The case of suffrage is interesting and important in its own right, but it also raises larger theoretical questions about the relationship between civic inclusion and civic participation. Suffrage expanded women's rights, but so did legislation enacted during the so-called second-wave women's movement nearly fifty years later. Did the two movements and their policy successes bequeath similar patterns in women's collective engagement on important public issues? Does more inclusion necessarily spell more participation? This study considers these questions. The suffrage case also calls our attention to what a "women's issue" is. How does the expansion of women's political incorporation shape the policy agendas that women's organizational representatives pursue? This study offers a suggestive answer.

This chapter focuses on the rich legacy of the Nineteenth Amendment on women's collective action. The chapter charts the long rise and ultimate decline of national-level policy engagement by US women's organizations from roughly 1880, four decades before suffrage, through 2000. As a measure of policy engagement, I consider the testimony of representatives of women's organizations before the US Congress. The appearances were compiled by hand from the Congressional Information Service's *CIS Index*, a series of hardbound volumes that catalogue congressional hearings (by subject matter and witnesses) going back to the early nineteenth century. These entries were then cross-checked with the online hearings database maintained by Lexis-Nexis (now Proquest). The present dataset contains every appearance by a women's organization from 1873 to 2000—nearly ten thousand five hundred appearances by some twenty-one hundred groups testifying across nearly two hundred policy domains.

Women's groups were those that fell into at least one of four categories: organizations whose name included a word or suffix connoting female membership (e.g., League of *Women* Voters, Alpha Kappa Alpha *Sorority*, American National Cow*belles*, American Legion *Auxiliary*); unions and professional associations representing overwhelmingly female employment categories (nurses, secretaries, garment workers, etc.); voluntary associations whose priorities represented disproportionately female concerns and whose leaders were women (i.e., playground associations in the Progressive Era; breast-cancer organizations in the late twentieth century); and citizens' groups working for abortion rights and family planning.

For interest groups seeking a voice in American democracy, appearing before Congress is a coveted means of political engagement. Testimony also serves as a reliable measure, over time, of the groups that Congress considers to be the key players in a policy debate—that is, which groups have the policy authority and political clout to warrant an invitation to appear. Note that the dataset does not capture certain types of women's organizational work, including advocacy on purely local or state issues, institutional building, litigation, administrative advocacy, election involvement, or service provision. What the data do provide, however, is a window into how women's civic place evolved over time.

To tell the story, I first provide a brief theoretical perspective on women's civic identities and illustrate how suffrage provided a platform for organizing around them. I then lay out conventional narratives surrounding two key decades—the 1920s and the 1950s—in which women's activism is said to have stalled. Next, I assess those narratives empirically, demonstrating that by three measures—the number of times that women's groups testified at congressional hearings, the number of women's organizations that appeared, and the breadth of issues to which the groups spoke—these groups' policy engagement actually expanded in the four decades after suffrage. Then I show that by these same measures, women's engagement surprisingly declined after the second-wave women's movement of the 1960s and 1970s. I evaluate promising yet ultimately unsatisfying explanations for this inverted-U pattern and lay out an account centered on the role of public policy.

Specifically, I argue that the discursive and tangible resources provided by policy helped structure and direct the organization of women's interests. For the first two-thirds of the twentieth century, interests were oriented around both women's group rights and women's civic responsibility; for the last third of the century, the focus was on group rights almost exclusively. This evolution had implications for the volume of women's voices in American democracy as well as the range of issues on which they were heard.

The Nineteenth Amendment and Women's Civic Roles

The Nineteenth Amendment conveyed two powerful ideas about women's relationship with the state. The first idea was that women were entitled to equal treatment with men; if a man could vote, the state should not deny the right to a similarly situated woman. The second idea was that women's voices were important in democratic governance. Thus, the amendment simultaneously validated women's rights and expanded their civic responsibilities. These concepts of rights and responsibilities course through American history, with its strains of liberalism and civic republicanism.

The rights-responsibilities dichotomy roughly maps onto a dichotomy long used to understand gender relations: the sameness-difference dichotomy. While a vast oversimplification, the sameness-difference dyad has served as the foundation for much fruitful theorizing about women's roles in American public life. The idea behind gender sameness is that to the extent possible, women are not or should not be considered "different" from men. Sameness arguments often underlie women's rights claims, such as the right to equal treatment under law and to equal access to economic, social, and political institutions. The idea behind gender difference is that women as a group have distinctive experiences and perspectives and that these differences help direct women's patterns of public engagement. Difference rationales sometimes fuel rights claims (e.g., only women get pregnant, so employment laws must protect women from discrimination). But more commonly, women's groups have deployed difference arguments in connection with civic responsibilities. The idea that women are different from men—more caring, more public spirited—has served as the rationale for robust participation in policy debates extending far beyond women's rights (Goss 2014; Goss 2013). While sameness rationales have served women-oriented interests, difference rationales often have served other-oriented interests.

The Nineteenth Amendment created a political and rhetorical space for both types of citizenship: the rights-oriented variant focused on the interests of women as a group and the responsibility-oriented variant focused on the interests of other groups and the public at large. The robust definition of women's citizenship envisioned by the Nineteenth Amendment—a definition that validated equality claims against the state and invited participation in the state—helped to fuel a burst of women's collective engagement that lasted for decades. The suffrage amendment didn't create women's political engagement—indeed, the amendment was a product of a protracted, well-organized, nation-spanning movement. But the amendment did provide both external validation for women's role in governance and an unprecedented political opportunity for continued wide-scale civic education and organizing.

Women's Organizing after Suffrage

For at least four decades after suffrage—roughly until the second-wave women's movement began in the mid-1960s—the conventional wisdom holds that American women were politically disengaged. Women of the 1920s were flirty flappers, exercising their liberation by wearing shortened skirts, not by storming the ballot box. Women of the 1940s tended to matters at home while the boys were away at war—they were "Rosie the Riveters" out of necessity rather than choice. Women of the 1950s happily returned to their wifely and motherly duties—like June Cleaver, the archetypal middle-American matriarch in the popular family television series *Leave It to Beaver*. Do these iconic images accurately portray women's public engagement? Is it right that nothing much happened of interest between suffrage and the second-wave movement? Scholarly answers to these questions have differed over the years; congressional data help us sort them out.

Predictions that women's political engagement and influence would drop with enfranchisement began even before the Nineteenth Amendment was ratified. Antisuffragists argued that enfranchising women would actually undermine their efforts to mobilize collectively for social reform by eliminating the separate, nonpartisan sphere in which women found the moral and organizational grounding for their public work (Jablonsky 1994; Marshall 1997). The concern was that women would be absorbed into the political parties and their demands would be diluted and dismissed (Kraditor 1971).

Many contemporary historians picked up this theme, arguing that 1920 marked the beginning of a gradual downward spiral in women's capacity to organize and speak with a collective voice. Barbara Ryan (1992: 37) concludes that there "was no clear direction after the suffrage victory." By "adopting formerly male values and behavior," newly enfranchised women "lost the basis for a separate political culture," leaving them without uniquely "women's issues" around which to organize and prompting their political fragmentation (Baker 1984: 644–645). Women's organizations were not tooled to conduct successful lobbying campaigns among newly enfranchised females (Harvey 1998), and the political climate of the 1920s "proved to be bad for women's organizing" (Banaszak 2006: 6). By 1924, just four years after universal suffrage, "little remained of a nationally organized women's movement" (Ferree and Hess 2000: 1). By 1930, women had "ceased to engage in autonomous political action on behalf of expanded state responsibility" (Sklar 1993). In sum, the "woman movement as a whole was dead" (O'Neill 1971: 263).

While elements of the decline narrative are plausible, skeptical historians have taken issue with the portrait of postsuffrage women as civic laggards. For example, Nancy Cott (1992) has argued that there was a great deal of continuity in the scope and volume of women's collective engagement in the decades after 1920. That year the National American Woman Suffrage Association transformed itself into the National League of Women Voters to provide women with a civic education, lobby for causes on which women were expert, and unify "the country's woman power into a new force for the humanizing of government."[2] Women's groups including the league formed the Women's Joint Congressional Committee, which by 1924 included twenty-one organizations with a combined membership of twelve million women (Wilson 2007). In his 1929 book, *Group Representation before Congress*, Pendleton Herring observed that women's lobbies were the second most common form of interest group, after trade associations.[3] Women's groups also were active on the state level, racking up numerous policy victories that belie the conventional story of women's waning influence (Andersen 1996; McCammon 2012).

The 1950s: Another Story of Decline?

After a brief mobilization to support the troops, women of the 1950s are often portrayed as gratefully embracing domesticity. Wifely and maternal obligations are said to have distracted women from fully exercising their rights and assuming the responsibilities of democratic citizenship. Betty Friedan's groundbreaking work, *The Feminine Mystique* (1963), described a world in which mid-century homemakers fixated on family and femininity while shunning positions of leadership in voluntary associations and other roles in the public sphere (Friedan 1963). Indeed, politically engaged women's voluntary associations of the sort featured in the present study barely figured into Friedan's book—and then more as forums for dissatisfaction than as vehicles for political empowerment (Friedan 1963).

Later scholars picked up this line, arguing that the conservative political climate of the 1950s "combined with a serious constriction of opportunities for women in education and the professions to severely limit the context in which women's organizations could function" (Levine 1995: 83). Perhaps as a result, "thoughts of political power . . . had no place in the 1950s' American housewife and mother image" (Ryan 1992: 36). A few accounts of "pockets" of women's political resistance notwithstanding, most histories of the 1950s "stress the postwar domestic ideal, the reassertion of a traditional sexual division of labor, and the formal and informal barriers that prevented women from fully participating in the public realm" (Meyerowitz 1994: 3). One scholar of the second-wave movement declared the 1950s "stifling for women" (Davis 1999: 9). Another suggested that, after three decades dominated by the "mythical ideal" of traditional family relations, "most people never even knew there had been a women's movement" in the late nineteenth and early twentieth centuries (Ryan 1992: 36).

And yet, as with the 1920s, there is evidence that women were more active in the 1950s than the standard *Leave It to Beaver* narrative of female domesticity would suggest. Robert Putnam (2000) saw the 1950s as the apex of twentieth-century civic engagement, with women occupying a central role as civic caretakers. The League of Women Voters, whose membership grew by 44% from 1950 to 1958, created myriad opportunities for women to engage in local, state, and national policy advocacy and to prepare themselves for elective office in later life (Young 1989; Ware 1992). In a study of interest groups at mid-century, David Truman (1951: 100) reported that women's associations were "both influential and numerous," while Ethel Klein (1984: 18) argued that mid-century women constituted an "established lobby" with "greater political sophistication" than had been present during more outwardly activist periods.

Thus, for both the 1920s and 1950s, there is some evidence challenging the prevailing view that women's activism crashed after suffrage. And yet, the narrative of women's retreat from politics has a powerful hold on the imagination. Congressional hearings data allow us to assess these competing accounts of women's policy engagement. Obviously, public testimony is only one form of political activity, but it is an important one. If women's groups were being invited to offer their analysis to the nation's most powerful policymaking body, one might reasonably infer that women did not pass into political obsolescence after winning the right to vote. After all, congressional testimony is an important indicator of who matters in Washington.

WHAT HAPPENED? WOMEN'S POLICY ADVOCACY ON CAPITOL HILL, 1920–1959

From the 1920s to 1960, the federal government grew in both the depth and range of its policy endeavors. So, too, did American women's organizations. Contrary to narratives of decline after suffrage, women's organizations enlarged their engagement in national policy debates. This impressive growth shows up in several ways. I focus on three measures, all of which tell basically the same story. These measures are (1) the number of times women's groups appeared as witnesses before congressional committees and subcommittees, (2) the number of different women's groups testifying, and (3) the range of policy domains in which women's collective voices were heard.

Figure 9.1 presents the simplest snapshot of the periods before and after suffrage: total appearances before Congress, as well as the number of appearances adjusted for the number of hearings that Congressional committees and subcommittees held. The two patterns tell a broadly similar story: a steady yet punctuated rise in women's appearances, peaking in the second half of the 1940s.

As the figure shows, the peak came in the period from 1945 to 1948, when women's groups were working on, and Congress was considering, a wide range of issues, including health insurance, foreign aid, European reconstruction, postwar housing, and the Equal Rights Amendment (ERA). Congress sought policy input and political intelligence on all these matters, and women's organizations were well prepared to provide it. Whether adjusting for number of hearings or not, the data make clear that these organizations did not fade away after suffrage. Rather, they continued to press their claims at a rate of roughly one-and-a-half to three times the presuffrage levels.[4]

As I show in my book (Goss 2013), much the same pattern appears when one considers women's organizations' participation in hearings on particularly

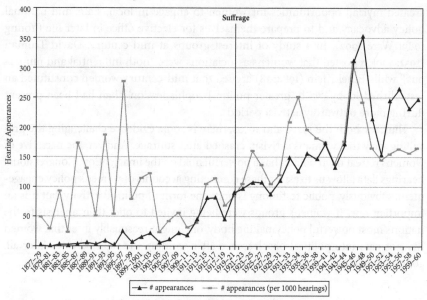

FIGURE 9.1 *The Rise of Women's Policy Advocacy, 1877–1960*
Goss 2013.

significant legislation. Congress took the women's lobby so seriously that its representatives were invited to testify on more than 40% of the nation's most important policy questions in the 1940s, and 34% in the 1950s—eras when women are often portrayed more as domestic helpmates than as authoritative political actors.

Figure 9.2 offers yet another way of evaluating the pattern of women's national policy engagement before and after suffrage: the number of groups testifying on Capitol Hill. Between the 1910s and the 1950s, the number of women's organizations appearing at congressional hearings grew by 135%—and by close to 75% from the 1920s.

These findings underscore the observation that the 1940s and 1950s saw the emergence of "an experienced women's lobby" that "provided an organizational context for maintaining or increasing pressure for women's rights in the future" (Klein 1984: 18). Compared to the presuffrage era, Congress by mid-century was hearing from a broad array of federated organizations and their state and local chapters—such as the League of Women Voters—as well as from a growing number of women's occupational groups. Growth in the number of hearings held no doubt contributed to the diversity of women's groups that were able to appear. But even so, the evidence challenges the conventional wisdom that women were home baking cookies during the supposedly placid 1950s.

A third and very important measure of women's policy engagement is the range of policy questions on which they were invited to testify. Figure 9.3 charts the rise in issue domains in which a women's group appeared at least once.

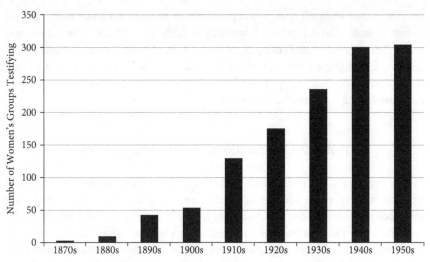

FIGURE 9.2 *Rise in the Number of Women's Groups Testifying, 1870s–1950s*
Goss 2013.

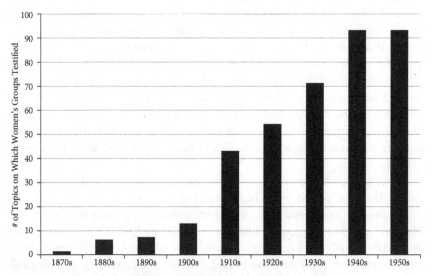

FIGURE 9.3 *Women's Groups' Issue Interest Widened, 1870s–1950s*
Goss 2013.

In the 1910s, women's groups were testifying on legislation spanning 43 issue domains, a figure that ballooned to 93 issue domains by mid-century. Congress in the 1950s held hearings in 197 policy domains, meaning that women had a voice in nearly half of them. The steady widening of these policy engagements reflects the federal government's expansion into social and economic life and the relevance of women's voices to those debates. As Congress expanded its engagement, it sought the counsel of women's groups—particularly in areas of long-standing concern to them, such as social welfare (especially relating to children, labor issues, and seniors) and international cooperation and aid. In addition, women's groups were insisting on having a voice on perennial questions of governance, such as foreign trade, nominations and appointments to high-level government positions, and relations among the branches of government.

Women's Organizations after the Second Wave

Just as the period from the late 1870s through the 1950s encapsulated a major women's movement, so too did the period from 1960 to 2000. The second wave took root in the mid-1960s, reached its heyday in the 1970s, and, depending on the account, either faded or was institutionalized by the early 1980s. The second-wave movement coalesced around policies to protect women from institutionalized discrimination and to facilitate their access to nontraditional gender roles. As in the suffrage era, the second wave produced a lively debate about whether policy victories would have lasting effects on women's voice in public affairs.

Not surprisingly, as was the case with the postsuffrage era, historians disagree about what happened to second-wave feminism. Early popular assessments, in the news media and in some scholarly works, proclaimed that the movement had died by the 1980s—and some went so far as to claim that feminism itself, as an identity frame for collective action, had likewise fallen into disrepute (for a review, see Hawkesworth 2004). By these accounts, the wave crashed. More recently, however, scholars have argued that feminism as a movement and an identity did not fade away but merely changed forms (Disney and Gelb 2000; Wolbrecht 2000; Costain and Costain 1987). The wave rolled on; it just looked different. Again, women's organizational presence on Capitol Hill helps us make sense of these differing accounts.

Figure 9.4 shows women's group appearances, per one hundred hearings, over the length of the period of study. By bringing in the pre-second-wave era, this graph affords a panoramic view of women's public engagement on Capitol Hill. Women's engagement grew rapidly after suffrage, peaked at mid-century, then plunged in the 1960s. While the feminist movement brought women's engagement back from the doldrums for a brief period, the downward spiral began again in the early 1980s, never to recover. By the late 1990s, women's groups were less prominent on Capitol Hill than they had been in the years immediately preceding suffrage, when women were still formally disenfranchised.

Note that congressional hearings became shorter in the latter decades of the twentieth century, which could raise questions about the trend line that adjusts for number of hearings per Congress. However, the decline in women's appearances is not simply an artifact of shorter hearings or other changes in congressional treatment of outside interests. Further analysis shows that appearances by women's groups declined relative to those by other interest groups and all types of witnesses.

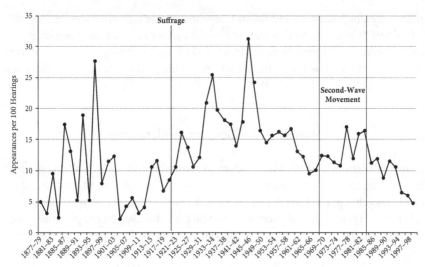

FIGURE 9.4 *Women's Group Appearances, 1887–2000*
Goss 2013.

Specifically, I assembled a dataset that counts and categorizes different types of witnesses in a random sample of hearings at five-Congress intervals from the 45th Congress (1877–1879) through the 95th Congress (1997–1998). The dataset includes 1,680 hearings and testimony from nearly 20,000 interest groups, corporations, governmental agencies, and private citizens.[5] The data suggest that the rise-and-fall pattern of women's groups' participation generally tracks that of interest groups more broadly. However, women's groups' rise after suffrage and fall in the second half of the twentieth century is more pronounced than is that of other interest groups or of congressional witnesses generally (Goss 2013). In other words, even after adjusting for any changes in lawmakers' appetite for policy input, the distinctive rise-and-fall pattern among women's groups remains.

The story of women's organizational weakening is evident, though later and less pronounced, in the count of women's groups appearing on Capitol Hill. As the feminism-in-decline narrative was taking hold in the 1980s—and as the number of women's group appearances was falling—the number of groups testifying actually rose a bit, before falling in the 1990s (Goss 2013). The same pattern is true for the range of policy issues on which women's groups testified (Goss 2013). These findings lend credence to assertions that women's groups indeed proliferated and specialized during the 1980s. Yet many of the groups weren't the large, politically influential interests likely to be called again and again to testify on a wide range of issues.

In sum, women's organizational engagement rose and fell over the course of the twentieth century. The pattern is most pronounced in the volume of these groups' appearances at congressional hearings, but it is also evident in the number of groups that testified and the range of issues on which they appeared. The pattern presents obvious puzzles: Women's collective action in the halls of Congress was rising when popular accounts tell us that women were retreating into domesticity, and it was falling in an era when women had never enjoyed more social, political, and economic status. How might we make sense of these perplexing patterns? Below I briefly review intriguing yet unconvincing possibilities and then lay out a more compelling explanation that puts public policy at the center.

Assessing the Obvious Explanations

Scholarly theories and popular wisdom propose three categories of explanations for the rise and fall of women's organizations on Capitol Hill: those focused on Congress (changes in lawmakers' tastes and practices), those focused on women (changes in their roles and perspectives), and those focused on the pressure-group system (changes in the system's composition, in organizational strategies, or in funding availability). I consider these in turn.

CONGRESS-RELATED EXPLANATIONS

One possibility is that the evolution of women's national policy engagement is less about women's groups per se than about Congress. A closer examination of the evidence casts doubt on four possible Congress-centered explanations. First, this is not a story of partisan favor: Access to women's groups did not wax and wane depending upon which party was in charge of Congress. Second, this is not a story of gains in female representation in Congress rendering women's groups obsolete: The decline in women's groups' testimony preceded large increases in female members of Congress, and in any event, studies show that strong women's groups and female lawmakers are complements, not substitutes (Thomas 1994; Reingold 1992). Third, this is not a story about how Congress shifted away from women's priorities: Congress actually *increased* its attention to issues of longstanding concern to women—such as gender equality, international affairs, and social legislation— and this shift happened at the same time that women's groups' presence was on the decline (Baumgartner and Mahoney 2005; Wolbrecht 2000; Costain 1988). Finally this is not a story about Congress's taste for input from interest groups generally: Women's groups gained and then lost ground both in an absolute sense and relative to other types of interest groups and congressional witnesses. In sum, changes in Congress do not explain the pattern of women's collective engagement over the twentieth century.

GENDER-RELATED EXPLANATIONS

Throughout the twentieth century, American women's lives were transformed as females began moving into the paid labor force and negotiating changes in their personal and family lives. Although these changes may have led to some shifts in American women's political engagement, they do not fully account for the observed patterns. This story is not fundamentally about the effects of women's move toward paid work. Women's labor force participation increased more or less monotonically throughout the twentieth century, while their organizational engagement experienced rises and falls. Studies also show that labor force participation is typically correlated with more engagement, not less, which would be consistent with the pre-1960 pattern but not with the post-1980 trend (Burns, Schlozman, and Verba 2001; Putnam 2000). Nor is it the case that women lost their sense of sisterhood and the impulse for gender-based organizing. Even as the media were heralding the "death of feminism," individual women continued to have high levels of solidarity and believe that collective action was important, at least on women's rights issues (Tolleson Rinehart 1992). Although such findings are ambiguous for post-baby-boom women, the patterns observed in my data would have preceded this generation's coming of age. In sum, changes in women's lifestyles and tastes do not seem to be the primary forces behind the evolution of women's organizations.

ORGANIZATIONAL EXPLANATIONS

Nor were the trends driven primarily by two seemingly plausible organizational-level possibilities. I examined whether the data simply reflect a shift among women's groups away from Congress as a focus of policy pressure and toward other institutions, such as the courts or administrative agencies. Evidence compiled by others suggests that women's groups were not shifting strategies; Congress remained their top target (Grossmann 2012). Another possibility is that women's groups' strength varied with the availability of patronage funding, and here the evidence paints a complicated story. Funding remained available and by some measures grew, meaning that women's groups did not fade from the congressional scene because they lacked money (Goss 2013). However, funders may have influenced women's groups' more specialized agenda (Goss 2007). I show below that focusing and specialization are related to the presence of women's groups on Capitol Hill.

The most compelling organizational-level explanation pertains to evolution of the interest-group universe itself. In the early twentieth century, women's groups played a major role in creating the pluralist, group-based politics that we see today (Cott 1987), and they were central to sustaining it for decades. But women's groups also may have fallen victim to their own success. With the "advocacy explosion" that began in the 1960s and accelerated in the 1970s (Berry 1997), specialized pressure groups began colonizing issue niches previously dominated by women's multipurpose, mass-membership groups. These developments provided incentives for women's groups to define policy interests narrowly to attract money from donors and recognition from political elites. The proliferation of interest groups coincided with feminist pressures to repeal discriminatory laws, enact legislation that would empower women, and end sexist practices in the social and market spheres. Thus, as women's groups were facing competition in their traditional policy niches, they were also getting pressure to focus on women's rights and status. As we shall see, changes in the interest-group environment worked hand in hand with policy changes operating on women's groups to produce dramatic changes in women's collective representation in debates over national issues.

What Explains the Evolution: A Two-Level Theory

Explaining major social transformations that unfold over long periods of time is always difficult. Thus, no single factor can account for the rise and fall—and the widening and narrowing—of women's organizational engagement over the twentieth century. Many forces contributed to these developments, some of which I already have mentioned. Here I offer a layered account that incorporates those factors and introduces a larger, fundamental driver: policy itself. First, I introduce the proximate causes of the observed patterns in women's organizational engagement: (1) changes in the types of groups that represented women and (2) changes in these groups' policy agendas. Next, I drill down to examine what drove these two interrelated changes. In so doing, I offer an explanation rooted in policy itself. Not only did women's groups seek to influence policy, but policy also influenced women's groups by providing incentives to organize in certain ways and focus on certain issues.

CHANGES IN THE TYPES OF ORGANIZATIONS SPEAKING FOR WOMEN

Theda Skocpol (2003, 1999, 1992) has argued that federated voluntary organizations—those with national, state, and local affiliates—played a critical role in the development of democratic citizens and the construction of the early welfare state in America. In the second half of the twentieth century, these groups began to decline as thriving hubs of civic activity for everyday citizens, only to be replaced by professionally staffed expert advocacy groups based in Washington. Skocpol (2003) has aptly described this pattern as the shift from "membership to management." This shift profoundly affected women's political representation by reducing the volume of women's public voice and narrowing the range of issues on which women were heard.

Consider appearances by the seven traditional federated women's associations, all formed in the late nineteenth or early twentieth century, that testified the most over the course of the dataset.[6] In the 1950s, these seven groups were responsible for 50% of all women's group appearances; by the 1990s, this fraction was just 8%. A similar pattern holds in the absolute number of appearances. These seven groups appeared five times as often in the 1950s compared to the 1990s, even though Congress held fewer hearings in the earlier decade.[7]

These findings in part reflect the declining memberships of these groups. Data assembled by Robert Putnam show that eight out of ten large, traditional women's groups suffered significant membership losses—generally from 60% to 90% in population-adjusted terms—between 1966 and 1996 (Goss and Skocpol 2006).[8] The groups that lost ground included such historically prominent associations as the Federation of Business and Professional Women (~84%, in terms of the fraction of the relevant population who belonged); the American Association of University Women (~80%); the General Federation of Women's Clubs (~73%); the Woman's Christian Temperance Union (~91%); and the League of Women Voters (~63%).

As these general-purpose organizations declined, several categories of groups enjoyed increasing prominence in Washington, but none grew prominent enough to offset the declines in women's mass-membership federations.

Occupationally based associations—such as labor unions, farm and agricultural organizations, professional associations, and occupational support entities—constituted roughly 10% to 25% of women's groups' appearances until the 1970s. With the second-wave movement and women's advancement in white-collar professions, occupational groups proliferated, constituting nearly 60% of all appearances by women's groups in the 1990s. However, these groups tended to be specialized along industry lines and were typically called to testify only when issues in their industry domains came before Congress.

Another sector of the women's group universe that posted growth in the 1960–1990 period is the feminist sector. Between 1966, when the National Organization for Women (NOW) was established, and 2000, more than six hundred newly formed feminist groups appeared before Congress. These included national advocacy groups and their local affiliates, such as the National Women's Political Caucus and the Lincoln, Nebraska, chapter of the Older Women's League; state organizations, such as the Pennsylvania Breast Cancer Coalition; local service providers, such as the Minneapolis Women's Center; and women's occupational groups, such as the Massachusetts Women's Bar Association. Contrary to the stereotype of the second wave as an elite women's movement, many of the groups appearing on Capitol Hill represented disadvantaged subpopulations: older women, blue-collar women, victims of domestic or sexual violence, and women of color.

While the leading feminist groups were visible on Capitol Hill, especially in the late 1970s and early 1980s, they never reached anywhere near the prominence of traditional mass-membership associations. Most of these new groups testified just once. Only twenty-five of them (4%) testified more than ten times, and only two (NOW and the Women's Equity Action League) testified more than one hundred times. The combined membership in feminist groups was only a small fraction of membership in the "old-fashioned" women's organizations. Gelb and Palley (1996) found four prominent feminist groups had a combined membership of just 250,000 in 1978; by contrast, the four largest "traditional" women's groups had about 10.7 million members that year, or forty-three times as many (Goss and Skocpol 2006).

The feminist movement spawned a backlash by conservative women, but again, these groups did not become an especially large and versatile advocacy force. Three prominent conservative women's groups appeared with some regularity on Capitol Hill in the 1980s and 1990s: the Eagle Forum, founded by Phyllis Schlafly in 1972; Concerned Women for America, founded by Beverly LaHaye in 1979; and the Independent Women's Forum, founded by three conservative women in 1992 in response to the controversy involving Supreme Court nominee Clarence

Thomas. These three groups appeared fifty-seven times between 1979 and 2000—or roughly five times per Congress. To put this in perspective, the three most prolific feminist groups—NOW, the Women's Legal Defense Fund, and the National Women's Political Caucus—appeared roughly five times as often in that time frame. Thus, while conservative women's groups brought important new perspectives to national debates, their prominence on Capitol Hill should not be overstated.

Groups representing women of color also made strong gains in the era of women's rights, but their growth was constrained by natural demographic limits. The 1970s–1980s period witnessed the birth of a wide range of feminist organizations specializing in advancing the interests of African American, Native American, Hispanic, and Asian American women. Yet just one organization—the National Council of Negro Women—was responsible for 43% of all appearances by minority women's groups. Issues on which the council testified included the minimum wage, housing, elderly assistance, juvenile delinquency, child care, pay discrimination, the status of black males, and television violence. With only three exceptions, minority women's groups never constituted more than 4% of all women's group appearances in any given Congress. Moreover, minority women's groups seemed to follow the same downward trajectory seen with other women's groups during the 1980s and 1990s, with the exception of a brief uptick in the 1993–1994 congressional session.

The changing fortunes of different types of groups, particularly the large multi-issue, mass-membership federations, affected the range of issues on which women's groups testified and, in turn, their prominence on Capitol Hill. The big federations declined in prominence from the 1970s onward, but no other types of groups—second-wave feminist groups, conservative groups, women-of-color groups, occupational organizations—ever grew large or numerous enough to equal the traditional organizations' prominence on Capitol Hill.

Indeed, the decline in the big women's associations drove much of the decline we observe in women's organizational representation in the latter decades of the twentieth century. Figure 9.5 shows the observed pattern compared to what it would have been if (a) traditional organizations had continued to testify at their peak levels and (b) second-wave feminist groups had done the same.

As the figure shows, if traditional women's groups had held their own, women's organizational representation would have dipped very little after its mid-century height. While the feminist movement clearly did elevate women's voice in Congress, the decline of those groups contributed little to the overall decline in women's collective representation.

TYPES OF ISSUES

The fading away of multipurpose federations had important consequences. It reduced the breadth of issues around which women's groups were actively engaged and as a result reduced the number of times that Congress called those groups to testify. As multi-issue groups declined, the women's organizational universe came to be dominated by smaller, more specialized groups dedicated to various aspects

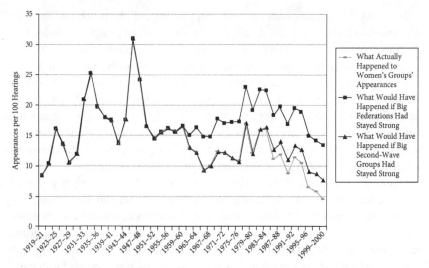

FIGURE 9.5 *Federations' Decline Depresses Advocacy, 1919–2000*

Note: Big Federations are the American Association of University Women, the General Federation of Women's Clubs, the League of Women Voters, the National Council of Jewish Women, the PTA, the Woman's Christian Temperance Union, and the YWCA. Big Second Wave groups are the National Organization for Women, the National Women's Law Center, the National Women's Political Caucus, the Older Women's League, the Women's Equity Action League, the Women's Legal Defense Fund, and the Women's Lobby.

Source: Goss 2013.

of women's rights, status, and well-being. Furthermore, as the types of groups speaking for women shifted, the range of issues on which women's voices were heard narrowed, and the scope of women's advocacy declined.

From suffrage through mid-century, women's groups appeared before Congress on a wide array of policy matters. Issue domains in which women's groups testified regularly included agriculture, alcohol abuse, child health, consumer safety, District of Columbia affairs, drug regulation, education, foreign aid, gender discrimination, government operations, housing, immigration, juvenile justice, labor, military manpower, national parks, price controls, tax policy—the list goes on (Goss 2013). Women's groups believed—and Congress evidently agreed—that virtually any issue was a women's issue.

With the advent of the second-wave women's movement, the range of issue domains remained broad—even expanded. Women's groups continued to testify at hearings focused on social welfare, health care, tax policy, and so forth. However, the dimensions of these multifaceted policies that women's groups addressed narrowed. To illustrate, I coded each of the roughly 10,500 appearances according to whether, within a broad policy domain, a women's organization was primarily advocating for women's interests. I defined such interests as women's legal rights, professional status, economic well-being, or physical welfare. Note that such issues are often feminist issues, but they need not be. Conservative groups might have taken positions—for example, against suffrage, legalized abortion, or the ERA—because they saw the policies as antithetical to women's well-being.

The story of women's issue interests after suffrage looks much like the story of women's presence on Capitol Hill. After 1920, women's groups expanded their role, moving assertively into a broader range of social, economic, and foreign policy debates. Women's groups continued to press for women's rights, status, and well-being, but a growing share of their testimony concerned nonfeminist issues, specifically relating to disadvantaged groups, the diffuse public interest, and the national interest. However, from the 1970s onward, women's organizations fundamentally reoriented their energies. In the middle decades, women's groups had advocated for women's rights, status, and well-being roughly 10% to 20% of the time; by the 1980s and 1990s, it was closer to 70% to 80% of the time.

Figure 9.6 shows the relationship between how broad women's policy interests were and how prominent these groups were on Capitol Hill. Reflecting policy breadth, the figure charts the percentage of appearances in which women's groups testified primarily on general (i.e., non-women-centric) issues. Reflecting prominence, the figure charts the number of hearing-adjusted appearances by these groups. (To facilitate presentation, these measures have been converted into standard units reflecting variation around their means; thus, readers are invited to pay attention to the patterns of the lines more than to the absolute numbers.) A visual inspection reveals that the two lines run strikingly in tandem: The more broadly leading women's groups defined their issue interests, the more frequently Congress summoned them to share their political intelligence and policy expertise.

Thus, we have a paradox. As women's groups moved away from other-oriented causes, they were able to provide expert knowledge and an intensive focus on women's equality. Feminist groups scrutinized existing laws and regulations across the policy spectrum to undo provisions that treated women unfavorably. Feminist organizations also advocated for important new policies to redress historic inequities and advance women's priorities. At the same time, by going deeper on feminist concerns, women's groups sacrificed the breadth of policy engagement for which they had long been known. A particular casualty was foreign affairs, a policy domain in which women's groups were quite active in the early and middle twentieth century (Goss 2009). The data show that by the last third of the twentieth century, women had become a collection of specialized interests. Their days as a public-interest lobby were largely behind them.

What Was behind Women's Group Specialization?

Political participation shapes public policy. Movements of politically engaged women brought suffrage in 1920 and women's rights advances in the 1970s. However, public policy also has the power to "feed back" and shape participation (Mettler and Soss 2004; Skocpol 1992). Feedback effects may be direct or indirect. In the case of American women, direct feedback effects include the increase in voting brought about by the Nineteenth Amendment and the rise in jury service facilitated by state laws and court rulings (McCammon 2012; Kerber 1998). Indirectly, policies can influence participation by altering resources available to

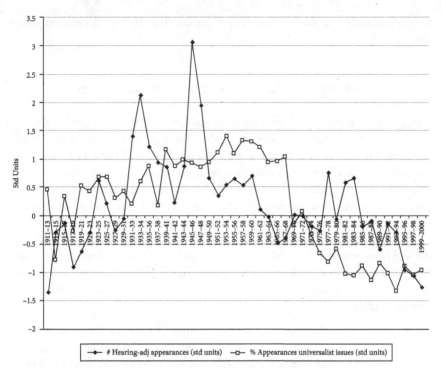

FIGURE 9.6 *Broader Agendas Mean Greater Presence, 1911–2000*

Note: Because the two measures are on different scales, the data have been converted into standard units representing each data point's deviation from its respective mean. Putting the two data sources into comparable units allows the patterns to be viewed side-by-side.

Source: Goss 2013.

constituencies and by changing their interpretations of their civic roles (Pierson 1993). Resource effects refer to endowments, such as money and educational access, that increase individuals' capacity to engage politically. Interpretive effects relate to citizens' "perceptions of their role in the community, their status in relation to other citizens and government, and the extent to which a policy affected their lives" (Mettler 2002: 352). When people feel more included and experience greater status as citizens, their participation should be expected to grow. The political and economic incorporation of women over the last century makes them an ideal case for examining feedback effects on civic engagement.

Consistent with feedback theory, laws advancing women had both resource and interpretive effects that directed female collective action toward certain types of policy claims and away from others. However, policy feedbacks did not operate the same way over time. The Nineteenth Amendment yielded an expansion in women's engagement, while the gender-equality laws of the 1960s and 1970s laid the groundwork for the narrowing of women's agendas and the eventual decline of their presence on Capitol Hill. What accounts for these different trajectories? Why in one era do inclusionary policies give way to greater participation, while in the next era inclusionary policies are followed by more constrained participation?

One logical answer is that feedback effects are contingent: They depend on policy design.

The Legacy of Suffrage: Rights and Responsibility

Suffrage was a public policy with the potential for broad feedback effects. Ratified in 1920, the Nineteenth Amendment reads, "The right of citizens of the United States to vote shall not be denied or abridged by the United States or by any State on account of sex." The amendment embodies the duality of American citizenship, which encompasses both rights (to ballot access) and responsibilities (to take part in collective decision-making). The amendment also embodied the parallel constructs in women's political history: women's claims to the same political status as men, as derived from natural law, and women's difference from men, as derived from maternal caregiving roles. Suffrage leader Carrie Chapman Catt captured women's understanding that the amendment provide a flexible and expansive platform for women to exercise both their equality rights and their caregiving responsibilities:

> The vote is the emblem of your equality, women of America, the guaranty of your liberty. . . . The vote is a power, a weapon of offense and defense, and a prayer. Understand what it means and what it can do for your country. Use it intelligently, conscientiously, prayerfully. No solider in the great suffrage army has labored and suffered to get a "place" for you. Their motive has been the hope women would aim higher than their own selfish ambitions, that they would serve the common good.[9]

Women's organizations took up this charge. Groups emphasizing the "rights/sameness" perspective used the amendment as a launch pad for their efforts to secure the next step in women's political inclusion: an equal rights amendment to the Constitution. The groups embracing this important item on the equality agenda included the National Woman's Party, the National Federation of Business and Professional Women's Clubs, the National Association of Women Lawyers, and the American Medical Women's Association (Rupp and Taylor 1987). At the same time, women's groups emphasizing the "responsibilities/difference" perspective saw the amendment as a potent new way for women to bring their distinctive sensibilities to bear on issues such as world peace and children's well-being. Women's assertion of a "duty to serve society as women" resonated as government increasingly assumed caregiving roles by initiating social welfare programs (Kraditor 1971: 52–53). Groups emphasizing women's public responsibilities of care included the National Consumers League, the Woman's Christian Temperance Union, the General Federation of Women's Clubs, the Young Women's Christian Association, and the American Association of University Women. These organizations and others formed the Women's Joint Congressional Committee, whose policy agenda throughout the 1920s included passage of a child and maternal health bill, a constitutional amendment giving Congress the power to regulate child labor, and two bills regulating food safety (Wilson 2007). The agenda reflected the maternal orientation of women's mass-membership groups and their desire for the state to assume and facilitate caregiving roles occupied by wives and mothers.

The Nineteenth Amendment's joint expression of women's sameness (rights) and difference (responsibility) created the context for a third, hybrid identity to emerge: one oriented around women as good citizens (Goss 2013). The good-citizen perspective shared with the difference perspective the idea that women are distinct in their concern for others' well-being and in transcending the self-interestedness of partisan politics. The good-citizen perspective shared with the sameness perspective the belief that women could and should participate on the same footing as men. Exponents of the good-citizen frame believed that the explicit invocation of gender difference, except in the context of discrimination, was unhelpful or even counterproductive to women's influence. This interpretation was developed and carried forth most prominently by the League of Women Voters, the top-testifying women's organization in American history. In 1949 the league's president summarized the sex-segregated group's orientation by averring that members "think of themselves as citizens first and as women incidentally" (Rupp and Taylor 1987: 49). This hybrid identity allowed women to be both equal to men, in their gutsy claims to authority across a broad range of salient issues, and different from men in their public performance of the civic virtues traditionally associated with and assigned to women. The frame took advantage of beliefs about sex difference but did not articulate them. It was implicitly, but not explicitly, gendered.

In sum, by embodying both women's sameness and women's difference, the amendment allowed women's groups regardless of their beliefs about women's nature to claim it as the moral foundation for policy advocacy. In advancing both rights and responsibilities for women, the amendment provided an expansive, flexible platform for women's collective action, allowing women to be the same as men, different from them, or some nimble combination of the two. In speaking to multiple identities, the amendment allowed women's groups to claim any issue as a women's issue.

1960–1980: How Rights Came to Eclipse Responsibility

As the major women's policy of the early twentieth century, suffrage conferred rights on individual women as well as conveying to them a responsibility for the commonweal. It legitimated women's advocacy for further policies benefiting women as a group, while providing a rationale for women's advocacy on behalf of other groups or the public at large. By contrast, the major women's policies of the 1960s–1970s, which were focused on women's legal equality, provided a less expansive platform for women's collective engagement down the line. Three significant policy enactments are of particular importance: the President's Commission on the Status of Women, formed in 1961, which quickly spawned two additional federal equal rights committees and commissions in all fifty states; the Equal Pay Act of 1963, which began the process of incorporating women as full participants in

economic life; and Title VII of the 1964 Civil Rights Act, which barred gender discrimination in employment. While these early-1960s policy innovations were not
the product of a women's movement, they laid the groundwork for one. Both the
Equal Pay Act and Title VII enshrined gender equality as a central orienting principle of women's collective action, directing women—in particular elite women—
toward an agenda of dismantling institutionalized inequalities. The President's
Commission pointed women's activists to where the problems were and provided
authoritative evidence of their scope. These three policies created both a discursive
context and a government apparatus for women to pursue the same rights that
men had. In short, they created a context for women's groups to view their mission
primarily as redressing inequities.

Policies can feed back into politics by providing resources and structures
for collective engagement (Mettler and Soss 2004). Exemplifying such feedback effects, two government institutions created by lawmakers—the Equal
Employment Opportunity Commission and the President's Commission on
the Status of Women—catalyzed the creation of the flagship organization of the
second-wave movement, the National Organization for Women. NOW's founding
Statement of Purpose held that "the time has come for a new movement toward
true equality for all women in America, and toward a fully equal partnership of
the sexes" (Carabillo, Meuli, and Csida 1993: 159). NOW's purpose was "to take
action to bring women into full participation in the mainstream of American
society now, exercising all the privileges and responsibilities thereof in truly equal
partnership with men" (Carabillo, Meuli, and Csida 1993: 159). Within a few years
of NOW's creation, a host of feminist advocacy groups sprang up, including
the Women's Equity Action League (1968), Federally Employed Women (1968),
the National Coalition of American Nuns and Church Women United (1969), the
Women's Rights Project of the American Civil Liberties Union (1971), the NOW
Legal Defense and Education Fund (1971), the National Women's Political Caucus
(1971), the Women's Legal Defense Fund (1971), the Network for Economic Rights
(1971), the Women's Lobby (1972), Equal Rights Advocates (1972), and the Center
for Law and Social Policy's Women's Rights Project (1972), which in 1981 would
become the National Women's Law Center (Rosenberg 1993). These organizations
relied on a mix of educational, advocacy, and litigation strategies, but they were
united in their pursuit of equality claims.

Second-Wave Feminism: Policy Feedbacks
on Women's Group Resources

Besides working through the identity mechanism, policy feedbacks encouraged
egalitarian feminism by conferring resources on, and enlarging the capacities
of, feminist groups. Most directly, the President's Commission on the Status of
Women provided resources, networks, legitimacy, and a political opportunity
for the emergence of the second-wave movement (Costain 1992; Davis 1999;
Klein 1984). After the commission had completed its work, it successfully urged

President John F. Kennedy to create the Citizens' Advisory Council on the Status of Women (made up in part of commission members). He also established the Interdepartmental Committee on the Status of Women, a Cabinet-level body composed of administration officials (Davis 1999). The two national status-of-women entities began holding national conferences of state commissions in 1964. These meetings brought together hundreds of feminist leaders from around the country to share information—and grievances—with one another and with sympathetic government officials, including feminists within the executive and legislative branches. Attendance nearly quintupled from the first to the second meeting, which Cabinet members and President Lyndon B. Johnson attended (Carabillo, Meuli, and Csida 1993). These conferences galvanized women, who were "mingling in workshops and expanding their knowledge beyond the boundaries of their individual states," providing "a forum for an expression of women's rising expectations for correcting injustices" (Carabillo, Meuli, and Csida 1993: 12).

With success at the national level, and at the urging of the Federation of Business and Professional Women, all fifty states and many counties created their own women's commissions, providing a platform for information-sharing, networking, and policy advocacy at the subnational level (Carabillo, Meuli, and Csida 1993; Davis 1999). State commissions, working with a newly energized base of women's organizations, were very successful in lobbying for policy changes. Between 1963 and 1965, state legislatures enacted a slew of laws to remove barriers to women's employment, jury service, and property rights. Thus, the President's Commission defined the problems and spun off organizations at the national and state levels that fed the broader movement and its lobbying groups. At the 1966 meeting of state commissions, grievances reached a boiling point, and NOW and the second-wave movement were born.

How the Equality Orientation Affected Women's Collective Engagement

A core assumption of democratic theory and practice is that more civic inclusion leads to more civic participation. After suffrage the assumption indeed held true. The women's lobby (or lobbies) grew in prominence on Capitol Hill and represented women's interests and perspectives on an ever-widening range of domestic and international policy issues (Goss 2013; Wilson 2007; Cott 1992). Yet the raft of policy victories of the 1960s and 1970s gave way to a decline in women's groups' prominence and a focusing of their policy interests. Why would two sets of policies, both so important to women's inclusion and status, have left such different patterns of democratic participation in their wake? Below I offer four answers that illuminate the complex interactions between policy, as a set of ideas and incentive structures, and organizational participation as an adaptive response to these ideas and incentives.

First, although suffrage and the equal rights policies of the 1960s and 1970s were both about inclusion, they were about fundamentally different kinds of inclusion.

Suffrage was about *political* inclusion: the right to take part in democratic decision-making. The landmark Equal Pay Act and Title VII of the 1964 Civil Rights Act—along with later successes such as Title IX of the Education Amendments (1972), the Women's Educational Equity Act (1974), the Equal Credit Opportunity Act (1974), and the Pregnancy Discrimination Act (1978)—were about *economic* inclusion, the right to reap the full rewards of one's effort and talent. Both types of inclusion are important, but only the first—political inclusion—conveys an expectation of responsibility to participate in matters of public concern. Economic inclusion provides incentives to participate, but around a much narrower set of questions bearing on access to and treatment in paid employment. Suffrage, as a policy encompassing both rights claims and expectations of civic duty, provided a platform for a more expansive policy agenda.

Second, the platform provided by suffrage was perfectly suited to multi-issue mass-membership groups, which flourished in the decades after the Nineteenth Amendment won ratification. Groups such as the League of Women Voters ("an everywoman's organization") and the General Federation of Women's Clubs created a space where civic-minded women with different policy interests could find a home (Mathews-Gardner 2005; Stuhler 2003; Ware 1992). The broad policy agendas pursued by these multi-issue groups paralleled the government's agenda, meaning that women were poised to jump into virtually any policy debate that arose. The League of Women Voters, for example, has positions on more than forty issues at the national level and hundreds more at the state and local levels (League of Women Voters 2015). As I have shown, the downward trajectory of women's engagement at congressional hearings would not have been nearly as steep had these multi-issue groups maintained their strength. Suffrage also left room for groups that wanted to mobilize around specific female identities—mothers, feminists, and so forth. Thus, the suffrage amendment's invitation to pursue both group rights and social responsibilities allowed women to advance a wide range of policy agendas, both within multi-issue federations and through specialized groups speaking to particular civic orientations.

On the other hand, the policy context of the 1960s and 1970s, coupled with larger political shifts, encouraged women's groups to think less expansively about their policy agendas. A raft of policymaking at the federal level, combined with the availability of patronage resources, encouraged new interest groups to proliferate (Skocpol 2003; Berry 1997; Walker 1991). The interest-group universe came to be dominated by specialized, niche-seeking organizations (Baumgartner and Leech 2001; Browne 1990). These new groups displaced multipurpose women's organizations that in an earlier era had been active across issue domains, from the environment to international relations to social welfare (Goss 2013). At the same time, equal rights policies enacted in the early 1960s provided new resources, networks, and ideational justifications for women's groups to defend and build upon those gains—that is, to think of women's issues as feminist issues (Goss 2013). These laws also reinforced a liberal feminist ideology that viewed social caretaking rooted in gender difference as anathema to women's equality. As Nancy Fraser (1997: 99) has noted,

> Equality feminists saw gender difference as an instrument and artifact of
> male dominance. . . . To stress gender difference is to harm women. It is to
> reinforce our confinement to an inferior domestic role, hence to marginal-
> ize or exclude us from all those activities that promote true human self-
> realization, such as politics, employment, art, the life of the mind and the
> exercise of legitimate authority.

Third, the focus on feminist issues advantaged certain types of groups, namely
those speaking the language of gender rights. These groups fared well in the
era when working women were coming up against laws and public policies that
clearly discriminated against or otherwise disadvantaged them. However, once
policy reforms had been enacted in the 1960s–1980s, women's groups were left
to defend against rare threats to the antidiscrimination laws and to seek the few
protectionist policies that feminists were comfortable supporting (such as policies to protect women from violence and provide family and medical leave).
By the 2000s, a growing chorus of feminists had come to believe that the second wave's unfinished business lay in marital bargaining over work and family (Sandberg 2013; Hirshman 2007; Rowe-Finkbeiner 2004), in the failure of
society to embrace diversity in all of its complex and intersecting forms (Henry
2004), and in the cultural treatment of sexual expression (Baumgardner and
Richards 2000). Such priorities do not easily lend themselves to congressional
hearings or lawmaking.

Finally, feminism's policy victories created the conditions under which gender-
based organizing became problematic. These triumphs helped make women better off in education, employment, credit markets, and government programs. In
addressing women's unequal treatment under law, these policies weakened griev-
ance claims that had served as a basis for feminist mobilization. At the same time,
the maternalist and civic-woman frameworks of the early and mid-twentieth
century had yet to stage a comeback (Goss 2013). While surveys suggested that
women maintained a high level of collective identity and continued to believe in
collective action, it had become harder to identify an agenda or even collective
action frame around which women's civic passions could coalesce.

THE FORESHORTENED LEGACY OF SUFFRAGE

From the 1870s, when this study begins, through 2000, when it ends, the United
States underwent profound changes in its economic, political, and social organization. The interest-group universe that women had played a central role in building was fundamentally reconfigured, with broad, mass-membership federations
losing clout to professional lobbies with niche agendas, including feminist issues.
With advocacy by women's groups, the national welfare and regulatory state was
"invented" and then expanded to encompass a broad array of policies—from
health care research to income support and pensions to worker protections—that
affected women's lives in profound and intimate ways. In key respects, women
embody the evolving relationship between Americans and the state.

The case of American women raises important questions about what these changes have wrought. On the positive side, the dismantling of discriminatory laws and antiquated belief systems has helped to free women to pursue their dreams and deploy their talents to their highest and best ends, both for the benefit of the woman herself and for the benefit of others. At the same time, women have suffered a loss in representation on Capitol Hill. The organizations that once served as their voice appear less often, and on a narrower range of issues, than they did during the supposedly docile 1950s.

To be sure, twenty-first-century women continue to exercise political voice as individuals in the voting booth, where they participate at higher rates than men, and through lawmaking bodies and policy agencies, where they exercise considerable power to shape agendas. Nevertheless, the fading of women's collective action outside the state is cause for concern. Women continue to hold different policy preferences from men on key issues, and yet the United States is not even close to gender parity in positions of political leadership, whether in Congress or policy advocacy groups (Goss 2013). Women's groups may help redress these issues by cultivating female leadership and magnifying women's voice (Burns, Schlozman, and Verba 2001). Indeed, research suggests that female political leaders are most responsive and effective when women's groups are strong (Keiser 1997; Weldon 2002).

After 2000, when this study ended, innovative female leaders began reinvigorating women's historic role as defenders and promoters of the public good, while not surrendering women's status as equal-rights-bearing citizens (Goss and Heaney 2010). If history is any guide, these groups' fortunes will depend powerfully upon both the policy context and the ways that women's leaders interpret and respond to it.

Notes

1. Maud Wood Park's Farewell Address, reproduced in Stuhler (2003): 109–112; quote appears on pp. 111–112.

2. "Why Join the League of Women Voters?" 1921, reproduced in Stuhler 2003: 37.

3. Herring 1929, cited in Truman 1951: 100.

4. One might reasonably ask whether women's organizational activities increased after suffrage—or simply congressional recognition of women's organizations. The data don't allow us to say definitively, but circumstantial evidence (including organizational censuses) suggests that the upward trend was driven by women themselves. Supporting that conclusion is the fact that there was no sudden jump in women's appearances after 1920, which we might have expected if Congress had suddenly become solicitous of newly enfranchised women's views. I thank Nancy MacLean for raising this important question.

5. A total of 19,732 witnesses appeared. Some of these witnesses may be double counted if they appeared at more than one hearing in the dataset.

6. The seven traditional groups are the League of Women Voters and affiliates (990 appearances); the General Federation of Women's Clubs and affiliates (524); the National

Congress of Mothers / PTA and affiliates (508); the American Association of University Women and affiliates (303); the National Council of Jewish Women and affiliates (264); the Woman's Christian Temperance Union and affiliates (220); and the YWCA and affiliates (166).

7. According to the Policy Agendas Project, Congress held 16,344 hearings in the 1990s, compared to 11,526 in the 1950s.

8. I thank Professor Putnam for making these data available for the Goss and Skocpol chapter cited here.

9. *The Woman Citizen*, September 4, 1920, reprinted in part in Stuhler 2003: 26.

References

Andersen, Kristi. 1996. *After Suffrage: Women in Partisan and Electoral Politics before the New Deal*. Chicago: University of Chicago Press.

Baker, Paula. 1984. "The Domestication of Politics: Women and American Political Society, 1780–1920." *American Historical Review* 89(3): 620–647.

Banaszak, Lee Ann, ed. 2006. *The U.S. Women's Movement in Global Perspective*. Lanham, MD: Rowman and Littlefield.

Baumgardner, Jennifer, and Amy Richards. 2000. *Manifesta: Young Women, Feminism, and the Future*. New York: Macmillan.

Baumgartner, Frank R., and Beth L. Leech. 2001. "Interest Niches and Policy Bandwagons: Patterns of Interest Group Involvement in National Politics." *Journal of Politics* 63(4): 1191–1213.

Baumgartner, Frank R., and Christine Mahoney. 2005. "Social Movements, the Rise of New Issues, and the Public Agenda." Pp. 65–86 in *Routing the Opposition: Social Movements, Public Policy, and Democracy*, edited by D. S. Meyer, V. Jenness, and H. Ingram. Minneapolis: University of Minnesota Press.

Berry, Jeffrey M. 1997. *The Interest Group Society*. Third edition. New York: Longman.

Browne, William P. 1990. "Organized Interests and Their Issue Niches: A Search for Pluralism in a Policy Domain." *Journal of Politics* 52(2): 477–509.

Burns, Nancy, Kay Lehman Schlozman, and Sidney Verba. 2001. *The Private Roots of Public Action: Gender, Equality, and Political Participation*. Cambridge, MA: Harvard University Press.

Carabillo, Toni, Judith Meuli, and June Bundy Csida. 1993. *Feminist Chronicles*. Los Angeles: Women's Graphics.

Costain, Anne N. 1988. "Women's Claims as a Special Interest" Pp. 150–172 in *The Politics of the Gender Gap*, edited by C. M. Mueller. Newbury Park, CA: Sage.

———. 1992. *Inviting Women's Rebellion: A Political Process Interpretation of the Women's Movement*. Baltimore: The Johns Hopkins University Press.

Costain, Anne N., and W. Douglas Costain. 1987. "Strategy and Tactics of the Women's Movement in the United States: The Role of Political Parties" Pp. 196–214 in *The Women's Movements of the United States and Western Europe*, edited by M. F. Katzenstein and C. M. Miller. Philadelphia: Temple University Press.

Cott, Nancy F. 1987. *The Grounding of Modern Feminism*. New Haven, CT: Yale University Press.

——. 1992. "Across the Great Divide: Women in Politics before and after 1920." Pp. 153–176 in *Women, Politics, and Change*, edited by L. A. Tilly and P. Gurin. New York: Sage.

Davis, Flora. 1999. *Moving the Mountain: The Women's Movement in America since 1960*. Urbana: University of Illinois Press.

Disney, Jennifer Leigh, and Joyce Gelb. 2000. "Feminist Organizational 'Success': The State of U.S. Women's Movement Organizations in the 1990s." *Women & Politics* 21(4): 39–76.

Ferree, Myra Marx, and Beth B. Hess. 2000. *Controversy and Coalition: The New Feminist Movement across Four Decades of Change*. Third edition. New York: Routledge.

Fraser, Nancy. 1997. "Equality, Difference, and Democracy: Recent Feminist Debates in the United States." Pp. 98–109 in *Feminism and the New Democracy*, edited by J. Dean. London: Sage.

Friedan, Betty. 1963. *The Feminine Mystique*. New York: Norton.

Gelb, Joyce, and Marian Lief Palley. 1996. *Women and Public Policies: Reassessing Gender Politics*. Charlottesville: University of Virginia Press.

Goss, Kristin A. 2007. "Foundations of Feminism: How Philanthropic Patrons Shaped Gender Politics." *Social Science Quarterly* 88(5): 1174–1191.

——. 2009. "Never Surrender? How Women's Groups Abandoned Their Policy Niche in U.S. Foreign Policy Debates, 1916–2000." *Politics and Gender* 5(4): 1–37.

——. 2013. *The Paradox of Gender Equality: How American Women's Groups Gained and Lost Their Public Voice*. Ann Arbor: University of Michigan Press.

——. 2014. "Gender Identity and the Shifting Basis of U.S. Women's Groups' Advocacy, 1920–2000." Pp. 170–201 in *Nonprofits & Advocacy: Engaging Community and Government in an Era of Retrenchment*, edited by R. Pekkanen, S. R. Smith, and Y. Tsujinaka. Baltimore: The Johns Hopkins University Press.

Goss, Kristin A., and Michael T. Heaney. 2010. "Organizing Women as Women: Hybridity and Grassroots Collective Action in the 21st Century." *Perspectives on Politics* 8(1): 27–52.

Goss, Kristin A., and Theda Skocpol. 2006. "Changing Agendas: The Impact of Feminism on Public Policy." Pp. 323–356 in *Gender and Social Capital*, edited by B. O'Neill and E. Gidengill. Oxford: Routledge.

Grossmann, Matt. 2012. *The Not-So-Special Interests: Interest Groups, Public Representation, and American Governance*. Stanford, CA: Stanford University Press.

Harvey, Anna L. 1998. *Votes without Leverage: Women in American Electoral Politics, 1920–1970*. Cambridge: Cambridge University Press.

Hawkesworth, Mary. 2004. "The Semiotics of Premature Burial: Feminism in a Postfeminist Age." *Signs* 29(4): 961–985.

Henry, Astrid. 2004. *Not My Mother's Sister: Generational Conflict and Third-Wave Feminism*. Bloomington: Indiana University Press.

Herring, E. Pendleton. 1929. *Group Representation before Congress*. Baltimore, MD: The Johns Hopkins University Press.

Hirshman, Linda R. 2007. *Get to Work*. New York: Penguin.

Jablonsky, Thomas J. 1994. *The Home, Heaven, and Mother Party*. Brooklyn, NY: Carlson.

Keiser, Lael. 1997. "The Influence of Women's Political Power on Bureaucratic Output: The Case of Child Support Enforcement." *British Journal of Political Science* 27(1): 136–148.

Kerber, Linda K. 1998. *No Constitutional Right to Be Ladies*. New York: Hill and Wang.

Klein, Ethel. 1984. *Gender Politics*. Cambridge, MA: Harvard University Press.

Kraditor, Aileen. 1971. *The Ideas of the Woman Suffrage Movement, 1890–1920*. Garden City, NY: Doubleday.

League of Women Voters. 2015. *Impact on Issues 2014–2016: A Guide to Public Policy Positions*. Washington, DC.

Levine, Susan. 1995. *Degrees of Equality: The American Association of University Women and the Challenge of Twentieth-Century Feminism*. Philadelphia: Temple University Press.

Marshall, Susan E. 1997. *Splintered Sisterhood: Gender and Class in the Campaign against Woman Suffrage*. Madison: University of Wisconsin Press.

Mathews-Gardner, A. Lanethea. 2005. "The Political Development of Female Civic Engagement in Postwar America." *Politics & Gender* 1(4): 547–575.

McCammon, Holly J. 2012. *The U.S. Women's Jury Movements and Strategic Adaptation: A More Just Verdict*. New York: Cambridge University Press.

Mettler, Suzanne. 2002. "Bringing the State Back into Civic Engagement: Policy Feedback Effects of the G.I. Bill for World War II Veterans." *American Political Science Review* 96(2): 351–365.

Mettler, Suzanne, and Joe Soss. 2004. "The Consequences of Public Policy for Democratic Citizenship: Bridging Policy Studies and Mass Politics." *Perspectives on Politics* 2(1): 55–73.

Meyerowitz, Joanne, ed. 1994. *Not June Cleaver: Women and Gender in Postwar America, 1945–1960*. Philadelphia: Temple University Press.

O'Neill, William L. 1971. *Everyone Was Brave: A History of Feminism in America*. New York: Quadrangle/New York Times.

Pierson, Paul. 1993. "When Effect Becomes Cause: Policy Feedback and Political Change." *World Politics* 45(4): 595–628.

Putnam, Robert D. 2000. *Bowling Alone: The Collapse and Revival of American Community*. New York: Simon and Schuster.

Reingold, Beth. 1992. "Concepts of Representation among Female and Male State Legislators." *Legislative Studies Quarterly* 17(4): 509–537.

Rosenberg, Gerald N. 1993. *The Hollow Hope: Can Courts Bring about Social Change?* Chicago: University of Chicago Press.

Rowe-Finkbeiner, Kristin. 2004. *The F Word: Feminism in Jeopardy*. Emeryville, CA: Seal Press.

Rupp, Leila J., and Verta Taylor. 1987. *Survival in the Doldrums: The American Women's Rights Movement, 1945 to the 1960s*. New York: Oxford University Press.

Ryan, Barbara. 1992. *Feminism and the Women's Movement: Dynamics of Change in Social Movement Ideology and Activism*. New York: Routledge.

Sandberg, Sheryl. 2013. *Lean In: Women, Work, and the Will to Lead*. New York: Knopf.

Sklar, Kathryn Kish. 1993. "The Historical Foundations of Women's Power in the Creation of the American Welfare State, 1830–1930." Pp. 43–93 in *Mothers of a New World: Maternalist Politics and the Origins of Welfare States*, edited by S. Koven and S. Michel. New York: Routledge.

Skocpol, Theda. 1992. *Protecting Soldiers and Mothers*. Cambridge, MA: Belknap/Harvard University Press.

———. 1999. "Advocates without Members: The Recent Transformation of American Civic Life." Pp. 461–509 in *Civic Engagement in American Democracy*, edited by T. Skocpol and M. P. Fiorina. Washington, DC: Brookings Institution Press and New York: Russell Sage Foundation.

———. 2003. *Diminished Democracy: From Membership to Management in American Civic Life*. Norman: University of Oklahoma Press.

Stuhler, Barbara. 2003. *For the Public Record: A Documentary History of the League of Women Voters*. Washington, DC: League of Women Voters of the United States.

Thomas, Sue. 1994. *How Women Legislate*. New York: Oxford University Press.

Tolleson Rinehart, Sue. 1992. *Gender Consciousness and Politics*. New York: Routledge.

Truman, David. 1951. *The Governmental Process: Political Interests and Public Opinion*. New York: Knopf.

Walker, Jack L., Jr. 1991. *Mobilizing Interest Groups in America: Patrons, Professions, and Social Movements*. Ann Arbor: University of Michigan Press.

Ware, Susan. 1992. "American Women in the 1950s: Nonpartisan Politics and Women's Politicization." Pp. 281–299 in *Women, Politics, and Change*, edited by L. A. Tilly and P. Gurin. New York: Russell Sage Foundation.

Weldon, S. Laurel. 2002. "Beyond Bodies: Institutional Sources of Representation for Women in Democratic Policymaking." *Journal of Politics* 64(4): 1153–1174.

Wilson, Jan Doolittle. 2007. *The Women's Joint Congressional Committee and the Politics of Maternalism, 1920–30*. Urbana: University of Illinois Press.

Wolbrecht, Christina. 2000. *The Politics of Women's Rights*. Princeton, NJ: Princeton University Press.

Young, Louise M. 1989. *In the Public Interest: The League of Women Voters, 1920–1970*. New York: Greenwood.

10

After Suffrage Comes Equal Rights?

ERA AS THE NEXT LOGICAL STEP

Tracey Jean Boisseau and Tracy A. Thomas

> The work of the National Woman's Party is to take sex out of law—to give
> women the equality in law they have won at the polls.
> ——ALICE PAUL, 1922

> The point of E.R.A. is to get people to recognize that change is already here.
> ——ELEANOR HOLMES NORTON, 1978

In July 1978, at the largest march for women's rights in the nation's history up to
that time, Equal Rights Amendment (ERA) supporters poured onto the mall at the
center of the nation's capital in a desperate plea for more time to get the remaining three states needed for ratification. Likely very few of these dedicated march-
ers fully realized the time span of the campaign of which they were now a part,
or were fully aware of its tortured history. In 1978 a push for an amendment to
the US Constitution guaranteeing women equal rights with men was over a half
century old, having started in the wake of a woman suffrage amendment passed
before many on the mall that day were born; few but the very eldest of the leaders
could have recalled the arguments that they or their predecessors may have once
mounted against the ERA. In the crowd of one hundred thousand—three times as
large as the largest suffrage parade held in the 1910s and twice the size of the first
historic march on Washington in support of the ERA in 1970—were virtually all
of the leaders of progressive women's organizations, representing a vast coalition
of interests and activist causes (National Organization for Women, n.d.). This time
around, few women identifying as feminists disagreed that it was time for a federal
amendment guaranteeing and constitutionally enshrining women's equality under
the law.

The provisions of the ERA were not what feminists gathered on the mall to
debate. All that activists were asking for on that hot day in July was more time
to bring three more states around and achieve the required two-thirds majority for ratification. Well aware of the historic nature of this watershed moment,
Eleanor Holmes Norton, recent chair of New York City's Commission on Human

Rights, newly appointed first female chairperson of the US Equal Employment Opportunity Commission, and future first African American congresswoman from the District of Columbia, queried the crowd, "How will people look at us fifty years from now if Congress doesn't even give us more time?" She continued, "We look back on history and wonder, what all the fuss was about over an issue. The point of E.R.A. is to get people to recognize that change is already here" (Dismore 2014).

In hindsight it appears Norton was right on her latter point at least—much of the change that an equal rights amendment to the US Constitution portended and promised was well under way in the 1970s, having been achieved in the decades since the adoption of women's suffrage in 1920. The acceleration of public readiness for such changes that Norton sensed seemed to suggest a new political opportunity for passage of the ERA (McAdam 1982). These achievements came in fragments and through the enormous efforts of thousands of recently enfranchised women pushing for legal and policy changes at the ballot box and in the context of the courts, state and federal legislatures, national and local educational institutions, the armed forces, workplaces, and the media. In the next half-century following the marches of the 1970s, a whole lot more would be accomplished in these areas still. But despite such progress, few feminists today would agree that sex inequalities have been eradicated in law or in society. The campaign for the ERA, as of this writing, remains an aspiration for many activist feminists and a dead dream to the point of irrelevancy for many more. The march on Washington in 1978 accomplished its immediate aim—an extension was granted—yet neither that limited extension, nor the persistence of diehard ERA activists subsequently, resulted in additional endorsements from the states, causing a "blanket amendment" to the US Constitution to fade from the agendas of most feminist organizations and from public view.

Yet the amendment proposition lives on. A campaign to ratify the ERA survives literally—in annual efforts that continue to this day to introduce the amendment into congressional committee. The spirit of the campaign endures—in legal battles over individual issues and points of law that have been taken up by state and federal legislatures and the US Supreme Court. Conflict and debate between women over the ERA and the principle of equal rights for women also persist—most strikingly in battles between progressives and conservatives who see women's interests in stunningly divergent ways. The history of disagreement and disunity among women concerning the ERA is as long-standing as the campaigns themselves.[1] Significantly, the logic of an equal rights amendment was never universally evident or endorsed—even by the suffragists who fought most vigorously for a constitutional right for women to vote.

The political wake left by the passage of the Nineteenth Amendment did nothing to smooth the way for unity among women activists on the subject of equal rights. Once ratified, the arguments among feminist organizers over tactics to achieve suffrage were replaced with arguments over whether an equal rights amendment would menace what many viewed as the most important accomplishments of female organizers apart from suffrage itself: protective legislation for women's employment. Even after the Fair Labor Standards Act of 1938 quieted the mainstay of labor advocates' concerns, virulent disagreement over ERA among women organizers continued throughout the middle decades of the twentieth century. Not until the late 1960s and 1970s would battle lines between women organizers be redrawn, and even then the fundamental question of women's difference from men—whether physical, psychological, or social—did not evaporate. Indeed, with ratification of the ERA as distant a goal as it seems at present, the politicized public culture and vigorous democratic debate over women's nature and role that have been inspired and sustained by a century-long effort to enshrine women's equal rights into the US Constitution may well be considered the ERA's principal if not singular achievement.

Almost a full century in the making, the campaign for an equal rights amendment has far exceeded in longevity the campaign for women's suffrage, however much a "logical next step" it seemed to some following the spectacular achievement of the Nineteenth Amendment (Neale 2013: 1). The ERA's history reveals how resistant to the idea of equality between men and women a political system—even one that includes women as voters—can be. In this chapter, we reexamine the route taken by the ERA through its many permutations in the century since the passage of women's suffrage. We begin by revisiting the sunset of the woman suffrage movement that also was the dawn of the first ERA campaign initiative.

In the Wake of Women's Suffrage, 1920–1925

The first ERA campaign is most closely identified with Alice Paul and a coterie of former suffragists she gathered around her to lead the National Woman's Party (NWP). The NWP formed in the several years preceding the achievement of women's suffrage in 1920 and was crucial to the success of that effort. For some like Paul, virtually simultaneous with women winning the right to vote came an ambition to expand on women's rights as citizens generally. Specifically, this meant undoing the 1875 US Supreme Court decision in *Minor v. Happersett* (1875) that confined women to a "special" class of citizenry under the federalist provisions of the Fourteenth Amendment.[2]

Though very much in the minority among feminist women, Paul and the NWP leadership were not entirely alone in viewing an equal rights amendment as a necessary next step to suffrage. Historian Nancy Cott (1989) points to an early manifestation of support for an equal rights amendment by the Feminist Alliance, a small group based in New York City. The alliance called for something similar to the ERA as early as 1914, six years before suffrage was achieved. No determined plan, however, existed for how to achieve equal rights for women in all areas of the law until March 1921 when the NWP voted in favor of a slate of equal rights objectives. The resolutions adopted at this meeting included the following simple statement: "That, the immediate work of the new organization be the removal of the legal disabilities of women" (*Vassar Miscellany News* 1921: 4). The wording of this resolution did not mention an equal rights amendment, but it was clear that this was the determined direction in which Alice Paul intended to move the NWP.

In opposition to the NWP's expressed intention to push for an equal rights amendment, major women's groups organized the Women's Joint Congressional Committee (WJCC), a national lobbying group, and chose Maud Wood Park to head it. As former head (1916–1920) of the Congressional Committee for the National American Woman Suffrage Association (NAWSA), Park had virulently opposed Alice Paul's sensationalist tactics that had brought the suffrage campaign to a controversial fever pitch in the late 1910s (Cott 1990). Park continued to oppose Paul and her decision to turn the political machinery of the NWP toward an equal rights amendment campaign, drawing the strength for her opposition from the threat that many female activists felt such an amendment posed to protective legislation for women in employment.

Once Park was chosen to lead the WJCC, little chance of reaching an agreement about an equal rights amendment across organizational lines was likely. This was not for lack of effort. Florence Kelley, a former NWP leader, onetime close ally to Alice Paul, and newly named director of the National Consumers League, attempted to bring the major women's organizations together in hopes of reaching a compromise position on the question of an equal rights amendment. In December 1921 Kelley coordinated a meeting between Alice Paul and the NWP leadership and leaders from the General Federation of Women's Clubs, the Woman's Christian Temperance Union, the National Women's Trade Union League, and the League of Women Voters to discuss the issue. Delegates left convinced more than ever that no compromise was possible, but such opposition did not dissuade Paul or her supporters from their decision to champion an equal rights amendment.

Within three years of the passage of the Nineteenth Amendment, Alice Paul formally kicked off a campaign for an equal rights amendment on July 21, 1923, in Seneca Falls, New York. Well-known for her flair for political theater and use of historical flourish, Paul chose her date and venue carefully. The occasion was a commemorative celebration of the Woman's Rights Convention held there seventy-five years prior on July 19–20, 1848, out of which had come the Declaration of Sentiments—a founding moment and document in the long campaign for woman suffrage. Paul's proposed amendment, named for a prominent nineteenth-century suffragist and women's rights activist, Lucretia Mott, read, "Men and women shall have equal rights throughout the United States and every place subject to its jurisdiction," and included a sentence endowing Congress with the power to enforce its provisions (Neale 2013: 2). Soon after introducing the initiative to enthusiastic supporters at the commemoration in July, Paul arranged to have her proposal introduced to the 68th Congress in December 1923 by both a senator and representative of Kansas, one of whom was the nephew of famed suffragist Susan B. Anthony (Woloch 2015).

As wrapped in history and resonant of collective women's activism as the rollout of the first ERA purposefully was, the proposed amendment was nonetheless deeply resented by most female organizers and even most former suffragists who viewed the logic of an equal rights amendment as, at best, flawed and the implications of it as dangerous to women's interests. Forming themselves into the nonpartisan and politically neutral League of Women Voters (LWV), many former suffrage workers in the aftermath of suffrage turned to the task of promoting women not only as voters but also as candidates for elected or appointed office. The league saw itself as a mechanism adding balance to the political landscape. Its initial primary concern lay with safeguarding the rights of women as enfranchised citizens whose full participation in an electoral system was still being widely questioned and even openly challenged by lawsuits such as *Lesser v. Garnett* (1922). The suit characterized the Nineteenth Amendment as an unconstitutional dilution of men's right to suffrage by rendering men's voting power "half strength." That logic was cursorily rejected by the Supreme Court, but the suit nonetheless put former suffragists on their guard against large and small challenges to women as voters and pushed them to find ways to institutionalize women's participation in local, state, and national politics. Their goal was not to create blanket legal equality for women with men on the national level, but to work state by state carving out space within the existing legal framework for women to participate as political actors.

Other former suffragists chose to lend their energy to organizations working for legislative reforms that seemed, to them, more germane to the struggles that women endured outside of the political sphere, especially at the workplace. Such women ignored Alice Paul's call to attend the 1923 Seneca Falls celebration and instead flocked to Washington, DC, that same year to attend the Women's Industrial Conference to discuss prospects for expanding protective legislation for women workers (Lipschultz 1996; US Department of Labor 1923). These women believed further political reform should hinge on women's seemingly inevitable gender-specific experiences as a distinct class of particularly vulnerable workers and as mothers with principal responsibilities for child rearing and homemaking. Whether as members of the increasingly prominent League of Women Voters or as determined labor rights advocates, most female activists and professional organizers either saw Paul's proposed ERA as a pipedream or as a specific and potent threat to the protective labor legislation that they had worked for several generations to put into effect.

The tendency of female activists and organizers to divide over the ERA depended more than any other factor on their class background and experience in the labor movement. According to Cynthia Harrison (1988), this is true even across racial lines, with black women's organizations splitting over the question of the ERA along much the same lines as white women's. As an example, Harrison points to the early endorsement for an equal rights amendment by the National Association of Colored Women (NACW) and attributes this to the influence of its founder and first president, Mary Church Terrell. Terrell's father was a self-made millionaire; she received an elite education at Oberlin College and went on to cofound the National Association of University Women (NAUW) as well as the National Association for the Advancement of Colored People (NAACP). In contrast, although Mary McLeod Bethune was an educator also—having founded the Bethune-Cookman College in Daytona Beach, Florida, in her public work she placed special emphasis on creating opportunities for black employment. During the Depression, Bethune served as the director of Negro affairs for the National Youth Administration in the Works Progress Administration under President Franklin Roosevelt. Unconvinced by Paul's insistence that an equal rights amendment would not endanger employment protections, Bethune kept the organization she founded, the National Council of Negro Women (NCNW), distanced from the ERA through the 1930s without making any public declarations of disavowal. After many years expressing the need for more sustained study of the matter, finally in 1944, the NCNW went on record as officially opposed to the amendment, specifically citing its "concern for protective labor legislation" (Harrison 1988: 11).

Experience in the labor movement did not automatically or inevitably lead to hostility to the ERA. Alice Paul had started out as a professional organizer advocating for women laborers, and at first was not unsympathetic to the view that there ought to be a way to retain some protective labor laws for women even within the context of equal rights for men and women under the law. Early on, in part to counteract the impression that the NWP and the ERA were anti–woman worker and with the hope of bringing pro-labor organizers and associations on board, Paul initially tolerated including a "construing clause" into the equal rights legislation that she and the NWP promoted in the 1920s (Zimmerman 1991). Though legal scholars and consultants at the time questioned how such a clause might be construed in practice (Hart 1994), such a clause would, presumably, exempt protective employment legislation for women workers from the imposition of gender-blind interpretations of equal rights otherwise mandated by the amendment. Throughout the 1920s Alice Paul and the lawyers and legal experts central to the leadership of the NWP experimented with the possibility of creating laws that could both sustain protective provisions for women in labor legislation while also serving the larger principle of women's equality to men. Compromise on this point, however, proved to be unsustainable.

While hoping to find the correct wording and argumentation sufficient to bring large numbers of women organizers around to support an equal rights amendment, in the 1920s the NWP through direct challenges chipped away at the problem of women's inequality under the law. As early as 1921 Paul chose Burnita Shelton Matthews, later the first woman to be appointed a federal district judge, to lead the NWP's Industrial Committee. The committee was composed of thirteen female attorneys charged with making a study of discriminatory laws in each state concerning women's property rights, child custody, divorce and marital rights, jury duty, education and professional employment, and national and citizen rights. Their mandate was to expose legal inequalities between men and women that were embedded in all facets of law. The committee was charged also with proposing new legislation to counteract such inequalities. According to Amelia Fry (1986), by the end of the decade, the NWP could point to about three hundred state laws changed out of the six hundred the committee had identified or targeted throughout the country. Pressing state by state for equal access to jury duty, guardianship, and fair wages, arguing that women should be treated equally with men, the activities of the NWP's Industrial Committee were not that far from the "specific bills for specific ills" program of the League of Women Voters (Mathews and De Hart 1990: 29). In addition, according to its own internal history, the NWP mirrored some of the league's primary emphasis on getting more women elected and appointed to office by launching two major Women for Congress campaigns in 1924 and 1926 and lobbying for women to be appointed to high federal office and prominent government positions (Library of Congress n.d.).

Paul's hope that shared ground between the NWP and postsuffrage organizations like the league could bring women activists en masse into the campaign for an equal rights amendment was emboldened by an early victory for women's equal rights in Wisconsin. Before Paul had even formulated an ERA campaign, in 1921 NWP leader Mabel Raef Putnam helped push through the first statewide equal rights law guaranteeing women equality under the law except where the law offered women "special protection and privileges which they now enjoy for the general welfare" (Lemons 1973: 187). It was not very long, however, before the wisdom of that clause would reveal itself as flawed in exactly the way Paul feared when, in 1923, the Wisconsin attorney general cited it in his refusal to strike down a 1905 law that barred women from employment in the state legislature due to the "very long and unreasonable hours" the work involved (McBridge 1993: 298). Supporters of equal rights for women were appalled by this application of the Construing Clause, interpreted in this instance, at least, to keep women literally out of the halls of power. Subsequently, Paul would come to see any sort of exemption as inadvisable. She viewed such clauses as inconsistent with her larger vision for an equal rights amendment, in part because of her belief that inevitably the inclusion of special exemptions would hold women back from advancement in employment as well as every other facet of social life. Soon after embarking on an equal rights amendment campaign, Paul as well as other leaders in the NWP came to accept as definitive the views of Gail Laughlin, an NWP lawyer and first president of the National Federation of Business and Professional Women, who contended that sex-based labor legislation was not, as women's labor advocates insisted, a lamentable but practical necessity. "If women can be segregated as a class for special legislation," she warned, "the same classification can be used for special restrictions along any other line which may, at any time, appeal to the caprice or prejudice of our legislatures" (Cott 1990: 47).

Although Paul and the NWP were adamant on this point, most female organizers and activists continued to support sex-based legislation and to have serious reservations about an equal rights amendment. The questions raised by an amendment—whether over its usefulness as a strategy, its feasibility within existing legal frameworks, or its foundational assumptions about men's and women's nature and experiences—were thoroughly aired in a series of debates held in 1924 between the amendments' proponents and opponents. The most commonly referenced of these, "The 'Blanket' Amendment—A Debate," held in August 1924 between Doris Stevens and Alice Hamilton, was sponsored by the Consumers League of New York and reported in its organ, *The Forum*. Several other heavily publicized debates took place on the issue, including one held earlier in March of that same year between Alice Paul and Mary Van Kleeck titled "Is Blanket

Amendment Best Method in Equal Rights Campaign?"—designed to suggest that the question remained open. A second debate held in August 1924, featuring Sophonisba Breckinridge and titled "Could Mothers' Pensions Operate under Equal Rights Amendment?" posed the question in a way designed to highlight women's presumably special needs as mothers and widows. Another debate held the following month put labor legislation at its center, posing the question, "Should There Be Labor Laws for Women? No, Says Rheta Childe Dorr, Yes, Says Mary Anderson" (*Good Housekeeping* 1925). Despite the seeming variety of focus in the structure of these debates, their substance echoed one another closely, as did the stalemate quality of their tone. As early as 1924, few minds appeared open enough to be changed by the ventilation of the intricacies of either side's arguments. Almost immediately after the passage of women's suffrage in 1920, the lines of battle between women passionately devoted to improving women's lives under conditions of inequality were clearly drawn and, by the middle of that decade, appeared to be unresolvable.

The Battle over Protective Labor Laws for Women, 1925–1940

The next fifteen years saw continued infighting among feminist activists, repeatedly pitting the ERA against protective labor laws for women. Social feminists like Kelley were dedicated to lobbying for labor laws for working-class women, to protect the "mothers of the race" from exploitation by industrial management and to compensate for women's disadvantage in the workplace (Lehrer 1987; Woloch 2015). In the first two decades of the twentieth century, most states had passed some type of women's labor laws of maximum hours, minimum wages, night prohibitions, and occupational exclusions. Legislatures and courts, however, resisted such laws for men as contradictory to notions of masculinity and physical strength and instead determined that men were entitled to liberty and freedom of contract in employment bargaining. Women, on the other hand, were deemed different—weaker and in need of special protection from the abuses of the workplace (Woloch 2015).

Social feminist reformers feared, correctly, that an equal rights amendment would prohibit different treatment of women workers and thus invalidate their efforts to enact special protective legislation. Leaders like Kelley wanted "to protect at least women and children from the worst ravages of capitalism" (Mansbridge 1986: 8). She worked to improve the economic conditions of working-class women who worked long shifts in unhealthy conditions and were paid less wages than men. Kelley's approach was to emphasize women's difference—their smaller, weaker bodies; their home demands of childcare and housekeeping; and the impact of working conditions on pregnancies (Becker 1981).

Egalitarian feminists also prioritized economic opportunity and autonomy for women, but they disagreed that special protective legislation for women was the appropriate legal means to that end. These legal-equality feminists refused to support any law classifying women separately based on their alleged inferiority, difference, or need for protection. "Protection" had been the common-law rationale for denying women civil and legal rights going back to eighteenth-century England. Equality feminists objected to any insertion of ideas of protection in the law. Practically, egalitarian feminists also feared that special employment rules for women would mean women's loss of work, as employers hired men who were free from these rules. If women faced restrictions on overtime or night work and required minimum wages or maternity leaves, they were less valuable to an employer than a male worker who had no such limitations. If employers were reluctant to hire women, then women were limited in their ability to support themselves and their families (Woloch 2015). Given the rift among women's organizations regarding an equal rights amendment, any shared agreement on specific legal reforms, like marital property and child custody, was lost by the conflict over a blanket amendment, with social feminists leveraging women's difference and separateness and egalitarians demanding formal equality (Woloch 2015).

Early in the twentieth century, the US Supreme Court endorsed social feminists' efforts by upholding protective legislation for women—but not men. In its seminal decision in *Lochner v. New York* (1905), a divided Court struck down a state law setting maximum hours for male bakers. The case established a new theory of substantive due process, holding that the Constitution did not authorize states to legislate in violation of an employee's freedom to contract. Three years later, however, a unanimous Court in *Muller v. Oregon* (1908) upheld a similar maximum-hour law for women, limiting their work in factories and laundries to ten hours per day.[3] The Court distinguished women from men in the need for protection in "woman's physical structure and the performance of maternal functions," including smaller physical size, maternity and menstruation, and housework demands (*Muller* 1908: 421). "Differentiated by these matters from the other sex, [woman] is properly placed in a class by herself, and legislation designed for her protection may be sustained, even when like legislation is not necessary for men, and could not be sustained" (*Muller* 1908: 422). The Court was influenced by the novel "Brandeis Brief," of data and sociological evidence of women's physical disadvantage submitted by lawyer and later justice Louis Brandeis and compiled by Florence Kelley and her NCL colleague Josephine Goldmark, Brandeis's sister-in-law (Woloch 2015). Despite the gendered focus of much of Kelley's evidence, a decade later, the Court extended this protectionist rationale to men by upholding a general maximum-hour law for all workers (*Bunting v. Oregon* 1917).

But *Lochner*'s theory of freedom of contract for employees and employer survived as well, subject to the caveat of protecting health. The Court refused to extend its reasoning to uphold protective labor legislation in the form of minimum wage standards, even for women. Following the ratification of the Nineteenth Amendment, the Supreme Court took the occasion to strike down a minimum wage law specifically for women, which strengthened women's equality rights. In *Adkins v. Children's Hospital* (1923), a split Court held that the Nineteenth Amendment exemplified a general guarantee of gender equality, altering the older legal cases of protection based on gender difference (Siegel 2002). The decision, written by newly appointed Justice George Sutherland, who had counseled Alice

Paul on suffrage and the proposed equal rights amendment (Zimmerman 1991), held that "the ancient inequality of the sexes, otherwise than physical," had come "almost, if not quite, to the vanishing point" (*Adkins* 1923: 553). The Court held that "while physical differences must be recognized in appropriate cases," like *Muller*, which concerned women's health, it rejected the "doctrine that women of mature age, sui juris, require or may be subjected to restrictions upon their liberty of contract which could not lawfully be imposed in the case of men under similar circumstances" (*Adkins* 1923: 449). To do so, the Court continued, would be to ignore all implications of trends in legislation and common thought "by which woman is accorded emancipation from the old doctrine that she must be given special protection or be subjected to special restraint in her contractual and civil relationships" (*Adkins* 1923: 553). An amicus brief submitted by the NWP helped the Court articulate this idea of women's equality (Woloch 2015). However, while *Adkins* represented a step forward in women's equality, just one year later, the Supreme Court returned to its endorsement of women-only protective legislation, upholding a state law banning women from night work in New York restaurants (*Radice v. New York* 1923).

Adkins was decided the same year Alice Paul introduced the ERA to Congress and the public. The decision helped solidify the battle between social and egalitarian feminists. Any hope of reconciling their approaches of formal equality and special protection was abandoned. (Cott 1989). As Harriot Stanton Blatch, onetime NWP member and daughter of feminist leader Elizabeth Cady Stanton, expressed, a middle-road approach was "the worst possible solution, doubling rather than neutralizing the damage" (DuBois 1997: 222). Blatch viewed the abstract guarantee of ERA as useless, believed in concrete worker protections for all workers, and despised any special classifications for women based on biological weakness (DuBois 1997). Egalitarians, on the other hand, opposed any classification by sex, and social feminists rejected equality as harmful to women. As social feminist Kelley wrote, "The cry Equality, Equality, where Nature has created inequality, is as stupid and as deadly as the Cry Peace, Peace, where there is no Peace" (Lemons 1973: 185). Political acrimony intensified, as egalitarian feminists found themselves in allegiance with Republicans and business interests against laboring women and Democrats, and social feminists prioritized questions of class over gender (Woloch 2015). The proposed ERA came to have a "symbolic association with white professional women single-mindedly devoted to formal equality and indifferent to the plight of poor women and women of color" (Mayeri 2004: 784).

The Supreme Court continued to reject minimum wage laws for all workers. In 1936 a split Court reaffirmed *Adkins* in *Morehead v. New York ex rel. Tipaldo* (1936), invalidating a New York minimum wage law for women and minors. Yet just one year later, in *West Coast Hotel Co. v. Parrish* (1937), the Court reversed that decision in another closely divided case, this time upholding the minimum wage law for women in favor of a female hotel maid. The *West Coast Hotel* Court affirmed that state legislatures could enact laws for workers' protection, particularly women workers, because of "the fact that they are in the class receiving the least pay, that their bargaining power is relatively weak, and that they are the ready victims of those who would take advantage of their necessitous circumstances" (*West Coast Hotel* 1937: 398). *West Coast Hotel* rejected *Lochner*'s absolutist theory of freedom of contract.

Importantly, though, this logic helped clear the way for protective legislation for all workers. The next year, Congress passed Roosevelt's Fair Labor Standards Act (FLSA) of 1938, shepherded by the first female secretary of labor, Frances Perkins. The new law established a minimum wage of twenty-five cents for all workers and a maximum forty-hour workweek.

In effect, Kelley had won. Her vision of protective legislation for women and all workers was accomplished. In so doing, much of the social feminists' opposition to the ERA evaporated, as women's equality and protection for women workers were now both accomplished by protective labor laws for women and men. One might expect, then, that the ERA would now experience smooth sailing. The FLSA had removed the impediment to the ERA for the social feminists that had bogged down the equality movement in the first decades after suffrage. With the infighting among feminists deflated, it seemed the ERA was ripe for action. Indeed, the amendment made initial progress. The ERA reported out of committee favorably in May 1936 for the first time since its introduction in Congress in 1923 (Fry 1986). But advocates clung to old allegiances, with labor and union feminists refusing to endorse what they increasingly viewed as a conservative, pro-business amendment (Woloch 2015).

Taking Sides during and after the War, 1940–1960

The FLSA and its affirmation by the US Supreme Court in 1941 (*United States v. Darby*), did not come close to demolishing the deep rift between the NWP and labor organizations. But, in the 1940s, the combination of the new law and a public relations campaign to drum up enthusiasm for women's entrance into nontraditional forms of employment after the outbreak of war altered the cultural landscape in ways that seemed to clear the way forward for some progress on the ERA. In the context of a nation at war captivated by "Rosie the Riveter," women's effective and experiential equality to men seemed less unimaginable as well as less objectionable. According to Cynthia Harrison (1988), in this period, the ERA appealed more to conservative and mainstream capitalists steeped in individualist rhetoric and confidence in America's commitment to free enterprise and individual opportunity as coextensive with the American Dream. She argues that a "pro-business" view of the ERA had its advantages as Roosevelt's New Deal drew to a close and at the end of a period during which labor achievements appeared to many to have gained too much of an upper hand. Unlike during the Depression when the Roosevelt administration pushed as far in the direction of labor as possible, the Cold War period saw more conservative presidential administrations scrambling to put forth a positive agenda of change of their own. This began as early as the war years, when both the Republican and Democratic Party began including endorsements of the ERA in their national platforms (1940 and 1944,

respectively) (Cott 1990). By the early 1940s several major women's organizations also had come around to supporting the amendment. Not only the National
Federation of Business and Professional Women's Clubs but also the extremely
large and ecumenical General Federation of Women's Clubs—after a ten-year
study and reconsideration of the question, according to an internal history of the
organization published in 1953—agreed to endorse (Freeman 1996; Stephensons
1944; Wells 1953).

Seizing on the opportunity that a change in the cultural zeitgeist appeared to
portend, Alice Paul reorganized the NWP's internal organization and amplified its
lobbying efforts (Harrison 1988). Rather than a mass-membership organization,
Paul saw the NWP's effectiveness as lying with the small, elite cadre of professional organizers and lobbyists at its core. This organizational philosophy, however, led to charges of elitism, adding fuel to the claims of its pro-labor opponents
that the NWP was out of touch with the conditions and experiences of the average American woman, who lacked the education, affluence, and independence
enjoyed by many in the NWP leadership.

To counteract such charges, and to "benefit from the power of numbers," Paul
created an umbrella organization, the Women's Joint Legislative Council (WJLC),
whose membership consisted of "all the organizations that endorsed the ERA,"
bringing, according to Harrison (1988: 17), the combined membership to "between
five and six million members, a formidable constituency." Taking place in an age of
media saturation and in the context of a public culture obsessed with celebrities,
Harrison (1988) notes that Paul sought endorsements from leading lights in fields
as disparate as aviation (Amelia Earhart), Hollywood film (Katharine Hepburn),
popular literature (Pearl S. Buck), and the fine arts (Georgia O'Keeffe) as well as
professional and academic fields such as social science (Margaret Mead), education (Mary Woolley, former president of Mount Holyoke College), public health
(Margaret Sanger), law (Judge Sarah Hughes), and politics (Congresswoman
Margaret Chase Smith). While the NWP was far from populist in its orientation as
well as its messaging, through high-profile endorsements it sought to attract public notice and appear as a big tent filled with the most influential and distinguished
of female allies that it could muster to its side.

In the hope of taking advantage of a change in the political climate, and to head
off opposition coming from southern states concerned with states' rights principles, in the early 1940s Alice Paul reconsidered the wording of the Lucretia Mott
Amendment. She consulted with members of Congress and male attorneys to produce the most effective while least objectionable amendment possible. The newly
worded proposal, unofficially dubbed the "Alice Paul Amendment," removed language that the earlier iteration had included that might have suggested the ascendancy of the federal government over individual states and echoed more perfectly
the Nineteenth Amendment in its structure: "Equality of rights under the law shall
not be denied or abridged by the United States or by any state on account of sex"
(Neale 2013: 2). Official sanction to the new wording and to the proposed ERA
was provided by a favorable review in 1942 by the US House and Senate subcommittees (*Congressional Digest* 1943). But, according to Jo Freeman (1996), once it

reached the House Judicial Committee in 1943, pressure from Catholic organizations, particularly the National Council of Catholic Women and the National Catholic Welfare Conference, appeared to sway the votes of key congressmen with large Catholic constituencies to reverse their support. The proposed amendment went down in a vote 11 to 15.

The closeness of this vote, followed by the endorsement in 1944 by the Democratic Party as well as the support of newly sworn-in President Truman in 1945, signaled an apparent shift in the responses of official institutions to the ERA. New support for the amendment piqued the concern of left-leaning feminists and those in the labor coalition, led by those in the Women's Bureau of the Department of Labor, which had long strenuously rejected an ERA. They responded to what they perceived as a new level of threat by forming an oppositional alliance specifically aimed at halting the ERA's advance (Berry 1988). The name of the alliance, the National Committee to Defeat the Un-equal Rights Amendment, left no room for doubt about what it considered the primary threat to women's rights at the close of World War II. The same year that the United States helped defeat the Axis powers, a committee hoping to defeat the ERA once and for all produced a brochure that outlined what women could lose if an equal rights amendment were passed. These potential losses included "family support," which might mean elimination of the right of wives to expect or demand husbands' financial support or might even, the pamphlet suggested ominously, require wives to support husbands. The brochure also listed protections for widows that would be at risk, such as Social Security benefits and allowances or creditor protection pending estate settlements. The brochure concluded its list of the implications of this "dangerous amendment" by insisting that the ERA was "misleading" because it "masquerades as a progressive measure, whereas it would actually destroy progress toward equal rights, and would undermine the foundations of family life" (National Archives 1945). The latter comment likely reflected the inclusion of groups in the National Committee such as the leadership of the YWCA and the national councils of Jewish, Catholic, and Negro women as well as the LWV and leaders from the American Federation of Labor (AFL) and Congress of Industrial Organizations (CIO; Steiner 1985). According to Steiner, this large alliance of anti-ERA forces was responsible for the narrow defeat of the ERA in July 1946, when, despite being fast-tracked past hearings in the House Committee of the 79th Congress, the amendment proposal made it out of senatorial committee only to be defeated on the floor of the Senate in a nail biter 38-35 vote against passage.

A few years later, in 1950, a fateful compromising clause, drafted by the leadership of the Women's Bureau, was added to the amendment following a heated debate regarding the proposal on the floor of the Senate. Senator Carl Hayden (D-AZ) proposed the addition of a clause thereafter known as the "Hayden rider" that read, "The provisions of this article shall not be construed to impair any rights, benefits, or exemptions now or hereafter conferred by law upon persons of the female sex" (Neale 2013: 3). According to Thomas H. Neale, the rider caught ERA proponents off guard, and according to Freeman (1996), many senators "took advantage of the opportunity to vote for both amendments," allowing the rider to pass 51-31 and the ERA with rider attached to pass 63-19. Only Senator Margaret Chase Smith (R-ME), the lone female senator at the time, opposed the addition (Neale 2013).[4] In the eyes of Alice Paul and the NWP, the rider compromised the principle of equality and thus had rendered the proposal utterly worthless. The NWP demanded it be withdrawn. In 1953, during the Eisenhower administration, according to Jo Freeman (1996), "history repeated itself" and the ERA with attached rider achieved congressional approval by a large margin. And again, the NWP insisted it be tabled.

The Eisenhower administration, devoid of the labor radicals who had supplied much of the energy and vision to the Roosevelt and Truman administrations, proved a good deal friendlier to the ERA than previous administrations. In place of Frieda Miller, whose long career as a strong labor organizer and whose longtime opposition of ERA was widely recognized, President Eisenhower appointed Alice Leopold as head of the Women's Bureau of the Department of Labor. Leopold was a former Connecticut secretary of state who, as a freshman member of the 1949 General Assembly, was instrumental in passing legislation providing "equal pay for equal work" in that state (Leopold 1955: 7; *Sunday Herald* 1953). Although Leopold was not able to orchestrate adoption of the ERA, she focused attention more on women's professional work in scientific and medical fields, and gave both tacit and nontacit support for the ERA, despite the Department of Labor's continuing official stance against it (O'Farrell 2015). Aside from Leopold, Eisenhower himself proved to be the most enthusiastic supporter of the ERA in his administration. Near the beginning of his second term of office, he included a rousing endorsement of "equal rights" for women in what historian Gilbert Yale Steiner characterizes as a "major campaign speech on civil rights"; Eisenhower did so again in his budget message to Congress in January 1957 (Steiner 1985: 10).[5] In 1958 Eisenhower asked a joint session of Congress to pass the ERA, but when the amendment was introduced, the wording included the Hayden rider, rendering it unacceptable to the NWP and again compelling its leadership to demand that it be withdrawn.

As a result of the impasse resulting from the introduction of the Hayden rider to the ERA, no real progress would be made to advance the ERA in the postwar period, including the few years of John F. Kennedy's presidency. The lack of action during the Kennedy administration was due, in part, to his appointment of a staunch labor advocate as assistant secretary of labor for labor standards. Esther Peterson, the first woman lobbyist for the AFL-CIO and a longtime advocate for the rights of working women, consistently opposed the ERA throughout her tenure as assistant secretary, although, according to Karen O'Connor, she would become a "driving force" behind the passage of the Equal Pay Act of 1963 (O'Connor 2010: 274). In the early 1960s, Peterson, like many others of her generation, saw equal pay for working women as a pro-labor initiative while continuing to view the ERA in terms of the rifts between women activists characterizing those first divisive years of the 1920s.

This entrenched pattern of opposition between women organizers endured for two generations until a pro-ERA campaign emerged in the second half of the 1960s in the wake of civil rights legislation that reconfigured political alliances and legal strategizing. By the 1970s, as a state-by-state ratification process unfolded, women split along very different lines from those that had prevailed mid-century. The issue of protective labor legislation ceased to divide feminist-minded women, even as some of the same ideas about women's difference from men and need for special protections and privileges that labor advocates once articulated as foundational to their arguments became even more pronounced in heated public debates between feminists and a new coalition of conservative women.

The Reemergence of the ERA in the Context of Civil Rights and Feminism, 1961–1982

Mayeri (2004: 757) explains that "after decades of bitter division over the Equal Rights Amendment," women's rights activists "overcame long-standing racial, class, and ideological rifts to unite around a dual strategy—the simultaneous pursuit of a constitutional amendment and judicial reinterpretation of the Fourteenth Amendment." The judicial front of the equality battle came out of the President's Commission on the Status of Women convened in late 1961, where participants were eager to develop an alternative legal strategy to circumvent the impasse over the ERA. The Supreme Court had just decided *Hoyt v. Florida* (1961), rejecting a Fourteenth Amendment challenge to women's exemption from state jury service because women were different from men as "woman is still regarded as the center of home and family life." The commission asked Pauli Murray, attorney and civil rights activist, to research and evaluate possible strategies, and Murray recommended a renewed litigation effort under the Fourteenth Amendment drawing heavily on the analogy between race and sex discrimination in the "Jane Crow" laws (Murray and Eastwood 1965). This flexible, case-by-case approach allowed for incremental movement that mediated the absolutist positions of feminists on the ERA and concretely and politically linked women's rights with the burgeoning civil rights movement. The American Civil Liberties Union (ACLU), a longtime opponent of the ERA due to its labor union allegiance, "enthusiastically embraced the Murray proposal" (Mayeri 2004: 766). Ardent ERA supporters initially resisted the judicial Fourteenth Amendment approach, thinking it to be an end run around the amendment; but following the success of the race-sex connection in the passage of Title VII, these opponents came around to accepting the alternative strategy.

Title VII of the Civil Rights Act of 1964 and its prohibition of employment discrimination on the basis of race or sex proved to be a crucial step in building support for an equality amendment (Mansbridge 1986). The original bill targeted race discrimination in private employment but was amended to include sex discrimination as well. Conservative segregationist Howard Smith (R-VA) introduced a bill to add sex, many believed as a tactic to defeat the legislation, though Smith supported some view of women's rights (Mayeri 2004). Representative Martha Griffiths (D-MI), a longtime women's rights advocate, allegedly authored the amendment but let Smith offer it, knowing that this approach might garner political support even if derived from racial prejudices (Berry 1988). Title VII passed with the addition of gender, though early enforcement by the Equal Employment Opportunity Commission (EEOC) gave lesser priority to sex discrimination complaints than to those of race discrimination (Mayeri 2004).

The National Organization for Women (NOW), newly formed in 1966 by Betty Friedan and Murray, pressed for full enforcement of the new Title VII and actualizing its mandate of equality in employment (Fry 1986). By 1970, federal courts, the Department of Labor, and the EEOC all interpreted Title VII as invalidating women-specific rules, including protective labor legislation and, more importantly, requiring extension of any protections like minimum wages to men rather than eliminating them for women (Mansbridge 1986). Union and social feminist opposition to the ERA finally began to wane, with the long-standing concern over worker protection laws now addressed (Mayeri 2004).

NOW quickly prioritized the ERA. The 1960s had seen few litigation successes with the judicial approach, and legal activists believed they needed the political leverage, if not the substantive right, of an equality amendment campaign (Mayeri 2004). NOW adopted the ERA as a top priority at its conference in 1967. It rejected Pauli Murray's alternative proposal for a human rights amendment that would have more broadly granted a "right to equal treatment without differentiation based on sex," potentially encompassing sexual orientation and explicitly addressing private action and reproductive rights (Mayeri 2004: 787). Long-standing ERA proponents, now much older, adamantly opposed any change in the wording of the ERA that might broaden it to more radical agendas, fearing it would jeopardize existing support. This had the effect of reducing feminist demands to "their lowest common denominator" rather than pursuing a wider social justice agenda (Mayeri 2004: 785). Pursuing a constitutional amendment, however, did not mean abandoning the Fourteenth Amendment litigation. By 1970 "most legal feminists had reached a consensus that the constitutional change they sought could and should be pursued simultaneously through the dual strategy" of amendment and litigation (Mayeri 2004: 800).

In early 1970 the Pittsburgh chapter of NOW used direct action to support its demand for the ERA, disrupting a hearing of the US Senate Subcommittee on Constitutional Amendment on another proposed amendment, with protesters demanding hearings on the long-proposed ERA (Mansbridge 1986; Mathews and De Hart 1990). A Citizens' Advisory Council on the Status of Women petitioned President Richard Nixon to endorse the amendment, and for the first time the US Department of Labor supported the ERA. In May, the Senate Amendment Subcommittee held hearings and referred the equality amendment positively to the Senate Judiciary Committee. There Senator Samuel Ervin Jr. (D-NC), a states' rights opponent of the civil rights' laws, and later of Watergate hearings fame, "became the amendment's chief antagonist" (Mathews and De Hart 1990: 36). He opposed the ERA because of its threat to social norms, concerned about losing the traditional physiological and functional differences of gender to what he characterized as a passing fad. He attacked "militant women who back this amendment," saying "they want to take rights away from their sisters" and pass laws "to make men and women exactly alike" (Mathews and De Hart 1990: 37–39). Ervin moved the debate beyond the abstract principles of equality to concerns with specific effects of gender equality, including the draft, divorce, family, privacy, and homosexuality. Harvard Law professor Paul Freund also testified about the "parade of horribles the ERA might produce, including the legalization of same-sex marriage, the abolition of husbands' duty of familial support, unisex bathrooms, and women in military combat" (Mayeri 2004: 808). The opposition succeeded, and the bill failed in the Senate (Mansbridge 1986).

Meanwhile, the ERA passed in the House. Martha Griffiths used a rare procedural move of the discharge petition to "pry the ERA out of the House Judiciary Committee," where it had languished for years while the liberal chair, Emanuel Celler (D-NY), "kept it in his bottom drawer" because of the persistent opposition by labor (Mansbridge 1986: 13). After only an hour's debate, the House passed the ERA by a vote of 350-15 on August 10, 1970. When the Senate failed to pass the bill, it was reintroduced the next year, when the House passed the ERA for a second time on October 12, 1971, by a vote of 354-23. This time the Senate passed the ERA on March 22, 1972, by a vote of 84-8 with a seven-year timeline for the required three-fourths of the states to ratify the amendment (Mansbridge 1986). States initially rushed to ratify the ERA. Hawaii was the first state to ratify the amendment, twenty-five minutes after the Senate vote. The next day, three states ratified, and two more the following day. By early 1973, less than one year after Congress's passage, twenty-four states had ratified, most unanimously or with quick hearings and debate.

This trajectory halted in 1973 with the Supreme Court's decision in *Roe v. Wade* finding a woman's constitutional right to choose abortion. *Roe* stopped the advancing ratifications, shifted the public discourse, and overturned previous support by Republicans (Ziegler 2015). "The battle against the ERA was one of the first in which the New Right used 'women's issues' to forge a coalition of the traditional Radical Right," of those concerned with "national defense and the Communist menace" (Mansbridge 1986: 5), and religious evangelicals to activate a previously apolitical segment of the working and middle classes that "was deeply disturbed by cultural changes" (Mansbridge 1986: 16). Through these groups, the ERA became linked with abortion as both were sponsored by radical "women's libbers" who were a threat to traditional women and family values. The debate became framed as women versus women.

The face of women's opposition to the ERA was conservative activist Phyllis Schlafly and her STOP ERA (Stop Taking Our Privileges) organization (Berry 1988; Neuwirth 2015). Schlafly, a mother to six children, offered herself to the anti-ERA movement as a voice for stay-at-home mothers in need of special privileges and protections under the law. The irony that she, much like all the most prominent reformers historically lining up on either side of the ERA amendment (such as Alice Paul, Florence Kelley, and Pauli Murray), held a law degree and enjoyed a flourishing decades-long career in the public eye, was utterly elided in her rhetoric. Doggedly focused on women's roles as mothers and homemakers, Schlafly trumpeted the cause of women's difference from men—championing the special rights of women as citizens who, ideally, did not work outside the home. She asserted that equality was a step back for women: "Why should we lower ourselves to 'Equal Rights' when we already have the status of 'special privilege'?" (Wohl 1974: 56). She and other ERA opponents reframed the issue as forcing women into dangerous combat, coeducational dormitories, and unisex bathrooms. Feminist advocates responded by clarifying that privacy rights protected concerns about personal living spaces in residences and bathrooms, but their counsel was unheard in the din of threat to traditional family and gender roles. Opponents equated the ERA with homosexuality and gay marriage, as the amendment's words "on account of sex," "were joined with 'sexual preference' or homosexuality to evoke loathing, fear, and anger at the grotesque perversion of masculine responsibility represented by the women's movement" (DeHart-Mathews and Mathews 1986: 49). Schlafly hurled insults at the ERA supporters, urging her readers to view photographs of an ERA rally and "see for yourself the unkempt, the lesbians, the radicals, the socialists," and other activists she labeled militant, arrogant, aggressive, hysterical, and bitter (Carroll 1986: 65). When ERA supporters "gathered at the federally financed 1977 International Women's Year Conference in Houston and endorsed homosexual rights and other controversial resolutions on national television, they helped to make the case for ERA opponents" (Berry 1988: 86).

The shift in debate slowed and then stopped ratification of the ERA. In 1974, three states ratified the amendment, one state ratified in 1975 and one in 1977, and then ended the campaign with only thirty-five of the thirty-eight required (Mansbridge 1986). At the same time, states began to rescind their prior ratifications, with five states voting to withdraw their prior approval (Neuwirth 2015). The legality of the rescissions was unclear, but these efforts had political reverberations in the unratified states (Mansbridge 1986).[6] When the deadline arrived without the required three-fourths approval, Congress voted in 1978 to extend the ratification deadline three years to June 30, 1982. Not a single additional state voted to ratify during this extension (Berry 1988). In 1980, the same year President Jimmy Carter proposed registering women for the draft, the Republican Party dropped ERA from its platform and newly elected president Ronald Reagan came out in opposition to the ERA. Businesses, manufacturers, and insurance companies all increasingly opposed the amendment (Burroughs 2015). ERA supporters escalated with more militant demonstrations of hunger strikes and marches. They chained themselves to the gates of the White House fence and Republican National Committee headquarters and trespassed on the White House and governors' lawns. But such protests had little effect, proving counterproductive as they alienated Republican sponsors and reinforced portrayals of the radicalness of the proposed amendment (Carroll 1986). Despite an extension, the ERA was defeated on June 30, 1982, three states short of the required super-majority of states. Congress immediately reintroduced the amendment, holding hearings in late 1983. The floor vote of 278-147 in the House came six votes short of the two-thirds needed for passage. Despite how close this generation of campaigners had come to achieving their goal, for most, the ERA was now dead (Farrell 1983; Mayeri 2009).

The broader goals of the ERA, however, were not dead or abandoned. All through the previous decade, legal feminists led by the ACLU and Ruth Bader Ginsburg had been pursuing the second front of litigation and doing so with some success. In 1971, the Supreme Court struck down a law for the first time as arbitrary sex discrimination under the Fourteenth Amendment. In *Reed v. Reed* (1971), the high court overturned a state law that presumptively made a father, and not a mother, the administrator for a deceased child's estate. Two years later in *Frontiero v. Richardson* (1973), a plurality of the Court applied heightened scrutiny to strike down a law automatically granting military benefits to wives, but requiring military husbands to show dependency. The pros and cons of the dual constitutional strategy played out in *Frontiero*. The Court's plurality endorsed strict scrutiny for sex-based classifications because of congressional passage of the ERA, thus harmonizing the two. But the concurrence held that the pendency of legislation weighed against judicial decision, and required waiting for the final outcome of the constitutional process. In 1976 a majority of the Court definitively applied equal protection to sex discrimination in *Craig v. Boren* (1976), adopting, however, only an intermediate judicial scrutiny, one more permissive than that for race.[7] As Mayeri (2004: 826) notes, "This Goldilocks solution" in *Craig* captured the "Court's ambivalence about both the procedural and the substantive aspects of a revolution in gender roles." The ambivalence is apparent in that while striking down the law in *Craig* denying young men equal access to 3.2% beer, the Court upheld other discriminatory laws, like veterans' preferences for men, statutory rape for minor women, and military pensions for men (*Schlesinger v. Ballard* 1975; *Kahn v. Shevin* 1974; *Geduldig v. Aiello* 1974). Equal protection proved an imperfect solution, and easily manipulable in the hands of the Court. For many activists, this indicated that perhaps an equal rights amendment was needed after all.

In the 1980s, at the time of ERA's defeat, polling found that a majority of the electorate remained in support of the amendment (*Businessweek* 1983; *Gallup Report* 1981; Mansbridge 1986). According to Pleck (1986: 107–108), "In the midst of a national conservative tide, popular support for the ERA was very strong." Most national leaders, political conservatives, and "major national organizations from the American Bar Association to the Girl Scouts had gone on record in favor of it" (Pleck 1986: 108). Then why did the ERA fail? Scholars and activists have searched for possible explanations. Some suggest that a rushed political process failed to build the necessary state consensus on women's rights to match the federal consensus, along with inadequate state organizational structure to secure ratification, outdated campaign tactics and failure to use mass media, and lack of legislative prioritization (Berry 1988; Carroll 1986; Mansbridge 1986; Mayo and Frye 1986; Pleck 1986; Steinem 1984). Other scholars point to deep substantive disagreements about women in military combat and revolutionary changes in traditional motherhood, which threaten women personally as they perceive a danger to themselves and their daughters (DeHart-Mathews and Mathews 1986). Berry (1988: 85) notes that "equality may have seemed simple to proratificationists, but to others it meant sexual permissiveness, the pill, abortion, living in communes, draft dodger, unisex men who refused to be men, and women who refused to be women. . . . And a fear that men would feel freer to abandon family responsibilities and nothing would be obtained in exchange." Legal scholar Catharine MacKinnon (1987: 770) thought ERA failed because it did not go far enough, and more radically "mobilize women's pain and suppressed discontent" derived from systemic, social realities of male supremacy. And still others questioned the need for an equal rights amendment, given intervening Supreme Court decisions extending equal protection to women and federal legislation like Title VII and Title IX of the Education Amendments (Mansbridge 1986; Mayeri 2004).

Congress continued to reintroduce the Equal Rights Amendment every year after its defeat, but it went nowhere. Glimmers of action appeared in 2007 when a bipartisan group of lawmakers rechristened the amendment the "Women's Equality Amendment" (Mayeri 2009: 1224) and in 2013 when Representative Carolyn Maloney (D-NY) proposed new language for an equality amendment to make the equality abstraction more concrete: "Women shall have equal rights in the United States and every place subject to its jurisdiction." But the time and urgency for an equal rights amendment seemed to have passed. If ERA was not politically dead, it was at least comatose (MacKinnon 1987).

Conclusion: Equal Rights One Hundred Years after Suffrage

In 2014 a new ERA Coalition of major women's rights organizations formed, fueled by a new generation of young people outraged at continuing inequality and energized to action (Neuwirth 2015). The year brought renewed grassroots interest in the ERA, sparking popular reconsideration of an equality amendment endorsed by celebrities like Meryl Streep and feminist icon Gloria Steinem (Babbington 2015). Justice Ruth Bader Ginsburg publicly called for the ERA to ensure future generations that women's equality is "a basic principle of our society," just as she had thirty-five years earlier (Schwab 2014).[8] Even legal feminist scholar Catharine MacKinnon (2014: 569), previously opposed to the ERA as a weak, formalistic attempt at equality, now believed that an ERA is "urgently needed, now as much as or more than ever." Surveys have shown over the last decade that most voters, as high as 96%, support equality for women, and 91% believe equality should be guaranteed by the Constitution (Neuwirth 2015), indicating perhaps a gendered cultural opportunity for change (McCammon et al. 2001). However, these surveys also show that 72% of people believe, *incorrectly*, that such rights are already included in the Constitution.

The ERA Coalition believes the time is ripe again for an equal rights amendment, given the next generation's interest and recent political activity (Neuwirth 2015). In 2014 Oregon passed a state ERA referendum with 64% of the vote. Illinois and Virginia also passed state ERA laws, two states that had not previously ratified the federal ERA. Federal ERA proponents advocate a "three-states-more" strategy, which assumes the continued validity of the prior ratifications and seeks ratification of the required three additional states. One state, Nevada, ratified the ERA in March 2017. This extended ratification strategy is supported by the delayed ratification of the Twenty-Seventh Amendment (salary change for Congress must take effect the following term), as it was sent to the states for ratification in 1789, but not ratified until 1992, when the last states joined (Burroughs 2015).

A key question is whether women legally need the ERA, or whether its goals of general equality and specific rights have effectively been accomplished through other means. The virtually unanimous consensus of legal scholars is that the ERA's goals have been effectively achieved through the Supreme Court's equal protection jurisprudence (Mayeri 2009; Siegel 2006). Courts now review gendered state action under intermediate scrutiny, requiring that any laws treating women differently be justified by important governmental interests and that the laws be closely tailored to those interests (*United States v. Virginia* 1996; *Mississippi University for Women v. Hogan* 1982). Other scholars, however, have emphasized the limitations of equal protection analysis for sex equality (Brown et al. 1971; MacKinnon 2014; Mansbridge 1986). For gender discrimination cases under equal protection, the Court utilizes a lower standard of intermediate scrutiny, rather than the strict scrutiny used in race and religious discrimination. This lower standard tolerates many of the continuing instances of less overt sex discrimination and laws that have discriminatory effect rather than textual prohibitions on gender (Siegel 2002). The equal protection approach is also limited because it requires proof of intent—defendants thinking bad thoughts about women—which, MacKinnon (2014: 572) notes, "doesn't address how discrimination mostly operates in the real world," where "the vast majority of sex inequality is produced by structural and systemic and unconscious practices" inherited from centuries of gender hierarchy. Equal protection law's formal classification structure, she explains, which rigidly treats only exactly similar things the same, is incapable of assessing the ways in which people "can be different from one another yet still be equals, entitled to be treated equally" or where affirmative diversity is needed to treat alike those whom are different (MacKinnon 2014: 571).

Some scholars (Schwab 2014; Hoff-Wilson 1986) also conclude that equality for women has essentially been achieved for women without the ERA because the specific substantive goals of the amendment were accomplished through a variety of federal legislation on specific issues as well as the parallel state constitutional amendments. Twenty-three states adopted mini-ERAs, and such amendments have helped strengthen women's ability to challenge discriminatory laws in those states. Courts often interpret the state ERAs to require strict scrutiny, and two states mandate an even higher absolute standard that presumes any discriminatory law to be unconstitutional (Burroughs 2015; Wharton 2005). In addition, federal legislation has mandated equal employment and education in the Equal Pay Act of 1963, Title VII of the Civil Rights Act of 1964, Title IX of the Education Amendments of 1972, the Pregnancy Discrimination Act of 1978, and the Violence Against Women Act of 1994. Such piecemeal legislation, however, is subject to the political ebb and flow and can be rolled back, as the Violence Against Women Act was when the Supreme Court held in *United States v. Morrison* (2000) that Congress had no power to address civil remedies for domestic violence (MacKinnon 2014).

The renewed campaign for an equal rights amendment emphasizes the continued systemic harms to women of economic inequality, sexual violence, and pregnancy discrimination and the limits of existing laws to address these concerns (MacKinnon 2014; Neuwirth 2015). Proponents of an equal rights amendment emphasize the need for a permanent constitutional guarantee to control an overarching legal and social principle of women's equality. The United States, unlike the majority of other countries, has refused to incorporate such an express guarantee in its written constitution or adopt the international women's bill of rights by ratifying the United Nations' treaty (MacKinnon 2014; Neuwirth 2015).[9] The absence of an express guarantee permits traditional literalists like Justice Antonin Scalia to opine, "Certainly the Constitution does not require discrimination on the basis of sex. The only issue is whether it prohibits it. It doesn't" (*California Lawyer* 2011). The ERA offers a corrective to this thinking and the equivocal state of women's rights under the law. It offers a textual guarantee of sex equality, an inspiration for public policy, and a powerful symbolic support of women's equality in all social and legal venues (Ginsburg 2014; MacKinnon 2014).

The equality amendment fulfills the hope first envisioned by proponents of a suffrage amendment to fully integrate women into every aspect of the citizenry with full recognition of their humanity (Siegel 2002). Now, almost one hundred years later, perhaps the time is right. Or perhaps the time is right to embrace the larger social justice legacy of the women's equality movement and expand the amendment to all human rights to include aspects of sexual orientation discrimination and reproductive rights. These broaden the concept of sex discrimination to encompass the ways in which gender is practiced and experienced in our society. Perhaps dovetailing with recent advances and political consensus in civil rights of same-sex marriage will give women's equality the final push it needs to be enacted.

Notes

1. Other scholars (e.g., Ghaziani 2008) have also written of the influence of conflict within social movements on the movement itself. Additional work (Meyer and Staggenborg 1996) notes the important role of opposition movements.

2. *Minor* (1875) held that the Privileges and Immunities Clause of the newly enacted Fourteenth Amendment includes women as "persons" and national "citizens," but that voting is a privilege of state, not national, citizenship.

3. *See also Riley v. Massachusetts*, 232 U.S. 671 (1914) (law similar to *Muller*); *Miller v. Wilson*, 236 U.S. 373 (1915; upholding eight-hour law for female hotel maids); *Bosley v. McLaughlin*, 236 U.S. 385 (1915; upholding maximum-hour law for female hospital workers).

4. According to Neale, while she voted against the rider, Senator Smith voted yes on final passage of the resolution as amended, which included the rider. Senate debate, *Congressional Record*, vol. 96, pt. 1 (January 25, 1950); *Congressional Quarterly Almanac*, 1950, p.420.

5. Steiner (1985) cites as sources the Republican Platform 1956, in Donald Bruce Johnson, comp. *National Party Platforms* (1978: 554), "Address in Madison Square Garden, New York

City, October 25, 1956," and "Annual Budget Message to the Congress for Fiscal Year 1958," *Public Papers of the President: Dwight D. Eisenhower, 1956* (GPO 1958: 1020) and *1957* (GPO 1958: 57).

6. One federal court upheld the rescissions, but expiration of the ERA ratification dead-line mooted the question before the Supreme Court could review the case. *Idaho v. Freeman*, 529 F. Supp. 1107 (1981), *stayed*, January 25, 1982. The evidence against the legality of rescis-sion is that states attempting to rescind their ratification of the Fourteenth Amendment were still included as enacting states (Berry 1988).

7. The *strict scrutiny test* requires that state laws based on race be justified with compelling interests that are narrowly tailored to necessary regulation, thus invalidating most laws based on race. *Loving v. Virginia*, 388 U.S. 1 (1967); *McLaughlin v. Florida*, 379 U.S. 184 (1964).

8. For Ginsburg's early pro-ERA writings, see Ruth Bader Ginsburg, "The Fear of the ERA," *Washington Post*, April 8, 1975: A21; Ruth B. Ginsburg and Kathleen W. Peratis, "Equal Rights for Women," *New York Times*, December 31, 1975: 21; Ruth Bader Ginsburg, "Let's Have E.R.A. as a Signal," *ABA Journal*, January 1977: 70; Ruth Bader Ginsburg, "Sexual Equality under the Fourteenth and Equal Rights Amendment," *Washington University Law Review* (1979): 161–178.

9. The United States is one of only seven countries that has not ratified the UN Convention on the Elimination of All Forms of Discrimination Against Women (CEDAW), including Iran, Somalia, Sudan, South Sudan, Palau, and Tonga. The treaty was signed by President Carter in 1980, but failed to get the two-thirds congressional vote necessary for ratification (Neuwirth 2015).

References

Adkins v. Children's Hospital of DC, 261 U.S. 525 (1923).

Babbington, Charles. 2015. "Meryl Streep Stumps for ERA." *U.S. News & World Report*, June 23. http://www.usnews.com/news/entertainment/articles/2015/06/23/capitol-hill-buzz-meryl-streep-asks-congress-to-revive-era.

Becker, Susan D. 1981. *The Origins of the Equal Rights Amendment: American Feminism between the Wars*. Westport, CT: Greenwood Press.

Berry, Mary Frances. 1988. *Why ERA Failed: Politics, Women's Rights, and the Amending Process of the Constitution*. Bloomington: Indiana University Press.

Bosley v. McLaughlin, 236 U.S. 385 (1915).

Brown, Barbara A., Thomas I. Emerson, Gail Falk, and Ann E. Freedman. 1971. "The Equal Rights Amendment: A Constitutional Basis for Equal Rights for Women." *Yale Law Journal* 80: 871–985.

Bunting v. Oregon, 243 U.S. 426 (1917).

Burroughs, Gaylynn. 2015. "ERA Yes." *Ms.*, Winter 2015: 34–37

Businessweek. 1983. "For Most Americans, Passage of the ERA is Just a Matter of Time." August 1: 92.

California Lawyer. 2011. "Legally Speaking: Antonin Scalia." January. http://www.callawyer.com/2011/01/antonin-scalia/.

Carroll, Berenice. 1986. "Direct Action and Constitutional Rights: The Case of the ERA." Pp. 63–75 in *Rights of Passage: The Past and Future of the ERA*, edited by J. Hoff-Wilson. Bloomington: Indiana University Press.

Congressional Digest. 1943. April: 22.

Congressional Quarterly Almanac. 1950. 420

Cott, Nancy F. 1989. *The Grounding of Modern Feminism.* New Haven, CT: Yale University Press.

———. 1990. "Historical Perspectives: The Equal Rights Amendment Conflict in the 1920s." Pp. 45–59 in *Conflicts in Feminism,* edited by M. Hirsch and E. F. Keller. New York: Routledge Press.

Craig v. Boren, 429 U.S. 190 (1976).

DeHart-Mathews, Jane, and Donald Mathews. 1986. "The Cultural Politics of the ERA's Defeat." Pp. 44–53 in *Rights of Passage: The Past and Future of the ERA,* edited by J. Hoff-Wilson. Bloomington: Indiana University Press.

Dismore, David. 2014. "July 9, 1978: Feminists Make History With Biggest-Ever March for the Equal Rights Amendment." Feminist Majority Foundation. https://feminist.org/blog/index.php/2014/07/09/july-9-1978-feminists-make-history-with-biggest-ever-march-for-the-equal-rights-amendment/.

DuBois, Ellen Carol. 1997. *Harriot Stanton Blatch and the Winning of Woman Suffrage.* New Haven, CT: Yale University Press.

Fair Labor Standards Act. 1938. 29 U.S. Code § 201.

Farrell, William E. 1983. "U.S. Amendment on Equal Rights Beaten in House." *New York Times,* November 16: A1.

Freeman, Jo. 1996. "What's in a Name? Does It Matter how the Equal Rights Amendment Is Worded?" (http://www.jofreeman.com/lawandpolicy/eraname.htm)

Frontiero v. Richardson, 411 U.S. 677 (1973).

Fry, Amelia R. 1986. "Alice Paul and the ERA." Pp. 8–24 in *Rights of Passage: The Past and Future of the ERA,* edited by J. Hoff-Wilson. Bloomington: Indiana University Press.

Gallup Report. 1981. "Public Support for ERA Reaches New High," August 9.

Geduldig v. Aiello, 417 U.S. 484 (1974).

Ghaziani, Amin. 2008. *The Dividends of Dissent: How Conflict and Culture Work in Lesbian and Gay Marches on Washington.* Chicago: University of Chicago Press.

Ginsburg, Ruth Bader. 1975. "The Fear of the ERA." *Washington Post,* April 8: A21.

———. 1977. "Let's Have E.R.A. as a Signal." *American Bar Association Journal,* January: 70–73.

———. 1979. "Sexual Equality under the Fourteenth and Equal Rights Amendment." *Washington University Law Review* 1979: 161–178.

Ginsburg, Ruth Bader, and Kathleen W. Peratis. 1975. "Equal Rights for Women." *New York Times,* December 31: 21.

Good Housekeeping. 1925. "Should There be Labor Laws for Women? No Says Rheta Childe, Yes Says Mary Anderson." September: 52–53.

Harrison, Cynthia. 1988. *On Account of Sex: The Politics of Women's Issues, 1945–1968.* Berkeley: University of California Press.

Hart, Vivien. 1994. *Bound by Our Constitution: Women, Workers, and the Minimum Wage.* Princeton, NJ: Princeton University Press.

Hoff-Wilson, Joan, ed. 1986. *Rights of Passage: The Past and Future of the ERA.* Bloomington: Indiana University Press.

Hoyt v. Florida, 368 U.S. 57, 62 (1961).

Idaho v. Freeman, 529 F. Supp. 1107 (1981), *stayed,* January 25, 1982

Johnson, Donald Bruce, comp. 1978. *National Party Platforms.* Champaign: University of Illinois Press.

Kahn v. Shevin, 416 U.S. 351 (1974).

Kelley, Florence. 1921. "The New Woman's Party," XLV *Survey* 827, March 5.

Lehrer, Susan. 1987. *Origins of Protective Labor Legislation for Women, 1905–1925.* Albany: State University of New York Press.

Lemons, J. Stanley. 1973. *The Woman Citizen: Social Feminism in the 1920s.* Champaign: University of Illinois Press.

Leopold, Alice K. 1955. "Federal Equal Pay Legislation," *Labor Law Journal* 6: 21–22.

Lesser v. Garnett, 258 US 130 (1922).

Library of Congress. n.d. "Historical Overview of the National Woman's Party." https://www.loc.gov/collections/static/women-of-protest/images/history.pdf.

Lipschultz, Sybil. 1996. "Hours and Wages: The Gendering of Labor Standards in America." *Journal of Women's History* 8: 114–136.

Lochner v. New York, 198 U.S. 45 (1905).

Loving v. Virginia, 388 U.S. 1 (1967).

MacKinnon, Catharine A. 1987. "Unthinking ERA Thinking." *University of Chicago Law Review* 54: 759–771.

———. 2014. "Toward a Renewed Equal Rights Amendment: Now More Than Ever." *Harvard Journal of Law and Gender* 37: 569–579.

Mansbridge, Jane J. 1986. *Why We Lost the ERA.* Chicago: University of Chicago Press.

Mathews, Donald G., and Jane Sherron De Hart. 1990. *Sex, Gender, and the Politics of ERA: A State and the Nation.* New York: Oxford University Press.

Mayeri, Serena. 2004. "Constitutional Choices: Legal Feminism and the Historical Dynamics of Change." *California Law Review* 92: 755–839.

———. 2009. "A New E.R.A. or a New Era? Amendment Advocacy and the Reconstitution of Feminism." *Northwestern University Law Review* 103: 1223–1301.

Mayo, Edith, and Jerry K. Frye. 1986. "The ERA: Postmortem of a Failure in Political Communication." Pp. 76–89 in *Rights of Passage: The Past and Future of the ERA,* edited by J. Hoff-Wilson. Bloomington: Indiana University Press.

McAdam, Doug. 1982. *Political Process and the Development of Black Insurgency, 1930–1970.* Chicago: University of Chicago Press.

McBridge, Genevieve G. 1993. *On Wisconsin Women: Working for Their Rights from Settlement to Suffrage.* Milwaukee: University of Wisconsin Press.

McCammon, Holly J., Karen E. Campbell, Ellen M. Granberg, and Christine Mowery. 2001. "How Movements Win: Gendered Opportunity Structures and the State Women's Suffrage Movements, 1866–1919." *American Sociological Review* 66: 49–70.

McLaughlin v. Florida, 379 U.S. 184 (1964).

Meyer, David S., and Suzanne Staggenborg. 1996. "Movements, Countermovements, and the Structure of Political Opportunity." *American Journal of Sociology* 101: 1628–1660.

Miller v. Wilson, 236 U.S. 373 (1915).

Minor v. Happersett, 88 U.S. 162 (1875).

Mississippi University for Women v. Hogan, 458 U.S. 718 (1982).

Morehead v. New York ex rel. Tipaldo, 298 U.S. 587 (1936).

Muller v. Oregon, 208 U.S. 412 (1908).

Murray, Pauli, and Mary O. Eastwood. 1965. "Jane Crow and the Law: Sex Discrimination and Title VII." *George Washington Law Review* 34: 232–256.

National Archives. 1945. "The Un-Equal Rights Amendment." http://recordsofrights.org/records/381/the-un-equal-rights-amendment.

National Organization for Women. n.d. "History of Marches and Mass Actions." http://now.org/about/history/history-of-marches-and-mass-actions/.

Neale, Thomas H. 2013. "The Proposed Equal Rights Amendment: Contemporary Ratification Issues." May 9. *Congressional Research Service.* https://www.fas.org/sgp/crs/misc/R42979.pdf.

Neuwirth, Jessica. 2015. *Equal Means Equal: Why the Time for an Equal Rights Amendment Is Now.* New York: New Press.

O'Connor, Karen. 2010. *Gender and Women's Leadership.* Thousand Oaks, CA: Sage Publications.

O'Farrell, Brigid. 2015. "American Women: Looking Back, Moving Ahead: The 50th Anniversary of the President's Commission on the Status of Women Report." *Women's Bureau, U.S. Department of Labor.* http://www.dol.gov/wb/PCSW-03-30-2015.pdf.

Pleck, Elizabeth. 1986. "Failed Strategies; Renewed Hope." Pp. 106–120 in *Rights of Passage: The Past and Future of the ERA,* edited by J. Hoff-Wilson. Bloomington: Indiana University Press.

Radice v. New York, 264 U.S. 292 (1923).

Reed v. Reed, 404 U.S. 71 (1971).

Riley v. Massachusetts, 232 U.S. 671 (1914).

Roe v. Wade, 410 U.S. 113 (1973).

Schlesinger v. Ballard, 419 U.S. 498 (1975).

Schwab, Nikki. 2014. "Ginsburg: Make ERA Part of the Constitution." *U.S. News & World Report,* April 18. http://www.usnews.com/news/blogs/washington-whispers/2014/04/18/justice-ginsburg-make-equal-rights-amendment-part-of-the-constitution.

Siegel, Reva B. 2002. "She the People: The Nineteenth Amendment, Sex Equality, Federalism, and the Family." *Harvard Law Review* 115: 947–1046.

———. 2006. "Constitutional Culture, Social Movement Conflict, and Constitutional Change: The Case of the De Facto ERA." *California Law Review* 94: 1323–1419.

Steinem, Gloria. 1984. "How Women Live, Vote, Think." *Ms.,* July: 54.

Steiner, Gilbert Yale. 1985. *Constitutional Inequality: The Political Fortunes of the Equal Rights Amendment.* Washington, DC: Brookings Institute.

Stephensons, Alice K. 1944. "Federation Poll Backs 'Equal Rights.'" *New York Times,* April 27: 20.

Sunday Herald (Bridgeport, CT). 1953. November 22: 7.

United States v. Darby, 312 U.S. 100 (1941).

United States v. Morrison, 528 U.S. 598 (2000).

United States v. Virginia, 518 U.S. 515 (1996).

US Department of Labor, Women's Bureau. 1923. *Proceedings of the Women's Industrial Conference* 33. Washington, DC: Government Printing Office.

Vassar Miscellany News. 1921. 5(33), March 2: 4.

Wells, Mildred White. 1953. *Unity in Diversity: The History of the General Federation of Women's Clubs.* Washington, DC: General Federation of Women's Clubs.

West Coast Hotel Co. v. Parrish, 300 U.S. 379 (1937).

Wharton, Linda A. 2005. "State Equal Rights Amendments Revisited: Evaluating Their Effectiveness in Advancing Protection Against Sex Discrimination." *Rutgers Law Journal* 36: 1201–1293.

Wohl, Lisa C. 1974. "Phyllis Schlafly: The Sweetheart of the Silent Majority." *Ms.*, March: 56–57.

Woloch, Nancy. 2015. *A Class by Herself: Protective Laws for Women Workers, 1890s–1990s.* Princeton, NJ: Princeton University Press.

Ziegler, Mary. 2015. *After Roe.* Cambridge, MA: Harvard University Press.

Zimmerman, Joan G. 1991. "The Jurisprudence of Equality: The Women's Minimum Wage, the First Equal Rights Amendment, and *Adkins v. Children's Hospital*, 1905–1923." *Journal of American History* 78: 188–225.

...

Diversity in Women's Social Movement Activism

ILLUSTRATIONS FROM ONE HUNDRED YEARS OF ENGAGEMENT

11

Black Women Cause Lawyers

LEGAL ACTIVISM IN PURSUIT OF RACIAL AND GENDER EQUALITY

Brittany N. Hearne and Holly J. McCammon

Many accounts have been written of legal activism aimed at gaining racial equality during the civil rights movement (Branch 1989; Greenberg 2004; Tushnet 1987) and gender equality during the women's rights movement of the late 1960s and 1970s (O'Connor 1980; Schneider and Wildman 2011; Strebeigh 2009). In these portrayals, scholars often detail the legal victories that mark progress toward limiting racial segregation in schools and challenging employment discrimination under the Civil Rights Act's Title VII. Others highlight the legal strategies of the women's rights movement and its successes in legal cases like the pivotal *Reed v. Reed* case in which the Supreme Court ruled that gender distinctions in law violated equal protection for women. Across these literatures, the names of prominent litigators (and later Supreme Court justices) Thurgood Marshall and Ruth Bader Ginsburg often emerge. Rarely, however, in accounts of the influential efforts of activist lawyers working to end racial and gender discrimination do scholars consider the role of black women lawyers (for exceptions, see Mayeri 2011, 2014; Randolph 2015; Smith 1998).

Yet black women have contributed in important ways to legal activism aimed at gaining racial and gender equality. Like the woman suffragists of a century ago, black women cause lawyers have also fought for greater rights under the law. Throughout the past century, the efforts of black women lawyers have centered largely on combatting the discrimination confronted by black women, discrimination resulting from combined systems of racial and gender oppression. In this chapter, we trace the struggle of black women activist lawyers as they combat racial and gender inequality in the United States over the last one hundred years. Their legal work has been influenced heavily by both the civil rights and second-wave feminist movements. Today, debates about women's rights at work and in their private lives have also influenced the activism of black women lawyers. For example, the highly contested confirmation of Clarence Thomas after Anita Hill accused him of sexual harassment in the workplace or the research that highlights an elevated risk of intimate partner violence for black women (West 2004) has shown the importance of ongoing activism for cause lawyers. Throughout the chapter, we show that these legal activists were and continue to be dedicated to gaining greater rights for both blacks and women, with efforts often focused specifically on black women. We consider them to be social movement cause lawyers and below discuss what it means to be a cause lawyer.

In tracing the temporal line of their efforts as well as the progression of their cause lawyering, we define four generations of lawyers, drawing on leading representatives from each legal generation. Our work follows in the tradition of Whittier's (1995) study of "feminist generations," as we discern generational cohorts of black women cause lawyers, the movement contexts shaping their legal efforts, and important accomplishments of each generation. We begin with the earliest cohort in the late nineteenth century, as black women struggled simply to achieve a place in the legal profession, confronting the societally-imposed subordinate status of black women. In the second generation of cause lawyers, black women worked for racial equality along with black men in the civil rights movement, centering their energies on the fight for racial justice, often within organizations like the National Association for the Advancement of Colored People Legal Defense and Educational Fund (NAACP LDF). A third generation of black women cause lawyers followed closely on the heels of the second generation and began to draw parallels between racial inequality and gender bias. They were influenced by and, in turn, importantly influenced an increasingly mobilized feminist movement in the 1970s. In recent decades, a fourth generation of black women lawyers has emerged, and their work allows us to see how race and gender combine to influence the lives of women of color. Separate discussions of race and gender equality have given way in this new paradigm to conversations about how racial and gender discrimination intersect to constrain the lives of black women.

The legal work of black women lawyers over the last century has significantly aided in establishing greater rights under the law for both blacks and women, and their efforts have also led to a paradigm shift allowing us to move away from a framework where "blacks" and "women" are understood as mutually exclusive categories and instead to see how interlocked systems of racial and gender oppression have historically limited and continue to circumscribe opportunities for black women.[1]

Cause Lawyering

Cause lawyering—or *political lawyering*, as Minow (1996: 289) calls it—describes the deliberate efforts and strategies used by lawyers to accomplish the goals of a larger social movement. In fact, cause lawyers often identify with and consider themselves a part of the social movement (Marshall and Hale 2014). They use their legal skills and expertise to mobilize the law, often through litigation but in other ways as well, such as by educating marginalized groups about their legal rights (Sarat and Scheingold 2006). Cause lawyers engage in legal work that protects and furthers the rights not only of their clients but of the larger group of beneficiaries of the social movement's agenda. Legal cases are chosen not only because of their likelihood of a successful outcome in the court system but also because of the potentially broad political and social implications that success in the specific case may have in society as a whole. Cause lawyers may be employed as part of a legal activist group, such as the NAACP LDF, or they may have a private practice that centers its work on using the law to bring about social, political, and/or economic change. Cause lawyers can also participate more broadly in social movement activism, as organizers and by engaging in protest events (Marshall 2006). Some cause lawyers are members of the legal academy and while they may litigate, they engage in scholarly writing, developing ideas often at the forefront of social movement legal activism (McCammon et al. 2017).

Few accounts of cause lawyering, however, have considered the roles of black women (see, e.g., Chen and Cummings 2013; Hilbink 2006). Yet black women lawyers have made important contributions in furthering the legal fight to combat racial and gender exclusion, particularly when racism and sexism combine to produce intersecting systems of bias. Given this limited attention, we seek to trace the history of black women's legal activism, to show how it developed over the last century, and to consider its impact. Our investigation into black women's cause lawyering reveals a progression in its forms over time across four generations of lawyers as well as an understanding of the ways in which key social movements— the civil rights and second-wave feminist movements—importantly influence black women's legal activism.

The First Generation: Black Women Lawyers at the Turn of the Twentieth Century

The first black woman to become a lawyer in the United States was Charlotte Ray, who graduated from Howard University Law School in 1872, just a few years after the first black man and white woman became lawyers (Smith 1997). After Ray's achievement, in 1883 Mary Ann Shadd Cary became the second black female lawyer, also graduating from Howard (Rhodes 1998).[2] There is some evidence that Howard University may have resisted admitting and graduating women from its law school, although the evidence has been disputed (McDaniel 2007; Rhodes 1998). Cary was sixty years old at the time she graduated and was a seasoned antislavery and woman's suffrage activist. Ray and Cary overcame the combined prejudice confronted by black women in a society steeped in traditions of both racial and gender oppression. With slavery ending only a handful of years earlier and deeply-rooted beliefs among whites about the appropriate roles for black women (as Smith [1997: 388] states, they were assumed to be "mammies, maids, or mistresses"), the professional accomplishments of these late-nineteenth-century lawyers are remarkable feats of individual triumph. While the historical record for both is limited, there is evidence that Ray and Cary were each able to set up law practices in Washington, DC, although neither practice survived very long due to limited clients and, most likely, rigid assumptions about whether black women should be practicing attorneys (Rhodes 1998; Smith 1997). For Cary, her early combined advocacy for race and gender equality is evident in her founding of a suffrage group, the Colored Women's Progressive Franchise Association, in 1880 (Yee 1997).

Early black female lawyers like Ray and Cary would pave the way for later black women who pursued law degrees early in the twentieth century. The exact number of black women lawyers in the United States at this time remains unclear. One 1935 count found only thirty-five black women practicing law (Sampson 1935). By 1941, another tally identified fifty-seven black women lawyers (McDaniel 2007). The 1935 count may have underestimated the number of these early lawyers. For example, one woman not included was Violette Neatley Anderson. Anderson earned her law degree in 1920 from the University of Chicago's law school, as the only woman in her law school class (Cook 1996).

Anderson's legal work shows that she, too, was one of the first black women cause lawyers in the United States. Historical accounts reveal that she litigated a wide range of legal cases, from criminal to contractual matters (McDaniel 2007). Anderson probably represented most clients who came to her law practice, in that it is unlikely she had the financial resources to strategically choose her clients. Yet her record indicates that she frequently worked on behalf of poorer blacks in both the Chicago region as well as nationally. In the 1920s, Anderson served as president of the Friendly Big Sisters League of Chicago, which provided housing for impoverished black women and their children (Cook 1996). Later Anderson concentrated her efforts on mobilizing support for the 1937 federal Bankhead-Jones Farm Tenant Act, which provided poor tenant farmers, including many black farmers, with low-interest loans and the means to purchase farmland. Anderson's legal activism prior to the 1950s on behalf of poor blacks provides a case of women's cause lawyering's involvement in the long civil rights struggle in the United States for racial economic justice.

Another early black woman cause lawyer, also in Chicago, was Edith Sampson. Sampson gained her law degree in 1925, just after Anderson, and then also a master of law degree from Loyola University. Like Anderson before her, Sampson was the only woman in the master's program at Loyola (*Chicago Tribune* 1962; Cook 1996). Both Anderson and Sampson pursued their legal education in an era still rife with barriers for black women who sought professional occupations (Smith 1997). Soon after receiving her law degree, Sampson organized the Portia Club in Chicago to provide impoverished black women and their children with free legal services (Jordan 2012). Later Sampson became a leader in the National Council of Negro Women and through this organization worked to influence Depression-era economic policy, urging that policy take into account the needs of black women, particularly concerning minimum wages, workplace hours laws, and regulations of working conditions. Here one can see an awareness of not only race and gender inequality but how these systems interlock with class oppression. The combined efforts of Anderson and Sampson show early black women lawyers' focus on aiding both black women and men. Like Mary Ann Shadd Cary before them, these early cause lawyers reveal their concern—in Anderson's involvement in the Friendly Big Sisters League and Sampson's leadership in the Portia Club—that black women's needs did not always align with those of black men or even other women.

The Second Generation: Black Women Cause Lawyers and the Civil Rights Movement

While the first generation of black women cause lawyers faced a difficult struggle simply to become practicing attorneys, a second generation of black women cause lawyers gained an opportunity for legal activism through the growing civil rights movement. Frankie Freeman and Constance Baker Motley were two leading black women lawyers active in the movement. Characteristic of each of these women's legal work is a focus on racial discrimination and activism toward gaining rights for black Americans that stems largely from their involvement in the civil rights movement.

The decision by black women lawyers of the civil rights movement to engage in legal activism aimed at securing greater racial equality was stimulated by frustrations with the ubiquitous nature of Jim Crow and white supremacy in their everyday lives, but also by the emerging civil rights movement. Constance Baker Motley, who grew up in New Haven, Connecticut, and would later work with the NAACP LDF, remembered her first overt encounter with segregation when she was denied access as a teenager to a beach reserved for whites only (Motley 1998). At fifteen years old, as a good student and influenced by her proximity to Yale University, Motley decided she would pursue a legal career, despite pressure from family members who encouraged her to pursue a career more in line with what was expected of women at the time (Motley 1998). In her description of attending Fisk University, a historically black university in Nashville, Tennessee, she mentions that she rarely left campus for social events in order to avoid the humiliation of racist practices, such as being denied admission to restaurants reserved for whites (Motley 1998). She then graduated from Columbia University law school in 1946.

In her autobiography, Frankie Freeman (2003), who grew up in Danville, Virginia, the last capital of the Confederacy, and who would conduct legal work for the local NAACP in St. Louis, writes that, while blacks sometimes lived in close proximity to whites, in a racially segregated society there was very little interaction between the two groups. She went on to graduate from a historically black university, Hampton Institute, and because she knew she wanted to be a lawyer, she moved to New York to pursue her goal at St. John's University. But her story reveals the ongoing difficulty in becoming a legal professional. Upon arriving at St. John's, she learned that the school did not accept credits from black colleges. The racial barrier at St. John's led her off her educational path, but she later continued in her efforts to become a lawyer after not being promoted in her jobs in Washington, DC. For instance, in her work at the Department of Treasury, she experienced a racially-insensitive culture and was reminded that blacks were second-class citizens (Freeman 2003). Freeman eventually turned to Howard University's law school, from which she graduated in 1947.

After law school, as these women sought occupations in the legal profession, they had to overcome multiple barriers stemming not only from racism but also sexism. In their cause lawyering, they focused on racial discrimination cases. In St. Louis, once Freeman established herself as a lawyer by taking on a wide range of cases, she decided to become more politically active (Freeman 2003). Freeman's race-based political consciousness led her to join the local NAACP chapter because, at the time, "the NAACP was viewed as the salvation for black people in terms of legislative activities and litigation" (Freeman 2003: 48). As a member of the St. Louis NAACP legal team, she became lead attorney in *Davis v. St. Louis Housing Authority*, a 1955 case that would end the St. Louis Housing Authority's refusal to rent to qualified blacks. Freeman filed the class-action suit and won.

In 1945 Constance Baker Motley joined the NAACP LDF as the organization's first female attorney. Early on at LDF, Motley was involved in a number of cases aimed at attacking racial segregation in schools, including *Brown v. Board of Education* (1954), and she led a lawsuit against the University of Mississippi when the school would not grant a black man, James Meredith, admission. Motley would go on to argue ten racial desegregation cases before the Supreme Court while working for LDF (Motley 1988, 1998). Of these, she won nine, with the tenth later overturned in her favor (Motley 1988). Her first Supreme Court case was *Hamilton v. Alabama* (1961); winning this case affirmed the right to counsel in a capital punishment case for a black defendant. Motley argued a number of cases in 1963, including *Gober v. City of Birmingham* and *Shuttleworth v. City of Birmingham*, which involved protests by civil rights movement activists. The cases concerned sit-ins by college students who were then charged with trespassing. Later that same year she argued *Watson v. City of Memphis*, challenging segregation in the municipal park system in Memphis, Tennessee.

Freeman and Motley contributed greatly to the civil rights movement's legal strategy aimed at reducing racial discrimination, and their contributions reveal their sole focus on racial discrimination in their cause lawyering. But as their biographies also show, they encountered gender discrimination along the way. For example, after law school Freeman quickly realized that none of the St. Louis law firms, including the black firms, would hire her because she was a woman. Freeman (2003) writes that law at the time was considered by most to be a male profession, and many believed her place should be in the home. Motley, too, confronted differential treatment because of her gender. Although she was extremely successful at LDF as an integral member of the legal team and later would argue numerous cases before the Supreme Court, she was passed over for the top leadership position. When Thurgood Marshall left and the organization's next director-counsel was selected, Jack Greenberg, a white man, was chosen over Motley for the position (Roisman 2016). Although Motley said little about this moment in her life, Roisman (2016) argues that Marshall hesitated to appoint a woman as his replacement in the male-dominated legal field.

Freeman and Motley experienced both racial and gender discrimination, yet their activism was primarily aimed at securing greater rights for black Americans. The social and legal context of the 1950s and 1960s shaped this focus in their legal activism. In addition to the pronounced racial discrimination of the time, the opportunity provided by the civil rights movement played a prominent role in steering their legal efforts, drawing their cause lawyering into organizations and legal cases devoted to litigation for racial justice.

As the women's movement gained momentum in the 1970s, many women would develop a feminist consciousness, including black cause lawyers like Freeman and Motley. However, Freeman's and Motley's politics did not completely align with the women's movement, even in this changing environment. MacLean (2002) argues that Motley was detached from the women's movement because she likely viewed it as favoring white women. She worried that other groups seemed to be profiting from the reform momentum that civil rights activists had generated, while black men and women continued to remain disadvantaged. Although there were race-based tensions in the women's movement, Freeman, as a member of the US Civil Rights Commission, testified before the House Judiciary Committee in 1978, urging extension of the ratification period for the Equal Rights Amendment (Frye et al. 1987). Further, one of the more notable court decisions made by Motley, who beginning in 1966 was a US District Court judge, was in the *Ludtke v. Kuhn* (1978) case, in which she ruled that Melissa Ludtke, a sports reporter, could not be barred from the New York Yankees' locker room simply because she was female.[3] With the rise of second-wave feminism, both Freeman and Motley shifted somewhat to recognize and use their now "insider" positions, for Freeman as a member of the US Civil Rights Commission and Motley as a federal judge, to work for greater gender equality, but the overall history of their legal careers attests to their deep and long-term commitment to the fight for racial justice.

The Third Generation: Race and Gender Comparisons

Pauli Murray and Florynce Kennedy represent a third generation of black women cause lawyers, a generation that followed closely on the heels of the second generation. The legal careers and legal thought of Murray and Kennedy reflect a growing awareness of the pronounced effects of both racism and sexism. Their thinking along with that of others (Collins 2015) provides evidence of earlier statements of black feminism, which in the 1960s and 1970s offers a precursor to the later intersectionality perspective (which we discuss below). Murray and Kennedy, like Freeman and Motley before them, were heavily influenced by civil rights movement activism. In fact, Kennedy at times prioritized black activism over feminism, stating at one point that "racism will always be worse than sexism" (Randolph 2011: 20), and both women also participated in civil rights movement protests (Murray 1987; Randolph 2011). But unlike the second generation of black women cause lawyers, Murray and Kennedy also devoted substantial efforts to developing legal frameworks for understanding gender discrimination and they pursued legal advocacy on behalf of women. Their core contributions came during the years just after those of Freeman and Motley, with Freeman and Motley working in the legal wing of the civil rights movement in the 1950s and early 1960s and Murray and Kennedy providing their legal activism in the 1960s and 1970s, at a time when the second wave of feminism emerged and was expanding.

Murray's and Kennedy's biographies reveal early experiences with both racial and gender discrimination. Both detail how their parents and other family members confronted white racism and hate groups during their childhoods (Kennedy 1976; Murray 1987). Kennedy, for example, writes of her mother and father standing up to a group of Klansmen who threatened violence and told the Kennedy family to move from their predominately white neighborhood (Kennedy 1976; Randolph 2015). Additionally, Kennedy was first rejected from Columbia University Law School because she was a woman (Kennedy 1976), and Murray writes that once in law school at Howard University as the only woman in her class, she faced discrimination from male professors and colleagues (Murray 1987). Early in their legal careers, both women, like Freeman and Motley before them, were drawn into legal work in the civil rights movement. Murray took on race-based discrimination research work in her newly established firm, including publishing the book *States' Laws on Race and Color* and an early law review article containing arguments later used by Marshall in *Brown v. Board of Education* (Mayeri 2011; Murray 1987). Kennedy defended black artists such as Billie Holiday against racial discrimination and worked with a civil rights organization in Mississippi (Randolph 2015).

But actions by early second-wave feminists provided Murray and Kennedy with opportunities to expand their arguments to consider gender discrimination as well as race-based bias, and here the efforts of second- and third-generation black women cause lawyers diverge. In 1961 Murray took a position with the President's Commission on the Status of Women (PCSW), a group coordinated by feminists inside the Kennedy administration (Duerst-Lahti 1989). Murray (1987: 347) later recalled that her involvement with the committee was an "intensive consciousness-raising process." As a member of PCSW, Murray began to develop a strategic race-gender analogy argument. She compared gender discrimination to racial discrimination, in order to allow audiences to see the similarities between the two. The strategy of comparing gender discrimination to the injustices endured by blacks was meant to expose legal policy that continued to exclude women while legal progress was being made to address racial discrimination (Mayeri 2011; Murray and Eastwood 1965). Legal scholar Serena Mayeri describes Murray's race-gender comparison as the legal currency of second-wave feminism, as feminist legal activists in the women's movement, including Ruth Bader Ginsburg in the *Reed* case, soon moved forward in the courts, challenging sex distinctions in law and drawing on Murray's race-gender analogies to do so. In 1962, based on a comprehensive analysis of previous judicial decisions, Murray's report to the PCSW proposed renewed litigation on behalf of women under the Fourteenth Amendment to challenge laws and practices that discriminated on the basis of sex. Her proposal was well received by the PCSW, and Murray's argument in the report launched the women's movement's litigation agenda to win Fourteenth Amendment protections for women, a campaign in the courts that, at the time, ran parallel to efforts to win an Equal Rights Amendment (Mayeri 2004).

Kennedy was more radical in her activism, explicitly challenging blacks to accept feminism and whites to confront racism (Randolph 2015). In 1968, as the women's movement was gaining traction, Kennedy participated in protests against the Miss America pageant, but she did so for both race- and sex-based reasons (Randolph 2015). Kennedy's objection to black-only activism was clear at the 1967 Black Power Conference when she became involved in a heated argument with fellow black leaders after they demanded that Kennedy's white female guests, Ti-Grace Atkinson and Peg Brennan, leave because the meeting was for blacks only (Randolph 2011). Only a few weeks later, Kennedy spoke out against black exclusion in white leftist organizations when she argued that, in order to be effective antiracist allies, whites had to comprehend the importance of black self-determination (Randolph 2011). Soon, Kennedy moved further into her feminist legal activism. She served as counsel in a class-action lawsuit, *Abramowicz v. Lefkowitz*, to repeal New York's restrictive abortion laws, and the lawyers in the case were the first to invite women who had suffered through illegal abortions to serve as expert witnesses (Randolph 2015; Siegel 2010). Though this case was ultimately dismissed in federal court as moot when the New York legislature changed its abortion law, the case later prompted challenges of abortion laws in other states using similar legal tactics.

While a pivotal development, Murray's race-gender discrimination analogies remain inherently limited. The language of the analogy comparing women and blacks treats race and gender as mutually exclusive categories, thereby excluding black women who experience the double burden of being both female and black. While the race-gender analogy worked well for women's rights litigation in the courts (Mayeri 2011), the idea of elevating the kind of discrimination encountered by black women—discrimination that Murray and Kennedy understood well from their everyday experiences—met resistance in black and predominately white women's social movement organizations at the time. The 1963 March on Washington, a demand for civil and economic rights for blacks, in which the NAACP was heavily involved, for example, is remembered as having largely excluded women from visible roles (Collier-Thomas 2001; see Robnett 1997 for a broader examination of the civil rights movement). Also, while Murray was a founding member and Kennedy an early member of the National Organization for Women (NOW), Murray found that NOW members would not adequately address the double jeopardy of being both black and female, and Kennedy perceived Betty Friedan to be dismissive of the Black Power movement (Mayeri 2011; Randolph 2015). Consequently, Kennedy and Murray both eventually left NOW.

Although Kennedy and Murray often found resistance in both black and feminist movement circles, their legal activism furthered both race- and gender-based advocacy. They labored on behalf of both movements, responding to the opportunities each movement offered and, for Murray especially, in leading the intellectual effort to highlight gender discrimination by drawing race-gender comparisons.

This third generation of black women cause lawyers set the stage for further intellectual developments and activism, efforts that would be propelled by a fourth generation of black women cause lawyers.

The Fourth Generation: The Intersectionality Approach

The earlier comparisons of racial and gender discrimination were influential particularly in litigation for gender equality (Mayeri 2011), but, again, such comparisons ignore black women's experiences that do not fit within the separate categories of black or female. Discrimination against black women goes unacknowledged in race-gender analogies. In ignoring the discrimination confronted by black women (and other women of color), the race-gender comparisons also fail to acknowledge differences among women—differences, for instance, linked to race, ethnicity, nativity, class, sexual orientation, and gender identity. Just as the efforts of earlier black women lawyers challenged oppression, the fourth generation of lawyers did so as well. As black women lawyers gained in legal prominence, they began to focus—and continue to do so—on how the law uniquely responds to discrimination against black women (Cooper 2016; Watson 2008).

By the late 1980s and early 1990s, black women made inroads into the legal academy (Watson 2008) and in doing so brought their cause lawyering for racial and gender equality into legal teaching and scholarship. Although barriers to gaining positions as legal scholars remained substantial (Greene 1990; Jordan 1990), black women lawyers achieved status in the academy, becoming legal intellectual leaders. Kimberlé Crenshaw is one of these intellectual legal leaders. She completed her law degree at Harvard in 1984 and joined the University of California, Los Angeles (UCLA) law faculty in 1986. Beginning in the late 1980s, she articulated the critical perspective of intersectionality in which she states that black women are "theoretically erased" when "single-axis analysis" of racial or gender discrimination is considered in antidiscrimination law (Crenshaw 1989: 139). Crenshaw's framework transcended comparisons of race and gender oppression and instead recognized that racialized and gendered systems intersect to oppress black women in ways distinct from the treatment of black men and white women. Crenshaw used the legal academy as a bully pulpit for her cause lawyering intellectual advocacy, arguing that the language of Title VII forces women to choose between making discrimination claims based on race or sex. This limitation in law restrains the legal capacity of black women, who can be and are discriminated against simultaneously because of their race and sex. The intersectionality framework today holds that multiple oppressed identities (e.g., race, gender, ethnicity, and sexual orientation) interact to influence the everyday experiences of those with politicized identities, which occurs in myriad ways (Cho, Crenshaw, and McCall 2013; Collins 2015; Cooper 2016).

While Crenshaw provided foundational intellectual leadership, other academic black women lawyers in this fourth generation were compelled to fight the cause-lawyering battle at a more practical level (Watson 2008). For instance, law professor

Anita Hill, who previously was employed at the Department of Education and then the Equal Employment Opportunity Commission (EEOC), testified against then–Supreme Court judicial nominee Clarence Thomas, stating that he sexually harassed Hill while they worked together in these government agencies. Shortly after publication of Crenshaw's pivotal 1989 article, in 1991 Hill became the public example of how black women are left at the margins of mutually exclusive legal categories of race and sex discrimination. Hill accused Thomas of sexual misconduct during their work together at the Department of Education and EEOC. Hill's testimony before an all-white and all-male US Senate Judiciary Committee sparked broader public awareness of sexual harassment in the workplace.

But Hill also encountered substantial criticism, including from blacks, because she, as a black woman, was charging a black man with sexual misconduct (Grier 1995). Years of race advocacy separated from gender advocacy had resisted perceptions of black men as sexual aggressors, because such perceptions serve the white purpose of undermining black men's stature in society (Grier 1995; hooks 2015). Hill's experience and public testimony challenged the logic of many black activists, pointing to the possibility of the subordination of black women by black men. As Crenshaw was developing her intersectionality approach, she assisted on the legal team representing Hill during the Senate hearings. Crenshaw later remarked that Hill's allegations against Thomas were met with confusion and hostility by many because the claims failed to fit easily within either the white female "rape narrative" or a black male "lynching narrative" (Crenshaw 1992: 405). Hill, however, did provide a *black woman's narrative*, and the resistance her narrative faced— including from the Senate committee that, in the end, recommended Thomas for appointment—attests to the still marginalized status of black women.

But the lives of Crenshaw and Hill also illustrate the recent accomplishments made by black women cause lawyers, in particular, their inroads into the legal academy and legal profession as well as their legal intellectual leadership. The progress on race and gender by both the civil rights and women's movements aided these women in their efforts by helping to open doors. Hill graduated from Yale University law school in 1980 and Crenshaw just after that from Harvard, both in an era after the preceding decades' waves of civil rights and feminist activism. Hill today is a professor at Brandeis University and counsel at a civil rights and employment practice law firm, while Crenshaw is Distinguished Professor of Law at UCLA and professor at Columbia University Law School. Their substantial personal achievements, like those of the women before them, help dismantle barriers that black women and other women of color have long confronted in the legal profession and in society. In her book published after the 1991 Senate hearings, Hill (1997) calls for an end to the dismissive and exclusionary treatment of black women, treatment that can even occur in rights activism, where often, she states, black men are placed at the center of efforts for racial progress and white women at the center of pressure for women's rights.

Both Hill and Crenshaw remain involved in cause-lawyering efforts through their scholarship to expand the inclusion and rights of the marginalized. In a law review article, Hill (2007) argues for an increase in women judges because of the unique views women can bring to the law. Hill states that a diversity of judges should be the norm instead of the exception and that the significant role the law plays in social life warrants the inclusion of women and racial minorities because of the difference they make in ensuring fairness in law. Crenshaw's more recent work continues to condemn the exclusion of black women. In a recent article, Crenshaw (2012) argues that black women, like black men, are also prisoners in a system of mass incarceration and victims of distinctive forms of heavy surveillance by law enforcement. Crenshaw's challenge to consider the position of black women in systems of social control is in response to discussions that often only consider the impact of surveillance, policing, and incarceration for black males. Crenshaw also challenged President Barack Obama to consider the roles of black girls when he proposed a five-year, $200 million initiative titled My Brother's Keeper, a new program to offer mentorship, summer jobs, and other support to boys and young men of color (Crenshaw 2014). Hill's and Crenshaw's most recent statements remind us, once again, of gender disparities and that girls and women of color need attention, just as do their male counterparts.

Hill and Crenshaw, as fourth-generation cause lawyers, have played and continue to play pivotal roles in shaping discourse around race and gender equality. Their intellectual contributions and front-line efforts in resisting the exclusion of the experiences and interests of black females and women of color more generally provide critical advancement in the struggle against intersecting systems of discrimination. Since Crenshaw's pivotal 1989 article and Hill's Senate testimony, the intersectionality paradigm has gained substantial traction and is deployed in a variety of realms, in academic disciplines such as history, sociology, psychology, political science, and legal studies, and in workplaces, the law, and social movements (Cho, Crenshaw, and McCall 2013; Chun, Lipsitz, and Shin 2013). Across multiple venues, the intersectionality perspective has been used to examine the experiences of not only black women but those with other intersecting marginalized identities (Collins 2015; hooks 2015).

Conclusion

Over the last one hundred years, black women have pursued law degrees and many have strategically used their legal skills as cause lawyers to advocate for black, women's, and black women's rights. The earliest of these activists were compelled to struggle simply to become lawyers in the face of systems of gender and racial oppression that sought to exclude black women (and black men and white women) from the profession of law. The earliest black women cause lawyers recognized, however, that the interests of black women were often distinct from those of other groups, precisely because black women bore the brunt of both racism and sexism (and class hierarchy as well). For a second generation of black women cause lawyers, in the context of a growing civil rights movement in the United States, their focus was largely on achieving race-based equality and using the court system to strive for black justice. Soon, however, with the rise of the second-wave feminist movement and black feminism, a third generation of black women cause lawyers emerged, reacknowledging gender inequality and articulating comparisons of race and gender discrimination to further our thinking about gender inequities. For a fourth and recent generation of black women cause lawyers, intersectionality as an analytic perspective has grown from the earlier discussions of similarities between race and gender discrimination and a history of black feminism to an intersectionality paradigm today that is used heavily not only in legal realms but in academia and social justice movements as well.

Black women cause lawyers are rarely considered in histories of cause lawyering in the United States, and yet they have made significant contributions over the past one hundred years, as they have combatted both racial and gender discrimination and especially have fought against systems of racial and gender subordination and the ways in which they interlock to oppress black women and other groups marginalized by intersecting oppressions. Like the suffragists, black women cause lawyers have fought for greater equality, but they have done so on behalf of a group experiencing multiple systems of subordination. The goal of our chapter has been to reveal the important efforts of black women cause lawyers as they have advocated for blacks and women and for equal rights and social justice for those whose lives are shaped by intersecting systems of bias. As we move into the second hundred years following the Nineteenth Amendment, the issues fueling the Black Lives Matter movement, coupled with the continued disproportionate experience by black women of intimate partner violence, rape, reproductive health limitations, and workplace discrimination show the ongoing need for the legal activism of black women cause lawyers (West 2004; Browne and Misra 2003; see also Roberts 1997).

Notes

1. While intersectionality began as an exploration and acknowledgment of the unique oppression of black women, today the paradigm can be applied to multiple politicized social categories (Collins 2015; Crenshaw 1989).

2. The achievements of Ray and Cary are part of an even earlier history of black women challenging legal norms in the United States and demanding greater rights under the law (Giddings 1984; McDaniel 2007; Pratt 2012).

3. Banaszak (2010) offers a useful discussion of how black lawyers, both women and men, were generally excluded from federal government employment well into the 1960s.

References

Abramowicz v. Lefkowitz (Hall v. Lefkowitz), 305 F. Supp. 1030 (S.D.N.Y. 1969).

Banaszak, Lee Ann. 2010. *The Women's Movement Inside and Outside the State.* New York: Cambridge University Press.

Branch, Taylor. 1989. *Parting the Waters: America in the King Years, 1954–63.* New York: Simon and Schuster.

Brown v. Board of Education of Topeka, Kansas, 347 U.S. 483 (1954).

Browne, Irene, and Joya Misra. 2003. "The Intersection of Gender and Race in the Labor Market." *Annual Review of Sociology* 29(1): 487–513.

Chen, Alan K., and Scott L. Cummings. 2013. *Public Interest Lawyering: A Contemporary Perspective*. New York: Wolters Kluwer.

Chicago Tribune. 1962. "Mrs. Sampson Making Negro History Again." October 21: 10.

Cho, Sumi, Kimberlé W. Crenshaw, and Leslie McCall. 2013. "Toward a Field of Intersectionality Studies: Theory, Applications, and Praxis." *Signs* 38(4): 785–810.

Chun, Jennifer Jihye, George Lipsitz, and Young Shin. 2013. "Intersectionality as a Social Movement Strategy: Asian Immigrant Women Advocates." *Signs* 38(4): 917–940.

Collier-Thomas, Bettye. 2001. *Sisters in the Struggle: African American Women in the Civil Rights–Black Power Movement*. New York: New York University Press.

Collins, Patricia Hill. 2015. "Intersectionality's Definitional Dilemmas." *Annual Review of Sociology* 41: 1–20.

Cook, Beverly. 1996. "Violette Neatley Anderson (1882–1937)." Pp. 12–15 in *Notable Black American Women*, volume 2, edited by J. C. Smith. Detroit: Gale Research.

Cooper, Brittney. 2016. "Intersectionality." Pp. 385–406 in *The Oxford Handbook of Feminist Theory*, edited by L. Disch and M. Hawkesworth. New York: Oxford University Press.

Crenshaw, Kimberlé W. 1989. "Demarginalizing the Intersection of Race and Sex: A Black Feminist Critique of Antidiscrimination Doctrine, Feminist Theory and Antiracist Politics." *University of Chicago Legal Forum* 14(1): 139–167.

———. 1992. "Whose Story Is It, Anyway? Feminist and Antiracist Appropriations of Anita Hill." Pp. 402–440 in *Race-ing Justice, En-gendering Power: Essays on Anita Hill, Clarence Thomas, and the Construction of Social Reality*, edited by Toni Morrison. New York: Pantheon.

———. 2012. "From Private Violence to Mass Incarceration: Thinking Intersectionally about Women, Race, and Social Control." *University of California Los Angeles Law Review* 59(6): 1418–1474.

———. 2014. "The Girls Obama Forgot; Kimberlé Williams Crenshaw: My Brother's Keeper Ignores Young Black Women." New York Times, July 29.

Davis v. St. Louis Housing Authority, 1 Race Rel. L. Rep. 353 (Civil No. 8637 E.D. Mo., 1955).

Duerst-Lahti, Georgia. 1989. "The Government's Role in Building the Women's Movement." *Political Science Quarterly* 104: 249–268.

Freeman, Frankie Muse. 2003. *A Song of Faith and Hope: The Life of Frankie Muse Freeman*. St. Louis: Missouri History Museum Press.

Frye, Jocelyn C., Robert S. Gerber, Robert H. Pees, and Arthur W. Richardson. 1987. "The Rise and Fall of the United States Commission on Civil Rights." *Harvard Civil Rights–Civil Liberties Review* 22(2): 449–505.

Giddings, Paula. 1984. *When and Where I Enter: The Impact of Black Women on Race and Sex in America*. New York: HarperCollins.

Gober v. City of Birmingham, 373 U.S. 374 (1963).

Greenberg, Jack. 2004. *Crusaders in the Courts: Legal Battles of the Civil Rights Movement*. New York: Twelve Tables Press.

Greene, Linda S. 1990. "Tokens, Role Models, and Pedagogical Politics: Lamentations of an African American Female Law Professor." *Berkeley Women's Law Journal* 6: 81–92.

Grier, Beverly. 1995. "Making Sense of Our Differences: African American Women on Anita Hill." Pp. 150–158 in *African American Women Speak Out on Anita Hill–Clarence Thomas*, edited by Geneva Smitherman. Detroit: Wayne State University Press.

Hamilton v. Alabama, 368 U.S. 52 (1961).

Hilbink, Thomas M. 2006. "The Profession, the Grassroots and the Elite: Cause Lawyering for Civil Rights and Freedom in the Direct Action Era." Pp. 60–83 in *Cause Lawyers and Social Movements*, edited by Austin Sarat and Stuart A. Scheingold. Stanford, CA: Stanford University Press.

Hill, Anita F. 1997. *Speaking Truth to Power*. New York: Anchor Books.

———. 2007. "The Embodiment of Equal Justice under the Law." *Nova Law Review* 31(2): 237–257.

hooks, bell. 2015. *Feminists Theory: From Margin to Center*. New York: Routledge.

Jordan, Emma Colman. 1990. "Images of Black Women in the Legal Academy: An Introduction." *Berkeley Women's Law Journal* 6: 1–21.

Jordan, Gwen. 2012. "Engendering the History of Race and International Relations: The Career of Edith Sampson, 1927–1978." *Chicago-Kent Law Review* 87: 521–548.

Kennedy, Florynce. 1976. *Color Me Flo: My Hard Life and Good Times*. Upper Saddle River, NJ: Prentice-Hall.

Ludtke v. Kuhn, 461 F. Supp. 86 (S.D.N.Y. 1978).

MacLean, Nancy. 2002. "Using the Law for Social Change: Judge Constance Baker Motley." *Journal of Women's History* 14(2): 136–139.

Marshall, Anna-Maria. 2006. "Social Movement Strategies and the Participatory Potential of Litigation." Pp. 164–181 in *Cause Lawyers and Social Movements*, edited by Austin Sarat and Stuart A. Scheingold. Stanford, CA: Stanford University Press.

Marshall, Anna-Maria, and Daniel Crocker Hale. 2014. "Cause Lawyering." *Annual Review of Law and Social Science* 10(1): 301–320.

Mayeri, Serena. 2004. "Constitutional Choices: Legal Feminism and the Historical Dynamics of Change." *California Law Review* 92(3): 755–839.

———. 2011. *Reasoning from Race: Feminism, Law, and the Civil Rights Revolution*. Cambridge, MA: Harvard University Press.

———. 2014. "Pauli Murray and the Twentieth-Century Quest for Legal and Social Equality." *Indiana Journal of Law and Social Equality* 2(1): 80–90.

McCammon, Holly J., Allison McGrath, Ashley Dixon, and Megan Robinson. 2017. "Targeting Culture: Feminist Legal Activists and Critical Community Tactics." *Research in Social Movements, Conflict and Change* 41: 243–278.

McDaniel, Cecily Barker. 2007. " 'Fearing I Shall Not Do My Duty to My Race If I Remain Silent': Law and Its Call to African American Women, 1872–1932." PhD dissertation, Department of History, The Ohio State University, Columbus.

Minow, Martha. 1996. "Political Lawyering: An Introduction." *Harvard Civil Rights–Civil Liberties Law Review* 31(1): 287–296.

Motley, Constance Baker. 1988. "Some Recollections of My Career." *Law and Inequality: A Journal of Theory and Practice* 6(1): 35–40.

———. 1998. *Equal Justice under Law: An Autobiography*. New York: Macmillan.

Murray, Pauli. 1987. *Pauli Murray: The Autobiography of a Black Activist, Feminist, Lawyer, Priest, and Poet*. Knoxville: University of Tennessee Press

Murray, Pauli, and Mary O. Eastwood. 1965. "Jane Crow and the Law: Sex Discrimination and Title VII." *George Washington Law Review* 34(2): 232–256.

O'Connor, Karen. 1980. *Women's Organizations' Use of the Courts.* Lexington, MA: Lexington Books.

Pratt, Carla D. 2012. "Sisters in Law: Black Women Lawyers' Struggle for Advancement." *Michigan State Law Review* 5: 1777–1795.

Randolph, Sherie M. 2011. "The Lasting Legacy of Florynce Kennedy: A Black Feminist Fighter." *Against the Current* 152. https://www.solidarity-us.org/site/node/3272.

———. 2015. *Florynce "Flo" Kennedy: The Life of a Black Feminist Radical.* Chapel Hill: University of North Carolina Press.

Reed v. Reed, 404 U.S. 71 (1971).

Rhodes, Jane. 1998. *Mary Ann Shadd Cary: The Black Press and Protest in the Nineteenth Century.* Bloomington: Indiana University Press.

Roberts, Dorothy. 1997. *Killing the Black Body: Race Reproduction and the Meaning of Liberty.* New York: Pantheon.

Robnett, Belinda. 1997. *How Long? How Long? African American Women in the Struggle for Civil Rights.* New York: Oxford University Press.

Roisman, Florence Wagman. 2016. "An Extraordinary Woman: The Honorable Constance Baker Motley: (September 9, 1921–September 28, 2005)." *Indiana Law Review* 49(3): 677–823.

Sampson, Edith Spurlock. 1935. "Legal Profession Followed by Nation's Best Known Socialites (1935)." Pp. 16–23 in *Rebels in Law: Voices in History of Black Women Lawyers*, edited by J. C. Smith. Ann Arbor: University of Michigan Press.

Sarat, Austin, and Stuart A. Scheingold. 2006. *Cause Lawyers and Social Movements.* Stanford, CA: Stanford University Press.

Schneider, Elizabeth M., and Stephanie M. Wildman. 2011. *Women and the Law Stories.* New York: Foundation Press.

Shuttlesworth v. City of Birmingham, 373 U.S. 262 (1963).

Siegel, Reva B. 2010. "Roe's Roots: The Women's Rights Claims That Engendered Roe." *Boston University Law Review* 90(4): 1875–1908.

Smith, J. Clay, Jr. 1997. "Black Women Lawyers: 125 Years at the Bar; 100 Years in the Legal Academy." *Howard Law Journal* 40(2): 365–397.

———. *Rebels in Law: Voices in History of Black Women Lawyers.* Ann Arbor: University of Michigan Press.

Strebeigh, Fred. 2009. *Equal: Women Reshape American Law.* New York: W. W. Norton.

Tushnet, Mark V. 1987. *The NAACP's Legal Strategy Against Segregated Education, 1925–1952.* Chapel Hill: University of North Carolina Press.

Watson v. City of Memphis, 373 U.S. 526 (1963).

Watson, Elwood D. 2008. *Outsiders Within: Black Women in the Legal Academy after Brown v. Board.* Lanham, MD: Rowman and Littlefield.

West, Carolyn M. 2004. "Black Women and Intimate Partner Violence: New Directions for Research." *Journal of Interpersonal Violence* 19(12): 1487–1493.

Whittier, Nancy. 1995. *Feminist Generations: The Persistence of the Radical Women's Movement.* Philadelphia: Temple University Press.

Yee, Shirley J. 1997. "Finding a Place: Mary Ann Shadd Cary and the Dilemmas of Black Migration to Canada, 1850–1870." *Frontiers: A Journal of Women Studies* 18(3): 1–16.

{ 12 }

American Mothers of Nonviolence

ACTION AND THE POLITICS OF ERASURE
IN WOMEN'S NONVIOLENT ACTIVISM

Selina Gallo-Cruz

One great contribution often overlooked in the examination of the successes of the early suffrage movement is the insight and tactical skills stemming from early women nonviolent activists—activists who advocated for nonviolence as the best way to couple the ends they sought with the most favorable means for achieving them. These women opposed violence as a form of conflict resolution, even and especially in the face of violence. So important was their commitment to a nonviolent philosophy, they sought to live their personal lives as nonviolently as possible while developing protest and political persuasion tactics that could effectively bring about social change.

In this chapter I explore the historical legacy of American women's contributions to nonviolence movements. I do so to acknowledge the conceptual, tactical, and organizational gifts of the unsung heroines of American nonviolence—which, I argue, stands among the great contributions women activists have made following early-feminist nonviolence among nineteenth-century suffragists. Because popular accounts of nonviolent movements tend to write out or ignore the important transformations spurred by feminist activism and thinking, I consider the politics of feminist activists' erasure from nonviolent histories—how and why women's contributions to American nonviolence have been omitted from the growing canon of nonviolent history. I also examine the unique role of feminists in developing a nonviolence repertoire through a distinctively gendered territory of resistance, asking how women's gendered experiences shape their nonviolent activism. Operative among these dynamics I discuss (1) the double standard of gendered invisibility—that women are expected to be passive even as they must advocate for their own freedoms, and that such political invisibility both facilitates women's effectiveness as activists and obscures them from the male academic gaze and thus biases historical memory; (2) a radical-feminist transformation of the politics of nonviolence organizing toward a more deeply democratic process;

and (3) the feminist-led transformation from a nonviolence that glorifies "self-sacrifice" to a nonviolence that values self-protection, preservation, and health in the realization of collective social justice.

Feminist Nonviolence from Early Suffragists to Today

The movements for US women's suffrage and nonviolence were born of the same social heart. Canonical histories of US women's suffrage typically begin somewhere around the 1848 Seneca Falls conference. In fact, this conference marks the splintering of women-led abolitionist activism—activism committed to nonviolence as both a method and an outcome—into a strand of activism that focused more explicitly on women's rights. Through their fervent dedication to abolishing the slave trade, early suffragists gained both their organizing skills and their critical comparative insights on both women's and black Americans' exclusion and political and social rights. Seneca Falls organizers Lucretia Mott and Elizabeth Cady Stanton generated the idea for a conference in London in 1840 at the World's Anti-Slavery Convention (which for Cady Stanton and her abolitionist husband was also their honeymoon!). Mott and Cady Stanton shared sentiments regarding their exclusion from speaking at the convention and the limits they experienced organizing in the movement. They were also strong proponents of what was then known as *nonresistance* but later developed into Gandhi's and others' formulations of what we now call *nonviolence*: the resolve to actively resist injustice by avoiding violence or harm to others, including those who oppress us with violence. Just as female abolitionists viewed both women's empowerment and slave liberation as mutual and necessary steps to a more egalitarian society, so too did they consider the methods of peaceful resistance a necessary means to an end to any form of power politics.[1]

Most popular and academic histories of nonviolence start with Gandhi, famed leader of the early 1900s Indian independence movement. Those histories readily identify Gandhi's conceptual forefathers as Thoreau (1849), who wrote on the political imperative of citizens' refusal to support unjust policies, what we now call *noncooperation*, in *Civil Disobedience*, and Tolstoy (1899), who formulated a similar theory of passive resistance (resisting injustice without violence) as the Christian moral high ground.[2] It is less often mentioned that Gandhi also learned a great deal from English and American suffragists, especially their tactics of fasting, public marches, and rallies, and their deep dedication to activism. In his personal commentaries, he reflected, "Undaunted, these women work on steadfast in their cause. They are bound to succeed and gain the franchise, for the simple reason that deeds are better than words" (Gandhi 1906, quoted in Offen n.d.).[3]

Conceptually, the coupling of nonviolence as a means to the end of violence is essential to identifying and understanding the American mothers of nonviolence I discuss here. In the words of abolitionist-feminist Lydia Maria Child, "Abolition principles and nonresistance seem to me identical. . . . The former is a mere unit of the latter. I never saw a truth so clearly insomuch that it seems strange to me that any comprehensive mind may embrace one and not the other" (quoted in Bacon 2005: 129). Discourse salient in the early-twentieth-century Women's League for Peace and Freedom reveals a methodological approach of "intelligent compassion," through which women organizers use their marginalized position as women to contemplate global others marginalized from organizers' privileged statuses of class, race, and citizenship (Confortini 2012). Feminist nonviolent studies scholar Pam McAllister echoes this sentiment:

> For me, means and ends need to be consistent. . . . Put into the feminist perspective nonviolence is the merging of our uncompromising rage at the patriarchy's brutal destructiveness with a refusal to adopt its ways, a refusal to give into despair or hate or to let men off the hook by making them the "Other" as they have made those they fear "Others." (1982: iii)

The Feminism and Non-Violence Study Group (1983) concludes that "resistance to war and to the use of nuclear weapons is impossible without resistance to sexism, to racism, to imperialism, and to violence as an everyday pervasive reality" (1983: 5). The War Resisters League similarly notes, "The view of women as the other parallels the view of our enemies as non-human available targets for any means of destruction or cruelty" (1989: 23).

The movements I discuss in this chapter span women's activism through the first, second, and third waves of feminist organizing across the twentieth century, late-nineteenth-century organizing through the World War II period, the 1960s through the 1980s, and the 1980s and 1990s to today.[4] These movements included those aimed at putting an end to violence and social justice movements that embrace nonviolence as both the ideal means and ends of mobilization. Through its presence in these groups, the nonviolence movement picks up new members whose commitment to nonviolence then outlasts any smaller issue-specific movement, and nonviolent activists are often dedicated to a broad range of social justice issue movements and campaigns at any one time. Harriet Hyman Alonso (1993) details suffragists' use of national and international networks to promote issues of abolition and slavery, civil rights and antiracism, equal pay, property and marriage rights, welfare and child labor issues, world peace and disarmament, antinuclear organizing, birth control and sexual orientation, and the myriad other initiatives toward peace and human rights in which suffragists were so actively involved. In fact, a clear break from suffrage into any of these other early movements is impossible because the main suffrage organizations were so deeply committed to these other causes alongside their commitment to gaining women's right to vote.

To examine women's roles in the nonviolence movement, and the politics of women's erasure, I utilize secondary sources on nonviolence in the United States. The major sources informing this discussion include those covering early abolition and nonresistance activism from the early to late 1800s (Ceplair 1989; Faulkner 2011; Alonso 1993; Bacon 1980, 1992, 2005; Sterling 1991), and several pieces covering the linkages between the suffrage and early-twentieth-century disarmament movements and the mid- to late-twentieth-century no-nuclear and peace movements (Boulding 2000; Foster 1989; Harris and King 1989; Alonso 1993; Lynd and Lynd 1995; Oldfield 1989). Other work covers women and nonviolent activism in the civil rights and labor movements (Collier-Thomas and Franklin 2001; Crawford, Rouse, and Woods 1993; Ling and Montieff 2004; Olson 2001; Robnett 1997). There are a range of pieces specifically addressing women and different facets of nonviolent activism in the environmental and human rights movements (Hill 2001; Griffin-Nolan 1991; Kaplan 2002; Nepstad 2004; Rowbotham 2002; Smith 1996). Additionally, several pieces address feminism and nonviolence (McAllister 1982, 1988, 1991; Riegle 2013) and feminism and peace specifically (Cockburn 2012; Foster 1989; Harris and King 1989; Swerdlow 1993; Oldfield 1989).

My analysis is also informed by insights from in-depth interviews with twenty activists in the women's rights, civil rights, antiwar, antinuclear, peace, human rights, and environmental movements. These interviews include women who have worked across these movements from the 1950s until today. I also utilize archival materials made available by several nonviolent and peace organizations, including the War Resisters League, the Movement for a New Society, and the Fellowship for Reconciliation, as well as from documents and manuscripts provided to me by the activists I interviewed.

In the discussion below, I introduce a framework for explaining women's erasure from and contributions to the history of the nonviolence movement. I then identify and analyze distinctive gendered experiences that have arisen in the overlapping of feminism and nonviolence in the United States. These include processes I discuss as gender and unexpected power; women's lived experiences and approaches to violence; the feminist transformation of protest, communication, and community dynamics; and a movement from a nonviolence that embraces self-sacrifice to one that embraces self-affirmation. Through an emergent coding of feminist contributions to the nonviolence movement in its various iterations I forward a sociological analysis of feminism as one vital expression of nonviolence that has reshaped the repertoire in both strategic and unintentional ways.

Gender, Action, and the Politics of Erasure

Both the questions raised here and my analytical tools are framed by feminist inquiry. Feminist historians caution us against the male bias of movement histories, warning that "history is a problem in sampling" (Boulding 1976: 3) and that "men tend to play up the part played by men" in these actions (King 1995). Boulding's paradigmatic corrective to this bias[5] has shown us that an "underside" of missing actors and missing actions lie waiting in the archives for someone with the right epistemological perspective to give those stories historical life. The women's histories of activism cited above give support to the general hypothesis that while women have contributed much, these contributions have not been included in the canon.

Lengermann and Niebrugge-Brantley (1998) explain that there are two notable qualities of the gendered erasure of women's legacies from popular histories. First, historians often apply a male gaze to their history-writing,[6] an emphasis on issues and actions that favor men. This bias subjectively defines what is important enough to gain a public legacy and effectively erases women's contribution from the record. Second, a "writing out" of women occurs in histories that fail to include women because women were neither adequately nor accurately publicly recognized due to their "invisibility," or lack of recognition, from influential but biased professional institutions (Lengermann and Niebrugge-Brantley [1998], discuss academia in particular). Although some of the earliest social theorists were highly active and widely published women (Harriet Martineau, for example, out-published Charles Dickens, and Jane Addams won the Nobel Peace Prize), their work eluded the male-biased canon because of the topics they addressed (e.g., Addams's concern with settlement houses or Wells's dedication to antilynching campaigns) and the context, sometimes nonacademic, in which it was produced.[7]

In reviewing the stories of women's contributions to nonviolence, I ask an epistemological question: why and how are some types of *actions* privileged over others? I then evaluate the sociological quality of effectiveness of those "gendered" actions—gendered in the sense that they are unique to women and women's communities and are filtered through a patriarchal interpretation of women's action.

I offer insight into the particular contributions of the women's movement to the nonviolence movement following US suffrage in two key ways. First, I highlight one branch of feminism that is wholly committed to nonviolent social change— a feminism that aims to disentangle patriarchy from the ways we identify social problems to the ways we work toward transformation. Next, I examine the ways in which engagement with nonviolent peacemaking has enhanced how women envision and work toward a more gender-egalitarian society. I begin my discussion with the qualities of actions that set women's nonviolence apart. Then I establish how gendered contributions have shaped the invisibility and writing out of women's nonviolence.

Gender and Unexpected Power

Preaching to what was commonly referred to as a "promiscuous" or mixed-race, mixed-gender crowd was a controversial exercise among abolitionists, especially when women were preaching. Only the most progressive abolitionist men supported this practice, and widely publicized events often were met with hostile, public opposition, such as the 1853 New York City Women's Rights Convention. This gathering was attended by early suffragist-abolitionist Lucretia Mott, among many other luminaries, including Sojourner Truth and William Lloyd Garrison. This particular convention circuit had been followed by angry mobs who publicly derided the "strong-minded women" who had gotten their "pluck up" (Bacon 1980). Mob backlash led to the burning of organizing offices and acts of violence against the organizers. When a drunken mob appeared outside this convention, physically threatened the attendees from leaving, and invited the men to fight, it was the small-framed but self-composed Mott who led the exit through the violent crowd. She did so by clutching for the gang leader himself, Captain

Rynders, who was stunned into courteously and safely escorting her out of the mob. She publicly approached him in a tavern the following day to thank him for his assistance only to leave him expressing dismay at how "kindly and sensible" she seemed to be for a woman so deeply derided as the loathed "Black Man's Goddess" (Bacon 1980).

One of the mechanisms considered key to effective nonviolence is inducing a state of surprise in the resisted attacker—that the attacked is neither expecting nor is he prepared for responding to the act of resistance (Gregg 1935). I argue that a gendered element of such surprise is the combination of boldness coupled with idealized markers of femininity, because gendered socialization dictates that feminine women act passively, especially in the face of conflict. Because women are often unexpected to be powerful in political conflict, the coupling of gendered notions of femininity with acts of bold nonviolent action constitute an unexpected form of nonviolent power. The ability for women activists to capitalize on men's expectations that they are passive and incapable of boldness may be called a "cloak of femininity," a performative demeanor women may take on and off for strategic efficacy. We might add age along with boldness and femininity to Mott's arsenal; her authority drew, in part, on her grandmotherly stature (Bacon 1980). The activism of Mary Harris "Mother" Jones provides another example. Mother Jones was a seventy-year old, deeply dedicated labor leader whose threatening reputation as an organizer outsized her physical appearance. In one instance, the town sheriff quietly confided to the labor leader, not realizing who she was among the crowd, "Oh Lord, that Mother Jones is sure a dangerous woman" (McAllister 1991: 13). Jones took advantage of his impaired judgment to query his plans for arrest. He blindly confessed he would not do so as the costs would be greater than the castigatory effect. She pried further to learn that the local militia had a catered breakfast planned at the town hotel. With that, Jones led her marching mothers to a full breakfast, compliments of the state; through the day of marching and organizing, hassle-free; and out of the town and back into the surrounding mountain towns from which they had mobilized!

In ways both positive and negative to the organizing efforts of women, this socially constructed cloak of femininity provides women shielding from the radar of violent attack and allows them to organize and act effectively, even in an unintentional way (distinctive from what Spivak discusses as "strategic essentialism" [1987]). We learn of several laudable successes of the youthful Diane Nash in York's *A Force More Powerful* (2000), which includes documentary footage of the 1960 Nashville sit-ins and march. The documentary details how capable Nash was in so many ways and how she blossomed as an organizer and activist. Nash, a young African American female student organizer, was fervently devoted to the cause of desegregation. She organized beyond her own fears of violence—even the threat of being killed. While Nash has become well-known for her skill, bravery, and many great successes in the civil rights movement, biographers' descriptions of Nash and interviews with Nash's activist peers point to how she is also often assessed through a gendered lens—biographers and peers note that Nash was a former beauty queen and that she was esteemed in the movement for her beauty.

Nash had not initially sought to be the leader of the pathbreaking movement. She was thrust into the position when male organizers could not commit to the meetings that she never missed.[8] Nevertheless, she rose to the occasion and soon became strategically savvy in responding to violent crackdowns against the movement. After the students' NAACP attorney's house was firebombed, Nash led the students on a march to confront the mayor. The protestors brazenly questioned his bigotry in failing to condemn the violent bombing following a string of sit-in protests at local lunch counters. At first, the mayor engaged in a heated argument with a young black minister. His argumentative demeanor suddenly shifted, however, to calm, respectful dialogue when approached by polite, eloquent Diane Nash. In her soft-spoken way, she straightforwardly challenged the mayor, asking, "Do you feel it is wrong to discriminate against a person solely on the basis of his race or color?" To this the mayor answered that he did believe it was wrong, and the first major desegregation success was won in the Nashville lunch counters.[9] That the mayor responded favorably to a young woman esteemed for her beauty and traditional feminine comportment points to an undertheorized form of what sociologists refer to as the gendered interruption of a social space (see Wade and Feree 2015), in this case when social norms demand courtesy from a male actor in a conflict situation, altering the aggressiveness with which the mayor responded to other male protesters.[10]

Because of the low expectations of women's power in a man's world and because of the norms of courtesy associated with expressions of femininity, women can disarm even those against whom they are protesting through gendered mechanisms of nonviolence. This is one reason women's contributions have been written out of the history of nonviolence. Too many of the heroines' great organizing contributions have been overshadowed by celebrations of charismatic male leaders who engage in more outward shows of dramatic, masculine resistance.[11]

Women's work also tends to be invisible in contexts in which women's leadership is implicitly or explicitly discouraged, even as their experiences as women enable them to contribute unique and valuable insights and tactics. Both the civil rights and antiwar movements were settings in which women struggled to gain respect and recognition. Women such as those who led the 1969 Women against Daddy Warbucks war resistance effort fought to combat these biases (Riegle 2013). When asked why they had decided to organize a women's only draft-resistance action, Maggie Geddes explains,

> Remember the poster with Joan Baez that says, "Girls say yes to men who say no"? People didn't use the word "women" in those days. . . . Yes there were long-standing women's organizations like Women Strike for Peace and Women's International League for Peace and Freedom, but we were young, we were active, and we wanted to be more active as women. (Riegle 2013: 99)

Geddes describes the sexist climate of draft-resistance organizing. The small group of women were immediately discouraged from carrying out their plan of breaking in and destroying draft files. They were told by male organizers that as women they had insufficient authority and experience to attempt such an action. They were accused of destroying the movement's solidarity by making an issue out of sexual politics in organizing without male leadership. Furthermore, Geddes described the general environment of war organizing as one in which women were actually "hooted down" when they got up to speak at rallies—not a far cry from the experience of early feminist abolitionists (Riegle 2013:99).

Several women and one male accomplice successfully organized and executed the action despite male leaders' hostility. Its creative design and orchestration speaks to the valuable insights offered by a woman's perspective and gendered experience. Some of the women entered the building during the day, hid in closets, and then opened the way for the others after hours. Instead of burning the draft cards, they methodically shredded about six thousand files covering seven or eight Manhattan draft boards, including the South Bronx and parts of Brooklyn where large populations of lower-income individuals and men of color resided. Additionally, the women removed the "1" and the "A" keys from all the typewriters—a secretary's insight—as 1A designated a draft priority. The action was then widely publicized in anticipation of an antiwar rally to be held in Rockefeller Square in front of the office of Dow Chemical and other war-related companies. Several women came to the rally and threw the draft board shreds out over the crowds. They were immediately arrested by federal agents who came looking for them after the shredded files appeared in mimeographed flyers.

The gendered reception of the women's action became most evident in their failed prosecution. The women who were taken into custody were not questioned about *their* involvement. Investigators wanted to find the male minds behind the action. The media also overlooked the women's leadership in the event, and although several of the women had taken public responsibility for the action, none of them were interviewed by journalists who covered the story. The grand jury even tried to coerce those arrested to revealing who had "put them up to it." Eventually, the case was dismissed in its entirety.

Women's Lived Experiences and Approaches to Violence

The legacy of women's contributions to nonviolence showcases a form of resistance that capitalizes on the gendered lives, and thus lived perspectives, of women claims makers. This is not to suggest that there exists some essential difference between women's and men's capacities for resistance, as is a common misconception when women's contributions are written out of nonviolence histories.[12] McAllister's two volumes on women's nonviolent activism (1988, 1991) offer a formidable refutation to the assumption that women do not play leading or formative roles in public protests, rallies, marches, and strikes typically covered in popular histories. She details the significant lifelong contributions of hundreds of individual women activists and women's communities, groups, and organizations doing just that with case after case of strategically savvy, women-led resistance throughout the Americas, Europe, Asia, Africa, Australia, and the Pacific. She notes how women have been deeply engaged in highly public and confrontational forms of nonviolence. Women have thrown themselves before kings and placed their bodies in the paths of cannons and tanks. Where there diverges a unique form of woman-inspired and woman-led protest, however, the gendered resources capitalized on by women resisters become clearer.

Among women-led actions that illustrate how women have profoundly shaped the US nonviolence movement, Women Strike for Peace and the Seneca Peace Encampment are notable. Women Strike for Peace (WSP) was an organization born of a 1961 march of thousands of women (on the nation's capital and around the world) to protest nuclear testing. The organization was founded on the idea that women should make a distinctively gendered statement as mothers—against the threat of nuclear war, and on behalf of their children's health and futures. The signing of the 1963 Nuclear Test Ban Treaty can be greatly attributed to WSP's nationwide marches and lobbying efforts. Among these was the famous Baby Tooth Survey in which women from around the country sent their babies' teeth to be tested for traces of fallout from nuclear testing (the results proved increased levels of radioactive substances). Later, the organization played a significant role in facilitating transnational solidarity with women in Vietnam in protest of the war and in advocacy for reconciliation. WSP remained a powerful voice against US interventions in Latin America in the 1980s and 1990s and continued to lobby against the arms race (Swerdlow 1993).

Just as the earlier international suffrage movement mobilized their authority as "moral mothers" to advocate for everything from the realms of labor rights to the threat of war into an era of women's public rights (see Berkovitch 1999), WSP continued the work of merging ideas of moral motherhood with other social justice issues on the crest of a second-wave feminist movement. The banners they carried express these themes in translation:

> "We can't eat guns. Cut military spending."
> "My son died in vain in Vietnam."
> "Let our children grow."
> "A toy should be a joy. A toy is to grow."
> "Children are not for burning."
> "Dear Mom and Dad, Your silence is killing me."
> "The women of Vietnam are our Sisters."

The infamous WSP banners depicted pictures of mutilated Vietnamese children and simply asked, "What for?" (Swerdlow 1993).

But WSP also challenged the downplayed importance of traditional women's roles in a patriarchal system that assumes such roles cannot be publicly influential or effect widespread social change. As cofounder Dagmar Wilson explained, "I wanted to emphasize that this [the housewife and the mother role] was an important role and it was time we were heard" (quoted in Swerdlow 1993: 55). Wilson's glimpse into political circles left her underwhelmed by the lack of fervency behind the male-led politics-as-usual of the Cold War. "I was not only disturbed by our policies but angered by the gutlessness of the professional men who were part of the social circle to which my husband and I belonged" (quoted in Swerdlow

1993: 56). She organized alongside cofounder Bella Abzug, who went on to serve in the House of Representatives (her 1970 campaign slogan was "Women Belong in the House"!). Later, she became a leader in a number of second-wave organizations and UN initiatives for development and human rights.

Following the model of the women's peace demonstration at Greenham Common, where women set up an encampment outside of a British nuclear testing site, the Seneca Women's Encampment for a Future of Peace and Justice was organized by US women's communities. This summer-long women's action took place at the Seneca Army Depot in upstate New York, from which Cruise and Pershing II missiles were scheduled to be deployed to Europe. The encampment lands were eventually purchased as "women's lands," and an annual demonstration convened. Twelve thousand women from around the world participated in the first Seneca Peace Encampment, and their nonviolent civil disobedience led to 950 arrests (Peace Encampment Herstory Project 2007).[13]

Organizationally and strategically, there was significant overlap between WSP actions and the Seneca Peace Encampment. WSP was among Seneca's organizational supporters, and together they fostered women's solidarity in leading the challenge against nuclear war. They also shared the foundational theme of women's unique position on issues of war and nuclear holocaust. As the 1983 Seneca Peace Mission Statement expressed,

> Women from New York state, from the United States and Canada, from Europe, and, indeed, from all over the world, are committed to nonviolent action to stop the deployment of these weapons. The existence of nuclear weapons is killing us. Their production contaminates our environment, destroys our natural resources, and depletes our human energy and creativity. But the most critical danger they represent is to life itself. Sickness, accidents, genetic damage and death, these are the real products of the nuclear arms race. We say no to the threat of global holocaust, no to the arms race, no to death. We say yes to a world where people, animals, plants and the earth itself are respected and valued. (Peace Encampment Herstory Project 2007)

The Seneca Peace Encampment, however, incorporated a different demographic characteristic of the multiculturalist thrust of third-wave feminism. Where WSP embraced traditional roles of motherhood and domesticity to call for inclusion and respect in political organizing, the Seneca Peace Encampment was situated in a culture of challenging the expectation that women adopt the traditional role of female domesticity and heteronormativity. There was active engagement by lesbian-feminist communities, and the culture of the camp, although often focused on the logistics of confrontations with local antagonists and legal authorities, incorporated an openness to goddess-centered paganism that could be translated into a firm political stance against a patriarchal culture of war making (Krasniewicz 1992).

Discursive and structural differences—the differences between ideas that women and men have and the different resources they have access to—explain the importance of woman-designed actions to the nonviolence repertoire, qualities that may be overlooked when male-centered actions are privileged. First, while women's actions mirror general tactics in targeting specific policy changes, they remain anchored in broader reflections on the deeper ontological foundations of war making and violent conflict as systems of competition and elimination, issues beyond the scope of any one campaign-centered action. Second, women activists design consciousness-raising actions, such as the provocative, deeply symbolic protests of dozens of women wailing at the gates of the missile storage site, tied in a giant "web of life" around the Pentagon, or wrapping thousands of handmade quilts around the Washington Monument. Finally, women's actions frequently weave together nonviolence objectives with overarching goals of social transformation as the above noted Seneca Peace Encampment mission statement so clearly articulates.

Feminist Transformations of Protest, Communication, and Community Dynamics

Second-wave feminism's popular slogan, "The personal is political," also aptly describes one of the invaluable contributions of American women to the nonviolence repertoire.[14] There are two particular dimensions of women-led process transformations that best illustrate women's contribution. The first is found in the functional mechanics of how to protest.

Several feminist nonviolent activists of the early-second-wave era pointed me to the occupation of the Seabrook Nuclear Power Plant as a turning point in feminist-led nonviolent actions. In 1977, over two thousand activists organized under a coalition of environmental groups known as the Clamshell Alliance attempted to block the construction of a nuclear reactor at Seabrook, New Hampshire. One thousand four hundred and fourteen activists were arrested and jailed for two weeks by the National Guard.[15]

Numerous aspects of this action signaled a turning tide in the dynamics of nonviolence organizing. First, although women in the United States had long been skilled trainers for nonviolent actions, many of the Seabrook preparations were led by these experienced women and thus showcased their training expertise. Second, and especially vital to those examining how actions have changed for the better, was the decentralized structure of Seabrook's tactical implementation. The action incorporated a form of small group organizing known as affinity groups. In the context of a direct action, an *affinity group* is defined as "an autonomous group of 5–15 persons . . . a group of people who not only have an affinity for each other, but who know each other's strengths and weaknesses and support each other as they participate . . . in a nonviolent campaign together" (War Resisters International n.d.). Representatives of these groups then convened in "spokescouncils"—groups of representatives for the affinities who met to incorporate decision-making input from each of the hundreds of smaller groups.

Two of my interviewees described how the women who led these trainings effectively innovated the use of affinity groups at Seabrook. The thousands of activists arrested had been trained for months before the action. So disciplined were they that when the governor flew in to negotiate with them in jail, the protestors insisted there were no leaders with whom he could talk without going through the lengthy process of consulting in the spokescouncils. This use of affinity groups dramatically reshaped the dynamics of protest. The organizational structure gave individuals a sense of community, solidarity, and support that made the psychological experience of risk easier. One activist, reflecting on Seabrook-style affinity groups versus other types of mass action, explained how much better it was to have a personal relationship with a small group of fellow activists. Knowing they were going into the action together and that each of them had an equal say in the collective decision of how to act created community and buy-in. She contrasted this with another protest experience in which one male leader walked up and down the sidewalk yelling at them through a bullhorn about what they should be doing. Only one individual directed the group, and there had been no preparatory work to build personal connections among the participants. The development of affinity groups also provided an effective check-and-balance system on the personal or sociological inclinations of certain types of people to dominate the course of an action. This was a substantial revision for high-stakes decisions that had to be made in the moment of protest where the context and the risk can radically change at any time.

Another important contribution handed down from feminist nonviolence innovators addresses nonviolent communication more generally and relationship dynamics among activist communities. Women organizers, from the abolitionists turned suffragists (the inspiration for Seneca Falls), through the civil rights and other related movements, have expressed grievances with the sexist dynamics of the collective organizing process itself. We see this frustration outlined in Casey Hayden and Mary King's (1965) critical memo to civil rights organizers titled "Sex and Caste," Dorothy Cotton's (2012) *If Your Back's Not Bent*, Dolores Huerta's interview on "58 sexist comments" (Makers n.d.)[16] and in the critical feminist reactions to the chauvinist dynamics of antiwar organizing described above. As second-wave feminism revved up, women of various social justice movements were getting fed up with the imbalance of power in those movements. The Movement for a New Society (MNS) was instrumental in developing an innovative way to address these contradictions through nonviolence.

MNS was a decentralized network of mostly urban activist communities. MNS was founded on the objective of developing "pre-figurative politics" through a commitment to nonviolence—an intention to live the new form of an egalitarian society that activists envisioned. Most of the activists heavily involved in the movement lived in collectively owned houses, operated food cooperatives, and shared bills and domestic duties. These practices freed availability for political activism. Sometimes this entailed direct action, but it also included campaign and coalition building and general social justice work. Activists spent an impressive amount of time and energy contemplating and experimenting with egalitarianism in their personal relationships; challenging gender dynamics was principal among these efforts.

MNS began with a community Life Center of houses and activist networks in Philadelphia. The movement grew in part out of a Quaker Action group, incorporating influences from the peace movement, Gandhian theory and practice, critical race theory, feminist theory, anarchist philosophy (in particular syndicalism), the environmental movement, and the personal growth movement (Miller 1980). MNS eventually grew to about thirty US communities at its height. MNS lasted from about 1970 to 1986 and, considering itself a "movement of movements," held trainings for a broad range of other social justice movements. MNS is now considered a midwife to the nonviolent protest routines common today (Cornell 2011).

Some remarkable signposts of MNS's success in democratizing communication and balancing gender politics can be seen in the many workshops on the topic of feminism and nonviolence. One Philadelphia men's collective known as Gentle Strength, for example, held numerous men's workshops in which they contemplated the meaning of feminist demands for men and reflected on their accountability toward those demands. The MNS archives are peppered with discussions of gender dynamics in living and professional arrangements, including "check-ins" on the balance of gender roles in meeting facilitation to serious, documented claims of blatant sexism in organizing actions. The early handouts from these innovations show a directed effort toward mitigating sexist tendencies to dominate communication. One flyer reads,

> More often than not, men are the ones dominating group activity. Such behavior is therefore termed a "masculine behavior pattern," not because women never act that way, but because it is generally men who do. Men are beginning to take responsibility for their behavior. (Movement for a New Society n.d.)

The flyer continues to detail a laundry list of common tendencies, including, but not limited to

> Hogging the show. Talking too much, too long, too loud.
> Problem-solver.
> Restating.
> Condescension and paternalism.
> Seeking attention and support from women while competing with men.
> Running the show.
> Speaking for others. (Movement for a New Society n.d.)

On a broader level, many MNS members deeply questioned the ways feminism should be incorporated into any movement for social change. One 1986 conference titled "Feminism and Nonviolence" mapped out goals, theories, strategies, and tactics of feminism, nonviolence, and a united feminist nonviolence. In conclusion, the participants advocated for a merging of insights that could move forth from the realizations that

> The polarization of the sexes into two different roles, two different psyches, and two different sets of standards is a major cause of oppression.

The forces that oppress women are deeply entrenched in every institution of society and also perpetuated personally by men and women.

Social/political problems need to be analyzed in terms of the significant gender, class, and race (etc.) differences in origin, perpetuation, and solution.

Oppressors interlock. None of the oppressive systems can be destroyed while leaving the others intact. (The Dandelion 1986)

Today, examples of women working for the realization of nonviolence in the process of their activism abound in efforts as diverse as nonviolent mothering (see Frida Berrigan's beautiful book on this topic, *It Runs in the Family* [2015]) to the movement of Roman Catholic Women Priests, to the practice and spread of training in nonviolent communication.

From Self-Sacrifice to Self-Affirmation

Finally, the intertwining of feminism and nonviolence has led to a profound sea change in how activist women embrace nonviolent action as a self-affirming orientation rather than the self-sacrificing nonviolence associated with the legacies of some male martyrs. This change can in part be traced to the second-wave discourse on feminism and nonviolence. In particular, several of the women I interviewed voiced the feeling of running into a wall when confronting what nonviolence could do about the problem of violence against women. In the early 1970s, nonviolence activists were actively engaged with the movement that developed rape crisis centers, "Take Back the Night" marches, and other rape advocacy and awareness campaigns and community support systems for domestic abuse. Six of my respondents told me of the experience they had of attending a training on nonviolent direct action that detailed how they should peacefully respond to targeted violence experienced at a protest; each left wondering how this orientation would help women defend themselves against private experiences of harassment and sexual assault.

This collective questioning ushered in explorations into the applicability of nonviolent resistance for self-defense. Three women trainers told me of trainings that were developed using active, engaged noncooperation against the threat of assault. "The key here is for women to move past the role of victim. Through talking she can sometimes maneuver the attacker's impression of her as a victim. She can refuse to take on that role. She can make him see her as a person" (respondent interview, spring 2014). Another respondent shared a pamphlet of stories of women who resisted assault through primarily nonviolent means. The pamphlet, titled "Whose Hand Is THIS? I Found It on My Ass!! And Other Tales of Resistance!" was distributed at one of the earliest Take Back the Night marches in 1979 (Hayes and Royer 1979). But the caveat given here is that while these techniques can often work, there is the risk they will not. For nonviolent feminists, this possibility left too much room for conceptual slippage on the concept of "self-sacrifice" into an implication that women *should* sacrifice their personal safety and integrity in the name of resisting violence against the other above all else.

In the flagship publication of MNS's then-fledgling New Society Publishers, *Reweaving the Web of Life: Feminism and Nonviolence* (McAllister 1982), Lynne Shivers provides a critical analysis of Gandhi's contradictory views of women. Shivers praises his liberal insights into the oppressiveness of child marriage, enforced widowhood, the dowry system, and sati, but she questions his essentialist notions of how women should protest and his assertion that women are by nature more capable of self-sacrifice than men. When the debate over the value of nonviolence to feminist objectives was sparked, women identified the limits of nonviolence to feminist causes when nonviolence pursued heroic notions of saving oppressed peoples in faraway lands while failing to address the oppressive cultures in which we live that disproportionately affect women.

To redirect the course of nonviolent action, women had to learn to embrace a transformative type of anger.

> This kind of anger is not in itself violent. . . . It contains both respect for oneself and respect for the other. To oneself it says: "I must change—for I have been playing the part of the slave." To the other it says: "You must change—for you have been playing the part of the tyrant." It contains the conviction that change is possible—for both sides; and it is capable of transmitting this conviction to others, touching them with the energy of it—even one's antagonist. . . . It communicates. (Deming 1971: 7)

It is not just embracing anger, though, that feminists have reclaimed as their right to bodily integrity and personhood. Moving through anger to self-affirmation and the possibility—indeed the right—that women can flourish has been embraced as an important goal for the nonviolent feminist movement. This distinctive approach seeks to balance a commitment to social justice with a celebration of personal potential. As Barbara Deming explains, nonviolence means, "No. You are not the other; and no, I am not the other. No one is the other" (quoted in McAllister 1979). In this vein, one of feminism's contributions to the nonviolence repertoire is to give "Some Ground to Stand On" (Warshow 1998), as the activist documentary film on the life of Blue Lunden is appropriately titled, detailing the development of a new platform for nonviolently advocating for gay rights. Specifically, in realizing collective justice, women may include their own security and happiness as valid goals. Nonviolent feminist theorist Barbara Deming and her partner, Jane Verlaine, were among a decentralized network of pioneers in the "women's lands" movement of the 1970s and 1980s. These lands offered communal living arrangements for lesbians and a life that would both affirm and allow them to celebrate their lesbian identities. Likewise, women who remain conscious of nonviolence in their everyday relationships bridge this dimension of self-affirmation and fulfilling a transformational process. As Barbara Deming eloquently stated, "The injunction that we should love our neighbors as ourselves means to us equally that we should love ourselves as our neighbors" (1974: 8).

Feminism and Nonviolence

Over the course of the long twentieth century and the changing shape of feminist movements, continuities and transformations among nonviolent feminists have taken different forms. That women have used their uniquely gendered experiences of oppression to challenge the systematic bases of inequality remains constant. That women use gendered forms of power and resistance is also seen across the time periods considered here. Women's frustration with their exclusion from other social justice movements has shaped their active investment in both the first and second waves of feminism; abolition work fed into the first wave, and anti-Vietnam and civil rights experience into the second wave. Women's nonviolent repertoires also carry strategic lessons and insights of their forebears. Women's Strike for Peace actively rooted their efforts in the ongoing legacy of the first wave of feminism by starting a Jeanette Rankin Brigade to honor the suffragist who became the first woman in Congress, and the only representative to vote against entry into both world wars. Today's active anti-war movement, Codepink, is testament to this effort to incorporate processual and systematic analysis into an expressly gendered public protest against war (Codepink 2014). From the early suffrage movement through a century of feminist organizing, American women have been astute innovators in forging a feminist nonviolence.

I argue that these women nonviolent activists have operated in a gendered territory of resistance. Women live, and thus resist, in a patriarchal world. And women activists have used the power of patriarchy to enhance their resistance—even when it means simply being powerful in ways one is socially expected not to be. These trailblazers contribute to nonviolence as a system though which all can refuse to cooperate with the "othering" and power differentials on which patriarchy rests. This has made women, across a century of feminist activism, incredibly successful organizers, yet the gendered territory of resistance in which they advocate has also shaped their exclusion from popular nonviolent histories.

In some ways, women's uniquely gendered territorial stance means it is much more difficult to make it in the man's world of action histories, where those histories continue to privilege male actors and male ways of entering into actions. The nonviolence movement has perpetuated gender biases through its male-favored writing-up, tactical practices (e.g., programs showcasing "legacy" trainers still privilege men over women despite the long list of possible experienced women trainers), and proclaimed objectives (e.g., toppling dictators and excoriating unfavorable policies over envisioning and building inclusive, favorable alternatives). Our historical rendering of the nonviolence movement and the dynamics of organization within that movement will only effectively overcome gendered biases when we can follow women nonviolence activists in transcending the rigidities of gender (Flinders 2006; Reardon 1996) and when we can expand understanding of how resistance of all forms of othering translates into broad, discursive, complex, self-affirming, and transformative forms of action. The history of women's activism following the legacy of suffrage must acknowledge the great work women have done in developing feminist tactics and strategies and how this work has followed from the broader objectives and experiences of fighting for feminist change.

Notes

1. There were also both violent strands of abolition work—those that would feed into the mobilization for the Civil War, and racist strands of suffrage activism—women who made the claim that if black men could vote, so should white women. Those branches of activity developed as countercurrents later in the lifetime of both movements.

2. The troubling sexist orientations of these influences are outside the scope of this chapter but have been addressed by others (see Harding [1991] on Thoreau and Dworkin [1987] on Tolstoy).

3. Gandhi's legacy as "father" of nonviolence is further complicated by what many historians have critiqued as serious biases in his approach, both in some of his views on and treatment of women as well as in his positions toward class and ethnic distinctions (see, for example, Ambedkar 2014; Desai and Vahed 2015; Shivers 1984).

4. Those periods often organized by feminist historians into significantly distinctive eras of organizing, though to divide feminist organizing into distinctive periods does not come without nuanced attention to continuity and overlap (Bailey 1997).

5. I particularly wish to refer here to Boulding's phenomenal history of women, *The Underside of History: A View of Women Through Time* (1976) and her groundbreaking *Cultures of Peace* (2000), although she has authored many other impressive works.

6. The term *male gaze* originates in a 1975 critical film analysis in which the author posits that artistic narratives too often place the audience in the view or biased experience of heterosexual males (Mulvey 1975). Feminist theorists now often use the term to critically reflect on how the empirical world is analyzed through a male perspective, thus shaping scholarship to favor a male experience.

7. Women who have challenged the male bias in the biological sciences have come to a similar conclusion. They argue that beyond the perfunctory imposition of sexist biases onto the selection and interpretation of scientific data in everything from biological and evolutionary to cultural theories of behavior (Herschberger 1970; Morgan 1972; Reiter 1975; Tavris 1993), male analysts favor a certain epistemology that privileges the abstract formulation of ideas over concrete applications, objectivity over advocacy, and the intellectual over the purposive (Harstock 1983).

8. Nash went on to lead a Freedom Ride bus protest in 1961, signing her last will and testament before getting on board. The previous bus had been firebombed by the Ku Klux Klan (KKK; PBS 2012).

9. Nash's bold leading of the Freedom Rides against the caution of Senator Robert Kennedy (D-NY), to which he famously responded "Who the hell is Diane Nash?" and her willingness to be imprisoned in civil rights protest even while pregnant, to which the judge responded by suspending her sentence purportedly to avoid negative publicity, also speak to the power of her resources as a woman confidently protesting in a man's world.

10. This mirrors findings in the study of how perceived physical attraction shapes preferential treatment in the workplace (see Wong and Penner 2016). Furthermore, as the

documentary *A Force More Powerful* reveals about the Nashville lunch-counter-strike preparations, the activists were quite strategic in using physical appearances for legitimacy in their protests. Activist meetings and interviews in this documentary reveal that activists planned to dress like "they were going to Sunday school" to appear as respectable as possible and that they also strategically avoided coupling men and women of opposite races so as to avoid the appearance of miscegenation, or interracial coupling, that one trainer noted was a "fight they didn't want to fight right now" (York 2000).

11. The foundational role played by all women of the movement has only recently begun to be detailed in a literature specially focused on women in the civil rights movement (Collier-Thomas and Franklin 2001; Crawford, Rouse, and Woods 1993; Ling and Montieff 2004; Olson 2001; Buss 2009; Robnett 1997). For example, Mary King (1995) highlights the great efforts of organizers like Ruby Doris Smith-Robinson, Diane Nash, Anne Braden, Dorothy Cotton, Gloria Richardson, Gloria Joyce Ladner, Jean Wheller Smith-Young, Judy Richardson, L. C. Dorsey, Euvester Simpson, Doris Derby, Helen O'Neal, June Johnson, and Connie Curry, among other prominent women of the movement (see also King's memoir *Freedom Song*, 1988).

12. Pam McAllister begins her women's nonviolent "herstory" corrective by recounting her invitation to guest lecture a class on nonviolence and, upon the male professor's request, inform the students if women "had ever contributed anything to the history of nonviolence" (1988: 9–13).

13. Eventually, the Seneca Army Depot announced the closing of its storage site and repurposed the land for non-army state usage.

14. I do not present this as an essentialist claim about gendered protest but a social trend. Gandhi and King each had their version of "living the talk": Gandhi's "constructive pro-gramme" (Metta Center n.d.) and King's "beloved community" (King Center 2014).

15. Unit 1 of the nuclear reactor was completed in 1986 and went into full operation in 1990. The second unit was never completed, reportedly due to insufficient funds.

16. It should be noted here that Huerta is often incorrectly historically construed as a sidekick to Cesar Chavez. Huerta was a strategically invaluable leader in the movement, having encouraged Cesar to boycott grapes over potatoes, the move that historically made the United Farm Workers a movement success, having coined the now universal-protest chant "Sí Se Puede," and having directly mobilized the UFW's field crew for many years.

References

Alonso, Harriet Hyman. 1993. *Peace as a Women's Issue: A History of the U.S. Movement for World Peace and Women's Rights*. Syracuse, NY: Syracuse University Press.

Ambedkar, B. R. 2014. *Annihilation of Caste: The Annotated Critical Edition*. London: Verso.

Bacon, Margaret Hope. 1980. *Valiant Friend: The Life of Lucretia Mott*. New York: Walker and Company.

———. 1992. *One Woman's Passion for Peace and Freedom: The Life of Mildred Olmsted*. Syracuse, NY: Syracuse University Press.

———. 2000. *Abby Hopper Gibbons: Prison Reformer and Social Activist*. New York: SUNY Press.

———. 2005. "Nonviolence and Women." Pp. 129–135 in *Nonviolence in Theory and Practice*, edited by R. L. Holmes and B. L. Gan. Long Grove, IL: Waveland Press.

Bailey, Cathryn. 1997. "Making Waves and Drawing Lines: The Politics of Defining the Vicissitudes of Feminism." *Hypatia* 12(3): 17–28.

Berkovitch, Nitza. 1999. *From Motherhood to Citizenship: Women's Rights and International Organizations*. Baltimore: The Johns Hopkins University Press.

Berrigan, Frida. 2015. *It Runs in the Family: On Being Raised by Radicals and Growing into Rebellious Motherhood*. New York: OR Books.

Boulding, Elise. 1976. *The Underside of History: A View of Women through Time*. Boulder, CO: Westview Press.

———. 2000. *Cultures of Peace: The Hidden Side of History*. Syracuse, NY: Syracuse University Press.

Buss, Fran Leeper, ed. 2009. *Moisture of the Earth: Mary Robinson, Civil Rights and Textile Union Activist*. Ann Arbor: University of Michigan Press.

Ceplair, Larry, ed. 1989. *The Public Years of Sarah and Angelina Grimké: Selected Writings, 1835–1839*. New York: Columbia University Press.

Cockburn, Cynthia. 2012. *Anti-Militarism: Political and Gender Dynamics of Peace Movements*. New York: Palgrave Macmillan.

Codepink. 2014. "About Codepink." http://www.codepink.org/about.

Collier-Thomas, Bettye, and V. P. Franklin, eds. 2001. *Sisters in the Struggle: African American Women in the Civil Rights–Black Power Movement*. New York: New York University Press.

Confortini, Catia. 2012. *Intelligent Compassion: Feminist Critical Methodology in the Women's International League for Peace and Freedom*. Oxford: Oxford University Press.

Cornell. Andrew. 2011. *Oppose and Propose: Lessons from Movement for a New Society*. Oakland, CA: AK Press.

Cotton, Dorothy F. 2012. *If Your Back's Not Bent*. New York: Atria Books.

Crawford, Vicki L., Jacqueline Anne Rouse, and Barbara Woods. 1993. *Women in the Civil Rights Movement: Trailblazers and Torchbearers, 1941–1965*. Bloomington: Indiana University Press.

The Dandelion. 1986. "Feminism and Nonviolence." Movement for a New Society Records, 1971–1988. Swarthmore College Peace Collection DG 154.

Deming, Barbara. 1971. "On Anger—A Talk by Barbara Deming." *Liberation,* November.

———. 1974. *We Cannot Live without Our Lives*. New York: Grossman.

Desai, Ashwin, and Goolem Vahed. 2015. *The South African Gandhi: Stretcher-Bearer of Empire (South Asia in Motion)*. Stanford, CA: Stanford University Press.

Dworkin, Andrea. 1987. *Intercourse*. New York: Perseus Books.

Faulkner, Carol. 2011. *Lucretia Mott's Heresy: Abolition and Women's Rights in Nineteenth-Century America*. Philadelphia: University of Pennsylvania Press.

Feminism and Non-Violence Study Group. 1983. *Piecing It Together: Feminism and Nonviolence*. London: Author.

Flinders, Carol. 2006. "Nonviolence: Does Gender Matter?" *Peace Power*, Summer: 20–21.

Foster, Catherine. 1989. *Women for All Seasons: The Story of the Women's International League for Peace and Freedom*. Athens: University of Georgia Press.

Gregg, Richard B. 1935. *The Power of Non-Violence*. Hartford, ME: Greenleaf Books.

Griffin-Nolan, Ed. 1991. *Witness for Peace: A Story of Resistance*. Louisville, KY: Westminster/John Knox Press.

Harding, Walter. 1991. "Thoreau's Sexuality." *Journal of Homosexuality* 21(3): 23–46.

Harris, Adrienne, and Ynestra King. 1989. *Rocking the Ship of State: Toward a Feminist Peace Policy*. Boulder, CO: Westview Press.

Hartstock, Nancy C. M. 1983. "The Feminist Standpoint: Developing the Ground for a Specifically Feminist Historical Materialism." Pp. 283–310 in *Discovering Reality: Feminist Perspectives on Epistemology, Metaphysics, Methodology, and Philosophy of Science*, edited by S. Harding and M. B. Hintikka. Dordrecht, Holland: D. Reidel.

Hayden, Casey, and Mary King. 1965. "Sex and Caste." *Liberation*, April: 35–36.

Hayes, Mary Brigid, and Judith M. Royer. 1979. "Whose Hand Is THIS? I Found It on My Ass!! and Other Tales of Resistance!" Unpublished manuscript.

Herschberger, Ruth. 1970. *Adam's Rib*. New York: Harper and Row.

Hill, Julia. 2001. *The Legacy of Luna: The Story of a Tree, a Woman and the Struggle to Save the Redwoods*. New York: HarperOne.

Kaplan, Temma. 2002. "Uncommon Women and the Common Good: Women and Environmental Protest." Pp. 28–45 in *Women Resist Globalization: Mobilizing for Livelihood and Rights,* edited by S. Rowbotham and S. Linkogle. New York: Zed Books.

King Center. 2014. "The King Philosophy." http://www.thekingcenter.org/king-philosophy.

King, Mary. 1988. *Freedom Song: A Personal Story of the 1960s Civil Rights Movement*. New York: Morrow.

———. 1995. "Women and Civil Rights—A Personal Reflection." Presented at the 12th Annual Fannie Lou Hamer Lecture Series for the Department of Political Science at Jackson State University, October 5, Jackson, Mississippi.

Krasniewicz, Louise. 1992. *Nuclear Summer: The Clash of Communities at the Seneca Women's Peace Encampment*. Ithaca, NY: Cornell University Press.

Lengermann, Patricia Madoo, and Jill Niebrugge-Brantley. 1998. *The Women Founders: Sociology and Social Theory, 1830–1930*. Boston: McGraw Hill.

Ling, Peter J., and Sharon Monteith. 2004. *Gender and the Civil Rights Movement*. Piscataway, NJ: Rutgers University Press.

Lynd, Staughton, and Alice Lynd. 1995. *Nonviolence in America: A Documentary History*. Maryknoll, NY: Orbis Books.

Makers. n.d. "Dolores Huerta: 58 Sexist Comments in the United Farm Workers Movement." Makers: The Largest Video Collection of Women's Stories. http://makers.com/dolores-huerta/.

McAllister, Pam. 1979. "Contradictions between Feminist Anger and Nonviolent Practice." *WIN*, April 26: 18–20.

———. 1982. *Reweaving the Web of Life: Feminism and Nonviolence*. Philadelphia: New Society Publishers.

———. 1988. *You Can't Kill the Spirit: Stories of Women and Nonviolent Action*. Philadelphia: New Society Publishers.

———. 1991. *This River of Courage: Generations of Women's Resistance and Action*. Philadelphia: New Society Publishers.

Metta Center for Nonviolence. n.d. "Constructive Program." Petaluma, CA: Metta Center for Nonviolence. http://mettacenter.org/definitions/constructive-programs/.

Miller, Demi. 1980. "Roots of MNS." P. 7 in *"No Nukes" to a People's Energy Movement: A Strategy for the 1980s*. Philadelphia: Movement for a New Society.

Morgan, Elaine. 1972. *The Descent of Woman: The Classic Study of Evolution.* London: Souvenir Press.

Movement for a New Society. n.d. "Working for a Change." Movement for a New Society Records, Swarthmore College Peace Collection DG 154.

Mulvey, Laura. 1975. "Visual Pleasure and Narrative Cinema." *Screen. Oxford Journals* 16(3): 6–18.

Nepstad, Sharon Erickson. 2004. *Convictions of the Soul: Religion, Culture, and Agency in the Central America Solidarity Movement.* New York: Oxford University Press.

Offen, Karen. n.d. "Gandhi, the English Suffragists, and Non-Violent Direct Action." San Francisco, CA: International Museum of Women. http://www.imow.org/community/blog/viewentry?id=34.

Oldfield, Sybil. 1989. *Women Against the Iron Fist: Alternatives to Militarism 1900–1989.* Oxford: Basil Blackwell.

Olson, Lynne. 2001. *Freedom's Daughters: The Unsung Heroes of the Civil Rights Movement from 1830 to 1970.* New York: Scribner.

PBS. 2012. "Diane Nash and the Sit-ins." Online interview. https://mass.pbslearningmedia.org/resource/imlo4.soc.ush.civil.nash/diane-nash-and-the-sit-ins/#.WbleTYWcHmI.

Peace Encampment Herstory Project: A Digital Archive of Oral Herstories, Photographs, Videos, Songs, and Articles from the Women's Encampment for a Future of Peace and Justice, 1983–2006, Seneca County, New York, USA. 2007. http://peacecampherstory.blogspot.com/.

Reardon, Betty. 1996. *Sexism and the War System.* New York: Syracuse University Press.

Reiter, Rayna R. 1975. *Toward an Anthropology of Women.* New York: Monthly Review Press.

Riegle, Rosalie G. 2013. *Crossing the Line: Nonviolent Resisters Speak Out for Peace.* Eugene, OR: Cascade Books.

Robnett, Belinda. 1997. *How Long? How Long? African-American Women in the Struggle for Civil Rights.* New York: Oxford University Press.

Rowbotham, Sheila. 2002. "Facets of Emancipation: Women in Movement from the 18th Century to the Present." Pp. 13–27 in *Women Resist Globalization: Mobilizing for Livelihood and Rights,* edited by S. Rowbotham and S. Linkogle. New York: Zed Books.

Smith, Christian. 1996. *Resisting Reagan: The U.S. Central America Peace Movement.* Chicago: University of Chicago Press.

Spivak, Gayatri Chakravorty. 1987. *In Other Worlds: Essays in Cultural Politics.* New York: Methuen.

Sterling, Dorothy. 1991. *Ahead of Her Time: Abby Kelley and the Politics of Anti-Slavery.* New York: W. W. Norton.

Swerdlow, Amy. 1993. *Women Strike for Peace: Traditional Motherhood and Radical Politics in the 1960s.* Chicago: University of Chicago Press.

Tavris, Carol. 1993. *The Mismeasure of Woman.* New York: Touchstone.

Thoreau, Henry David. 1849. *Civil Disobedience.* Blacksburg: Virginia Tech.

Tolstoy, Leo. 1899. *The Kingdom of God Is within You. What Is Art? What Is Religion?* New York: T. Y. Crowell.

Wade, Lisa, and Myra Marx Feree. 2015. *Gender: Ideas, Interactions, Institutions.* New York: W. W. Norton.

War Resisters International. n.d. "Affinity Groups." http://wri-irg.org/de/node/5164.

War Resisters League. 1989. *Handbook for Nonviolent Action*. New York: War Resisters League.

War Resisters League. 2003. *Handbook for Nonviolent Action*. New York: War Resisters League.

Warshow, Joyce. 1998. *Some Ground to Stand On*. New York: Women Make Movies.

Wong, Jaclyn S., and Andrew Penner. 2016. "Gender and the Returns to Attractiveness." *Research in Social Stratification and Mobility* 44: 113–123.

York, Steven. 2000. *A Force More Powerful*. York Zimmerman, Santa Monica Pictures, and WETA.

13

Women in White Supremacist Movements in the Century after Women's Suffrage

Kathleen Blee

The passage of the Nineteenth Amendment coincided with a decided shift in the connection of white women to white supremacist politics in the United States. Until the early twentieth century, white womanhood was a symbolic foundation of racist politics since white men justified their defense of white privilege as necessary to protect white women from the sexual predations of nonwhite men (Blee 1991; McVeigh 2009). Yet women rarely participated directly in presuffrage racist movements. After women's enfranchisement, the symbolic importance of white womanhood to racist politics continued in varied ways, but white women were included as full members in most movements of white supremacism.

White women did not become participants in white supremacist movements in the early twentieth century simply by virtue of possessing the right to vote, although enfranchised white women were attractive recruits for those racist movements that contested for electoral office. Rather, the sociohistorical factors that ushered in women's suffrage—such as women's increased place in civic activism and paid employment—also opened the door to women's full engagement in the politics of white supremacism. So did changes in white supremacist organizations, especially decisions by racist leaders about the place of women in their movements. To understand the role of women in white supremacist politics, therefore, it is necessary to look broadly at the social contexts in which these movements operate, as well as to look narrowly at the inner workings of racist groups. The broader context of gender includes women's political and economic status in a particular era. The relevant aspects of the inner workings of racist groups are how they recruit and incorporate women. Both affect historical shifts in whether and how women participate in organized white supremacism. This chapter explores the changing role of women in white supremacist politics in the century since women's suffrage by focusing on four eras: the decades immediately prior to the Nineteenth Amendment, the postsuffrage 1920s, the mid-twentieth-century, and the 1970s to today.

Decades Immediately Prior to the Nineteenth Amendment

The women's suffrage amendment did not mark the beginning of white women's efforts to uphold white supremacism. For decades before, white women had supported the racial disparities embedded into the nation's economic and political life in a variety of ways. In the antebellum South, white women played a substantial role in maintaining the system of slavery by managing slave labor in plantation households (Fox-Genovese 1998), and white women's centrality in the system of slavery became even more pronounced during the Civil War. As southern plantation owners were called into military service, their wives were left to oversee the slaves. As Drew Faust (1996: 54) notes, white women "necessarily served as a pillar of the South's political order." In the postbellum era, white women participated in the mobs that inflicted violence and terror against African Americans, including those that lynched thousands in the late nineteenth and early twentieth centuries (Blee 2005; Clarke 1998; Dunn 2013). Women also participated in collective rightist movements that did not have explicit racist agendas, particularly those that opposed extending suffrage to women. Like their male colleagues, antisuffragist women argued that women could exert political influence only if they remained separate from the corruption and unruliness that characterized the country's elections and political parties (Marshall 1997).

The symbolic deployment of white women as a symbol of imperiled white privilege was evident across the landscape of racial conflict and violence in the centuries before women's suffrage. The logic linked sexuality to the fraught issues of race and gender: increased racial equity would empower nonwhite men to violate the sexual purity of white women while also disturbing the unfettered control that white men had historically exercised over white women (Durham 2007). Even before the establishment of the republic, white settlers justified their violent attacks and legal assaults on Native Americans as necessary defensive measures that were occasioned by the imminent threat that Native American men would sexually enslave white women (Nagel 2010). Anti-alien and nativist movements such as the Know Nothings of the mid-nineteenth century similarly claimed to be supporting pure white womanhood; for them, the threat was posed by immigrants, Catholic priests, and foreign influences (Bennett 1975). The many incidents of racial violence in the nineteenth and twentieth centuries, organized or spontaneous, also were commonly prompted by rumors among whites about African American men's sexual predations or attraction to white women.

The motif of terrorized white women became a foundation of the first Ku Klux Klan, which was organized immediately after the Civil War as a loose network of white men determined to inflict terror against former slaves and their northern allies who threatened the monopoly of white male power in the former Confederacy. This Klan mobilized white men to enact violence across the rural South by insisting that white southern women living on geographically isolated plantations were subject to sexual attack by formerly enslaved black men and needed the protection of the Klan.

The Postsuffrage 1920s

Although white women had been implicated in racial extremism and violence long before the advent of women's suffrage, the Nineteenth Amendment was a turning point in women's relationship to white supremacism. In the century that followed, women not only were symbols or ancillary participants in white supremacist movements and actions but were openly welcomed and recruited as active participants in significant movements of collective racism. The incorporation of white women in racial extremism was not uniform. In some movements, women were relegated to minor helping roles or recruited into auxiliary roles that were clearly subordinate to male members and leaders. But after 1920, there was a decided shift in women's position in racial extremism, from symbols of white endangerment used to mobilize white men to active participants.

The Nineteenth Amendment did not initiate women's involvement in racist politics, but it reshaped how many movements of racial extremism considered women's place in their efforts to exert influence, create racial terror, and safeguard white supremacism. Having the vote to a large degree legitimated women's place in the public world of power and politics for racist ends, although whether, how, and how extensively women were incorporated into racial extremism depended on the structure and ideology of episodes of white supremacism as well as the broader environments in which these episodes occurred. These factors are evident in one of the largest episodes of organized participation of women in racist politics in US history, the 1920s Ku Klux Klan.

The second wave of the Ku Klux Klan was formed in the 1910s and grew explosively into the early 1920s, enlisting approximately 3 million to 5 million white Protestant native-born members, including at least a half-million women. Although the first Klan operated only in the South, its second incarnation spread throughout much of the country. It took root in urban areas as well as small towns and the countryside and established a presence across the North from the East to the West Coast. The first Klan primarily targeted African Americans and their allies, but the second Klan trafficked in hatred of Catholics, immigrants, and Jews along with all nonwhites (MacLean 1995).

Many factors explain the astounding growth of the second Klan, especially the fear that the political and economic privileges of race, native birth, and religion were being eroded by changing social and moral codes, the large numbers of Catholic immigrants arriving from southern and eastern Europe, and the vast migration of African Americans from the rural South to the urban North (Chalmers 1987; McVeigh 2009). Yet such factors largely explain the participation of white, native-born, and Protestant men who had an established place in the economy and political life of the United States.

To explain the massive influx of women into the 1920s Klan requires attention to other factors, particularly the changing possibilities for women in public life posed and represented by women's suffrage. The enfranchisement of women opened the door for women's involvement in politics of all sorts, from progressive to the Klan—as voters, party activists, and elected officials. It also signaled broader shifts in US society that were important in bringing women into the Klan. By the 1920s the idea that women could be active in public life had become widely acceptable. So had the notion that women could take public action (by voting or joining political groups) without the permission or accompaniment of their husband or fathers. These social changes, together with decades of struggle, made women's suffrage possible. They also paved the way for white, Protestant, native-born women to join the Klan.

Women's enfranchisement proceeded unevenly across the country and across levels of government. If women's electoral support of progressive causes, women's rights, and social reform politics after enfranchisement was disappointingly thin for suffrage advocates (Chafe 1972; Cott 1987; Ware 1981; but see McCammon 2012), the number of women who joined the second Ku Klux Klan was nothing less than staggering. As only white, native-born Protestants were allowed to be in the Klan, a half-million women from a population in which immigrants constituted a substantial fraction represented an astonishing percentage of those eligible.

Women's participation in the Klan seems an odd outcome of the woman suffrage movement, which, at its beginning, adamantly supported broad principles of both racial and gender equity. Indeed, issues of racial justice were paramount at the birth of woman suffrage politics, which emerged from the effort to abolish racial slavery in the United States. Support for gender equity was also a hallmark of women's suffragism from the first. For example, the legendary 1848 convention in Seneca Falls, New York, organized by Elizabeth Cady Stanton and other pioneers of women's rights affirmed, "We hold these truths to be self-evident: that all men and women are created equal" (Cohen 1996: 713; DuBois 1978).

By the late 1860s, the link between equality and suffrage had begun to fracture. In place of equality, ideas of gender difference appeared in the discourse of suffragists who argued that women needed the vote because they would exercise it differently, and perhaps better, than their male counterparts (McCammon, Hewitt, and Smith 2004). Such discourse opened the door for other ideas of social difference, and soon some suffragists were espousing support for the citizenship rights of only those women who were white, while opposing comparable rights for other women (Blee 1991).

The idea of a racially distinct enfranchisement for women gained traction with the ratification of two amendments to the US Constitution, the Fourteenth Amendment in 1855, which removed racial restrictions on citizenship and equal protection, and the Fifteenth Amendment in 1870, which gave all men the right to vote (Cohen 1996). From that point forward, one faction of the woman suffrage movement adopted an explicitly racist position. Stanton declared the Fourteenth Amendment a "desecration" that "elevated the 'lowest orders of manhood' over the 'highest classes' of women" and, in an 1871 speech, professed her opinion that woman suffrage was required to "outweigh the incoming tide of poverty, ignorance, and vice that threatens our very existence as a nation," a statement that Philip Cohen notes (1996: 714–715) assumes that both women and the nation are white. Those associated with Stanton and this faction favored restrictions on suffrage for African American men, some even arguing that women's votes were needed to ensure the supremacy of the white race (Giddings 1984; also see Montoya's chapter in this volume).

This racist edge of the woman suffrage movement paved the way for women to enter the second Ku Klux Klan. When it began, the second Klan, like its Reconstruction-era predecessor, was a firmly masculinist organization, admitting only men whose manhood it found unquestionable. It proclaimed itself a crusade to ensure the supremacy of those who were "100% American," that is, native-born, Protestant, white, and male. But by the early 1920s, the Klan's ideological commitment to gender-exclusivity gave way to more pragmatic politics as the Klan realized that it could benefit from women's suffrage (McVeigh 2009). One reason that newly enfranchised women were attractive to the Klan was as a source of cash. The second Klan was not only a political movement but also a moneymaking scheme. Its initial promoters introduced modern advertising techniques and a system of pyramid financing to build an organization from which they could profit handsomely. Indeed, as the Klan swelled, money poured in from the dues of members and sales of Klan robes and hoods. By including women, Klan promoters and officials could add to their coffers significantly (Blee 1991).

Another reason the Klan wanted women was for their votes. Unlike the first Klan or subsequent eras of the Klan, the 1920s Klan aspired to win state and local office and even influence presidential elections. Throughout its decade of activity, it actively vetted candidates to find those who would support its agenda of white supremacism, urged members to run for office without openly revealing their Klan affiliations, and distributed approved lists of candidates to its members and supporters. Women in the Klan could add to the votes for Klan candidates and those who supported its agenda of white supremacy.

The practical considerations of money and votes shifted the Klan's public position on issues of gender. Rather than insisting that politics needed "real men" and a fraternity of white manhood, male Klan leaders began to make tentative comments in favor of empowering (white) women, including by granting women's suffrage. As one Klansman stated, "Woman has now come into her own through the 19th Amendment" (McVeigh 2009: 109). Klan newspapers occasionally heralded campaigns for women to serve in Congress and in the legislative body of the Presbyterian Church, positively covered women's rights efforts, and applauded women who took out legal documents in their birth surname rather than married surname (Blee 1991). Yet the male Klan's verbal endorsement of some aspects of women's rights did not extend into the contentious area of women's economic advance. They consistently regarded women as a threat to men in the labor force and urged women to leave paid work and return to their proper place in the home and family and the pursuit of charity work (McVeigh 2009).

To preserve the klannish masculinity that was so central to its identity while benefitting from women's votes and dues, the Klan decided to create distinct organizations for women. This would allow white women to be active on behalf of white supremacism but without "sacrifice of that womanly dignity and modesty we all admire" (Blee 1991: 31). The women's Klans it created were designed to be both separate and subordinate. Under names like Kamelia and Women of the Ku Klux Klan (WKKK), these female Klans operated with the same strict hierarchy of national organizations and local affiliates that characterized the men's Klan. The secrecy and paucity of surviving organizational records from the 1920s Klan make it impossible to determine the number of women's Klan chapters or members with any precision. However, the WKKK claimed 125,000 women members in June 1923, doubling to 250,000 in four months. Within a year, Klan periodicals were reporting news from women's Klans in twenty-two states in all regions of the country, and national women's klonvokations (conventions) attracted as many as 1,600 delegates. In the single state of Indiana, in which the Klan was quite sizeable and records more available, an estimated 250,000 women joined a women's Klan, constituting 32% of the eligible population of white, native-born Protestant women in the state.

In their structure and ritual, women's Klans hewed carefully to the models of the male Klans. They had similar militaristic hierarchies of officers with titles such as klaliff (vice president), klokard (lecturer), and kludd (chaplain). Like their male comrades, Klanswomen enacted elaborate sets of rituals that ranged from naturalization klonklaves (gatherings that initiated new members) to cross-burnings. They also embraced the male Klan's ideology and agenda in most respects. The women's Klans avidly supported restrictions on immigration and parochial school and fought to preserve racial segregation, antimiscegenation laws, and the privileges of whites and Protestants.

Despite the efforts of the male Klan to keep Klanswomen under their leadership, the WKKK and similar groups quickly carved a more independent path. Instead of the male Klan recruiting women to serve its political and monetary goals, Klanswomen began to join women's Klans to pursue their own agendas. In so doing, they resisted Klansmen's approach to some political issues even when they agreed on the ultimate goals. For example, Klansmen extolled women's life as mother and homemaker as central to the nation's greatness while the WKKK dissented, describing the home as the place of women's "monotonous and grinding toil and sacrifice" (Blee 1991: 51). More significantly, while Klansmen supported women's political and legal rights for instrumental reasons, to increase the strength of the movement for white supremacy, Klanswomen insisted that these were just the foundation for the more comprehensive equality between white men and women that could be achieved in a white Protestant nation. Other points of contention between male and female Klans were organizational autonomy and money. Women's Klans routinely argued that they were not under the control of the male Klan, and their leaders chafed when pressed into service cooking or serving food at Klan rallies. In a number of locations, women's and men's Klans battled over their shares of dues and sales, taking their claims into court and even into physical fighting on the street.

Why did 1920s Klan women have greater autonomy of action than women in the later racist movements discussed below? One reason is that the 1920s women's Klan built on the foundation of existing movements in which women had been key activists, especially woman suffrage and the anti-alcohol temperance movements. These movements gave women skills and confidence in independent political action. They also created political networks that women who entered the Klan could mobilize to find recruits and supporters. Not surprisingly, therefore, women earlier affiliated with the racist and nativist edges of women's suffragism became some of the spokeswomen and leaders of the 1920s women's Klan. They knew how to organize a political campaign. They had experience traveling, speaking in public, and asserting themselves as political agents and decision-makers. And they believed that America was intended to be a white nation.

A prominent example of the route from suffragism to the Klan was Daisy Barr, a Quaker preacher from Indiana who first entered politics through the temperance movement and became active in efforts to combat vice and corruption and secure for women the right to vote. Barr was attracted to the Klan as a means to protect white, native-born, Protestant women from the abuse she thought they suffered as a result of the alcohol industry and sexual depravations of Catholic, Jewish, African American, and immigrant men. She also may have seen the Klan as a route to political influence. Barr quickly rose to prominence in the women's Klan, attracting large audiences across the East and Midwest and securing an invitation to address the national meeting of male Klan leaders in 1923. A less prominent example of a woman who moved from suffragism to the Klan was Lillian Rouse, a well-educated writer in Indiana who published in socialist and progressive journals. Rouse saw her support of women's suffrage and the Klan as fully compatible ways to be an active citizen, recalling the women's Klan as essentially "a club stressing good government" (Blee 1991: 117). The Klan's success in recruiting women in the 1920s came about in part because it followed the massive movement for woman suffrage.

A second reason for the size and relative autonomy of women's participation in the second Klan is that the messages of justice and reform that were circulated by and in the woman suffrage movement (McCammon, Hewitt, and Smith 2004) laid a foundation for the Klan's efforts to mobilize women in the years after the passage of the Nineteenth Amendment. By insisting both that women, like men, were citizens with political rights and that women, differently from men, possess attributes and insights that are particularly needed to promote social reforms, the movement for woman suffrage (as well as temperance) provided a rationale for including women in a crusade for white supremacy that had earlier been understood as exclusively masculine.

Finally, the large influx and measure of independence of Klanswomen in the 1920s, compared to later Klans, may reflect its separate organization of women and men. Although the male Klan adopted this strategy to signify that women's Klans were auxiliary to the men's Klan, it allowed women to design their own tactics and direction. Some of these were complementary to the male Klan, as, for example, Klanswomen's use of organized gossip to destroy the livelihoods and reputations of Catholics, Jews, and African Americans who were targeted for other forms of attack and abuse by Klansmen. But Klanswomen also moved in different ways than did their male counterparts. They invited electoral candidates opposed by the male Klan to speak to their conventions, railed against white Protestant men who did not support women's rights, and insisted that women should work no longer than an eight-hour day (Blee 1991).

The second Klan collapsed precipitously in the late 1920s as the result of internal conflict, sensationalized sexual and financial scandals that engulfed its major leaders, and the Klan-aided imposition of a federal immigration quota system that removed one of its major issues. In the movements of racial extremism that followed, women played a very different role.

Mid-Twentieth-Century

The effects of women's enfranchisement were more muted in the movements of racial extremism that followed the second Klan, as these generally did not have electoral aspirations for which women might provide candidates or votes. To the contrary, most racist movements after 1930 deliberately avoided electoral politics. They regarded the US government, especially at the federal level, as inalterably controlled by enemies of the white race, such as Jews and African Americans on whose behalf the government implemented laws and policies of racial integration, affirmative action, lax immigration, and social welfare to support peoples of color.

Women's involvement in racial extremism after the 1920s Klan also seemed to have no direct link to women's rights politics or other mainstream social movements. The genealogy of women's activism in the second Klan is clear: the woman suffrage movement built on abolitionism, and the 1920s women's Klans built on suffrage and temperance movements. But no similar genealogy has been documented for women's racist activism after 1930. One reason may be that mid-century racist movements were much more politically marginal than was the 1920s Klan. The Klan, Nazi, and fascist movements that attracted women in this period operated at the edge of the law and were dismissed as irrelevant or dangerous by most whites. There was less opportunity for activists to move between racial extremism and more mainstream movements, as Klanswomen had done in the 1920s. There is also no indication that mid-century racial extremism had the substantial abeyance structures of social ties and informal networks among women (Taylor 1995) that allow female activism to linger between peak periods of mobilization and remerge later and that ideas, tactics, and even identities were passed on from one generation of activists to the next (Evans 1979; Whittier 1995).

Women were significantly involved in two major racist movements in the mid-twentieth century, the anti-Semitic and pro-fascist movements before and during World War II and the white supremacist groups that fought against racial desegregation and protection of African American voting rights in the 1960s and 1970s. Beyond explicitly racist movements, women were highly involved in the antifeminism and antiradicalism of the first Red Scare of the late 1920s, which, among other agendas, worked to combat social reforms that extended rights to women and children (Nielsen 2001).

ANTI-SEMITIC AND PRO-FASCIST MOVEMENTS

A major mid-century racist women's movement was the mothers' movements and their organizational affiliates. One example is the America First movement, which emerged in the late 1930s as a "vast network of right-wing mothers' groups opposed to American involvement in World War II" (McEnaney 1994: 47). This female antiwar movement was decidedly isolationist, drawing in millions of mostly white and middle-class women opposed to sending their sons into war. Unlike feminist peace groups from World War I, the peace campaign of America First was linked to deeply conservative beliefs. Its fifty to one hundred mothers' anti-interventionist groups defended the traditional family and gender roles and a strong military defense as essentially American. Their racist edge came in the embrace of the politics of anti-Semitism. Chapters and spokespersons cited Jewish international bankers as the force behind internationalist foreign policies and global wars, promoted persecution of Jews in the United States, and allied with the Reverend Gerald L. K. Smith, the far-right evangelical preacher and politician (Jeansonne 1996; McEnaney 1994; Ribuffo 1983). Some openly supported Hitler and German Nazism.

A related effort was the National Legion of Mothers of America (NLMA). Founded in 1939, NLMA began as an anticommunist but not anti-Semitic movement that was open to women of all races and faiths. If its first agenda was to organize women against war, over time and with leadership changes, anti-Semitic attitudes came to the surface. Some members and chapters declared that Jews were responsible not only for internationalism and war but also for moral decline. Others, including some that split from the NLMA over its views on race, denounced US Jews as not American and urged that Jewish refugees be deported (Jeansonne 1996).

Perhaps the most prominent early leader of the right-wing mothers' movement was Elizabeth Dilling, a fervent anticommunist lecturer and author whose 1934 pamphlet *The Red Network: A Who's Who and Handbook of Radicalism for Patriots* identified 460 organizations that were subversive and more than 1,300 individuals whom she regarded as "red." She attacked President Franklin D. Roosevelt for his supposed alliance with Reds and denounced the New Deal policies as Roosevelt's "Jew Deal" (Benowitz 2002; Jeansonne 1996). Another major figure, Agnes Waters, an incendiary speaker for gatherings of mothers' groups, was even more outspoken in her anti-Semitism. She argued that mainline Christianity was against Hitler because it was controlled by Jews and blacks and embraced the well-known anti-Semitic tract *The Protocols of the Elders of Zion* as fact.

Women also had a place in the related pro-fascist and Nazi movements that emerged in the United States during World War II, such as the German American Bund, which tried to merge Nazism with Americanism. Since the Bund presented itself as an organization of families, women and children were brought into the movement along with their husbands and fathers. Strongly patriarchal, the Bund restricted women from most leadership roles. Although their primary occupation was regarded as taking care of home and family, Bund women, some from the

mothers' movement, took part in boycotts of Jewish merchants and rallies in support of Nazi Germany (Diamond 1974; Durham 2007; Jeansonne 1996). Women
also poured into other anti-Semitic movements in the 1930s and 1940s, such as
those inspired by Father Charles Coughlin, a Detroit priest and radio broadcaster
who developed into a virulent anti-Semite (Jeansonne 1996).

Media coverage of the Holocaust of European Jews and the end of World War
II served to undermine the popularity of anti-Semitic politics in the United States.
The mothers' and fascist groups declined and then collapsed in the late 1940s.
When women's right-wing politics next became a significant force, in the 1950s, it
took the form of anticommunism and economic conservatism rather than racism
(Benowitz 2002).

MOVEMENTS AGAINST RACIAL EQUALITY

The civil rights movement and racial desegregation provoked the next significant
era of organized racism, in the form of a revival of the Ku Klux Klan. This Klan
enrolled about fifty thousand men and women, mostly in the South, to defend
white supremacy by fomenting a racial war. It was intensely violent, responsible
for a number of murders of civil rights workers and their supporters as well as
uninvolved African Americans (Chalmers 1987).

Although the mid-century Klans appear to be part of a lengthy Klan tradition, this sense of continuity may be inflated by a pattern among racist leaders
to present white supremacism as a continuous movement. For example, the Ku
Klux Klan appears as a single movement from the 1870s to the present in part
because each era of the Klan mimics the rituals and costumes of the original Klan.
They dedicate Klan units at Stone Mountain, Georgia, in honor of the first KKK;
set crosses ablaze to intimidate racial minorities; and cloak members in white
robes and pointed hoods little changed since Reconstruction (Blee 2002; 2012).
Although there is some evidence of intergenerational transmission of Klan membership from father to son (Cunningham 2007), the records are quite fragmentary
and only include male members. Nazi groups similarly work to create the illusion
of historical continuity. Nazis up to the present adopt the symbols of World War
II–era German and German American Nazism. They brandish swastikas and sign
documents with 88, a code for "Heil Hitler," as H is the eighth letter of the alphabet.

The 1960s Klans, which operated in a number of state and local organizations
with varying connections to each other, largely returned to the explicit view of
male superiority that characterized the Reconstruction-era Klan. To be in the Klan
was to express the highest level of white manhood as a defender of family and race.
As David Cunningham (2013: 67) notes, a popular slogan in the United Klans of
America was, "Be a Man—Join the Klan." The mid-century Klan generally allowed
only men to be formal members, but as a movement determined to integrate family and political time, many Klan chapters sponsored ladies' auxiliaries for the
wives and daughters of Klansmen.

In this Klan, women's role was decidedly auxiliary. They were assigned responsibility for serving food and collecting money at Klan events and for doing charity

work on behalf of the sick and needy, tasks that Klanswomen seemed to take up without dissent. David Cunningham (2013: 66) cites as the motto of a 1967 meeting of a North Carolina ladies' auxiliary that "every Klanlady should at all times look and act like a lady." The few Klanladies who became public speakers for the Klan shared Klansmen's bitter anger at African Americans and their Jewish and federal government supporters. Yet their subordinate role in the organization may have kept women largely away from the practice of the Klan's most visible forms of violence and terrorism. One exception was Kathy Ainsworth, a fifth-grade teacher and member of the Mississippi White Knights of the Ku Klux Klan, who was killed in 1967 as she attempted to bomb the home of a Jewish Anti-Defamation League leader (Durham 2007). For the most part, however, women in the mid-twentieth-century white supremacist movements were considered marginal by male leaders and generally incorporated into racist movements to keep Klansmen content, learn the racist beliefs they could impart to their children, and ensure they would not become involved with nonwhite men. White womanhood remained a potent symbol of what Klansmen were determined to protect, but actual white women were kept securely in the background.

The 1970s to Today

The most recent resurgence of organized racism began in the 1970s. David Duke, later a racist candidate who amassed considerable votes in his bid to become governor of Louisiana, took charge of the Knights of the Ku Klux Klan and asserted that federal policies in support of racial minorities had made white Americans an oppressed racial group. He also attempted to modernize the white supremacist movement, insisting that women should be more prominent in the Klan (as well as dropping its historic antipathy toward Catholics; Durham 2007). The ensuring decades witnessed women's participation in a variety of white supremacist organizations, including neo-Nazi groups that trace their ideology to German Nazism, dozens of Ku Klux Klan chapters with contending leaders, white power skinheads that recruit young people attracted to their intense culture and practice of violence, and assorted racist organizations. These groups have fluctuating connections and overlaps with each other, but all share an ideology of intense anti-Semitism and racism. Many also have an allegiance to the doctrines of Christian Identity, a vicious doctrine that regards Jews as evil beings who are literal descendants of Satan and nonwhites as descendants of prehuman ("pre-Adamic") beings (Barkun 1994).

Contemporary white supremacist groups express variable and often conflicting messages about white womanhood and specific white women. Across the many groups that constitute the landscape of modern organized racism, masculinity is central. Racists are motivated by the fear that white men are in danger of losing their proper place in economic and political life, they insist that white men are called to white supremacism to defend their race, and they argue that manly traits like aggression make the racial warrior. In this racial politics, the place of white women is unclear. If maleness is asserted through racial politics on behalf of one's racial family, then femininity—its opposite—must be passive. Yet the desire to bring women into the racial movement directs its leaders to insist that femininity also can propel racist activism. Little wonder that the images of white women circulated by racial movements are contradictory. White women are portrayed as passive, but also as manipulative. They are racial warriors but also innocents in need of white male protection. Women are mothers and breeders, as well as sexual objects. They are independent race warriors, yet also race traitors who betray racist men (Blee 2002; Daniels 1997).

The movement's diverse images of white womanhood and white women are reflected in women's variable roles in contemporary white supremacism (Ferber 2004). In some groups, women operate primarily as subordinate assistants to white supremacist men; in others, they are active and even mid-level leaders. For some white supremacist groups, women serve to bring new members in the group, but women also play a significant role in helping racist men exit the movement (Blee 2002; Blazak 2004). Women are involved in some aspects of the paramilitary orientation in much of modern organized racism. They encourage people to correspond with and send resources to imprisoned racial warriors, whom they term "POWs"; are involved in weapons training; and learn emergency medical care to care for wounded comrades. Yet throughout modern organized racism, women also are expected to create a home life for men and raise children to see racist activism as normal by teaching them slogans like *Sieg heil* (a German Nazi salute) and how to commemorate racist holidays like Hitler's birthday (Simi and Futrell 2010).

In many white supremacist groups, women are confined to clearly supportive roles, serving as what Raphel Ezekiel (2002: 54) describes as "servants and nurturers." In these groups, women are likely to be the girlfriends and wives of male members, and their input into the group's direction and tactics is minimal. As the racist publication the *Rational Feminist* notes, "The Movement is dominated by men and should be" (in Dobratz and Shanks-Meile 2004: 118). Racist women are charged with creating a collective social life so that members can do most of their socializing within the movement. As a Klanswoman related, "Once you get into the Klan, it becomes your whole family, all your socializing, all your parties" (Blee 2002: 130). For women, this means balancing the needs of their own family and children with those of the collective family of organized racism. For both families, they are responsible for emotional support, the logistics of meals, clothing repair and recreation, and the socialization of children and new members (Blee 2002).

In a few groups, women are central figures. Although almost all white supremacists oppose feminism because they trace its modern roots to Jewish women like Gloria Steinem, some groups also insist that women can work "side by side" with racist men (Blee 2002: 121). In such groups, women are regarded as "white sisters" and treated more as racist activists than as mothers and wives. This is evident in both the tasks assigned to racist women and their place in racist organizations. These groups tend to deploy women as recruiters, expecting that they will be less threatening to mainstream people than are racist men, and white supremacist women are often effective in this role. They approach potential recruits in the normal settings of everyday life—at the grocery, at parties, in medical clinics, at the playground while their children have fun. This recruitment strategy allows the ideas of white supremacism to be introduced gradually as the recruiter gains the trust of the potential recruit. It also fits the wary stance of most racist groups today, which only accept members who are known to a current member. Racist groups that regard women as white sisters also cede some leadership functions to women. In almost no group are women allowed to take formal leadership roles or serve as movement spokespersons. Yet women in the middle levels of racist groups act as leaders by creating cohesion among members, mediating conflicts, shaping strategies, and nurturing a collective identity among members. Such leadership functions are vital in a movement in which members drift in and out and internecine conflict is a mainstay of group life (Blee 2002).

How women participate in racist movements also depends on the particular part of the movement. The contrast between the Ku Klux Klan and neo-Nazis is particularly striking. The Klan today is generally quite traditional in its approach to issues of gender. Women are members in the dozen or so Klan chapters that still exist, although generally because a husband or boyfriend has joined the Klan. In most Klans, women are in the background, providing ancillary services at Klan rallies and events and being responsible for family and children. Recently a few Klans have marketed themselves as more modern by allowing women to assume some leadership roles. As one Klansman said, "Gone are the days of the Women's Auxiliary groups. Today women are active along with the men in meetings, in the Klan office and in public activities" (Dobratz and Shanks-Meile 2004: 118). How accurately that describes the Klan more broadly is unclear. In any case, Klans have been in decline in recent decades as the result of intense internal conflict, legal actions brought against Klan groups by antiracist organizations, infiltration and prosecution by government authorities, and its reputation as ineffectual. As a result, many Klan chapters are quite tiny and unable to attract young members outside the families of current Klan members.

Neo-Nazism is more complex in its relationship to gender (Dobratz and Shanks-Meile 1997). Its organizations range from Christian Identity–dominated communities and compounds to white power skinheads. As a whole, neo-Nazi groups are more active and able to attract younger members than are the Klans. Many adopt a dual approach to women members. One example is the World Church of the Creator (WCOTC), which sponsored a women's organization under the name Women's Frontier (WF). WCOTC/WF was known for its recruitment of violent racists, especially neo-Nazi skinheads, and for providing weapons training for members at its headquarters. The group was also renowned for its efforts to recruit women through a newsletter and website published under the auspices of Women's Frontier. In these media, WF set out a vision for white supremacist women, bemoaning the absence and invisibility of women in white supremacist groups and calling for a new form of women's activism on behalf of the white race. The details of this new vision were vague. Although WF insisted that white supremacist women should not simply be used as breeders for the new white generation, they also underscored the critical role of women in the traditional gendered tasks of bearing white babies and raising children as race warriors through home schooling (Rogers and Litt 2004).

A very different example is racist skinheads. Many skinheads are violently masculinist, referring to women in their groups as "oi toys" and taking pride in their ability to dominate their girlfriends and wives. These skinheads take heed of the prediction from Friedrich Nietzsche that begins their *Code of the Skinhead*, "a more manly, war-like age is coming, which will bring valor into honor!" (*Code* ca. 1993). In this world, women's place is to support warrior-men and recognize that they fight for her. However, in some skinhead groups, women refuse to conform to the image presented in skinhead propaganda. They confront male comrades over issues of sexism and demand a different place in the racist movement. As one woman asked, "Why do so many male skinheads and other males in the white resistance simply degrade women . . . The answer is these are not Aryan warriors" (Blee 2002: 149). There are even rare all-women skingirl groups that project an image of female aggression and revel in their ability to fight and inflict violence.

Conclusion

The enfranchisement of women provided opportunities for white supremacists, but only for a limited time. The 1920s Klan took advantage of women's new status as voters, as well as the political skills and networks that some women acquired in the campaign for woman suffrage, to mount an electoral strategy. But these efforts lasted less than a decade, and subsequent white supremacists largely abandoned electoral politics. Suffragism also established the notion that women could be independent political actors, creating the opportunity to bring women into separate Klans in the 1920s. This effect was longer-lasting if episodic, as masculine dominance and female passivity are central to white supremacist ideologies and organizations.

Women were accorded some measure of independent political action in organized racism primarily in the 1920s and after 1980; in the intervening years women in white supremacism were kept firmly in the background. The fluctuating role of gender in racist movements in the century after women's suffrage was the result of both pressures and opportunities that were generated in the larger social and political environment. Women had a larger role in racist movements that coincided with significant movements for women's rights in the broader society. This is true for the 1920s, when the Klan was able to build from the racist edge of the woman suffrage movement. It is also the case for the post-1980 era of white supremacist activity, which coincided with the second wave of feminism. The temporal association between women's white supremacist activity and mainstream women's movements in recent decades is particularly striking as there was not an explicitly racist segment of women's rights politics in the post-1980 period from which racist movements could build. At the same time, the changing expectations about women's place in public politics that occurred in mainstream society also impacted racist movements, even those that are highly insular and reject virtually all mainstream political and social ideas.

The women who were attracted to white supremacism rarely embraced any aspect of women's rights or feminist politics directly. Yet some of them carried expectations about how women should be treated in public life that reflected these broader concerns. When skingirls denounced their male comrades for mistreating women, or when Klanswomen asserted their rights to be considered for leadership positions historically monopolized by men, they were adapting the rhetoric and understandings of gender honed in progressive feminism for quite different political purposes. When scholars analyze the boundary between far-right politics and mainstream politics, they invariably focus on how right-wing extremism can influence more moderate politics, as in studies of the effects of paramilitary militias on immigration reform policies or the consequences of the Tea Party for the establishment Republican Party. Less studied, but no less interesting, are how mainstream ideological and political trends, including movements to expand women's rights, shape right-wing extremism such as racist movements.

How (and even if) women participated in racist movements in the last century also depended on internal opportunities such as fluctuations in the structure of white supremacism and the nature of racist ideology over time. Whether women are recruited into full membership, separate female auxiliaries, or as limited or secondary members changed what the always-male leadership of racist movements regarded as their roles and limitations. So did racist ideologies about women's place in the home and as racial warriors.

The male-centric nature of white supremacism, with its defense of social inequalities of gender as well as race, sets limits on how fully integrated women will ever become in racist movements. So does the persistent reliance of such movements on the symbol of white womanhood to denote the perquisites of racial privilege that white supremacism seeks to defend. Continuing advances of women in political and economic life may allow the further entry of women into organized racism, but their place in this movement is likely to remain fairly limited.

References

Barkun, Michael. 1994. *Religion and the Radical Right: The Origins of the Christian Identity Movement*. Chapel Hill: University of North Carolina Press.

Bennett, David H. 1975. "Women and the Nativist Movement." Pp. 71–89 in *"Remember the Ladies": New Perspectives on Women in American History. Essays in Honor of Nelson Manfred Blake*, edited by C. V. R George. Syracuse, NY: Syracuse University Press.

Benowitz, June Melby. 2002. *Days of Discontent: American Women and Right-Wing Politics, 1933–1945*. Dekalb: Northern Illinois University Press.

Blazak, Randy. 2004. "'Getting It': The Role of Women in Male Desistance from Hate Groups." Pp. 161–180 in *Home-Grown Hate: Gender and Organized Racism*, edited by A. Ferber. New York: Routledge.

Blee, Kathleen M. 1991. *Women of the Klan: Racism and Gender in the 1920s*. Berkeley: University of California Press.

———. 2002. *Inside Organized Racism: Women in the Hate Movement*. Berkeley: University of California Press.

———. 2005. "Racial Violence in the United States." *Ethnic and Racial Studies* 28(4): 599–619.

———. 2012. "Does Gender Matter in the United States Far-Right?" *Politics, Religion, and Ideology* 13(2): 253–265.

Chafe, William H. 1972. *The American Woman: Her Changing Social, Economic, and Political Roles, 1920–1970*. New York: Oxford University Press.

Chalmers, David. 1987. *Hooded Americanism: The History of the Ku Klux Klan*. Durham, NC: Duke University Press.

Clarke, James W. 1998. "Without Fear or Shame: Lynching, Capital Punishment, and the Subculture of Violence in the American South." *British Journal of Political Science* 28(2): 269–289.

Code of the Skinhead. ca. 1993. n.p.

Cohen, Philip N. 1996. "Nationalism and Suffrage: Gender Struggle in Nation-Building America." *Signs: Journal of Women in Culture and Society* 21(3): 707–727.

Cott, Nancy F. 1987. *The Grounding of Modern Feminism*. New Haven, CT: Yale University Press.

Cunningham, David. 2007. "Paths to Participation: A Profile of the Civil Rights–Era Ku Klux Klan." *Research in Social Movements, Conflicts and Change* 27: 283–309.

———. 2013. *Klansville, U.S.A.: The Rise and Fall of the Civil Rights–Era Ku Klux Klan*. New York: Oxford University Press.

Daniels, Jessie. 1997. *White Lies: Race, Class, Gender, and Sexuality in White Supremacist Discourse*. New York: Routledge.

Diamond, Sander. 1974. *The Nazi Movement in the United States, 1924–1941*. Ithaca, NY: Cornell University Press.

Dobratz, Betty A., and Stephanie L. Shanks-Meile. 1997. "The White Separatist Movement in the United States: 'White Power, White Pride!'" Baltimore, MD: The Johns Hopkins University Press.

———. 2004. "The White Separatist Movement: Worldviews on Gender, Feminism, Nature, and Change." Pp. 113–142 in *Home-Grown Hate: Gender and Organized Racism*, edited by A. Ferber. New York: Routledge.

DuBois, Ellen. 1978. *Feminism and Suffrage: The Emergence of an Independent Women's Movement in America, 1848–1869*. Ithaca, NY: Cornell University Press.

Dunn, Marvin. 2013. *The Beast in Florida: A History of Anti-Black Violence*. Gainesville: University Press of Florida.

Durham, Martin. 2007. *White Rage: The Extreme Right and American Politics*. New York: Routledge.

Evans, Sara. 1979. *Personal Politics: The Roots of Women's Liberation in the Civil Rights Movement and the New Left*. New York: Random House.

Ezekiel, Raphael S. 2002. "An Ethnographer Looks at Neo-Nazi and Klan Groups: The Racist Mind Revisited." *American Behavioral Scientist* 46(1): 51–71.

Faust, Drew Gilpin. 1996. *Mothers of Invention: Women of the Slaveholding South in the American Civil War*. Chapel Hill: University of North Carolina Press.

Ferber, Abby, ed. 2004. *Home-Grown Hate: Gender and Organized Racism.* New York: Routledge.

Fox-Genovese, Elizabeth. 1988. *Within the Plantation Household: Black and White Women of the Old South.* Chapel Hill: University of North Carolina Press.

Giddings, Paula. 1984. *When and Where I Enter: The Impact of Black Women on Race and Sex in America.* New York: Bantam Books.

Jeansonne, Glen. 1996. *Women of the Far Right: The Mothers' Movement and World War II.* Chicago: University of Chicago Press.

MacLean, Nancy. 1995. *Behind the Mask of Chivalry: The Making of the Second Ku Klux Klan.* New York: Oxford University Press.

Marshall, Susan. 1997. *Splintered Sisterhood: Gender and Class in the Campaign Against Woman Suffrage.* Madison: University of Wisconsin Press.

McCammon, Holly. 2012. *The U.S. Women's Jury Movements and Strategic Adaptation: A More Just Verdict.* New York: Cambridge University Press.

McCammon, Holly J., Lyndi Hewitt, and Sandy Smith. 2004. "'No Weapon Save Argument': Strategic Frame Amplification in the U.S. Woman Suffrage Movements." *Sociological Quarterly* 45(3): 529–556.

McEnaney, Laura. 1994. "He-Men and Christian Mothers: The American First Movement and the Gendered Meanings of Patriotism and Isolationism." *Diplomatic History* 18(1): 47–57.

McVeigh, Rory. 2009. *The Rise of the Ku Klux Klan: Right-Wing Movements and National Politics.* Minneapolis: University of Minnesota Press.

Nagel, Joane. 2010. "Masculinity and Nationalism: Gender and Sexuality in the Making of Nations." *Ethnic and Racial Studies* 21(2): 242–269.

Nielsen, Kim E. 2001. *Un-American Womanhood: Antiradicalism, Antifeminism, and the First Red Scare.* Columbus: The Ohio State University Press.

Ribuffo, Leo. 1983. *The Old Christian Right: The Protestant Far Right from the Great Depression to the Cold War.* Philadelphia: Temple University Press.

Rogers, JoAnn, and Jacquelyn S. Litt. 2004. "Normalizing Racism: A Case Study of Motherhood in White Supremacy." Pp. 97–112 in *Home-Grown Hate: Gender and Organized Racism*, edited by A. Ferber. New York: Routledge.

Simi, Pete, and Robert Futrell. 2010. *American Swastika: Inside the White Power Movement's Hidden Spaces of Hate.* Lanham, MD: Rowman and Littlefield.

Taylor, Verta. 1995. "Social Movement Continuity: The Women's Movement in Abeyance." *American Sociological Review* 54(5): 761–775.

Ware, Susan. 1981. *Beyond Suffrage: Women in the New Deal.* Cambridge, MA: Harvard University Press.

Whittier, Nancy. 1995. *Feminist Generations: The Persistence of the Radical Women's Movement.* Philadelphia: Temple University Press.

14

Women, Leadership, and the U.S. Environmental Movement

Holly J. McCammon, Allison McGrath, David J. Hess, and Minyoung Moon

Women's leadership in the US environmental movement over the last one hundred years in many respects reflects the larger gendered hierarchy of society. In ways similar to women's historical subordination in the larger culture, women's roles in the environmental movement have been constrained. Yet, at the same time, an examination of women's leadership in this movement, as well as shifts in these roles over the last one hundred years, reveal women leaders with substantial influence on environmentalism and significant efforts by women to challenge the traditional gender hierarchy. Just as woman suffragists challenged traditional gender norms, women in the environmental movement have agitated to put women on equal par with men. Women's environmental leadership has taken myriad forms: white women's early efforts in the conservation and preservation movement, black women mobilizing for environmental justice, Native American women's attempts to protect biodiversity, to name just some examples. In our chapter, we examine developments in women's leadership in the US environmental movement over the last one hundred years. We find similarities and differences in their efforts over time and across different environmental groups. Ultimately, however, we conclude that, while women's contributions have often been restricted by traditional gender norms, women's leadership has challenged those norms and had a fundamental influence on the environment.

Traditional definitions of leadership, as Klenke (1996: 1) tells us, conjure up images of the man on the white horse. This great-man conceptualization of leadership results, of course, in highly gendered understandings. Moreover, the traditional view often defines leaders as those holding titled and formal positions in large organizations and wielding substantial formal authority to direct the actions of subordinates. In the political arena, women historically have often been considered "outsiders" in what has been deemed a male sphere of action, and thus women and political leadership have not gone hand in hand (Carroll and Fox 2014). Even in the study of social movement political activism, few scholars consider women's leadership in any detail (for exceptions, see Banaszak 2010; McCammon 2012; Reger and Staggenborg 2006; Robnett 1997), while many accounts tend to focus predominantly on male leadership (Aminzade, Goldstone, and Perry 2001; Barker, Johnson, and Lavalette 2001; Nepstad and Bob 2006).

The difficulty, of course, in defining leadership in the traditional great-man way is that women's leadership is overlooked. In the environmental movement, if we perceive leaders as only the formal heads of the largest and most visible environmental organizations, then the long history of women's dominion remains obscured. In our chapter, we take a different approach, one often utilized by scholars studying women's political leadership (O'Brien and Shea 2010; Robnett 1997; Thomas 2003). These scholars argue that leadership can occur in a variety of ways and in a multitude of settings. As US senator Barbara Mikulski states, leadership is "creating a state of mind in others" (cited in Klenke 1996: 7). At the heart of social movement leadership is motivating others to participate in activism and guiding them as they do so, and the historical record easily reveals a wide range of instances of women's environmental leadership. Tracing women's environmental leadership over one hundred years shows both continuities in their leadership through time as well as developments illustrating that women's leadership in the earlier years was different, at least in some ways, than in the later years.

For instance, as our investigation reveals, throughout the past century, women leaders in environmentalism often have invoked traditional gendered roles, framing their environmental work as extensions of their domestic interests. Women in environmentalism speak of protecting children, future generations, home and family life, and people in their communities. Another continuity running through the history of women's environmental leadership is that some leaders over the one hundred years have engaged in environmentalism in women-only groups, from the early women's clubs to more recent ecofeminism. But the one-hundred-year history also reveals shifts over time, and these developments point to new dimensions of women's environmental leadership, which render the present different from the past. For example, today women have become leaders of prominent, sometimes national environmental organizations; they have been recognized as scientific experts; and they are now viewed as respected spokespersons on critical environmental issues. Such occurrences were exceedingly rare one hundred years ago. We find that the story of women's leadership in the environmental movement over the last one hundred years is one of both continuities and changes over time. The narrative is also one of a growing, diverse, and influential presence of women in the movement.

We divide our discussion of women's leadership in the environmental movement into two sections: women's leadership in the early- and mid-twentieth-century movement and their leadership in contemporary environmentalism. We rely on the historical record of women's environmental activism to formulate our account, including recent scholarly investigations, various biographies, and environmental organizational sources. Our discussion is somewhat chronological as we trace the variety of types and changing nature of women's environmental leadership. Many scholars who write about leadership focus their study on formal leaders located at the top of an organizational or institutional hierarchy, but we broaden this definition of leadership, as some social movement scholars (Kuumba 2001; Robnett 1997) explicitly encourage, to consider the complexity and changing nature of women's leadership in the environmental movement. Our study shows that a racially, ethnically, and class-diverse set of women have led in a range of ways, through individual discursive, artistic, and scientific efforts; through leadership in women-only organizations; in mobilizing maternalist grassroots efforts in local communities; and increasingly as leaders in top positions in national environmental organizations.

Women in Early-
and Mid-Twentieth-Century Environmentalism

By the end of the nineteenth century, and well prior to women winning the Nineteenth Amendment, women's organizations were beginning to stake out a role in the emerging environmental preservation and conservation movement. Late in the nineteenth century, with the frontier largely settled, interest turned to conservation of natural resources and preservation of the beauty and history of wilderness lands. Accounts of the early conservationists often tell of a white-male movement of hunters and campers, preserving nature for the benefit and enjoyment of a wealthier class (Merchant 1984; Riley 1999; Taylor 1997). But the participation of white women, often members of women's clubs, helped turn a narrow, early environmental movement into a broad-based movement, with thousands of women, primarily white and middle- and upper-class, who possessed the wealth and leisure for such pursuits.

While some women joined the male-led Sierra Club in their efforts to protect the land and wildlife, a larger segment of women engaged in preservationist politics through women's-only organizations, one of the most active of which was the General Federation of Women's Clubs (GFWC; Kaufman 1996; Merchant 1984; Rimby 2012; Unger 2012). Individual women often took the lead spurring the GFWC into action. For instance, writer and lecturer Virginia Donaghe McClurg appealed to the Colorado branch of the GFWC to help preserve the Native American cliff dwellings that later would become Mesa Verde National Park (Kaufman 1996; Robertson 2003). In time, GFWC groups across the country engaged in environmental advocacy by lobbying Congress and state legislatures to set aside land for parks and to protect waterways. Riley (1999) reports that by the 1920s most women's clubs embraced environmentalism as part of their mission, and this change of mission significantly broadened the early environmental movement. Women also publicized preservation and even pressed for programs to educate schoolchildren on the environment, aligning environmental and maternalist interests. GFWC leaders became prominent in the national movement and were on occasion recognized by the federal government for their efforts. For example, in 1908 Sarah Platt Decker from the Colorado Federation, was invited to join the White House Governors' Conference on Conservation (Merchant 1984). In the early twentieth-century, when a separate-spheres ideology directing women to stay home running households and rearing children continued to dominate, these early-twentieth-century female environmentalists pushed gender boundaries and revealed that women could provide public leadership on environmental issues.

A growing element in women's environmentalism in the early decades of the twentieth century emerged in urban areas. Although some wealthier white urban women simply followed male leaders in advocating for city parks, others pursued deeper reforms (Taylor 1997). During the century's early Progressive era, these women addressed growing overcrowding and related ills in the nation's largest cities. Late in the nineteenth century, Jane Addams and Ellen Gates Starr founded Hull House in Chicago and infused their work with social justice ideals, arguing that workers should not be exposed to workplace hazards and neighborhoods should be cleaner and safer environments for families (Addams 1911).

Middle-class black women's clubs, too, were proponents of urban reforms to create healthier communities, typically directing their efforts at poorer neighborhoods (Gilmore 1996; Smith 1995). Lugenia Burns Hope organized the Atlanta Neighborhood Union in 1908, a group that until 1935 sponsored efforts to interview neighborhood residents, assessing their sanitary needs and implementing reforms (Rouse 1989). Racially segregated southern cities and white political leadership relegated most black residents to neighborhoods without adequate water, sewer, and garbage-removal systems, resulting in higher rates of disease, particularly in poor black neighborhoods. Black women's environmental efforts during this period thus were often combined with public-health initiatives (Smith 1995). In some instances, black and white women's groups worked together to promote a better urban environment (Gilmore 1996), but often black women community leaders were compelled to take a self-help approach in responding to the environmental and health needs of black neighborhoods, particularly when combatting racial prejudice among city leaders proved futile and there were few governmental responses to their activism. Smith (1995) recounts that, although many African American men also led and did so by holding positions of formal authority in the early black environmental and health organizations, black women leaders worked more closely in the communities, educating and interviewing residents. Black women, then, demonstrated their ability to lead publicly by fighting a racialized battle to improve the urban environment, and they did so by taking a hands-on leadership role in communities.

Numerous women in the early part of the twentieth century engaged in environmentalism in other, more individualist ways that also helped demonstrate women's influence and break down gendered barriers concerning leadership. Many white women continued the nineteenth-century tradition of women's naturalist writing and artistic work (Riley 1999). Mary Hunter Austin, for example, wrote of the natural beauty of the southwestern desert and combined it with feminism, conveying that this was a "place where women could 'walk off' the societal dictates that hampered them" (Riley 2003: 86). Novelists like Willa Cather helped redefine women's relationship to nature, rejecting the belief that women feared nature and instead promoting female characters who gained strength and autonomy from their roles on the land. Mabel Osgood Wright's meditations on gardening drew female audiences and, as Philippon's (2004) investigation relates, relocated conservation environmentalism from the western frontier to the backyard garden. Rural African American women also pursued gardening, raising vegetables to contribute to the family economy, and black women led in Home Demonstration Work in the Negro Cooperative Extension Service, teaching women the science behind home cultivation (Glave 2003).

Some women led through scientific pursuits and dissemination of their expert knowledge of the public health dangers of pollutants and toxins in the environment, including in the workplace environment. Musil (2014) charts Rachel Carson's precursors, women who led the way in mid-twentieth-century environmental science. Ellen Swallow Richards is often identified as the nineteenth-century pioneer for women in environmental science, helping define home economics. With her expertise in chemistry, she also led the first water-quality survey in Massachusetts and advocated for water quality laws and sewage treatment. By the mid-twentieth century, others had followed, such as Alice Hamilton of Harvard Medical School, with research on human exposure to industrial metals and chemicals. Hamilton's expertise also helped publicize the link between the radium powder used to coat watch and clock faces to make them luminous in the dark and the deaths of women workers like Grace Fryer at the New Jersey US Radium Company (Kovarik 1996; Sicherman 1984). The women factory workers were told to lick their paint brushes in their application of the radium to give the brush a pointed tip, but the exposure to radium in time killed them. Scientists like Hamilton were pioneers, not only in developing the science of workplace environmental toxins, but also in helping redefine scientific work as a domain in which women as well as men could provide important insights.

These early female environmentalists challenged traditional roles for women by engaging in public environmentalism, either working through women-only organizations or becoming leaders in urban community environmental efforts, in literary and artistic pursuits, or in scientific endeavors. In later years, as we show, women-only groups continue to provide opportunities for women to prove their leadership skills. Women also continue their community environmental leadership, now in the environmental justice movement. Women's environmentalism in recent decades, as we also discuss, is at the same time distinct from the past in that women's leadership in environmental organizations grows substantially over time, including women leading a variety of types of environmental groups.

Women's Leadership in the Contemporary Environmental Movement

Scholars identify the 1960s as the beginning of the contemporary environmental movement (Dowie 1996; Dunlap and Mertig 1991; Sale 1993; Taylor 2014). The modern movement is characterized by an increasing diversity of women's leadership roles. Although more women today assume leadership positions in contemporary environmental organizations, their ability to claim the highest posts is often dependent on the type of organization with which they are affiliated (Cable 1992; Taylor 2014, 2015). There are various ways to distinguish types of contemporary environmentalism. Often a distinction is made among organizations oriented toward preservation and conservation and toward industrial transitions and reduction of environmental risks and hazards, on the one hand, and those oriented toward environmental justice, ecofeminism, and direct action, on the other (Dunlap and Mertig 1991; Dowie 1996; Gottlieb 2005). Typically, organizations of the first type—such as the World Wildlife Federation, Nature Conservancy, the Sierra Club, Friends of the Earth, the Natural Resources Defense Fund, and the Environmental Defense Fund—are characterized as "mainstream environmentalism." These organizations pursue approaches to reform based on institutionalized repertoires of action such as litigation, legislative lobbying, ballot initiatives, and campaigns for corporate responsibility. In contrast, we use the term *alternative environmentalism* below to characterize environmental justice, ecofeminist, and direct action groups (Dowie 1996; Gottlieb 2005; Kline 2011; Merchant 1996).

The different types of environmental organizations are associated with differences in women's leadership in the environmental movement. Mainstream groups have been more impervious to women's leadership compared to their alternative counterparts, and mainstream environmental leadership has historically been largely white, upper-middle-class, and male (Cable 1992; Gottlieb 2005; Taylor 1997, 2015). In contrast, alternative environmental organizations—such as the direct-action group Earth First!, community-based grassroots organizations of the environmental justice movement, and ecofeminist groups—have less hierarchical and more democratic organizational structures that often emphasize the importance of diversity in leadership (Dunlap and Mertig 1991; Unger 2012). As such, women in alternative environmental groups, including women of color particularly in environmental justice groups, have played a substantially greater role as leaders (Gottlieb 2005; Kline 2011; Taylor 2015).

In the following sections we explore developments in women's contemporary environmental leadership in greater detail. The discussion first turns to mainstream organizations and then to alternative branches of contemporary environmentalism.

WOMEN'S LEADERSHIP IN MAINSTREAM ENVIRONMENTAL ORGANIZATIONS

As noted by many researchers (Gottlieb 2005; Musil 2014; Unger 2012), Rachel Carson's 1962 book, *Silent Spring*, was a landmark moment in the diversification of the mainstream American environmental movement from its historical focus on preservation and conservation. The book identified the problem of persistent chemicals in the biosphere and presented important research on the role of pesticides in the food chain. Trained as a scientist, Carson spent her career as a government science writer, and she knew how to communicate science to a broad readership (Dreier 2012). Her book challenged conventional notions of environmental progress and is credited with helping galvanize public attention to chemicals and their harms to humans, both in industry and the home. These concerns became a hallmark of contemporary mainstream environmentalism as it emerged during the 1960s and 1970s.

Carson and *Silent Spring* also received widespread criticism and faced attacks from agricultural chemical companies and the mass media, much of which drew on traditional stereotypes of women (Smith 2001). For example, Carson's critics labeled her emotional and hysterical, disparaged her work as unscientific, and argued that she had no place in the male world of science. Smith (2001) writes that the harshest criticisms came from pesticide companies, which had a clear economic stake in the debate. Critics used gender stereotypes in an attempt to discount her work, but in the end they did so unsuccessfully. Carson's efforts helped propel a shift in how the American public viewed its relationship to the natural world. Her prominence as a scientific spokesperson also demonstrated to a broad public the contributions of women to scientific debates about the state of the environment, challenging traditional gender norms and empowering future female environmentalists (Musil 2014). Current evidence, however, reveals that resistance to women in scientific research, including in environmental science, is far from over (Martin 2012), and Carson's reputation as a mother of modern American environmentalism has undergone a second generation of attack from conservative organizations promoting disinformation about the effects of pesticide bans (Oreskes and Conway 2010).

Throughout much of the twentieth century, mainstream conservation and preservation environmental organizations tended to portray environmentalism through the lens of middle-class recreational uses of nature (Gottlieb 2005). This view of nature as a passive object to be enjoyed by an active citizenship resonated with long-standing historical depictions of nature as a feminized object (Merchant 1996). Mainstream environmental groups had few women in leadership positions until women began to make inroads starting in the 1970s (Taylor 2015). For example, Schrepfer (2005) recounts the difficulties faced by women in their repeated attempts to gain election to leadership roles in the Sierra Club, where women's contributions were restricted primarily to volunteer roles. Also, the male-led and hierarchically structured staffs of mainstream environmental organizations usually overlooked a range of concerns voiced by women. One example is the Sierra Club's response when Carson sounded the alarm in *Silent Spring* (Hazlett 2004). Carson articulated the interconnections between humans and nature, a view that in time would be embraced and further developed by ecofeminists. Although the Sierra Club in the 1960s responded to the harm of pesticides for the wilderness, Carson's arguments pointing to the dangers for humans as well as the home were left "at the margins—or even untouched" by Sierra Club leaders (Hazlett 2004: 718).

With the rise of the second-wave feminist movement beginning in the late 1960s, women began questioning the lack of female leadership and the limited attention to women's environmental concerns in the mainstream environmental organizations (Kline 2011; Merchant 1996; Unger 2012). This emergent feminist consciousness helped women environmentalists challenge the exclusion of women from leadership. A handful of women, primarily white, were able to move into leadership roles in mainstream environmental groups beginning in the 1970s, and they did so in a variety of ways (Gottlieb 2005; Taylor 2014).[1] For example, from 1972 to 1986 Louise Dunlap held the presidency of the Environmental Policy Institute and Environmental Policy Center, large environmental lobbying organizations, and Janet Welsh Brown led both the Environmental Defense Fund and Friends of the Earth during this period. Both Brown and Dunlap encountered negative sex stereotyping of women in their organizations and sometimes faced attempts by male leaders to exclude them from important meetings with government officials. They responded by adopting traditionally masculine styles of leadership to gain acceptance from their male peers. In effect, they used an assimilationist strategy in their leadership, and for the most part they relegated any focus on issues in environmental policy of specific interest to women to the back burner. Gottlieb (2005: 301) reports that such matters in these mainstream groups at the time were simply considered "irrelevant."

But other female leaders used a more feminist strategy to make inroads into mainstream organizations during the early years of the contemporary movement. For example, Helen King Burke, the sole woman on the Sierra Club's executive committee in the 1970s, sought to bring increasing gender awareness to mainstream environmental groups and did so by leading the formation of a coalition between women from mainstream environmental organizations and various feminist groups (Robinson 1978). Marcia Fine and Charlene Dougherty, both staff members at the Environmental Defense Fund, joined Burke in her pursuit, believing a coalition would help encourage more women to work on environmental issues in the government and would allow women to gain greater leadership in the environmental movement itself (Gottlieb 2005). Teaming up with the National Organization for Women, Burke and her fellow female environmentalists established the Women for Environmental Health Coalition. The coalition focused on drawing awareness to environmental issues that directly affected women, with a specific emphasis on environmental concerns related to women's reproductive health. Although the coalition eventually dissolved, the work of Burke and her colleagues demonstrated women's efforts to change the conversation in mainstream organizations and widen the discourse to include advocacy on behalf of women and gender-specific environmental issues.

Still other women simply moved away from the mainstream environmental organizations to form their own groups, especially as the 1960s and 1970s wave of protest unfolded and many activist organizations emerged (Schrepfer 2005; Unger 2012). For example, some women were becoming ecofeminists (which we discuss below), and some played active leadership roles in the growing anti–nuclear weapons movement, two strains of mobilizing that were closely intertwined (Gaard 1998; Nelkin 1981). Under the leadership of Ynestra King, women engaged in the 1980 and 1981 Women's Pentagon Action protest marches outside the Pentagon. The protesters' Unity Statement linked antimilitarism with environmentalism, characterizing the US military and its weapons as "the imperial power which threatens us all," including "the life of this planet, our earth, and the life of the children who are our human future" (Paley 2008: 461).

In recent decades, diversity in leadership in mainstream environmental organizations—both in terms of gender and race—has grown, although the majority of leadership and staff positions remain occupied by men, and the women who hold leadership positions are primarily white and middle class (Gottlieb 2005; Taylor 2014, 2015). As noted by Taylor (2015), even as late as the 2010s over 70% of mainstream presidents are male, more than half of all executive directors are male, and nearly 65% of board members in these organizations are male.

But women's presence in leadership continues to expand in mainstream environmental organizations, and the growth in their leadership suggests women's increasing centrality in the mainstream environmental movement. Today, for example, both Frances Beinecke and Kathryn Fuller have held multiple leadership positions and are well-networked into the mainstream environmental movement, with work spanning both environmental organizations and government environmental efforts (Alcoa 2015; Beinecke 2014; Herles 2010). Another important leader illustrating women at the hub of the mainstream environmental movement network is Laurie David, who has been a vocal advocate for the climate change movement and environmental sustainability. Author of the book *Stop Global Warming* and producer of Al Gore's *An Inconvenient Truth,* David currently serves as a trustee for the National Resource Defense Counsel and is a regular contributing environmental blogger to the Huffington Post (Herles 2010). She also worked closely with politicians to organize the Stop Global Warming Virtual March (David 2015). Female environmental leaders in the United States, such as Osprey Orielle Lake, along with leading environmental women from around the world—many of whom are women of color—are at the forefront of building transnational environmental networks, such as that initiated at the 2013 International Women's Earth and Climate Summit, once again broadening the environmental movement, this time globally (Dankelman 2002; Hemmati and Röhr 2009; International Women's Earth & Climate Action Network 2016; Lake 2016).

While early in the century almost no women led in mainstream environmental organizations, since the 1970s women's leadership in mainstream environmental organizations has grown. Women now lead some of the largest US environmental groups and are visible activists on core environmental issues, like climate change. But racial and ethnic diversity among women leaders in mainstream groups remains limited, and thus there is a continuing need for more growth in women's leadership in mainstream organizations, particularly among women of color.

ENVIRONMENTAL JUSTICE AND GRASSROOTS ACTIVISM

By the late 1970s a distinctive grassroots environmental movement was launched in the United States, and the activism increasingly gained momentum. From its inception, the environmental justice movement has had a significant female leadership, with leaders coming from a variety of racial and ethnic backgrounds (Rainey and Johnson 2009). Taylor (1997: 56) estimates that 50% of leaders in people-of-color environmental justice organizations are women; other estimates are as high as 70% (Bullard 2000). Today, women make up nearly 80% of the executive directors of environment justice groups and 50% of their presidents (Taylor 2015). But as some researchers point out, the movement has often not received broader public attention, in part because of an unwillingness to "see" women's leadership, but also due to the intersection of gender with racial, ethnic, and class biases (Krauss 1993; Taylor 1997). The women leaders themselves comment that their grievances, testimony, and knowledge are often not taken seriously by male political leaders (Gibbs 2011; Hamilton 1990; Krauss 1993; Schlossberg 2003). Women report that they are referred to as "hysterical housewives" and told to "get back in your kitchen" (Merchant 1996: 161; Rome 2003: 540). Although women's leadership in environmental justice is pronounced, these leaders have experienced gendered (and racially and ethnically based) resistance to their efforts.

Environmental justice mobilizations typically emerge when a local community is compelled to respond to toxic hazards in the air, water, or land, and sometimes in all three. One early leader, Hazel Johnson, was an African American woman who organized People for Community Recovery in 1979 to fight for the removal of asbestos from local public housing in her Chicago neighborhood (Pellow 2002; People for Community Recovery 2015). Her leadership developed as she and other local activists pressed government officials to consider local landfills, waste lagoons, and incinerators as superfund sites. Lois Gibbs, a white woman, was another early leader in a grassroots protest against toxic waste, whose environmental activism began in Love Canal, New York (Gibbs 2011). Winona LaDuke, a Native American, has led the White Earth Land Recovery Project for twenty-five years, an organization working to return land to the White Earth Indian Reservation in Minnesota to prevent deforestation.

Women have been important leaders in environmental justice activism, and their efforts have succeeded in making communities safer and healthier places for individuals and families. The women leading these mobilizations often reside in lower-income, working-class communities that have been targeted for waste disposal or chemical dumping (Krauss 1993; Taylor 1997; Unger 2012). City leaders or corporate entities select these neighborhoods because they believe residents lack the political resources to resist toxic exposure. These environmental practices can also be racist when communities of color are specifically targeted by political or corporate leaders for toxic wastes or other forms of degradation (Bullard 2001; Pulido 2000; Rainey and Johnson 2009).

Women who lead the environmental justice movement are often initially motivated by their status as mothers, and their desire to protect their families and even nurture their broader communities (Krauss 1993; Peeples and DeLuca 2006; Petit 2001; Prindeville 2004; Sze 2004). Women, especially mothers, often witness first-hand the negative health consequences of environmental toxins experienced by families. They draw the connections between environmental poisons and their children's health problems. Studies show that motherhood can motivate environmental activism across diverse groups of women, from Native American women in the Mohawk Nation at Akwesasne (LaDuke 1999); to white women in the coalfields of Appalachia (Bell and Braun 2010); to black activists in Atlanta, Georgia (Gomez, Shafiei, and Johnson 2011); to Latinas in the "Madres de Este Los Angeles" (Pulido 1997). Men may be less inclined to join and lead environmental justice activism because of the salience of their identities as breadwinners, and often they are tied directly as workers to the economic organizations the movement opposes (Bell and Braun 2010). Furthermore, when men are involved, their motivations can be different from those of women. For example, they often focus on protecting property values (Unger 2012). Some scholars (Gottlieb 2005) comment that women's environmental justice leadership does not originate in the women's movement or stem from a feminist perspective, but rather is a separate stream of women's social movement engagement. But others (Kaalunk 2004; Merchant 1996; Prindeville and Bretting 1998; Verchick 2004) remark that a broader definition of feminism, one encompassing maternalist political action, indicates that women's environmentalism is feminist at its core.

Women's identities as mothers and caregivers in their communities can draw them into activism, but their experience in the movement can politicize them and lead to a broadening of their actions. Women then organize and administer new grassroots environmental groups, develop leadership skills based on building communities with strong solidarity, mentor the next generation of environmental activists and experts, and become social commentators and media spokespersons (Cable 1992; Gomez, Shafiei, and Johnson 2011; Hamilton 1990; Krauss 1998; Newman 2001). For example, Lois Gibbs began her activism as a concerned mother in Love Canal but then founded and led the Center for Health, Environment, and Justice, which addresses environmental problems across the nation (Gibbs 2011). Margie Eugene Richard became involved when she saw the illnesses in her family and the fatal pipeline explosions in her Norco, Louisiana, community resulting from a Shell Oil refinery in "Cancer Alley" (Greene 2008). She went on to lead the Concerned Citizens of Norco for fifteen years in a successful community relocation campaign.

Researchers debate whether framing women's environmental justice leadership as motivated by maternalism is a benefit or disadvantage for the environmental justice movement. Some scholars (Di Chiro 1992; Peeples and DeLuca 2006) argue that a motherhood frame allows diverse women to come together and pursue a common goal of protecting children and communities from environmental hazards. Hickey (2013) tells us that motherhood conveys "respectability," which benefits women leaders and the movements themselves. Others indicate that maternalist rhetoric can oversimplify complex issues and instead can anchor and limit women to their traditional domestic roles (Petit 2001; Stearney 1994). This limitation invites others both inside and outside the movement to devalue women's contributions. In either case, the maternalist frame is prevalent in environmental justice politics and it provides a voice in the broader polity for politicized motherhood. Invoking motherhood as a rationale for women's activism also reveals continuity with an earlier generation of woman suffrage advocates, who also argued that a political voice for women, including mothers, would lead to greater protections for children and family life (Kraditor 1981).

Many women leading the environmental justice movement also invoke racial, ethnic, and even religious identities in support of their activism, in some cases even more so than motherhood identities (Prindeville 2004; Rainey and Johnson 2009). African American women come to understand that black neighborhoods are exposed to environmental hazards at higher rates than white neighborhoods, and their activism becomes a struggle against environmental racism (Taylor 1997). A number of African American women leading the environmental justice movement can trace their activism back to the civil rights movement, in which earlier political training helped them identify racial injustices (Krauss 1993; Peeples and DeLuca 2006). Religion and spirituality also hold a prominent place in the environmental justice movement (Kaalunk 2004). Prindeville (2004) indicates that more than three-quarters of the Native American women activists she interviewed cited a sacred and spiritual connection to nature, and Gomez et al. (2011) find that black women activists frequently mentioned their religious beliefs as a motivation for their environmental efforts. Likewise, Taylor (1997: 52) draws our attention to religious leadership in the environmental justice movement, pointing out that the book *Toxic Waste and Race*, published by the United Church of Christ in 1987, "did for people of color and the environmental justice movement what *Silent Spring* did for middle class whites in the 60s."

The women who lead environmental justice groups engage in a variety of strategies and tactics, relying heavily on grassroots organizing built on a foundation of family and community networks (Krauss 1993; Prindeville 2004; Rainey and Johnson 2009). Many acknowledge the importance of building coalitions and connections across groups, communities, and regions. Given the diversity of the movement, leaders often work to build collaborative ties across racial and ethnic groups to bolster the movement's strength (Di Chiro 1992; Gutiérrez 1994; Hamilton 1994; Prindeville 2004). In addition, increasingly leaders see merit in establishing ties with the women's movement, pointing out that environmental issues can deeply affect human reproduction. Unger (2012), for example, describes how the concerns of the Native American women's group Women of All Red Nations (WARN) with uranium mining's impact on women's reproduction are linked to its ties to the women's movement. Also, Di Chiro (2008) discusses links between two groups, Asian Communities for Reproductive Justice and the Environmental Justice and Climate Change Coalition.

But leaders of the environmental justice movement also contend with divisions in the movement. Sometimes tensions exist between women and men, where constraints are placed on women's leadership or women have been compelled to take up the reigns of leadership when men resign their posts. As Bullard (2002) points out, such resignations only enhance women's position in the movement. Less success has occurred in creating strong links between leaders in the environmental justice movement and those in the mainstream environmental groups such as the Sierra Club (Prindeville 2004; Taylor 1997, 2014). Environmental justice advocates argue that mainstream groups do not fully grasp the racial, ethnic, and class disparities that underpin environmental practices. As environmental justice leader Cora Tucker states,

> This white woman from an environmental group asked me to come down to save a park.
>
> She said that they had been trying to get Black folks involved and that they won't come.
>
> I said, "Honey, it's not that they aren't concerned, but when their babies are dying in their arms they don't give a damn about a park." I said, "They want to save their babies. If you can help them save their babies, then in turn they can help you save your park." And she said, "But this is a real immediate problem." And I said, "Well, these people's kids dying is immediate." (cited in Krauss 1993: 256)

Environmental justice advocates explain that leaders in these other environmental groups do not always understand that communities of color and poor and working-class neighborhoods often bear the brunt of environmental degradation. As Taylor (2014: 33) notes, these other leaders continue to maintain "a false dichotomy between environment and social justice." In the end, the efforts of women in environmental justice groups highlight a larger pattern of power relations and subordination rooted in race, ethnic, class, and gender relations. Some segments of the environmental movement, as well as larger society, have yet to confront this problem and make appropriate changes (Krauss 1993; Taylor 2014, 2015).

Women's leadership in the contemporary environmental justice movement is similar to that of an earlier generation of female environmentalists who fought to make urban areas more environmentally hospitable for residents. Also similar to earlier women's activism, today's environmental justice movement continues to draw heavily on gendered, maternalist activist frames. But the continuities do not end there; women in the environmental justice movement today also continue to confront and challenge the intersecting barriers posed by class, racial, and ethnic bias. At the same time, however, women's environmental justice activism provides a space for women's leadership to develop and even flourish within the broader environmental movement, and a diverse set of women's participation in environmental justice importantly diversifies the movement's composition.

WOMEN'S LEADERSHIP IN ECOFEMINIST
AND DIRECT-ACTION GROUPS

Like environmental justice organizations, ecofeminist and direct-action groups also call attention to the need for multiple voices in agenda setting and leadership, and in this sense they can be conceptualized as alternatives to mainstream environmental organizations. One such category of groups, ecofeminism, emerged beginning in the 1970s and articulated an alternative ideational framework, one linking patriarchy and the subordination of women to the destruction of nature (Merchant 1996; Mallory 2006; Mann 2011). Ecofeminism is female-led and is largely a critical community of intellectuals and activists who combine feminism and environmentalism to explain how the beliefs and values that underlie the oppression of women and other groups also lead to environmental degradation. The earliest ecofeminist philosophies were articulated by leaders such as Mary Daly (1978), Susan Griffin (1978), and Carolyn Merchant (1980), although the term "ecofeminism" was coined by the French feminist Françoise d'Eaubonne in 1974 (d'Eaubonne 1980; Mallory 2006; Warren 1987; for an extended history, see Mann 2011).

While some environmental organizations, such as World Women in Defense of the Environment, have consciously characterized themselves as ecofeminist, ecofeminism has also shifted the discourse in environmentalism more broadly to incorporate feminist principles and to critique power relations between dominant and marginalized groups (Brulle 2000; Leach 2007; Sturgeon 1997). During the 1980s, ecofeminist leaders held Women and Life on Earth conferences to create a discursive space for introducing and elaborating ecofeminist beliefs. However, some (e.g., Kirk 1997) argue that ecofeminist organizations do not give enough attention to the role of race and class oppression, which then can hinder connections to the environmental justice movement.

Another type of alternative environmental group, direct-action environmental organizations, also provide opportunities for women's leadership. The growing involvement of women in these groups has brought a feminist perspective into this formerly male-dominated form of radical environmental activism (Mallory 2006). For example, Judi Bari, a feminist and leader of Earth First!, a direct-action group committed to saving the Redwoods of Northern California, joined the radical environmental organization during the late 1980s. She became involved with Earth First! after finding out that lumber she used as a carpenter came from the Redwoods. She encountered staunch opposition to her environmentalism from outside the movement, often violent resistance that specifically targeted her as a woman (Bari 1992).

As a member of Earth First! she dramatically influenced the previously male-led organization and encouraged more women to join (Coleman 2005; Shantz 2002). Drawing on her feminist and working-class background and experience as a labor organizer, Bari was aware of tendencies within leftist organizations to treat concerns of gender as subordinate to the larger movement. She instead encouraged Earth First! members to consider the role of sexism in the organization and how gender influenced the group's tactical choices (Bari 1992; Coleman 2005; Sturgeon 1997). Bari saw a heavy reliance on what she referred to as "he-man" "individual acts of daring," such as when activists chained their bodies to logging equipment and engaged in tree spiking and monkeywrenching in an effort to prevent the work of timber companies. Bari counseled an alternative approach that emphasized "long-term community-based organizing" in place of these individual acts that damaged property. She argued that a nonconfrontational approach of building community support for Earth First!, including among some timber workers, would strengthen the organization and its impact. In her words, this was a "feminization of Earth First!" (Bari 1992), and scholars (Sturgeon 1997) credit her efforts in making Earth First! a leading radical environmental organization, more receptive to feminist ideas.

Another important female figure in the direct-action network of activists was Julia Butterfly Hill, who also drew attention to the destruction of the Redwoods and did so with the highly visible tactic of tree sitting (Delicath and DeLuca 2003; DeLuca 2001; Ingalsbee 1996). In the 1990s Hill occupied an old-growth Redwood named Luna for over two years to convince authorities to preserve it. Substantial women are involved in direct-action environmental efforts in the Pacific Northwest, where they form groups such as Forest Defenders with both women and transgender members who disrupt the work of logging companies (Mallory 2006). Most of the women in these groups are young and white, but some are older women, who are more likely to participate in direct-action environmentalism than are older men (Mallory 2006). Forest Defenders creates a forum for women and transgender individuals to learn activist skills for protecting the forests, such as "climbing, knot-tying, treesit[ting] and blockade construction" (Mallory 2006: 40). Mallory (2006) states that these spaces allow women and transgender women and men to avoid misogynistic and heterosexist behaviors in the broader direct-action community, a culture that Judi Bari (1994: 220) has described as a "big man goes into big wilderness to save big trees" mentality. Female leaders comment on a historical gender division of labor within the direct-action environmental movement, with women, for some time, being limited to support roles, such as providing food, coordinating transportation, and answering phones.

Unlike some of their mainstream female counterparts, women involved in ecofeminism and direct-action environmental groups are resistant to assimilation strategies. Rather than adopting traditionally male styles of leadership, women in alternative organizations are likely to embrace nonhierarchical organizational structures founded on the intersection of feminism and environmentalism to illustrate the relationship between the oppression of women and environmental degradation. However, these alternative environmental groups, along with environmental justice groups and mainstream organizations, taken all together clearly illustrate the growing diversity over time in women's environmental leadership. Unlike in the early part of the century where women led primarily in women-only organizations, today we see women leading in a variety of environmental activist venues.

Conclusion

Women's environmental activism is, of course, first environmental activism. But as our examination of women's leadership in the environmental movement demonstrates, women leaders in the environmental movement have also been part of the struggle to challenge traditional stereotypes about women and their capacity to lead. Women in the environmental movement have engaged in public political activism, and their ongoing leadership contests beliefs that leadership, political engagement, environmental philosophy, and even environmental science are solely male domains. Their leadership helps us set aside great-man understandings of leadership (and many of the other chapters in this volume that reveal women's leadership in other areas help us to do this as well). Although traditional gender beliefs have constrained women's environmental work, developments over the last one hundred years show that attempts to limit women's contributions have not succeeded. Rather, women in the environmental movement have guided, shaped, and expanded the movement, successfully challenging traditional and limiting gender norms, all while protecting the natural environment in a diverse set of ways.

The past one hundred years of women's leadership in the environmental movement also reveals a number of similarities in women's leadership over time and across groups, while providing evidence of changes through time and differences across groups. The historical continuities in women's environmental leadership are numerous. One pronounced continuity is an ongoing, rich racial, ethnic, and class diversity among women environmental leaders, with important advances by African American, Asian American, Latina, Native American, and working-class women to protect their communities from environmental harm. Throughout the history of women's environmental leadership, we also see continuing commitment to social justice environmental activism, from white women leading Hull House in Chicago at the turn of the twentieth century to early-twentieth-century black women's clubs in southern cities to the large, racially and ethnically diverse environmental justice movement today. Other similarities in women's leadership over time exist in women's use of maternalism to support their claims and in their use of women-only groups to conduct their activism. Perhaps the most pronounced continuity is women's enduring influence on the movement and the environment. From the movement's earliest stages, women have been important actors in expanding movement participation and in protecting the earth.

Our investigation also reveals developments in women's environmental leadership over the past century that illustrate less continuity and instead show changes in women's leadership. Most noticeable is the growth in women's leadership over time, as women have claimed significant positions in nationwide and local environmental organizations, contributed to the development of scientific knowledge, increased their presence in radical activism, and become public spokespersons on crucial environmental issues. Another indicator of variability in women's environmental leadership, this time across groups and among leaders more so than a trajectory over time resides in the degree to which women draw upon traditional gender roles or feminism in their environmental claims making. Some women leaders draw heavily on women's traditional domestic roles as mothers and nurturers to support their environmental demands while other leaders do so less or not at all. Additionally, some leaders tackle environmental concerns explicitly as feminists and others do not. There is also substantial variation among women environmental leaders in the strategies and tactics they pursue, running the gamut from radical environmental activism to political and corporate lobbying.

Finally, our examination of women's leadership in environmentalism reveals that barriers to women in leadership positions have not been experienced in the same way by all women in the movement. For instance, while women have achieved substantial leadership in the environmental justice movement, including if not especially women of color and working-class women, leadership for women has been more elusive over the past one hundred years in national-level mainstream environmental groups. Today, while white, middle-class women are making gains in mainstream groups, women of color and working-class women continue to confront barriers in their efforts to gain leadership roles. There is ongoing evidence that race, ethnicity, and class continue to combine with gender to create intersectional barriers to women's efforts to lead. Women's environmental leadership has been most pronounced in local, grassroots environmental groups that do not have large-scale, hierarchical organizational structures, which often fall into our category of "alternative" and environmental justice organizations, and, of course, women have led throughout the century in women-only groups. Our examination of women's environmental leadership shows that the barriers have not been constructed only on the basis of gender, but they also involve race, ethnicity, and class, as well as organizational type.

In the end, while a number of continuities in a century of women's environmental leadership can be pointed to, so can numerous changes over time and substantial differences across groups. Our examination of women's leadership in the environmental movement over the last one hundred years, however, is less a story of women's subordination and far more a narrative of women's agency. As women did in the suffrage movement, women in the environmental movement have pressed vigorously for social change, and they have done so while contesting traditional views attempting to subordinate women. A diverse group of women have taken up the reigns of leadership in the environmental movement in myriad ways over the last one hundred years. Their leadership has broadened the goals, strategies, analyses, philosophies, and organizational forms of the environmental movement, and they have contributed significantly to saving the environment.

Note

1. As Kristin Goss documents in her chapter in this volume, the rise of second-wave feminism contributed to a decline in membership in traditional women's organizations, including the General Federation of Women's Clubs. As Goss acknowledges, the rise of the contemporary environmental movement in the 1960s and 1970s drew women out of the GFWC and into environmental activism instead.

References

Addams, Jane. 1911. *Twenty Years at Hull House*. New York: Macmillan.

Alcoa. 2015. "Board of Directors: Kathryn S. Fuller." https://www.alcoa.com/global/en/about_alcoa/corp_gov/directors/Kathryn_Fuller.asp.

Aminzade, Ronald R., Jack A. Goldstone, and Elizabeth J. Perry. 2001. "Leadership Dynamics and Dynamics of Contention." Pp. 126–154 in *Silence and Voice in the Study of Contentious Politics,* edited by Ronald R. Aminzade, Jack A. Goldstone, Doug

McAdam, Elizabeth J. Perry, William H. Sewell Jr., Sidney Tarrow, and Charles Tilly. New York: Cambridge University Press.

Banaszak, Lee Ann. 2010. *The Women's Movement Inside and Outside the State.* New York: Cambridge University Press.

Bari, Judi. 1992. "The Feminization of Earth First!" *Ms.*, May/June: 84.

———. 1994. *Timber Wars.* Monroe, ME: Common Courage Press.

Barker, Colin, Alan Johnson, and Michael Lavalette. 2001. *Leadership and Social Movements.* New York: Manchester University Press.

Beinecke, Frances. 2014. *The World We Create: A Message of Hope for a Planet in Peril.* Lanham, MD: Rowman and Littlefield.

Bell, Shannon Elizabeth, and Yvonne A. Braun. 2010. "Coal, Identity, and the Gendering of Environmental Justice Activism in Central Appalachia." *Gender & Society* 24: 794–813.

Brulle, Robert J. 2000. *Agency, Democracy, and Nature: The U.S. Environmental Movement from a Critical Theory Perspective.* Cambridge, MA: MIT Press.

Bullard, Robert D. 2000. *People of Color Environmental Groups 2000 Directory.* Environmental Justice Resource Center, Clark Atlanta University, Atlanta, GA.

———. 2001. "Environmental justice in the 21st Century: Race Still Matters." *Phylon* 49(3/4): 151–171.

———. 2002. "Crowning Women of Color and the Real Story Behind the 2002 EJ Summit." http://www.ejrc.cau.edu/SummCrowning04.html.

Cable, Sherry. 1992. "Women's Social Movement Involvement: The Role of Structural Availability in Recruitment and Participation Processes." *The Sociological Quarterly* 33: 35–50.

Carroll, Susan J., and Richard L. Fox. 2014. *Gender and Elections: Shaping the Future of American Politics.* New York: Cambridge University Press.

Carson, Rachel. 1962. *Silent Spring.* Boston: Houghton Mifflin.

Coleman, Kate. 2005. *The Secret Wars of Judi Bari: A Car Bomb, the Fight for the Redwoods, and the End of Earth First!* New York: Encounter Books.

Daly, Mary. 1978. *Gyn/Ecology, the Metaethics of Radical Feminism.* Boston: Beacon Press.

Dankelman, Irene. 2002. "Climate Change: Learning from Gender Analysis and Women's Experiences of Organizing for Sustainable Development." *Gender and Development* 10(2): 21–29.

David, Laurie. 2015. "About Laurie." http://lauriedavid.com/about-laurie/.

d'Eaubonne, Francoise. 1980. "Le Feminisme ou la mort." Pp. 64–67 in *New French Feminisms: An Anthology*, edited by Elaine Marks and Isabelle de Courtivron. Amherst: University of Massachusetts Press.

Delicath, John W., and Kevin Michael DeLuca. 2003. "Image Events, the Public Sphere, and Argumentative Practice: The Case of Racial Environmental Groups." *Argumentation* 17: 315–333.

DeLuca, Kevin Michael. 2001. "Trains in the Wilderness: The Corporate Roots of Environmentalism." *Rhetoric and Public Affairs* 4: 633–652.

Di Chiro, Giovanna. 1992. "Defining Environmental Justice: Women's Voice and Grassroots Politics." *Socialist Review* 22: 93–131.

———. 2008. "Living Environmentalisms: Coalition Politics, Social Reproduction, and Environmental Justice." *Environmental Politics* 17: 276–298.

Dowie, Mark. 1996. *Losing Ground: American Environmentalism at the Close of the Twentieth Century.* Cambridge, MA: MIT Press.

Dreier, Peter. 2012. "How Rachel Carson and Michael Harrington Changed the World." *Contexts* 11(2): 40–46.

Dunlap, Riley E., and Angela G. Mertig. 1991. "The Evolution of the U.S. Environmental Movement from 1970 to 1990: An Overview." *Society & Natural Resources* 4: 209–218.

Gaard, Greta. 1998. *Ecological Politics: Ecofeminists and the Greens.* Philadelphia: Temple University Press.

Gibbs, Lois Marie. 2011. *Love Canal and the Birth of the Environmental Health Movement.* Washington, DC: Island Press.

Gilmore, Glenda Elizabeth. 1996. *Gender and Jim Crow: Women and the Politics of White Supremacy in North Carolina, 1896–1920.* Chapel Hill: University of North Carolina Press.

Glave, Dianne D. 2003. "'A Garden So Brilliant with Colors, So Original in Its Design': Rural African American Women, Gardening, Progressive Reform, and the Foundation of an African American Environmental Perspective." *Environmental History* 8: 395–411.

Gomez, Antoinette M., Fatemeh Shafiei, and Glenn S. Johnson. 2011. "Black Women's Involvement in the Environmental Justice Movement: An Analysis of Three Communities in Atlanta, Georgia." *Race, Gender & Class* 18: 189–214.

Gottlieb, Robert. 2005. *Forcing the Spring: The Transformation of the American Environmental Movement.* Washington, DC: Island Press.

Greene, Ronnie. 2008. *Night Fire: Big Oil, Poison Air, and Margie Richard's Fight to Save Her Town.* New York: Amistad Publishers.

Griffin, Susan. 1978. *Woman and Nature: The Roaring Inside Her.* New York: Harper and Row.

Gutiérrez, Gabriel. 1994. "Mothers of East Los Angeles Strike Back." Pp. 220–233 in *Unequal Protection: Environmental Justice and Communities of Color,* edited by Robert D. Bullard. San Francisco: Sierra Club Books.

Hamilton, Cynthia. 1990. "Women, Home, and Community: The Struggle in an Urban Environment Race." *Poverty and the Environment* 1: 3, 10–13.

———. 1994. "Concerned Citizens of South Central Los Angeles." Pp. 207–219 in *Unequal Protection: Environmental Justice and Communities of Color,* edited by Robert D. Bullard. San Francisco: Sierra Club Books.

Hazlett, Maril. 2004. "'Woman vs. Man vs. Bugs': Gender and Popular Ecology in Early Reactions to *Silent Spring.*" *Environmental History* 9(4): 701–729.

Hemmati, Minu, and Ulrike Röhr. 2009. "Engendering the Climate-Change Negotiations: Experiences, Challenges, and Steps Forward." *Gender and Development* 17(1): 19–32.

Herles, Cecilia M. 2010. "Women's Leadership the Environmental Movement." Pp. 218–225 in *Gender and Women's Leadership: A Reference Handbook,* edited by Karen O'Connor. Thousand Oaks, CA: Sage Publications.

Hickey, Georgina. 2013. "The Respectability Trap: Gender Conventions in 20th-Century Movements for Social Change." *Journal of Interdisciplinary Feminist Thought* 7(1): 1–12.

Ingalsbee, Timothy. 1996. "Earth First! Activism: Ecological Postmodern Praxis in Radical Environmentalist Identities." *Environmental Conflict* 39: 263–276.

International Women's Earth and Climate Action Network. 2016. "IWECI Summit." http://wecaninternational.org/pages/summit.

Kaalunk, Valerie Ann. 2004. "Witness to Truth: Black Women Heeding the Call for Environmental Justice." Pp. 78–92 in *New Perspectives on Environmental Justice: Gender,*

Sexuality, and Activism, edited by Rachel Stein. New Brunswick, NJ: Rutgers University Press.

Kaufman, Polly Welts. 1996. *National Parks and the Woman's Voice: A History*. Albuquerque: University of New Mexico Press.

Kirk, Gwyn. 1997. "Ecofeminism and Environmental Justice: Bridges across Gender, Race, and Class." *Frontiers* 18(2): 2–20.

Klenke, Karin. 1996. *Women and Leadership: A Contextual Perspective*. New York: Springer.

Kline, Benjamin. 2011. *First along the River: A Brief History of the U.S. Environmental Movement*. Lanham, MD: Rowman and Littlefield.

Kovarik, Bill. 1996. "Mainstream Media: The Radium Girls." Pp. 33–52 in *Mass Media and Environmental Conflict: America's Green Crusades*, edited by Mark Neuzil and William Kovarik. Thousand Oaks, CA: Sage Publications.

Kraditor, Aileen S. 1981. *The Ideas of the Woman Suffrage Movement, 1890–1920*. New York: W. W. Norton.

Krauss, Celene. 1993. "Women and Toxic Waste Protests: Race, Class and Gender as Resources of Resistance." *Qualitative Sociology* 16: 247–262.

———. 1998. "Challenging Power: Toxic Waste Protests and the Politicization of White, Working-Class Women." Pp. 129–150 in *Community Activism and Feminist Politics: Organizing across Race, Class, and Gender*, edited by Nancy A. Naples. New York: Routledge.

Kuumba, M. Bahati. 2001. *Gender and Social Movements*. Walnut Creek, CA: Alta Mira Press.

LaDuke, Winona. 1999. *All Our Relations: Native Struggles for Land and Life*. Cambridge, MA: South End Press.

Lake, Osprey Orielle. 2016. "Osprey Orielle Lake." http://therightsofnature.org/tag/osprey-orielle-lake/.

Leach, Melissa. 2007. "Earth Mother Myths and Other Ecofeminist Fables: How a Strategic Notion Rose and Fell." *Development and Change* 38(1): 67–85.

Mallory, Chaone. 2006. "Ecofeminism and Forest Defense in Cascadia: Gender, Theory and Radical Activism." *Capitalism Nature Socialism* 17(1): 32–49.

Mann, Susan. 2011. "Pioneers of U.S. Ecofeminism and Environmental Justice." *Feminist Formations* 23: 1–25.

Martin, Laura Jane. 2012. "Where Are the Women in Ecology?" *Frontiers in Ecology and the Environment* 10(4): 177–178.

McCammon, Holly J. 2012. *The U.S. Women's Jury Movements and Strategic Adaptation: A More Just Verdict*. New York: Cambridge University Press.

Merchant, Carolyn. 1980. *The Death of Nature: Women, Ecology, and the Scientific Revolution*. San Francisco: Harper and Row.

———. 1984. "Women of the Progressive Conservation Movement: 1900–1916." *Environmental Review* 8: 57–85.

———. 1996. *Earthcare: Women and the Environment*. New York: Routledge.

Musil, Robert K. 2014. *Rachel Carson and Her Sisters: Extraordinary Women Who Have Shaped America's Environment*. New Brunswick, NJ: Rutgers University Press.

Nelkin, Dorothy. 1981. "Nuclear Power as a Feminist Issue." *Environment: Science and Policy for Sustainable Development* 23(1): 14–39.

Nepstad, Sharon Erickson, and Clifford Bob. 2006. "When Do Leaders Matter? Hypotheses on Leadership Dynamics in Social Movements." *Mobilization* 11(1): 1–22.

Newman, Rich. 2001. "Making Environmental Politics: Women and Love Canal Activism." *Women's Studies Quarterly* 20: 65–84.

O'Brien, Erin E., and Jennifer Shea. 2010. "Women's Leadership within Their Communities." Pp. 41–49 in *Gender and Women's Leadership: A Reference Handbook*, edited by Karen O'Connor. Thousand Oaks, CA: Sage Publications.

Oreskes, Naomi, and Erik Conway. 2010. *Merchants of Doubt.* New York: Bloomsbury Press.

Paley, Grace. 2008. "Women's Pentagon Action Unity Statement." *Massachusetts Review* 49(4): 461–464.

Pellow, David Naguib. 2002. *Garbage Wars: The Struggle for Environmental Justice in Chicago.* Cambridge, MA: MIT Press.

People for Community Recovery. 2015. "History." http://www.peopleforcommunityrecovery.org/history.html.

Peeples, Jennifer A., and Kevin M. DeLuca. 2006. "The Truth of the Matter: Motherhood, Community and Environmental Justice." *Women's Studies in Communication* 29(1): 59–87.

Petit, Angela. 2001. "Domestic, Virtuous Women: Examining Women's Place in a Public Environmental Debate along Louisiana's Cancer Corridor." *Technical Communication Quarterly* 10: 365–386.

Philippon, Daniel J. 2004. *Conserving Words: How American Nature Writers Shaped the Environmental Movement.* Athens: University of Georgia Press.

Prindeville, Diane-Michele. 2004. "The Role of Gender, Race/Ethnicity, and Class in Activists' Perceptions of Environmental Justice." Pp. 93–108 in *New Perspectives on Environmental Justice: Gender, Sexuality, and Activism*, edited by Rachel Stein. New Brunswick, NJ: Rutgers University Press.

Prindeville, Diane-Michele, and John G. Bretting. 1998. "Indigenous Women Activists and Political Participation." *Women & Politics* 19: 39–58.

Pulido, Laura. 1997. "Community, Place, and Identity." Pp. 11–28 in *Thresholds in Feminist Geography: Difference, Methodology, Representation*, edited by John Paul JonesIII, Heidi J. Nast, and Susan M. Roberts. Lanham, MD: Rowman and Littlefield.

———. 2000. "Rethinking Environmental Racism: White Privilege and Urban Development in Southern California." *Annals of the Association of American Geographers* 90: 12–40.

Rainey, Shirley A., and Glenn S. Johnson. 2009. "Grassroots Activism: An Exploration of Women of Color's Role in the Environmental Justice Movement." *Race, Gender & Class* 16: 144–173.

Reger, Jo, and Suzanne Staggenborg. 2006. "Patterns of Mobilization in Local Movement Organizations: Leadership and Strategy in Four National Organization for Women Chapters." *Sociological Perspectives* 49(3): 297–323.

Riley, Glenda. 1999. *Women and Nature: Saving the "Wild" West.* Lincoln: University of Nebraska Press.

———. 2003. "Conservation Movement, 1870–1940." Pp. 83–91 in *Encyclopedia of Women in the American West*, edited by Gordon Morris Bakken and Brenda Farrington. Thousand Oaks, CA: Sage.

Rimby, Susan. 2012. *Mira Lloyd Dock and the Progressive-Era Conservation Movement.* University Park: Pennsylvania State University Press.

Robertson, Janet. 2003. *The Magnificent Mountain Women.* Lincoln: University of Nebraska Press.

Robinson, Gail. 1978. "A Woman's Place Is in the Movement." *Environmental Action* 9(22): 12–13.

Robnett, Belinda. 1997. *How Long? How Long? African-American Women in the Struggle for Civil Rights.* New York: Oxford University Press.

Rome, Adam. 2003. "'Give Earth a Chance': The Environmental Movement and the Sixties." *Journal of American History* 90(2): 525–554.

Rouse, Jacqueline Anne. 1989. *Lugenia Burns Hope: Black Southern Reformer.* Athens: University of Georgia Press.

Sale, Kirkpatrick. 1993. *The Green Revolution: American Environmental Movement, 1962–1992.* New York: Hill and Wang.

Schlossberg, David. 2003. "The Justice of Environmental Justice: Reconciling Equity, Recognition, and Participation in a Political Movement." Pp. 77–108 in *Moral and Political Reasoning in Environmental Practice*, edited by Andrew Light and Avner De-Shalit. Cambridge, MA: MIT Press.

Schrepfer, Susan. 2005. *Nature's Altars: Mountains, Gender, and American Environmentalism.* Lawrence: University Press of Kansas.

Shantz, Jeffrey. 2002. "Judi Bari and 'The Feminization of Earth First!': The Convergence of Class, Gender, and Radical Environmentalism." *Feminist Review* 70: 105–122.

Sicherman, Barbara. 1984. *Alice Hamilton, a Life in Letters.* Cambridge, MA: Harvard University Press.

Smith, Michael B. 2001. "'Silence, Miss Carson!' Science, Gender, and the Reception of *Silent Spring.*" *Feminist Studies* 27(3): 733–752.

Smith, Susan Lynn. 1995. *Sick and Tired of Being Sick and Tired: Black Women's Health Activism in America, 1890–1950.* Philadelphia: University of Pennsylvania Press.

Stearney, Lynn M. 1994. "Feminism, Ecofeminism, and the Maternal Archetype: Motherhood as a Feminine Universal." *Communication Quarterly* 42: 145–159.

Sturgeon, Noël. 1997. *Ecofeminist Natures: Race, Gender, Feminist Theory, and Political Action.* New York: Routledge.

Sze, Julie. 2004. "Gender, Asthma Politics, and Urban Environmental Justice Activism." Pp. 177–190 in *New Perspectives on Environmental Justice: Gender, Sexuality, and Activism*, edited by Rachel Stein. New Brunswick, NJ: Rutgers University Press.

Taylor, Dorceta E. 1997. "American Environmentalism: The Role of Race, Class and Gender in Shaping Activism, 1820–1995." *Race, Gender & Class* 5: 16–62.

———. 2014. "The State of Diversity in Environmental Organizations." Report prepared for Green 2.0, July.

———. 2015. "Gender and Racial Diversity in Environmental Organizations: Uneven Accomplishments and Cause for Concern." *Environmental Justice* 8(5): 165–180.

Thomas, Sue. 2003. "The Impact of Women in Political Leadership Positions." Pp. 89–110 in *Women and American Politics: New Questions, New Directions*, edited by Susan J. Carroll. New York: Oxford University Press.

Unger, Nancy D. 2012. *Beyond Nature's Housekeepers: American Women in Environmental History.* New York: Oxford University Press.

Verchick, Robert R. M. 2004. "Feminist Theory and Environmental Justice." Pp. 63–77 in *New Perspectives on Environmental Justice: Gender, Sexuality, and Activism*, edited by Rachel Stein. New Brunswick, NJ: Rutgers University Press.

Warren, Karen J. 1987. "Feminism and Ecology: Making Connections." *Environmental Ethics* 9: 3–20.

15

Women Occupying Wall Street

GENDER CONFLICT AND FEMINIST MOBILIZATION

Heather McKee Hurwitz and Verta Taylor

The Occupy Wall Street movement (Occupy; OWS) has been one of the most widespread mobilizations in the United States to critique increasing economic inequality in the wake of a global financial crisis (Gamson and Sifry 2013). Like many recent social movements in the United States, Occupy has been shaped by the networks, identities, and tactics of second-wave feminism, contemporary feminism, and antifeminist backlash (Haiven 2011; Meyer and Whittier 1994; Reger 2012). But it is striking that even one hundred years after enactment of women's suffrage, Occupy was weakened by gender conflict produced by gender inequalities, male dominance, and sexual harassment, which drove women away from the main movement organizations into separate feminist groups (Butler 2011; Haiven 2011; Pickerill and Krinsky 2012; Reger 2015).

The dynamics of gender conflict within Occupy are reminiscent of the relations between the emergent suffrage movement and the abolitionist movement in the mid-nineteenth century. As in Occupy, women found their voices silenced or ignored in the campaign to end slavery, prompting them both to fight for their right to be heard in the abolitionist struggle and to forge their own movement for the rights of women. Prior research suggests that gender conflict in the abolitionist movement played a critical role in the rise of the suffrage movement, just as gender conflict in the New Left and civil rights movements helped fuel the second-wave women's movement (Epstein 1991; Evans 1979). Occupy, in contrast, was comprised, at least in part, of networks of women that spilled over from the feminist movement. Social movements spill over into each other when they contribute to *and* benefit from each other. Despite its commitment to participatory democracy and nonhierarchical leadership, like many postfeminist movements, the Occupy movement had gender conflict deeply stitched into its fabric.

In this chapter, we use the concept of *gender conflict* as an umbrella term for conflicts that disadvantage, threaten, or harm women, genderqueer persons, and sexual minorities. Gender conflicts are a form of contention and infighting over issues pertaining to gender inequality. Gender conflicts develop primarily when, in response to gender inequality, subordinated groups—including women, transpersons, and sexual minorities—challenge male domination and vocalize the exclusion and oppressions they face in social movements. Gender conflicts may also spark feminist mobilization and the formation of feminist organizations. To understand the role of gender conflict and how feminism influences movement dynamics, we address two research questions: What role did feminist identity, tactics, and leadership play in the emergence and development of Occupy? And how did feminist mobilizing structures outside Occupy contribute to the movement?

Our analysis demonstrates how spillover and movement-to-movement influence between Occupy and women's and feminist movements inspired the emergence of a variety of feminist spin-off organizations within Occupy. We begin with an overview of the history and literature on gender conflict within a broad range of social movements, from suffrage to the present day. Next we describe briefly the data sources on which the study is based. Then we trace Occupy's emergence. As our analysis demonstrates, gender conflict plagued the movement almost from the outset, leading to the creation of distinct feminist spin-off organizations, that is, separate groups that formed within Occupy to redress women's grievances and their exclusion from leadership positions in the larger movement. We then describe three processes that we consider to be key to the persistence of feminism in social movements that are not principally mobilized around gender and sexuality issues: the development of feminist collective identity, feminist free spaces, and feminist bridge leaders. We conclude by arguing that gender conflict and feminist mobilization have influenced a variety of social movements not purportedly about gender issues throughout the one-hundred-year history since ratification of the Nineteenth Amendment, and Occupy provides a recent example of this conflict, an example illustrating that gender conflict within movements continues today. We suggest that future research focus on gender conflict in social movements to analyze when it emerges, how it unfolds, and its consequences, as well as the persistence of feminism.

Gender Conflict in Social Movements through Time

Many times over the last hundred years, women's movements in the United States have emerged in or spilled over into a variety of different social movements (Meyer and Whittier 1994; Staggenborg and Taylor 2005). One can see a pattern in a variety of movements by examining them side by side: one cause of women's activism has been gender conflict within other movements. For example, the first wave of feminism emerged out of gender exclusion in the abolitionist movement to end slavery. When Elizabeth Cady Stanton and Lucretia Mott attended the World's Anti-Slavery Convention in 1840, they were denied seats and voting privileges at the convention because they were women (Stanton, Anthony, and Gage 1881). In response, they organized the Seneca Falls convention with its sole focus on women's rights. Feminists have also mobilized within the labor movement, expanding this movement by addressing women's specific grievances and forming separate organizations to end sexual harassment and unionize female-dominated occupations like home health care workers (Boris and Klein 2008; Cobble 2007). As McCammon and colleagues document in their chapter in this volume, women in the environmental movement over the last century have confronted and resisted gendered hierarchies in environmentalism. Likewise, in HIV-AIDS organizing that started in the 1980s, the movement largely focused on gay men's issues and was dominated by male leadership. Feminists formed separate women's caucuses to advocate for women's health and promote women's leadership in the main social movement organization, AIDS Coalition to Unleash Power (ACT UP); Roth 1998; Schneider and Stoller 1994).

In most instances, mixed-gender movements have been characterized by gender inequality, which has both limited the movements and inspired feminists within them. The US civil rights movement marginalized women's formal leadership (as Hearne and McCammon in this volume also comment on), yet women played a major role in grassroots organizing for a variety of mass protests, including the Montgomery Bus Boycott (Robinson 1987). The segregation of women and gender conflict in the civil rights movement weakened the movement but also sparked spin-off organizations to address women's rights that helped catalyze the reemergence of a mass women's movement in the 1960s and 1970s (Polletta 2002; Robnett 1997). Additionally, in a variety of New Left social movement organizations in the 1960s, an opportunity for women to organize on behalf of women's rights was created by the stark contrast between the movement's professed belief in participatory democracy and the sexual exploitation of women and marginalization of women from leadership (Evans 1979; Polletta 2002). Ultimately, many women discovered that leaving civil rights and New Left organizations (including anti–Vietnam War organizations, Students for a Democratic Society, and the Student Non-Violent Coordinating Committee) opened an opportunity to merge the ideals of feminism and participatory democracy. Women's desire for a new democratic society and opposition to gender conflict in the civil rights and New Left movements contributed to the emergence of feminist movements of the 1960s and 1970s (Evans 1979; Polletta 2002; Taylor and Rupp 1993).

Since women's suffrage was granted one hundred years ago, one can find repeated examples of women's and feminist movements mobilizing within other social movements, using these movements as opportunities to press for women's and feminist goals. Social movement scholars have viewed gender inequality and male dominance within movements both as a political opportunity for the emergence of women's and feminist organizing and as a form of infighting that has the potential to weaken a movement and contribute to its decline (Gamson 1975; Robnett 1997; Roth 1998).

Considering the myriad ways that women's and feminist movements have contributed to many different US social movements, even those suffused with gender conflict, it is surprising there has been so much debate and skepticism about the involvement of women and feminists in the Occupy movement. Some scholars and journalists argue that women participated in all aspects of movement work and that feminist organizations contributed significantly to Occupy protests (Brunner 2011; Maharawal 2011; Milkman, Luce, and Lewis 2013; Seltzer 2011). Others argue that Occupy was dominated by white males, that sexism was rampant but ignored in the encampments and in movement organizations, and that feminism was peripheral to the movement (Butler 2011; Pickerill and Krinsky 2012; Reger 2015). We view this debate as symptomatic of the current state of feminism, which Reger (2012) has characterized as "nowhere-everywhere," meaning that feminist beliefs and protest simultaneously appear both trivial and "dead" or "nowhere" and yet, at the same time, persist among women as a basis of identity, solidarity, and mobilization. The goals of contemporary feminists are numerous and may be enigmatic and diverse, ranging from fighting for the rights of transgender persons, to support for fat-positive beauty standards (Reger 2012), to advocating sexual liberation and an end to sexual harassment by marching in "slutwalks" (Reger 2015). Similarly "gaga feminism" (Halberstam 2012) embraces gender fluidity and lesbian and gay politics, but is also a flashy caricature of feminism, inspired by capitalism, shared via social media, and infused with sexual liberation, like its namesake, popstar Lady Gaga. Women who support feminist claims may even appear to espouse antifeminism such as when participants claim the "I'm not a feminist but" identity in response to backlash (Crossley 2010). Although we know that feminism spills over into movements whose claims are not principally concerned with gender and sexual politics and that contemporary feminism may appear to be "nowhere-everywhere" because it takes a variety of new forms, we argue here that it is necessary to examine more systematically the persistence of gender conflict in existing social movements to fully understand the significance and continuity of feminism for contemporary social movements.

Data and Methods

The study is based on field research conducted between June and December 2012 in New York City and the San Francisco Bay Area, as well as at the first Occupy National Gathering (NatGat) in Philadelphia. While New York City sparked the nationwide movement, Bay Area activists in and around Occupy Oakland contributed heavily to cultivating it (Mahler 2012). NatGat was an assembly of participants from the nationwide movement. Data were obtained through participant observation, movement documents, and seventy-three in-depth semistructured interviews with participants.

In each location, Hurwitz conducted participant observation, paying attention to conflict over gender and feminist issues, and wrote field notes daily. She also collected data on the activities of the most significant feminist, women's, lesbian, gay, queer, and people of color groups and events that played a prominent role in each of the sites including Oakland Occupy Patriarchy, Safer Spaces committees, Women Occupying Wall Street, feminist general assemblies, and Women Occupy, a national clearinghouse of feminist and women's groups. From each field site and a variety of movement websites, we compiled an archive of paper and electronic documents about each group and the movement as a whole. The archive includes flyers, pamphlets, forum posts, articles, audio and video recordings of explicitly feminist events, and every newspaper issued by the *Occupied Wall Street Journal, Occupy! An OWS Inspired Gazette,* and *Tidal* (the main movement newspapers).

The seventy-three key informants were involved in these movement organizations and networks. They included speakers, group meeting facilitators, writers and bloggers, and active protesters. Interviewees initially were located by advertising the study on the email networks of Occupy Oakland, Women Occupy, and the New York General Assembly of Occupy. In the course of participant observation, Hurwitz met and recruited additional key informants through snowball sampling. The majority of the interviews were conducted with women, persons of color, and/or sexual minorities, although a few men were also interviewed: 80% of all respondents identified as female, 7% as genderqueer, 7% as male, and 6% declined to answer. Approximately 64% of participants were white, 11% Latin@/Chican@, 3% black, 5% Asian, and 17% other race / mixed-race / declined to answer. With respect to sexuality, 42% of participants identified as heterosexual; 19% as gay, lesbian, or bisexual; 25% as queer or other sexuality; and 14% declined to answer. The participants ranged in age from eighteen to seventy-seven years old. Forty-seven interviewees indicated that they had stayed overnight in an Occupy encampment. Interviews lasted from forty-five minutes to four hours (averaging about two hours) and were conversational but followed an interview guide. Interviews focused on the historical trajectory of each individual's participation over the first year of the movement, activities in which the participant felt particularly included or excluded, inequalities the participant experienced or observed in Occupy, and their prior involvement in feminist organizations and networks. Because the study focuses on infighting and conflicts, interviewees selected a pseudonym that we have used throughout the chapter to ensure their anonymity.

Field notes, interview transcripts, and documents were coded and analyzed using ATLAS.ti. The analysis focused on identifying the nature, frequency, and impact of gender conflict on Occupy and on the role it played in feminist mobilization. Of course, social movements are not homogenous. By focusing on movement centers and NatGat, which served as Occupy's radical flanks, we may underestimate the experiences of more moderate participants and organizations. In addition, we do not address the literally hundreds of local protests or conflicts about a range of other identities—such as class, race, sexuality, ability, and student concerns—and goals—such as anarchism and labor union mobilization (Lewis and Luce 2012) that also contributed to nationwide action.

The Emergence of Occupy

In response to an ad in the activist *Adbusters* magazine in the summer of 2011 and a series of community organizing meetings in Lower Manhattan parks, Occupy emerged in New York City on September 17, 2011, in an around-the-clock rally in the city's financial district in Zuccotti Park, a concrete city block dotted with a few trees and picnic tables. "We are the 99%" became the key slogan of the movement, symbolizing class-based solidarity in opposition to the most wealthy 1%, the government, corporations, and banks. By late October 2011, the movement's signature protest tactic—encampments or "occupations"—had spread across the United States and globally to more than one thousand town squares.

As protesters provided self-help or mutual aid to each other and the surrounding community, the encampments became a mechanism for participants and adherents to pool their resources, create solidarity and oppositional consciousness to the 1%, formulate and debate strategy and tactics—in short, to create a movement. They rallied and marched; held town hall meetings or "general assemblies"; and enjoyed free food, education, arts, and even mental health services and yoga at the camps (Milkman, Luce, and Lewis 2013). The movement amassed labor and monetary resources that included creating a counterculture with its own language and hand signals, operating procedures and structure (Gitlin 2012), and became a utopian experiment or an example of a "prefigurative world" guided by egalitarian values (Gitlin 2012). A growing body of literature analyzes the role of media and digital activism in creating a participatory culture (Costanza-Chock 2012) and how facilitators (masters of ceremonies) and stackers (people who organized a list of speakers) orchestrated democratic consensus-based decision making (Szolucha 2013). Occupy mobilized in part by utilizing personnel, tactics, and strategies from earlier waves of participatory democracy movements in the United States including the civil rights, New Left, antiglobalization, and women's movements (Leach 2013; Piven 2013; Polletta 2002). Some scholars have celebrated Occupy as the first successful consensus-based "structureless" participatory democracy movement in the United States in decades (Piven 2013). But our analysis will show that the movement's gender hierarchy kept the movement from living up to its claims.

Gender Conflict

A considerable body of research suggests that gender hierarchies and inequalities have frequently influenced mixed-gender social movements in the United States (Taylor 1999). Although Occupy did not designate formal leaders and was considered a "non-hierarchical" participatory democracy, gender hierarchy persisted. The most widespread gender conflicts occurred when individuals challenged men who monopolized organizing meetings and interviews with the press. The following statement made by one activist sums up the views of many women who participated in the early phases of Occupy: "10 people were interviewed [on the morning news]. . . . 1 of them was a woman. . . . The 99 percent is not 90 percent men!" (Butler 2011: 71). CODEPINK and other feminists responded to the lack of women's opportunities to speak to the press by organizing speak-outs against gender inequality and writing articles in *Ms.* magazine both about women's participation and subordination in Occupy. In an early article in the *Occupy N+1* newspaper, Audrea Lim describes the intensity of gender conflict within organizing meetings:

> Several weeks into OWS, a meeting of the People of Color caucus degenerated into a shouting match, and it made me want to leave for good. Three black men had jumped to their feet, pointing fingers and yelling over everyone else. . . . One of them [was] clearly an instigator. . . . The facilitator, an articulate Asian-American woman adept at being simultaneously kind and firm . . . attempted to referee.

Men challenged the woman facilitator, interrupting the agenda and frustrating Audrea, who left the meeting. Also, gender conflicts broke out over where women and genderqueer persons could sleep at the encampments or "occupations" and whether these spaces were safe enough for women, genderqueer people, and sexual minorities. As evidence of just how soon in the movement's history these gender dynamics began to play out, the very first issue of *Occupy! N+1* highlighted the problem of male dominance and a growing concern for gender inequality in the movement: "I've never felt as marginalized and unsafe as the first night I arrived at OWS. . . . There were men everywhere. I would estimate men outnumbered women sleeping in the park three to one." Smith and other women occupiers formed a Women's Caucus within the first two weeks of the encampment to create a safer designated space for women to sleep so they would not wake up sleeping next to strange men. Gender conflict was common in the form of sexual harassment; women's marginalization in meetings, as movement spokespersons; and within the encampments.

From its inception, men held a dominant position in the movement as far as leadership was concerned, and the culture of the movement was coded masculine. Illustrative of the culture of male dominance that pervaded the movement during its formative stages is the website "Hot Chicks of Occupy Wall Street" (http://hotchicksofoccupywallstreet.tumblr.com/) created by a few male Occupy participants in New York City. The site became popular thanks to a viral video: soft music plays in the background as the camera pans an Occupy encampment, pausing on close-ups of women laughing, bearing their midriffs and cleavage, and tossing their hair. The filmmakers interviewed some of the women, but others are mainly pictured as models in fashion magazines. In addition to the video, the website featured a series of photos and profiles of female activists. The website encouraged visitors to "like" or vote for their favorite women, as if it were a beauty contest. The website reaffirms gendered, racial, and sexual hierarchies, portraying women primarily as sexual objects rather than as full-fledged activists and asserts racial hierarchy by communicating that white is beautiful. Perhaps the most egregious examples of male dominance in the movement were about a dozen reported cases of sexual harassment and gender-based violence in the New York City encampment, several instances of violence against women and sexual minorities in Oakland, and episodes of harassment in smaller cities (see, for example, Lomax 2011; Newcomb 2011). Forms of violence and gendered harassment included catcalling, unwanted sexual invitations, and even rape. Minutes from a November 6,

2011, Women Occupying Wall Street (WOWS) meeting explain how the movement prioritized the participation of men protesters: "Three members shared personal experiences, one of which had occurred earlier that day and entailed a man physically grabbing her arm while he had alcohol on his breath and declaring that she was sexy while several Occupiers looked on and laughed. We were unanimously disgusted by such incidents." Aggressive men in the encampments acted on the belief that men are superior to women by objectifying and sexually harassing women.

Everyday life in the movement was also male-dominated. Participants repeatedly described the movement's incessant drum circles, heated discussion in the face of police presence, men's conversational domination of meetings and general assemblies, the threat of and actual sexual harassment, and men's interruptions of women in meetings as performances of male dominance intended to ensure men's power over movement spaces, leadership, and decisions about tactics and strategies. For example, Prakash was involved in several Occupations on the West Coast and NatGat and describes her experience with men leaders:

> Guys were doing good things like taking leadership roles, making stuff happen, leading the direction of the message or a march, but their voices were substantially more dominant than female voices in organizations and in everything that we did—it was very male oriented.

Similarly, despite the movement's nonhierarchical orientation, Danielle reveals that white radical men in her Occupy group in the West belittled women's authority and legitimacy: "I came expecting, 'Everybody is welcome in the 99%, let's work together, and support each other,' but it was totally not what happened. It was more like, 'Well you're not radical enough,' and one guy even said 'Go back to your couch in the suburbs, you stupid housewife.'" Both Prakash and Danielle observed and experienced gender conflict as a result of men's domination of leadership tasks. A 2012 issue of the feminist zine *Quarrel* sums up the deep inequalities within Occupy: "The encampments established were often a microcosm of the problematic structures that plague society at large: racism, sexism, homophobia . . . challenges of dealing with these issues, particularly gendered violence and sexual violence, were intensified by threat of police intervention and the perceived greater cause of social change." Gender conflicts, debates, and infighting over the role of women, gays, lesbians, and transgender persons in the movement frequently erupted over who could lead or speak, where to sleep, and whether women, genderqueers, and sexual minorities were safe in the urban encampments.

As this brief overview suggests, Occupy was built on the legacy of participatory democracy. One of the most prominent problems with collectivist democratic movements and of all mixed-gender social movements is that the pervasiveness and resilience of gender inequality in the larger society inevitably gets replicated in the organizational logic of social movements. This frequently counteracts even the best efforts of activists who claim to operate in a manner consistent with the principles of consensus decision making and participatory democracy (Polletta 2002; Taylor 1999). The culture of male dominance and variety of gender conflicts that broke out in Occupy were similar to those that women experienced in the New Left, HIV-AIDS, labor, and civil rights movements (Evans 1979; Polletta 2002; Robnett 1997; Roth 1998). However, Occupy acted quickly to address gender inequalities and mitigate gender conflicts. Benefiting from second-wave and contemporary feminist personnel, Occupy developed a variety of feminist organizations and networks to mobilize women's participation in the movement. They responded to gender conflict with the goal of strengthening Occupy by building a larger base of support inclusive of women and their interests.

The Emergence of Feminist Organizations in Occupy

Although gender conflict and the culture of male dominance was a source of infighting for the movement, Occupy provided a political opportunity for feminist mobilization. Gender conflict in combination with the large number of protest events—especially the diffusion of encampments as a tactical repertoire, Occupy's open and formally "leaderless" organizational structure, and the participation of women with histories of activism in second-wave and contemporary feminist organizations and networks—led to the formation of feminist spin-off organizations. Frustrated by the male-dominated leadership and direction of Occupy and the sexual harassment of women in the encampments, women, sexual minorities, genderqueer and transgender participants, and feminists turned first to existing feminist organizations and networks to mobilize. Over time, however, feminist participants increasingly began to create separate organizations.

Preexisting feminist mobilizing structures played an important role in rallying feminists within Occupy. Local feminist reading circles, self-defense collectives, nongovernmental organizations, lesbian and gay organizations, and other feminist networks in New York City and the San Francisco Bay Area joined with national organizations, such as the Feminist Peace Network and CODEPINK, to recruit increasing numbers of feminists to Occupy. Influential feminists such as Eve Ensler, Angela Davis, Alice Walker, Gloria Steinem, Jo Freeman, Ursula K. Le Guin, and many more blogged, wrote articles, visited, and spoke at occupations to support feminist activists. Women's studies programs and women's cultural communities provided knowledge, leadership, membership, and other resources to local Occupy organizers. Both CODEPINK and the Feminist Peace Network sponsored websites (womenoccupy.org and occupypatriarchy.org, respectively) that served as communication hubs to provide toolkits for feminist organizing. For example, within the first two weeks of the New York City encampment, feminists from CODEPINK were agitated by the exclusion of women from leadership. Although based in New York City, which allowed them to play a particularly active role in the New York movement center, CODEPINK sponsored actions throughout the country through their existing activist network.

Occupy participants also formed new feminist organizations unique to the movement. Within the first two weeks of Occupy's emergence, women and feminists found themselves confronted by male dominance, and the ensuing gender conflict provoked women to establish separate organizational spaces. In the New York City Occupy Wall Street movement, a variety of groups emerged that were inspired by feminist politics. Many took names that signaled their identities and interest, including the Speakeasy Caucus, Women Occupying Wall Street (WOWS), the Feminist General Assembly (FemGAs) group, Women Occupying Nations, Divine Feminine, the Queer Caucus, Anti-Racism Allies, Strong Women Rules, the People of Color Caucus, and a group that encompassed a broad spectrum of sexual and gender identities: the Queer Lesbian Gay Bisexual Transgender Intersex Queer or Questioning Asexual or Allies Two-Spirited Zhe, Zher, Gender Neutral Pronouns Caucus or "Queer/LGBTIQA2Z" for short. For example, at a New York City General Assembly in October, feminists publicized that the Speakeasy caucus was "open to both male-bodied and female-bodied individuals for the purpose of discussion, for how to make this community a safe space for everyone to have their voices heard truly equally." The group had a significant influence on the New York City Occupy press team, fielding women and queer speakers for national interviews. For example, they recruited a man *and* a woman for the *Colbert Report* television show on October 31, 2011. In addition, FemGAs contributed to the continuation of and mobilization of feminism and also served to recruit women, gender, and sexual minorities to mobilize for Occupy, as Shirin explains:

> The FemGA concept really arose from the idea of turning into an outreach organization where people who were already working on feminist issues in New York could come and have an assembly. Basically it was for Occupy but we can connect to [feminists] who are already doing this work and get more people connected with Occupy in that way.

FemGAs flourished in the spring and summer of 2012, a time when most Occupy encampments had been dismantled. Notably, FemGAs mirrored Occupy's tactic of organizing general assemblies and also encouraged feminists outside the movement to join Occupy. By building on the momentum of Occupy, FemGAs simultaneously mobilized support for feminism.

In the San Francisco Bay Area, the main feminist spin-off organizations were the SF Women's Alliance, Oakland Occupy Patriarchy (OOP), the People of Color / Queer People of Color Caucus, and Decolonize Oakland. The SF Women's Alliance created safe spaces within the San Francisco encampments. They built solidarity and oppositional consciousness among participants by sharing their reasons for being a part of Occupy and revealing their sexist, racist, and homophobic experiences at the encampment and in their lives in general.

Feminists in the movement also began to resist male dominance more publicly. The SF Women's Alliance spearheaded a rousing International Women's Day march in 2012, rallied in front of the Federal Reserve and other banks, advocated for reproductive rights, and protested sexual harassment and sexism in the banking industry. OOP headed up key marches and actions of Occupy in Oakland; for example, they led one of the contingents in the massive Oakland general strike on November 2, 2011, that collectively stopped all truck traffic and effectively all commerce at the Port of Oakland, one of the largest in the United States. OOP played a central role in attempts by Occupy Oakland to reclaim and reoccupy their encampment in Frank H. Ogawa Plaza (also known as Oscar Grant Plaza) and occupy other spaces in 2011 and 2012. They organized as a "feminist bloc" or a "glitter bloc," using gendered tactics such as donning glittery, pink, and/or purple clothing; wearing sequined facemasks (instead of the black facemasks typically worn by Black Bloc anarchists); and carrying banners with slogans such as "Disarm Cops, Arm Feminists" or "Feminists and Queers Against Capitalism." OOP was another example of a feminist group committed to organizing for feminism *and* Occupy as evident in an excerpt from their points of unity: "Women, Trans people, Queers, Fags, Dykes, need a space that is OURS. We are marginalized, harassed, and attacked in other spaces all the time. . . . We think we can support each other and increase our power by working together."

The Decolonize Oakland spin-off group evolved from the People of Color caucus and the Queer People of Color Caucus in Occupy Oakland. Decolonize Oakland critiqued the name of Occupy as signifying the European "occupation" or colonization and enslavement of Native Americans and African Americans. Decolonize Oakland aligned with a variety of people of color and immigrants' organizations in the city and provided a place where women of color feminists organized to draw attention to issues of race and class. The group supported activities such as an immigrants' rights march on May Day 2012, a coalition against a rate swap deal between the city of Oakland and Goldman Sachs that has cost Oakland residents millions of dollars, and internal movement activities such as a group discussion of Gloria Anzaldúa's classic feminist text *Borderlands / La Frontera: The New Mestiza*. Participants in Decolonize Oakland often participated in other spin-off groups, such as Occupy the Hood and Roots that drew heavily on existing mobilizing structures in African American communities in Oakland, including civil rights and antiracist organizations and the network of black churches. Bystanders and adherents of Occupy who felt excluded by white male dominance in Occupy shifted their support to Decolonize, as Jesse explains:

> Some of the white Occupy guys think this is the moment where we have to deal with the cops and anticapitalism. And we've been told things like—I can't even believe that people have said things like—you guys have to wait until after we deal with this and then we can deal with race and gender. And I'm like, are you serious? That's what people thought in the '60s. That's so old school, like women of color feminism never happened.

Although not all women or feminists, the majority of participants in Decolonize Oakland incorporated antiracist, intersectional, and feminist analyses in protests for economic justice. These protests opposed color-blind, antifeminist approaches to organizing that failed to recruit women of color or to take into account the specific disadvantages and interests of women of color. Nationwide, Decolonize organizations sparked critiques of white domination in Occupy, pressured Occupy chapters to issue statements of support and solidarity with the rights and self-determination of indigenous peoples, and sometimes introduced and performed indigenous traditions in Occupy encampments, such as smudging ceremonies, which is a Native American ritual to cleanse spaces of negative feelings.

One key example of national feminist organizing was the NatGat FemGA, a collaborative effort between the New York City WOWS and FemGA groups, the Philadelphia-based NatGat planning committee, and womenoccupy.org, a clearinghouse of feminist organizations. Through Internet-based conference calls participants across the nation discussed the purpose of the FemGAs and their potential impact on social justice. Hundreds of diverse Occupiers participated in the NatGat FemGA on July 1. Then, to put the national spotlight on Philadelphia with both a feminist and Occupy presence, several activists who had participated in the FemGA decided to "Occupy the 4th of July" by interrupting the annual reading of the Declaration of Independence on Independence Mall, standing up in the front row in silent protest wearing pink letters that spelled "Revolution Now." Many of the activists who met at the NatGat FemGA reconvened as the FemForce affinity group for the first anniversary of Occupy protests in the New York City financial district on September 17, 2012. During the several days of action that included antibanking, antifracking, and pro-Occupy marches and encampments, it was not uncommon for women, queer people, or even straight men who participated with the feminist affinity group to use gendered tactics, such as wearing brassieres and bustiers as they chanted, "Bust up big banks," stopping along the march routes to fling the bras at Bank of America branches.

As the evidence reveals, within the first year of the movement a variety of feminist organizations and protests emerged with goals both to increase a feminist presence in Occupy and to mobilize larger numbers of participants to Occupy as a whole. In the following sections of the chapter, we explore how gender conflict sparked three processes that were essential to the mobilization of feminism within the movement. In the conclusion, we argue that these processes have also been fundamental to other movements not specifically focused on gender and feminism that have experienced significant gender conflict.

Three Processes Mobilizing Feminism

FEMINIST COLLECTIVE IDENTITY

Gender conflict provided an opportunity for feminists to forge feminist collective identity. Feminist collective identity is the process of creating solidarity among feminists within a social movement. By developing feminist collective identity, activists erect a boundary between themselves and antifeminist beliefs and practices, in order to support the empowerment of women, genderqueer, and sexual minorities. Participants developed feminist collective identity to promote feminist tactics in opposition to the male-dominated culture and gendered and sexual oppressions they faced within the movement. For example, gender and sexual harassment triggered feminist solidarity, frequently contributing to the development of oppositional consciousness. Imogen explains how gender conflict inspired feminist organizing and forms of online consciousness-raising:

"We got broadsided with reports of people saying I feel really intimidated, I was harassed, I was hit upon, whatever, all of these reports. And we put up the Facebook page really quickly and people started migrating there and sharing stories. . . . I think that forged a number of opportunities for people to work together.

Imogen goes on to encapsulate how gender conflict sparked feminist solidarity on a Facebook page dedicated to airing gender conflicts and resisting male domination.

Offline, in the encampments, feminist participants and survivors of sexual assault also mobilized feminist solidarity. On November 4, 2011, a group within the New York encampment calling themselves members of a sexual assault survivors' team issued a statement on the New York General Assembly website, stating, "We are creating and sharing strategies that educate and transform our community into a culture of consent, safety, and well-being. At OWS, these strategies currently include support circles, counseling, consent trainings, safer sleeping spaces, self-defense trainings, community watches, awareness campaigns, and other evolving community-based processes to address harm." Members of this group formed a Safer Spaces Working Group to develop feminist consciousness about sexual assault. Over the course of the following three months, they negotiated a "Community Agreement" to spread feminist consciousness more broadly in the movement by advocating awareness about gender conflict, male dominance, and homophobia. The Community Agreement was a kind of pledge for movement participants to, among other commitments, "support the empowerment of each person in order to subvert the histories and structures of oppression that marginalize and divide us, such as racism, sexism, classism, heterosexism, transphobia, religious discrimination, ageism, & ableism." Participants became on-the-ground spokespersons pushing to recognize the Community Agreement, and they often served as confidants and advocates for other survivors, such as Ivy:

I tried to be a mediator for this kind of thing. I was trying to be an advocate for speaking out in the park. I was really trying to reach out to these kids who had been sexually assaulted, but it was so hard to get them to go to the authorities. They didn't want to do a rape kit test and they didn't want to deal with the police, so a lot of those instances, you know, were just left to speculation by the media. I knew all of the instances that happened to these kids. They would come to me and they would tell me, but they wouldn't do anything about it so I was forced to listen to them telling me these horrific scenarios and there was no justice for them. I couldn't force them, you know.

Transient youth who experienced sexual assaults often could not pay for medical services and were reluctant to seek the help of the police who surveilled and limited free speech in the encampments. In a response reminiscent of early underground rape crisis volunteers, Ivy drew on her feminist consciousness to provide counseling support and raise awareness against sexual harassment and rape.

Outrage about gender conflict, women's subordination, and sexual violence against women and sexual minorities sparked the development of feminist collective identity and solidarity, including consciousness about how to create a feminist movement culture (Taylor and Whittier 1995). The meaning of the gender conflicts that plagued the movement from its inception were both familiar and intelligible to women who had participated in second-wave feminism or contemporary feminist organizations, or had taken feminist studies classes in colleges and universities. As a result, feminists were able to use gender conflict as an opportunity to build on and extend existing feminist identities to bring feminist solidarity to bear against gender subordination and oppression within Occupy.

FEMINIST FREE SPACES

In addition to confronting male domination and sexual violence by developing feminist collective identity, women, transgender, and genderqueer participants formed feminist free spaces to prevent, impede, and resist gender conflict. Scholars have tended to study free spaces as sites for social movement emergence; however, prefigurative free spaces can also develop within ongoing movements as sites for participants to express a distinctive collective identity, a utopian way of living, or an innovative culture, or mount opposition to the movement overall (Polletta 1999). Prefigurative free spaces allow participants to mobilize around issues related to their own unique grievances and collective identities by creating a distinct boundary between themselves and dominant movement actors. Segregated feminist free spaces have been a strategy used by feminists to explicitly confront and diffuse gender conflict while developing a feminist collective identity and forging strategies to counter male domination. In Occupy, feminist free spaces served as a base for mobilizing feminist support for Occupy's goals and strategies and to promote participation in feminism and the larger Occupy movement. Within Occupy, free spaces for the expression of feminism and the prefiguring of a feminist culture in opposition to male dominance, gender hierarchy, and gender conflict took several forms, including segregated spaces for feminists where explicitly feminist tactics could be deployed.

Feminists created segregated spaces explicitly for women, genderqueer, and sexual minorities both within the encampments and also in virtual spaces in order to both avoid gender conflicts and create spaces led by women free of male dominance and sexual harassment. In larger encampments, it was not uncommon for feminists to sleep in sex-segregated tents and to create and designate sectors of encampments for women and members of "queer" communities. In the Zuccotti Park encampment in New York City, a group of women, transgender, and lesbian and gay participants decided to sleep overnight together in a large army tent designated by the Safer Spaces committee as a "safe space" explicitly for women and queer people. Similarly, in Oakland, feminist free spaces included OOP barbeques and feminist areas within the Oakland encampment at Frank Ogawa (Oscar

Grant) Plaza to nurture a feminist culture. Feminist free spaces also formed on the Internet and through conference calls such as the WOWS discussion forum and email list.

Feminist participants continually created and monitored the boundaries of both physical and virtual spaces to ensure that they were free of male domination. Segregated feminist free spaces provided opportunities for feminists to discuss and debate the importance of gender and sexuality issues and to raise the gender consciousness of participants since the majority of participants in the free spaces considered themselves feminists. As the comments of one woman illustrate, feminists consciously and continually engaged in maintaining a boundary between the feminist free spaces dominated by feminists, women, and queer communities in opposition to spaces that were dominated by heterosexual males. Jessica explains,

> Hurwitz: When you say a feminist occupation—I'm trying to understand— what made it feminist?
> Jessica: What made it feminist? It was organized by feminists so that it would be an autonomous space for women and queer people and transfolks. That was always the thing, it was always a little bit unclear but by and large it was a space without many hetero-cis-men, if any.
> Hurwitz: Was that ever defined by the group that this is the place for people who do not identify as hetero-cis men?
> Jessica: No—and sometimes. I actually feel like I'm oversimplifying. But I think the point was that it was not about making rules that people had to follow. It was about creating a culture.

Jessica goes on to explain that segregated zones for feminists, especially women and queer people, became sites where a feminist culture flourished. They provided safe spaces for feminists and gender and sexual minorities by limiting the participation of hetero-cis-men or men who were assigned male at birth, who have embraced male and heterosexual identities, and who typically enjoy privilege on the basis of their dominant gender and sexual identities. Participants in the feminist free spaces curbed the involvement of hetero-cis men, allowing participants to embrace a feminist culture that was inclusive, welcoming, and open only to individuals who did not identify as hetero-cis men, including women, lesbians, gay men, transgender persons, and other gender and sexual minorities. In Occupy Oakland, the feminist free space, for example, embraced a radical antipatriarchal, antiracist, and antihomophobic politics. Segregated feminist free spaces were online and offline sites controlled by women, queer people, and feminist participants who sought refuge to pose fundamental challenges to a movement that often appeared to be dominated by white men.

Feminist free spaces allowed feminist participants to organize events separate from those sponsored by the main Occupy organizations but that promoted both feminist beliefs and objectives, as well as the politics and goals of Occupy. Exemplary are the FemGAs. WOWS and the FemGA group held four assemblies in New York City between May 17 and August 18. The first national FemGA took place at NatGat. Occupy groups in Boston, Chicago, Los Angeles, and a handful of smaller cities held similar gatherings. New York City groups created the FemGA concept. Also, groups followed a FemGA format advertised as a "toolkit" on womenoccupy.org. Each New York City FemGA had a different theme to encourage a diversity of participation; they included speak-outs on defining feminism, LGBTQ issues, and the interests of people of color. The majority of FemGAs practiced consciousness-raising, a tactical innovation of second-wave feminists (Freeman 1975). Feminist free spaces mobilized feminists not only to participate in the larger movement that became known as Occupy, but they also were used as a mobilizing tool to draw feminists from beyond Occupy into the movement.

Feminist segregation in Occupy is a repertoire used not only by women's movements, but also by genderqueer, lesbian, gay, and other sexual minorities to erect boundaries that set them apart from male-dominated groups and networks in order to have the autonomy to embrace feminist politics, tactics, practices, and leadership styles (Taylor and Rupp 1993; Taylor and Whittier 1992). While feminist free spaces within Occupy were initially a response to white male domination of the movement and to the gender conflict that plagued the movement, ultimately they became opportunities for feminists to form solidarity, promote feminist consciousness, and practice feminist politics.

FEMINIST BRIDGE LEADERS

Gender conflict and white male dominance in the main movement organizations that constituted Occupy contributed to the marginalization of feminists and gender and sexual minorities. This resulted in a leadership hierarchy dominated mainly by white men. Like other "leaderless" movements that practice participatory democracy, Occupy was subject to latent and persistent status hierarchies based on ability and identity (Leach 2013; Polletta 2002; Freeman 1975). As a result, women found limited opportunities for leadership in the larger movement. Instead, feminists served primarily as grassroots and indigenous leaders, or what Robnett (1997) describes in her study of the civil rights movements as "bridge leaders." Although women assumed leadership in the separatist feminist organizations within Occupy, women functioned primarily as Occupy bridge leaders who did the work of mobilizing grassroots participation by the wider feminist community and connecting feminist participants and communities to the larger male-dominated movement. Helen explains a widely held sentiment among women in the movement: "I found in meetings a lot, that, you know, who shouts the loudest gets the most space. It seems like men being leaders is acceptable whereas if a woman wants to bottom-line something, it's like, 'Get in your place.'" Helen explains that men who spoke for a longer period of time and with a louder voice became informal leaders within the movement. Men who spoke more frequently and more loudly than women were trusted to *bottom-line* actions, the term the movement used to describe taking responsibility to oversee and implement tasks. Women's ability to lead or bottom-line was questioned and devalued because of societal expectations that women be submissive.

Nevertheless, the success of many of the general assemblies, occupations, and protest events that were led and dominated by white men often depended on women leaders' ability to mobilize grassroots participation by feminists. Esther, who participated in the planning of key marches and protest events on October 5, 2011, and November 17, 2011, epitomizes a strong leader and organizer who was marginalized because of her gender. She recounts the sexism she confronted at a meeting to plan the November 17 protest:

> I saw that people were being really dismissive and really doubtful of everything that I was saying, but I was the one who had been on the phone and who had been doing all the work. And at one point I looked around and I realized I was the only woman and I was like, 'We need more women here.' And I felt like I was being silenced and it led to this discussion happening right there on the spot that was very unsafe for me. I was the only woman, I started crying. At one point this one guy was like, 'I feel like you're silencing me because you're talking too much.' And someone else was like, 'She's the one doing the work!'"

Esther explains that her contributions to the movement were undermined because she was not taken seriously as a woman. Although she was an effective organizer, as the only woman who attended these organizing meetings, she was subjected to sexism and made to feel like an outcast.

Likewise, Derby was constrained by male-dominated leadership and a male hierarchy in decision making about protests. Derby expresses frustration over being excluded by the movement's male-dominated leadership, explaining that the only leadership opportunities open to her and other women were as bridge leaders when she argues,

> It's so dumb. When you want to get anything done there's a white guy somewhere that you need to talk to. The two guys that run [a particular protest planning group] keep telling me it has to be a small group of people [but in actuality] I won't be put on this committee because of those dudes who don't work with women. They just don't. And I was told by those dudes that the movement had to grow and accommodate for these different ways that decisions are made. That we can't do everything through consensus.

Although Derby was an experienced organizer, a formal leader in other movements, and a student leader at her university, she was excluded from the formal leadership of the protest planning. Both Esther and Derby exemplify the experience of bridge leaders who were marginalized and denied formal leadership status. They had to struggle to take part in meetings about movement strategy and tactics and were never treated as legitimate leaders, even though they contributed extensively to grassroots mobilization.

Although many women, queer people, people of color, and feminists may have been formal leaders in other institutions (such as in schools or workplaces) or in other social movements, in the context of Occupy they became mainly grassroots, indigenous, and informal leaders. Kite, a participant in progressive, lesbian, and feminist communities on the US East Coast observes, "It's almost like a service capacity thing that women are doing [as meeting facilitators], rather than I think one that shapes an agenda." Kite explains that women participated in and performed tasks during meetings such as organizing speakers, but were never permitted to structure the meetings or hold Occupy leadership roles. Although Kite had held formal leadership roles in lesbian and feminist organizations and was a key force in recruiting these constituencies to participate in Occupy, she never assumed a formal leadership role in Occupy because of its tokenization of women.

Family commitments also deterred Kite from consistently sleeping at the encampments, which illustrates the extent to which the movement's key tactic—encampments—by its very nature tended to exclude women and others with family responsibilities. Another woman, Jade, who has worked extensively with a national feminist organization, assumed a bridge leader role, concentrating on grassroots organizing instead of seeking a formal leadership position in Occupy, as she explains: "I'm a lifetime local organizer and I was like, 'I don't live in that community [in New York City], I live in another smaller community in another state.' So then I came back and I started an Occupy in my local neighborhood." Furthermore, Laura explains the kind of grassroots leadership and organizing that many women engaged in to connect women, lesbian, gay, bisexual, and transgender activist networks to Occupy in the San Francisco Bay Area: "I helped to mother the Occupy Pride [by finding them meeting space] and helped mother the SF Women's Alliance." Laura uses the term "mother" to describe how she used her connections as a feminist bridge leader to connect groups focused on gender and sexuality to mobilize for Occupy. Feminist bridge leaders drew on resources from feminist mobilizing structures created by generations of feminists who had been active in second-wave and contemporary feminist mobilizations. Although excluded from formal leadership in Occupy, bridge leaders' access to the resources and membership of preexisting feminist organizations and networks, online and off-line, allowed these women to function as grassroots leadership to expand Occupy's base of support.

In this analysis, we have extended Robnett's term *bridge leaders* (1997) to understand one of the ways that gender conflict contributes to the persistence of feminism. Like bridge leaders in the civil rights movement, bridge leaders in Occupy developed as a consequence of women's marginalization and exclusion from a leadership structure dominated by white men. Because women were not legitimated by formal movement leaders or frequently even by the movement's targets, they functioned primarily as bridge leaders connecting feminist and sexual minority communities to Occupy. While women bridge leaders were formal leaders in other institutional settings and in other movements, their opportunities for leadership in the context of Occupy were mainly as grassroots, indigenous, and informal leaders.

Conclusion

Prior studies of Occupy have tended to analyze conflict using a gender-blind lens (for example, Leach 2013; Lewis and Luce 2012; Smith and Glidden 2012); however, as this study suggests, gender identity and gender oppression are important factors in women's formation of collective identity in mixed-gender movements. With the decline of mass feminism as a social movement, feminist organizing has moved into new terrains, including social movements not specifically focused on gender inequality. In Occupy, women raised complaints about sexism and white male dominance in movement committees, organizations, newspapers, and general assemblies, and they used explicitly feminist spaces and meetings to challenge gender inequality in the movement's daily activities, goals, and tactics (Brunner 2011; Butler 2011; Maharawal 2011). Women, genderqueer, and sexual minorities faced gender subordination, such as being silenced in meetings or denied interviews with the press. For some women and queer participants, whether they could sleep safely at the urban protest encampments and grievances about sexual harassment, rape, belligerent males, and the lack of democracy in Occupy due to the loose structure of the movement (Freeman 1975; Smith and Glidden 2012) sparked feminist mobilization that took several forms. Occupy was rife with male dominance and gender inequality, but feminist activists engaged in gender conflict. Their feminist efforts spilled over into and persisted within the Occupy movement as they struggled against gender subordination.

In this chapter, we have examined gender conflict in one of the most recent and wide-ranging participatory democracy movements in the United States in decades. Our analysis finds that gender conflict sparked the development of feminist collective identity, feminist free spaces, and feminist bridge leaders in Occupy. Since suffrage, such processes have emerged in a variety of social movements troubled by gender conflict. Our analysis has demonstrated that contention around women's subordination in a larger movement creates an opportunity for feminists to use the broader movement's momentum both to recruit new women to feminism and to organize within the existing movement to challenge gender hierarchies and subordination. These findings are consistent with prior research by social movement scholars who have argued that gender conflict has been a major factor influencing the mobilization, composition, collective identity, tactics and strategies, and outcomes of a variety of social movements over the past one hundred years (Cobble 2007; Meyer and Whittier 1994; Robnett 1997; Roth 1998; Taylor 1999). Thus far, studies of social movements (for example, Ghaziani 2008) have paid significant attention to the way conflict over goals, framing, and collective identity influences movement emergence, goals and targets, and tactics and strategies. Our analysis here suggests that gender conflict is another crucial area of conflict, infighting, and debate that has yet to receive significant attention.

Gender conflict and the spillover of feminist mobilization into movements that are not principally concerned with gender or sexuality issues are processes experienced by women activists over the last one hundred years (and before this as well [Sinclair 1965; Stanton et al. 1881]). Like the feminist mobilizations that formed out of Occupy, the suffrage movement, too, had its origins in gender exclusion and gender conflict in the abolitionist movement, where women were marginalized and even attacked for speaking in public (Zaeske 1995). In Occupy, feminist and other participatory democracy movements played a fundamental role in the

2010–2012 global cycle of protest, and gender conflict and infighting over gender inequalities within the movement contributed to the persistence of feminism.

We join a range of gender scholars who endeavor to understand the persistence of gender conflict and gender hierarchy, even in organizational settings that presumably are dedicated to creating egalitarian relationships and promoting feminist claims (Acker 1990; Katzenstein 1990; Polletta 2002; Roth 1998). To understand the persistence of feminism, future research on the next one hundred years of women's activism should pay closer attention to gender conflict and debates about feminism in a wide variety of democratic movements that purportedly are not about gender.

References

Acker, Joan. 1990. "Hierarchies, Jobs, Bodies: A Theory of Gendered Organizations." *Gender & Society* 4: 139–158.

Boris, Eileen, and Jennifer Klein. 2008. "Labor on the Home Front: Unionizing Home-Based Care Workers." *New Labor Forum*, July: 32–41.

Brunner, Mikki. 2011. "Who Are the Black Women Occupying Wall Street?" Pp. 76–77 in *The 99%: How the Occupy Wall Street Movement Is Changing America*, edited by D. Hazen, T. Lohan, and L. Parramore. San Francisco: AlterNet.

Butler, Melanie. 2011. "Finding Our Voices and Creating Safe Spaces at Occupy Wall Street." Pp. 71–73 in *The 99%: How the Occupy Wall Street Movement Is Changing America*, edited by D. Hazen, T. Lohan, and L. Parramore. San Francisco: AlterNet.

Cobble, Dorothy Sue, ed. 2007. *The Sex of Class: Women Transforming American Labor.* Ithaca, NY: Cornell University Press.

Costanza-Chock, Sasha. 2012. "Mic Check! Media Cultures and the Occupy Movement." *Social Movement Studies* 11: 375–385.

Crossley, Alison Dahl. 2010. "'When It Suits Me, I'm a Feminist': International Students Negotiating Feminist Representations." *Women's Studies International Forum* 33(2): 125–133.

Epstein, Barbara. 1991. *Political Protest and Cultural Revolution: Nonviolent Direct Action in the 1970s and 1980s.* Berkeley: University of California Press.

Evans, Sara. 1979. *Personal Politics: The Roots of Women's Liberation in the Civil Rights Movement.* New York: Vintage.

Freeman, Jo. 1975. *The Politics of Women's Liberation: A Case Study of an Emerging Social Movement and Its Relation to the Policy Process.* New York: Longman.

Gamson, William A. 1975. *The Strategy of Social Protest.* Homewood: Dorsey Press.

Gamson, William A., and Micha L. Sifry. 2013. "The #Occupy Movement: An Introduction." *Sociological Quarterly* 54: 159–163.

Ghaziani, Amin. 2008. *The Dividends of Dissent: How Conflict and Culture Work in Lesbian and Gay Marches on Washington.* Chicago: University of Chicago Press.

Gitlin, Todd. 2012. *Occupy Nation.* New York: Harper Collins.

Haiven, Max. 2011. "Feminism, Finance and the Future of #Occupy—An Interview with Silvia Federici." *ZNet magazine*, November 26. http://zcomm.org/znetarticle/feminism-finance-and-the-future-of-occupy-an-interview-with-silvia-federici-by-max-haiven/#.

Halberstam, J. Jack. 2012. *Gaga Feminism: Sex, Gender, and the End of Normal.* Boston: Beacon Press.

Katzenstein, Mary F. 1990. "Feminism within American Institutions: Unobtrusive Mobilization in the 1980s." *Signs* 16: 27–54.

Leach, Darcy K. 2013. "Culture and the Structure of Tyrannylessness." *Sociological Quarterly* 54: 181–191.

Lewis, Penny, and Stephanie Luce. 2012. "Labor and Occupy Wall Street: An Appraisal of the First Six Months." *New Labor Forum* 21(2): 43–49.

Lomax, Tamura. 2011. "Occupy Rape Culture." *Feminist Wire*, November 5. http://thefeministwire.com/2011/11/occupy-rape-culture/.

Maharawal, Manissa. 2011. "Standing Up." Pp. 34–40 in *Occupy! Scenes from Occupied America*, edited by A. Taylor, K. Gessen, and editors from n + 1, Dissent, Triple Canopy, and The New Inquiry. Brooklyn: Verso.

Mahler, Jonathan. 2012. "Oakland, the Last Refuge of Radical America." *New York Times*, August 1. http://www.nytimes.com/2012/08/05/magazine/oakland-occupy-movement.html?pagewanted=all&_r=0.

Meyer, David S., and Nancy Whittier. 1994. "Social Movement Spillover." *Social Problems* 41: 277–298.

Milkman, Ruth, Stephanie Luce, and Penny Lewis. 2013. "Changing the Subject: A Bottom-Up Account of Occupy Wall Street in New York City." The City University of New York Murphy Institute, New York.

Newcomb, Alyssa. 2011. "Sexual Assaults Reported in 'Occupy' Camps." *ABC News/ World News*, November 3. http://abcnews.go.com/US/sexual-assaults-occupy-wall-street-camps/story?id=14873014.

Pickerill, Jenny, and John Krinsky. 2012. "Why Does Occupy Matter?" *Social Movement Studies* 11: 279–287.

Piven, Frances Fox. 2013. "On the Organizational Question." *Sociological Quarterly* 54: 191–193.

Polletta, Francesca. 1999. "'Free Spaces' in Collective Action." *Theory and Society* 28: 1–38.

———. 2002. *Freedom Is an Endless Meeting: Democracy in American Social Movements.* Chicago: University of Chicago Press.

Reger, Jo. 2012. *Everywhere and Nowhere: Contemporary Feminism in the United States.* New York: Oxford University Press.

———. 2015. "The Story of a Slut Walk: Sexuality, Race, and Generational Divisions in Contemporary Feminist Activism." *Journal of Contemporary Ethnography* 44: 84–112.

Robinson, Jo Ann G. 1987. *The Montgomery Bus Boycott and the Women Who Started It.* Knoxville: University of Tennessee Press.

Robnett, Belinda. 1997. *How Long? How Long? African-American Women in the Struggle for Civil Rights.* New York: Oxford University Press.

Roth, Benita. 1998. "Feminist Boundaries in the Feminist-Friendly Organization: The Women's Caucus of ACT UP/LA." *Gender & Society* 12(2): 129–145.

Schneider, Beth E., and Nancy E. Stoller, eds. 1994. *Women Resisting AIDS: Feminist Strategies of Empowerment.* Philadelphia: Temple University Press.

Seltzer, Sarah. 2011. "Where Are the Women at Occupy Wall Street? They're Everywhere." Pp. 80–84 in *The 99%: How the Occupy Wall Street Movement Is Changing America*, edited by D. Hazen, T. Lohan, and L. Parramore. San Francisco: AlterNet.

Sinclair, Andrew. 1965. *The Emancipation of the American Woman*. New York: Harper and Row.

Smith, Jackie, and Bob Glidden. 2012. "Occupy Pittsburgh and the Challenges of Participatory Democracy." *Social Movement Studies* 11: 288–294.

Staggenborg, Suzanne, and Verta Taylor. 2005. "Whatever Happened to the Women's Movement?" *Mobilization* 10: 37–52.

Stanton, Elizabeth Cady, Susan B. Anthony, and Matilda Joselyn Gage, eds. 1881. *History of Woman Suffrage*. Volume 1. New York: Fowler and Wells.

Szolucha, Anna. 2013. "Learning Consensus Decision-Making in Occupy: Uncertainty, Responsibility, Commitment." *Research in Social Movements, Conflicts and Change* 36: 205–233.

Taylor, Verta. 1999. "Gender and Social Movements: Gender Processes in Women's Self-Help Movements." *Gender & Society* 13: 8–33.

Taylor, Verta, and Leila J. Rupp. 1993. "Women's Culture and Lesbian Feminist Activism: A Reconsideration of Cultural Feminism." *Signs* 19(1): 32–61.

Verta, Taylor, and Nancy Whittier. 1992. "Collective Identity in Social Movement Communities: Lesbian Feminist Mobilization." Pp. 104–129 in *Frontiers in Social Movement Theory*, edited by A. Morris and C. Mueller. New Haven, CT: Yale University Press.

———. 1995. "Analytical Approaches to Social Movement Culture: The Culture of the Women's Movement." Pp. 163–187 in *Social Movements and Culture*, edited by H. Johnston and B. Klandermans. Minneapolis: University of Minnesota Press.

Zaeske, Susan. 1995. "The 'Promiscuous Audience' Controversy and the Emergence of the Early Women's Rights Movement." *Quarterly Journal of Speech* 81: 191–207.

16

Epilogue

WOMEN'S ACTIVISM FROM ELECTORAL CAMPAIGNS TO PROTEST ACTION: INTO THE NEXT 100 YEARS

Lee Ann Banaszak and Holly J. McCammon

As the chapters of this volume reveal, US women's political engagement over the past one hundred years has simultaneously been characterized by progress and setbacks, opportunities and limits, sharp increases in activism and demobilization. Consequently, no one single theme characterizes this rich history; rather, the last century is both one of great achievements by women and one of ongoing struggles. Women's electoral participation, for example, is substantial today, and it has grown and broadened over the course of the century, both in voting and office holding. In the 2016 US presidential election, the highest glass ceiling was challenged when the Democratic Party nominated a female candidate for the presidency. In a setback for women's political equality, however, Hillary Clinton lost the election, even as she won the popular vote by a significant margin. In a strong reaction to the election of a man with a history of derogatory behavior toward women (Barbaro and Twohey 2016; Tolentino 2016), women once again demonstrated their capacity for protest activism. The 2017 Women's March, just one day after the inauguration of Donald Trump, by many counts was the largest protest in US history, with estimates that 3 to 4 million people mobilized in more than five hundred cities across the nation (Waddell 2017). Indeed, as the chapters of this volume demonstrate, women have been a forceful presence in US politics. Women mobilized the suffrage movement and succeeded in winning the Nineteenth Amendment in 1920, and their political presence has been influential since that time, as our volume shows, in both electoral politics and social movement activism. And in the coming hundred years, there is much to suggest that women will continue this forceful presence in politics.

In this epilogue, we return to the central and varied themes developed in previous chapters. We consider growing gender equality and remaining inequality, and the increasing influence of women as well as their continuing marginalization. We do so by revisiting women's participation in electoral politics and social movement activism. We also explore the ways in which politics continues to be a deeply gendered sphere of action. Important to all of these is the rich diversity of women's engagement in political action. Women from a variety of backgrounds and political views play significant roles in both electoral politics and movement activism; significant insights can emerge from an intersectional approach to understanding women's political action. We conclude with thoughts, which must be speculative at best, of what may lie ahead for the second hundred years of women's enfranchisement.

A Century Later, Gender Equality and Inequality Are Both Evident in Electoral Politics

When the vote was won in 1920, women's presence in politics was still disputed, even though women had had a long prior history of political engagement (Hoffert 1995; Zaeske 2003). As Kevin Corder and Christina Wolbrecht's chapter in our volume shows, commentators debated whether women would vote or participate in electoral politics in any form, and whether they were a voice for change—voting for the Progressive Party—or whether they would reinforce the major parties. Women as political candidates were a relatively rare phenomena, and in 1920 only one woman—Jeanette Rankin—was serving in the US Congress. On the other hand, women's movement mobilization was at an all-time high, with suffrage activists, African American women's groups, union women, and club women active on political issues of all types. The contributions here show that even as much has changed since 1920 with women's greater participation in politics of all types and increasing numbers of women in elected office, a hundred years after suffrage electoral politics and political activism are still highly gendered, and women's progress has not been linear. As Celeste Montoya shows, the establishment of voting rights is not absolute, nor have the years since the adoption of the Nineteenth Amendment been years of unmitigated progress. Similarly, Kristin Goss shows that this trajectory has not been one-way; women's groups have less influence on congressional policy making today than they did in the forty years immediately after suffrage.

One of the most interesting positive changes has been the increases in women's voting participation. As Nancy Burns and her colleagues note, in the early 1960s (i.e., during the first years of the modern polling industry) men's voting rates were higher than women's. Since 1980, however, women have turned out in higher rates than men. Because voting like other forms of political participation is associated with activity in the workforce, higher socioeconomic class, and higher education, women's higher voting turnout rates are somewhat mysterious since on each of these factors women either lag behind men or, in the case of education, are at best equal to men. Nonetheless, women's turnout rate in the 2016 presidential election was 4% higher than men's. Only 59.3% of the citizen voting-age men cast ballots in the 2016 presidential election compared to 63.3% of the citizen voting-age women.[1] While gaps still exist in some forms of participation (for example, men are more likely to contact a government official), many of these gaps appear to be closing over time.

One of the largest remaining gaps has been the representation gap: women run less for public office, and men outnumber women significantly in all elected offices. Indeed, the United States currently ranks 104th in the world in terms of women's representation in national parliaments (Inter-parliamentary Union 2017). As Susan Welch's chapter details, the growth of women's representation in state legislatures started before 1920. Yet since 2009, the number of women serving in state legislatures has stagnated at a level below 25% (Center for American Women in Politics 2016a). In the 2016 election that number increased only by twenty-three women state legislators nationwide—an imperceptible change. Similarly, the number of women elected to the 115th Congress remains the same as the number who served in the 114th Congress, although women of color made significant gains in the 2016 election, with nine new women of color voted into office (Center for American Women in Politics 2016b). Importantly, 2016 saw the election of the first Latina into the US Senate. One of the complexities of the last hundred years of women's political engagement is that while women have made substantial gains toward equality, much inequality is still in evidence.

Women Are Influential in Social Movements yet Are Often Still Marginalized

The word *politics* often conjures notions of political parties, voting, and electoral politics, but political action is more far ranging, encompassing as well social activism, that is, activities in associations and protest activism. Positive change combined with the continued inequality evident in electoral politics can also be seen within the social movement sector. Moreover, protest politics plays a large role in both framing the political debate and in discussions around women's equality. This was particularly true during and after the 2016 electoral process, where both Donald Trump and Bernie Sanders discussed their bids for the presidency as a form of movement politics. Particularly after Donald Trump's statements about grabbing women were made public, women from Michelle Obama to informal groups on Facebook and Twitter mobilized in protest (Cillizza 2016; *The Guardian* 2016). This activism intensified after the election of Trump, as women proved to be the strongest mobilizers of opposition against his presidency (Waddell 2017). While many different action groups mobilized after election day, from protests surrounding the Electoral College to more violent protest on election day, it was the large-scale and broad-based intersectional mobilization of the Women's March that exemplified the postelection opposition (Hess 2017).

Women have participated in many forms of movement politics in the last hundred years, either individually or within formal or informal organizations. This volume provides an overview of women's roles in a number of important social movements, from the far right (see the chapter by Kathleen Blee) through the environmental movement (see Holly McCammon and colleagues), the civil rights movement (see the contribution by Brittany Hearne and Holly McCammon), and movements for nonviolence (see Selina Gallo-Cruz's chapter), to the Occupy movement (see Heather Hurwitz and Verta Taylor, this volume). In many cases, existing discussions of these movements are devoid of a focus on the women within them (see, for example, Gallo-Cruz's discussion in this volume), and the women activists themselves have been marginalized by the movement (see the chapters by Hurwitz and Taylor and McCammon et al.). Yet women's contributions have been significant in terms of both organizing and activism, as well as in terms of the intellectual leadership that has allowed these movements to advance. Similar stories could have been told, if space in our volume permitted, about numerous other major social movements, such as the labor and lesbian/gay/bisexual/trans/queer (LGBTQ) movements.

Equally important is a focus on women's organizations and feminist movement activism, which actively pursue both women's equality and other important issues. While the rise of feminist activism has been extensively chronicled and analyzed by scholars (Barakso 2004; Ferree and Hess 2000; Freeman 1975; Rupp and Taylor 1987; Ryan 1992), the contributors to this volume focusing on feminist activism also show that there are fresh perspectives to be had on feminist activism. Some of those perspectives come from taking a longer view of women's activism than is normally taken. Laura Nelson shows that our understanding of consciousness-raising tactics and activities of second- and third-wave activism disregards these activities among feminist activists at the time of the Nineteenth Amendment. Kristin Goss provides equally surprising information that the influence of women's organizations—at least measured by their testimony at congressional hearings—has been greatly reduced since the rise of the second wave. Tracey Jean Boisseau and Tracy Thomas help us see why a vigorous and successful campaign for an equal rights amendment is needed just as much today as it was in the 1970s.

Several of the pieces also reinforce analyses suggesting that feminist activism occurs within political institutions as well as outside of them (Banaszak 2010; Katzenstein 1998). Chapters by Goss and by Hearne and McCammon illustrate the importance of activism within the state by focusing on women's activism within the legislative and the judicial branch respectively. Goss notes that the thirty years immediately following the adoption of the Nineteenth Amendment were characterized by extensive legislative activism on important issues, including women's rights, but also on a wide range of issues, including foreign policy. Hearne and McCammon show how African American women lawyers acting for both the civil rights and women's movements were vital leaders in litigation and other legal strategies seeking racial and gender equality. Similarly, Jessica Monforti notes that Latinas' participation in the US Congress has brought a distinctive voice to that institution. In all of these cases, women's activism within institutions has led to substantive changes in women's representation.

What explanations do we have, however, for the continued marginalization of women within a variety of social movements, even in later years after several generations of women have protested such actions within movements (Evans 1979; Fonow 1998; Schrepfer 2005)? Hurwitz and Taylor discuss the assertion by heterosexual white men of gender, racial, and sexual hierarchies in the recent Occupy movement, and Hearne and McCammon and McCammon et al. note that male leaders in social movement organizations often reserve those positions for only men. But the limits on women's activism are even more complex. Goss, for instance, suggests that some of the reductions in women's associations' political influence at the national level are a result of the changing nature of the focus of women's groups (particularly after the second wave of feminism) and of the organizational activism itself, particularly the demise of large federated women's organizations. Once again, the story is a complex one, and no simple narrative fits.

Political Participation, Social Activism, and Political Institutions Are Gendered

From the form of women's political participation and social activism to the fundamental nature of political institutions, this volume also highlights the ways that gender has been and is imbued in the political process over the last hundred years. The gendered nature of political participation is highlighted particularly by the gender gap in vote choice and partisanship (as discussed in Heather Ondercin's chapter) that align women more with the Democratic Party. Partisan difference between men and women continued to play a role in the 2016 election. Exit polls indicate a thirteen-point gap between men and women's overall support for Hillary Clinton, with 54% of women but only 41% of men voting for her (Dittmar 2017: 24). This represents the largest gender gap since the term was initially coined in the 1980s (Center for American Women in Politics 2012; *The New York Times* 2016). As we discuss below, this generalization hides important differences among women, but nonetheless it suggests that women's activism and political behavior is still, one hundred years after the adoption of the Nineteenth Amendment, gendered in important ways.

The importance of gender issues as a mobilizing force for individuals on all parts of the ideological spectrum also reflects the ongoing gendered political context. At the turn of the twentieth century, women mobilized to fight for the vote, and at the time they faced a countermobilization of those opposed to voting rights for women (Marshall 1997). One hundred years later, gender issues are still motivating activism. Within the course of the 2016 election, many women (and men) mobilized against the Trump candidacy. Trump's recorded comments about sexually assaulting women generated a social media mobilization around the hashtag #notokay, which revealed ongoing discussion of sexism and sexual harassment in the months after the election (Beck 2016). The groundswell of tweets by people describing myriad experiences with sexual assault accompanied a longer standing increase in attention to sexism and sexual violence on college campuses and in other venues (Johnston 2015; see also the specific example in Mangan 2016).

One hundred years later, the power of women's mobilization continues to generate counter-responses on the other side. On social media, #Repealthe19th and #whywomenshouldnotvote exploded as hashtags during the 2016 presidential election. While a *Washington Post* article noted that the former hashtag was perpetrated by a small number of Trump supporters potentially with humorous intent (Ohlheiser 2016), it nonetheless suggests that continuing contradictions exist a century after the passage of the Nineteenth Amendment. Just as women's participation and mobilization are ongoing, so too are strongly antifeminist rhetoric and mobilization. These calls for a removal of women's right to vote in some far-right circles are not the only antifeminist activism we see today. While the form and rhetoric have changed over the years, during the one hundred years since the Nineteenth Amendment, calls for returning women to traditional roles have been largely continuous (Marshall 1997; Schreiber 2002). Importantly, this countermobilization against the rise of feminism is not a battle of the sexes; women and men can be found on both sides.

Our volume also examines the gendering of elected officials and candidates in elections in several respects. Jessica Monforti, writing about Latina members of Congress, argues that their family connections to politics, along with their careers of service, become important touchstones in their decisions to run for Congress. She also shows how the policies they choose to emphasize develop from their experiences as women. These experiences both create an identity that includes a gender component and help inform policy emphases that focus on families and communities. Gender experiences are unique, depending on one's place in the political and social context. While we discuss race shortly, the two political parties also provide differential gendered experiences for candidates and elected officials. Structurally, the Republican and Democratic Parties provide different contexts, as Welch indicates, noting that since the adoption of the Nineteenth Amendment, a sea change has taken place in the connection between women office holders on the state level and the political parties. While the Republicans were initially the party of women's rights, since 1971 there have been more Democratic than Republican women serving in elected office. In 2017, for example, three times as many women from the Democratic Party serve in Congress than from the Republican Party. Republican women candidates face very different experiences negotiating the gendered challenges that arise from campaigns, expectations of constituencies, and their policy emphases (Dolan 2010; Sanbonmatsu and Dolan 2009).

Social activism outside political parties, campaigns, and elections also is influenced by the gendered nature of society and politics (Costain 1992; McCammon et al. 2001; Taylor and Whittier 1998). As McCammon and colleagues in this volume note, women leaders in the environmental movement often ended up utilizing connections to traditional gender roles to frame their activism, particularly in the environmental justice movement, as women draw on maternalism to motivate their activism. Blee notes the contradictory role femininity plays in both mobilizing and suppressing women's activism and leadership within white supremacist groups like the Ku Klux Klan. For Gallo-Cruz and Nelson, the gendered experiences of women activists influence their activism. The radical feminist theory that inspired the activities in the 1920s and 1960s that Nelson studies often started from women's oppression in a gendered hierarchy, while Gallo-Cruz notes that women nonviolent activists often utilized gender in their activism.

Movement activities, organizations, and ideologies also carry a gendered component that influences the place of women within the movements. In its most obvious example, Blee shows how the white supremacist movements seeking to incorporate newly enfranchised women into their groups segregated the women by creating separate women's auxiliaries. But in many cases the gendered component is built into the culture, ways of doing things, or general patterns of interpersonal interaction. Hurwitz and Taylor for example, provide vivid examples of the ways that gender hierarchies of the Occupy movement permitted the objectification and harassment of women and LGBTQ activists of the movement. Women as a group also become the underlying symbols around which other movements mobilize. Blee notes, for example, that gendered images of vulnerable women were often held up as a reason for white supremacists to mobilize. When women organize as women—one hundred years ago during the suffrage movement or today as during the 2017 Women's March—gender drives that activism, and women reveal that they are a clear force in the political realm.

Thus, the political activism of women both inside partisan politics and in their external activism within women's movements as well as other social movements exhibits the continued gendered nature of women's political participation. That gendering can be seen both in the activism of women themselves, and in the nature of the movements, parties, and other political institutions that exist around them. This gendering also reveals both the progress women have made in moving into activism spaces where they had previously been absent, even as it illustrates the degree to which the climb into those spaces continues to be difficult. To more fully understand the role of gender, though, we must turn to a more intersectional analysis.

Understanding the One Hundred Years since the Nineteenth Amendment Requires an Intersectional Analysis

As the Nineteenth Amendment was adopted, those fighting for women's rights were also divided by race, with some white suffrage activists accepting and others embracing the exclusion of African American women from the vote (Spruill Wheeler 1993). The 2017 Women's March, on the other hand, took an explicitly intersectional approach, purposefully trying to build a broad coalition across groups of women who differed by race, class, citizenship, and sexuality. This change reflects a long history of the development of a clearly intersectional feminism; that history is marked by the development of intersectional theories (see, for example, Crenshaw 1989; Collins 2000) as well as differential recognition at different times and among different feminist organizations of the necessity of a broad intersectional feminism (Breines 2006). Understanding the changes that have occurred in the last hundred years requires careful analysis of the activism of different and diverse categories of women as well as the recognition that race, class, citizenship, heteronormativity, and other factors mediate the way these changes play out in women's lives.

Celeste Montoya reminds us in her chapter that the voting rights that women gained in the Nineteenth Amendment were withheld from many groups of women. Mexican American, Native American, Asian American, and African American women were often denied the franchise, either through the denial of citizenship or through forms of voter suppression like poll taxes and intimidation. The advent of voter identification laws and the rollback of the Voting Rights Act of 1965 suggest that issues of voter suppression continue to remain current. As Montoya notes, many of these forms of voter suppression—like voter identification laws—affect women differently, depending, in particular, on their position within race, ethnic, and class hierarchies.

The volume also points to the power of intersectional identities in promoting women's leadership and activism. McCammon et al. note that African American, Native American, and Latina women have long organized around issues of the environment and in recent years have been on the forefront of the environmental justice movement. Indeed, these authors argue that invoking intersectional identities helps strengthen the movement. Similarly, Hearne and McCammon chronicle the significant roles in changing policy through litigation and the law spearheaded by African American women lawyers like Frankie Freeman and Pauli Murray. They describe as well the intellectual leadership that later African American women cause lawyers provided in developing a more intersectional understanding of inequality and oppression.

Intersectionality also helps us understand trends in elected office and electoral participation. While women's numbers in Congress remained constant between the 114th and 115th Congresses, the number of women of color in Congress increased greatly and now constitutes over one-third of all women in Congress (Center for American Women in Politics 2016b). Monforti's analysis of Latinas in the House of Representatives shows that their multiple and intersecting identities shape their activities in Congress, particularly their legislative and political activities. Ondercin's chapter shows as well that women's experiences shape their partisanship, with African American women leaning much more Democratic than either white women or African American men.[2] Ondercin's work indicating that education affects women's partisanship also suggests that the intersection of class and gender may be important for understanding women's place in electoral politics—particularly as the costs of college education have made it less obtainable for working-class and poor women. The intersection of a wide array of identities and oppressions is a significant and fundamental part of the story of women's political participation over the last hundred years.

Turning to a Second Hundred Years of Women's Enfranchisement

In this book we have explored the changes and continuities in women's electoral participation and social movement mobilization since the adoption of the Nineteenth Amendment. The volume takes a wide view of women's political engagement, examining both women's participation in electoral institutions and elected office, and their collective efforts in social movements. These explorations have focused on the century since the Nineteenth Amendment. But what can these analyses tell us about the second hundred years after the Nineteenth Amendment? What will be women's achievements going forward? What further setbacks might they experience? When will gender parity in elected office occur? How will presidential, congressional, and state lawmakers continue to be influenced by the gendered nature of politics and current movement activism? How will women continue to lead and fight in social movement struggles? How will intersectional identities further unfold in the coming century? Will the coalition of intersectional movement groups that is cementing itself today continue over the longer term?

It is, of course, not possible for us to answer these important questions definitively. The future is unknown. But we can look to the last hundred years to discern important lessons in order to offer our best guess about what may come next. Women have long struggled for political equality and voice in the United States, and that struggle is not over. Women remain underrepresented in elected office, and even after generations of collective effort, they continue to confront gender bias in political activism as well as a variety of other domains. One clear message from the last hundred years is that women will not give up the fight for a greater political presence. The women in the suffrage movement continued their collective efforts for seventy years. Women civil rights activists along with their male allies fought even longer for inclusion of African Americans in the American electorate. Today we see significant successes in Latinas' ongoing struggle for a formal voice in elected political institutions and beyond. And the list of women's unrelenting efforts, both individual and collective, could go on and on, across many political districts, activist mobilizations, and issue and policy domains. The history of women's political engagement tells us that women will continue to fight these battles in the coming decades, so that their views and goals are represented in US politics.

Another indication of what the future may hold can also be discerned from the past history of women's political engagement. What this history clearly shows is that the setbacks and important defeats will continue as well. The 2016 presidential election was a fundamental setback for women who hoped for the first female president and for a political culture of coming together to be stronger, to paraphrase the Clinton campaign slogan "Stronger Together." Clinton won the popular vote, and a majority of women voters supported her candidacy. However, when we examine gender and race together, white women were more likely to support Trump, and only because of the opposition of women from minority racial and ethnic groups did women as a whole vote for Clinton. This speaks to the importance of intersectional coalitions among women going forward, but in the one hundred years since the Nineteenth Amendment, such broad-based coalitions have been rare. Important for the next hundred years will be the ability of women to build and maintain such coalitions. Women as a whole face many difficulties in maintaining such alliances: women's interests are diverse, and the history of women's movements has as much of a tradition of abandoning the broad-based coalition as maintaining it.

Partnerships among groups of women are built on fundamental assumptions of how the category of *women* is defined, and what constitutes their interest. Conflict within such coalitions often occurs when decisions are made to prioritize or denigrate an interest expressed by a group of women in order to engage the political system as a whole. These pressures on coalition building are not likely to dissipate in the coming century. Among other things, globalization and the increased recognition of the fluidity of a person's gender increase the variety of interests that are subsumed under the general category of *women*. This is likely to create even more differences among women, raising new challenges for women's representation and the women's movement.

Women have experienced other challenges over the last century. Significant challenges to equality have come in the form of the savage repression of civil rights activists; the defeat of the Equal Rights Amendment; losses in legal battles experienced by lesbians, transgender, and gender nonconforming individuals in their fight for equality; immigrant women's ongoing struggles to gain acceptance; working women's long battle for equal pay; and Muslim women's fight against discrimination. While the list of setbacks and barriers is, of course, much longer, there is no reason to believe that it should become shorter in the future. Nonetheless, social movement research suggests that setbacks and barriers are an impetus to mobilization. Research on how movements react to countermovements or loss suggests that mobilization is often aided by the sense of loss and threat that comes from such setbacks or losses (Banaszak and Ondercin 2016; Beckwith 2015; McGirr 2001; McVeigh 1999). Thus, even with concerns about coalition building among women and unfriendly political contexts, it seems likely that we will see continued mobilization of the women's movement and the continued engagement for feminist issues.

The history of women's past political engagement has much to teach us about what may lie ahead in the next hundred years. Women's movements and women in the political realm have overcome many defeats through their resilience and ability to adjust their tactics. For example, the past reveals that women have been strong agents for progressive social change both inside and outside of political institutions, adjusting their strategies to political circumstances (Banaszak 2010; Cobble 2007; Flexner 1959; Freeman 1975; Pardo 1998; Robnett 1997; Rosen 2000; Stokes-Brown and Dolan 2010; Swers 2002; Thomas 1994). McCammon's (2012) study of the actions of mid-twentieth-century women's fight to gain the right to sit on juries is a case in point. Women's groups, which ultimately won, confronted defeats not with resignation but rather with renewed and strategically tailored political activism, with tactics chosen specifically to offset the resistance to their cause.

Women today seeking greater equality for women must, therefore, be bold and inclusive. The authors of our volume suggest a glass half full and a glass half empty. Women over the past century have attained exhilarating achievements, but bias against women and their marginalization by some continues, sometimes vigorously. The intersecting oppressions that often target women of color and working-class women are pronounced. Past history of women's efforts suggests that women will continue to be a part of the mobilization for equality and justice for all, advocating, mobilizing, and engaging in electoral politics at increasing levels. Yet, as a diverse group, their interests may not always overlap. Hence, we can anticipate that their work will champion a diverse set of interests underlying the variety among women. Even in the face of a polarized and hostile political environment, women may encounter many defeats, but they must not be defeated.[3]

Notes

1. The 2016 election turnout figures are taken from the United States Census Bureau's Current Population Survey (see https://www.census.gov/data/tables/time-series/demo/voting-and-registration/p20-580.html.

2. Her data, which end in 2010, also suggest that there was a significant increase in African American men's support for the Democratic Party in 2008, corresponding with the Obama presidency.

3. The final quote paraphrases a statement from Maya Angelou (2009).

References

Angelou, Maya. 2009. "An Interview with Maya Angelou." *Psychology Today*, February 17. https://www.psychologytoday.com/blog/the-guest-room/200902/interview-maya-angelou.

Banaszak, Lee Ann. 2010. *The Women's Movement Inside and Outside the State.* Cambridge: Cambridge University Press.

Banaszak, Lee Ann, and Heather Ondercin. 2016. "Explaining the Dynamics between the Women's Movement and the Conservative Movement in the United States." *Social Forces* 95(1): 381–410.

Barakso, M. 2004. *Governing NOW: Grassroots Activism in the National Organization for Women.* Ithaca, NY: Cornell University Press.

Barbaro, Michael, and Megan Twohey. 2016. "Crossing the Line: How Donald Trump Behaved with Women in Private." *New York Times,* May 14. https://www.nytimes.com/2016/05/15/us/politics/donald-trump-women.html?_r=0.

Beck, Christina. 2016. "In Fury Surrounding Trump Allegations, Signs of a Changing America." *Christian Science Monitor*, October 13. http://www.csmonitor.com/USA/2016/1013/In-fury-surrounding-Trump-allegations-signs-of-a-changing-America.

Beckwith, Karen. 2015. "Narratives of Defeat: Explaining the Effects of Loss in Social Movements." *Journal of Politics* 77(1): 2–13.

Breines, Winifred. 2006. *The Trouble between Us: An Uneasy History of White and Black Women in the Feminist Movement.* New York: Oxford University Press.

Center for American Women in Politics. 2012. "The Gender Gap: Voting Choices in Presidential Campaigns." Fact sheet. http://www.cawp.rutgers.edu/sites/default/files/resources/ggpresvote.pdf.

———. 2016a. "For Women in State Legislatures and Statewide Offices, Not Much Change." Press release, November 21. http://www.cawp.rutgers.edu/sites/default/files/resources/press-release-post-election-stateleg-2016.pdf.

———. 2016b. "No Breakthrough at Top of Ticket, but Women of Color Gain in Congress." Press release, November 9. http://www.cawp.rutgers.edu/sites/default/files/resources/press-release-post-election-2016.pdf.

Cillizza, Chris. 2016. "Michelle Obama's Speech on Donald Trump Was Remarkable." *Washington Post*, October 13. https://www.washingtonpost.com/news/the-fix/wp/2016/10/13/michelle-obama-just-put-a-huge-and-emotional-exclamation-point-on-trumps-hot-mic-tape/?utm_term=.8220e9030ee6.

Cobble, Dorothy, ed. 2007. *The Sex of Class: Women Transforming American Labor*. Ithaca, NY: ILR Press.

Collins, Patricia Hill. 2000. *Black Feminist Thought: Knowledge, Consciousness, and the Politics of Empowerment*. Second edition. New York: Routledge.

Costain, Anne N. 1992. *Inviting Women's Rebellion: A Political Interpretation of the Women's Movement*. Baltimore, MD: The Johns Hopkins University Press.

Crenshaw, Kimberle. 1989. "Demarginalizing the Intersection of Race and Sex: A Black Feminist Critique of Antidiscrimination Doctrine, Feminist Theory, and Antiracist Politics." *University of Chicago Legal Forum* 140: 139–167.

Dittmar, Kelly. 2017. *Finding Gender in Election 2016: Lessons from the Presidential Gender Watch*. Barbara Lee Family Foundation and the Center for American Women in Politics.

Dolan, Kathy. 2010. "The Impact of Gender Stereotyped Evaluations on Support for Women Candidates" *Political Behavior* 32: 69–88.

Evans, Sarah. 1979. *Personal Politics: The Roots of Women's Liberation in the Civil Rights Movement and the New Left*. New York: Vintage Books.

Ferree, Myra Marx, and Beth Hess. 2000. *Controversy and Coalition: The New Feminist Movement across Three Decades of Change*. Third edition. New York: Routledge.

Flexner, Eleanor. 1959. *Century of Struggle: The Woman's Rights Movement in the United States*. New York: Atheneum.

Fonow, Mary Margaret. 1998. "Protest Engendered: The Participation of Women Steelworkers in the Wheeling–Pittsburgh Steel Strike of 1985." *Gender & Society* 12: 710–728.

Freeman, Jo. 1975. *The Politics of Women's Liberation: A Case Study of an Emerging Social Movement and Its Relations to the Policy Process*. New York: McKay.

The Guardian. 2016. "Trump's Groping Boasts Inspire Thousands of Women to Share Sexual Assault Stories on Twitter." October 9. https://www.theguardian.com/us-news/2016/oct/09/women-share-sexual-assault-stories-on-twitter-after-donald-trump-comments.

Hess, Amanda. 2017. "Forces in Opposition." *New York Times Sunday Magazine*, February 7: 36–42.

Hoffert, Sylvia D. 1995. *When Hens Crow: The Woman's Rights Movement in Antebellum America*. Bloomington: Indiana University Press.

Inter-Parliamentary Union. 2017. "Women in National Parliaments: Situation as of 1 January 2017." http://www.ipu.org/wmn-e/classif.htm.

Johnston, Angus. 2015. "Student Protests, Then and Now." *Chronicle of Higher Education*. December 11. http://www.chronicle.com/article/Student-Protests-ThenNow/234542?cid=rclink.

Katzenstein, Mary Fainsod. 1998. *Faithful and Fearless: Moving Feminist Protest inside the Church and Military*. Princeton, NJ: Princeton University Press.

Mangan, Katherine. 2016. "A Wave of Sexual Assault Cases Kindles Anger on Baylor's Campus." *Chronicle of Higher Education*, March 27.

Marshall, Susan E. 1997. *Splintered Sisterhood: Gender and Class in the Campaign against Woman Suffrage*. Madison: University of Wisconsin Press.

McCammon, Holly J. 2012. *The U.S. Women's Jury Movements and Strategic Adaptation: A More Just Verdict*. New York: Cambridge University Press.

McCammon, Holly J., Karen E. Campbell, Ellen Granberg, and Christine Mowery. 2001. "How Movements Win: Gendered Opportunity Structures and U.S. Women's Suffrage Movements, 1866 to 1919." *American Sociological Review* 66(1): 49–70.

McGirr, Lisa. 2001. *Suburban Warriors: The Origins of the New American Rights*. Princeton, NJ: Princeton University Press.

McVeigh, Rory. 1999. "Structural Incentives for Conservative Mobilization: Power Devaluation and the Rise of the Ku Klux Klan, 1915–1925." *Social Forces* 77(3): 461–496.

The New York Times. 2016. "Election 2016: Exit Polls," November 8. http://www.nytimes.com/interactive/2016/11/08/us/politics/election-exit-polls.html.

Ohlheiser, Abby. 2016. "Yes, #Repealthe19th Trended—But Not for the Reasons You Think." *Washington Post*, October 13.

Pardo, Mary. 1998. *Mexican American Women Activists: Identity and Resistance in Two Los Angeles Communities*. Philadelphia: Temple University Press.

Robnett, Belinda. 1997. *How Long? How Long? African American Women in the Struggle for Civil Rights*. New York: Oxford University Press.

Rosen, Ruth. 2000. *The World Split Open: How the Modern Women's Movement Changed America*. New York: Viking.

Rupp, Leila J., and Verta Taylor. 1987. *Survival in the Doldrums: The American Women's Rights Movement, 1945 to the 1960s*. New York: Oxford University Press.

Ryan, Barbara. 1992. *Feminism and the Women's Movement*. New York: Routledge.

Sanbonmatsu, Kira, and Kathy Dolan. 2009. "Do Gender Stereotypes Transcend Party?" *Political Research Quarterly* 62: 485–494.

Schreiber, Ronnee. 2002. "Injecting a Women's Voice: Conservative Women's Organizations, Gender Consciousness, and the Expression of Women's Policy Preferences" *Sex Roles* 47: 331–342.

Schrepfer, Susan R. 2005. *Nature's Altars: Mountains, Gender, and American Environmentalism*. Lawrence: University Press of Kansas.

Spruill Wheeler, Marjorie. 1993. *New Women of the New South: The Leaders of the Women Suffrage Movements in the Southern States*. New York: Oxford University Press.

Stokes-Brown, Atiya, and Kathy Dolan. 2010. "Race, Gender, and Symbolic Representation: African American Female Candidates as Mobilizing Agents." *Journal of Elections, Public Opinion, and Parties* 20: 474–494.

Swers, Michelle. 2002. *The Difference Women Make: The Policy Impact of Women in Congress*. Chicago: University of Chicago Press.

Taylor, Verta, and Nancy Whittier. 1998. "Guest Editors' Introduction: Special Issue on Gender and Social Movements: Part I." *Gender & Society* 12: 622–625.

Thomas, Sue. 1994. *How Women Legislate*. New York: Oxford University Press.

Tolentino, Jia. 2016. "Trump and the Truth: The Sexual-Assault Allegations." *New Yorker*, October 20. http://www.newyorker.com/news/news-desk/trump-and-the-truth-the-sexual-assault-allegations.

Waddell, Kaveh. 2017. "The Exhausting Work of Tallying America's Largest Protest." *The Atlantic*, January 23. https://www.theatlantic.com/technology/archive/2017/01/womens-march-protest-count/514166/.

Zaeske, Susan. 2003. *Signatures of Citizenship: Petitioning, Antislavery, and Women's Political Identity*. Chapel Hill: University of North Carolina Press.

{ CONTRIBUTORS BIOS }

Lee Ann Banaszak is professor of political science at The Pennsylvania State University.

Kathleen Blee is Bettye J. and Ralph E. Bailey Dean of the Kenneth P. Dietrich School of Arts and Sciences and Distinguished Professor of Sociology at the University of Pittsburgh.

Tracey Jean Boisseau is associate professor of women's, gender, and sexuality studies at Purdue University.

Nancy Burns is Warren E. Miller Collegiate Professor and chair of the Department of Political Science at the University of Michigan.

J. Kevin Corder is professor of political science at Western Michigan University.

Selina Gallo-Cruz is assistant professor in the Department of Sociology and Anthropology at the College of the Holy Cross.

Kristin A. Goss is Kevin D. Gorter Associate Professor of Public Policy and Political Science at the Sanford School of Public Policy at Duke University.

Brittany N. Hearne is a graduate student in sociology at Vanderbilt University.

David J. Hess is the James Thornton Fant Chair in Sustainability Studies and Professor of Sociology at Vanderbilt University.

Heather McKee Hurwitz is the postdoctoral fellow in the Department of Sociology and the Athena Center for Leadership Studies at Barnard College, Columbia University.

Ashley Jardina is an assistant professor of Political Science at Duke University.

Holly J. McCammon is Cornelius Vanderbilt Professor of Sociology at Vanderbilt University.

Allison McGrath is a graduate student in sociology at Vanderbilt University.

Jessica Lavariega Monforti is dean of California Lutheran University's College of Arts and Sciences.

Celeste Montoya is associate professor of women and gender studies at the University of Colorado, Boulder.

Minyoung Moon is a recent PhD in the Department of Sociology at Vanderbilt University.

Laura K. Nelson is assistant professor of sociology at Northeastern University.

Heather L. Ondercin is visiting assistant professor of political science at The College of Wooster.

Kay Lehman Schlozman is J. Joseph Moakley Professor of Political Science at Boston College.

Shauna Shames is assistant professor of political science at Rutgers University, Camden.

Verta Taylor is Distinguished Professor of Sociology and Affiliated Professor of Feminist Studies at the University of California, Santa Barbara.

Tracy A. Thomas is the Seiberling Chair of Constitutional Law and director of the Center for Constitutional Law at the University of Akron School of Law.

Sidney Verba is the Carl H. Pforzheimer University Professor Emeritus and Research Professor of Government at Harvard University.

Susan Welch is dean of the College of the Liberal Arts and professor of political science at The Pennsylvania State University.

Christina Wolbrecht is professor of political science at the University of Notre Dame.

{ INDEX }

Tables and figures are indicated by an italic *t* or *f* following the page number.

rights-responsibilities dichotomy, 200
right-wing extremism, moderate politics
    and, 309
Riley, Glenda, 314
Roberts, Barbara, 82
Roberts, John, 120
Robnett, Belinda, 349, 351
Rodgers, Cathy McMorris, 137
Roe v. Wade, 243
Roisman, Florence Wagman, 262
Roman Catholic Women Priests, 286
Roosevelt, Eleanor, 152, 183
Roosevelt, Franklin Delano, 156, 232, 237, 303
Roosevelt, Theodore, 22, 49
Roosevelt (Franklin D.) administration, 237, 240
Ros, Emilio, 134
Ros family, 134–35
Rosie the Riveter, 201, 237
Ros-Lehtinen, Amanda (Rodrigo), 143
Ros-Lehtinen, Ileana, 128, 131, 134, 135, 137, 139
Rouse, Lillian, 301
Roybal, Edward R., 115, 136
Roybal-Allard, Lucille, 136, 137–38, 140–41
Ruffin, Josephine St. Pierre, 107
Ryan, Barbara, 201
Rynders, Captain, 277–78

same-day voter registration, 121
sameness-difference dichotomy, 200
sameness perspective, rights and, 217
Sampson, Edith, 260–61
Sánchez, Linda, 131, 136, 138, 141
Sánchez, Loretta, 136, 138, 141–43
Sandberg, Sheryl, 189, 194n8
Sanders, Bernie, 358
Sanger, Margaret, 238
Sarachild, Kathy, 186
#SayHerName, 179, 189
Scalia, Antonin, 120, 248
Schlafly, Phyllis, 211, 243–44
Schneider, Monica C., 53
Schrepfer, Susan, 318
Seabrook Nuclear Power Plant, occupation
    of, 283–84
second-wave feminism, 5, 52, 176, 177, 178, 185,
    188t, 191, 192, 257
  assessments of, 206
  birth of, 219
  black women cause lawyering and, 263,
    264, 268–69
  environmentalism and, 318–19
  feedback effects and, 218–19
  moral motherhood and, 281
  motivation for, 334
  nonviolence and, 283, 286
  unfinished business of, 221

women's liberation and, 178
  women's organizations and, 206
  women's rights and, 178
Sedition Act of 1918, 190
self-help groups, 177, 187
Seneca Falls convention (1848), 3, 108, 178, 230,
    274, 298, 335
Seneca Women's Encampment for a Future of
    Peace and Justice, 281, 282, 283
separate-spheres ideology, 315
settlement houses, 178
sex discrimination, 245, 248
sexism, 11
sexual assault, peaceful response to, 286
sexuality, linked to race and gender, 296
sexual revolution, 191
Shaw, Anna, 108
Shelby County v. Holder, 120–21
Sheppard-Towner Act, 191
Shivers, Lynne, 287
Shuttleworth v. City of Birmingham, 262
Sierra Club, 314, 317, 318, 319, 323
Silent Sentinels, 180
Silent Spring (Carson), 317–18, 323
Simpson, Euvester, 290n11
Sixteenth Amendment, 47
skingirl groups, 308, 309
skinheads (white power), women and, 305,
    307, 308
Skocpol, Theda, 210
slavery, abolition of. *See* abolitionist
    movement
  white women's overseeing of, 296
SlutWalk demonstration, 179
Smith, Ethel, 5
Smith, Gerald L. K., 303
Smith, Howard, 241–42
Smith, Linda, 136
Smith, Margaret Chase, 238, 240, 248n4
Smith, Michael B., 318
Smith, Susan Lynn, 315
Smith-Robinson, Ruby Doris, 290n11
Smooth, Wendy, 111
social activism, gendered nature of, 361–62
social caretaking, gender and, 220–21
social feminists, 234–37
Socialist Party (US), 36, 178
social justice issues, nonviolence and, 275
social justice movements
  power imbalance in, 284–85
  women's exclusion from, 288
social movements, 6, 9, 10, 48
  cause lawyers and, 259
  continuity of, 177
  feminism in, 335
  gender conflict in, 335–37